MY STAIRW

Anthony Bright-Paul

A H u m m i n g b i r d   B o o k

UNDISCOVERED WORLDS PRESS

First published in the United States in 1965
by Dharma Book Company Inc.

website: www.undiscoveredworldspress.com
email: admin@undiscoveredworldspress.com

Copyright © by Anthony Bright-Paul 2005

Anthony Bright-Paul
anthony.bright@ntlworld.com

Introduction, page 6

Part 1

Preface to Part One, page 9
Chapter 1 The Question of God, page 11
Chapter 2 Vedanta: God Within Man, page 19
Chapter 3 Gurdjieff: Man as a Machine, page 33
Chapter 4 J. G. Bennett: Life at Coombe Springs, page 56
Chapter 5 Further Studies with J.G.Bennett, page 98
Chapter 6 The Arrival of Subud , page 115
Chapter 7 Who am I? page 179

Part 2

Introduction   The Awakening of the Soul, page 188
Chapter 8   The Philosophy of Subud, page 191
Chapter 9 — Extracts, page 201
Mangoendjaja: *My Inner Guidance*
Varindra Vittachi: *Corked*
From Ivan Vos: *The Greatest Gift*
Sudarto's Experience
From Ivan Vos's book
Bapak on Jesus
I. Gerson: *Icksan Ahmed*
Letters of Rainier Gebers
Ridwan (Bill) Aitken: *The first 400*
Bennett's Opening
Varindra Vittachi: *Fate and Destiny*
Email from H. Rofé
Husein Rofé again
From Bob Prestie's Autobiography
Soeparto in Japan
Bapak in Paris
Hussein Rawlings *Water of Life*
Lucius Perham *Into the Light*

Part 3

Chapter 10 Forty-six Year On, page 245
Chapter 11 Pergi ke California!, page 252
Chapter 12 Return to England, page 270
Chapter 13 Family Matters, page 289
Chapter 14 Retirement: A New Beginning, page 305
Chapter 15 Wisma Subud, Cilandak, Indonesia, page 311
Chapter 16 Beyond the White Magician, page 321

List of Photos

Cardinal Wolsey's Spring House, Coombe Springs, page 59

Djamichoonatra, the nine-sided building at Coombe Springs. (Now demolished), page 95

Icksan Ahmed, page 116

Pak Subuh, Ibu, John Bennett, Mrs. Sheila Ross, Sjafrudin, Ismana, Rahayu, Asikin, 1957, page 116

First Subud World Congress, page 145

Spanish group at Madrid, page 163

Anthony Bright-Paul, Harjono, Ismana and the McLeods, page 171

Robert Prestie, page 234

The author and his wife on an anniversary jaunt to London, page 310

SUBUD is a way of living not a theory or teaching. Statements about SUBUD should be considered as reflecting the author's own personal experience and understanding. They are not to be regarded as authoritative pronouncements nor are they intended to be a SUBUD doctrine.

Subud(r) and the Seven Circles Symbol are marks of the World Subud Association.

My Stairway to Subud

"Between 'Life' and the 'Way' there is the Stairway."
P. D. Ouspensky

Introduction

"Stairway to Subud" was first published by my friend Dan Cahill of the Dharma Book company of New York in 1964, and in England by the Coombe Springs Press.

The Stairway is like a series of steps leading up to a different floor or level, if you like. The first step was a question, which arrived with me as a 14 year old schoolboy in a big dormitory when most everybody had fallen asleep. What is the meaning of life?

This awakening was so powerful that it led me on to other questions and so began my studies of the major Religions of the World. At the same time, the Great War was coming to a close, I was faced with yet another question. Were Wars inevitable? Was there a way in which the vicious circle could be stopped? And from them, it was no great step to becoming an admirer of Mahatma Gandhi and a belief in nonviolence.

So taken was I by Hindu philosophy that I dreamed of going to India to become a *sannyasin,* but something held me back. I was loaned a book, *"In Search of the Miraculous"* by P. D. Ouspensky, and this acquainted me with the Teachings of George Ivanovitch Gurdjieff, and what is called The Fourth Way. This required that a man remained in life, but began an Inner Work called "Work On Oneself."

Quite by chance, Mr. Watkins of Watkins Bookshop in Charing Cross Road, gave me the address of one J. G. Bennett, who ran study Groups, working on the ideas and methods of this same Gurdjieff. Thus began in 1950 just before my 21st birthday, what I might call the adventure of my life.

For seven years I studied with John Bennett in this great house near Kingston in Surrey, meeting with Seekers of the Truth from all over the world. For three of those years, I lived at Coombe Springs, and then moved to Manchester where I acted as a sort of lieutenant to Bennett in relation to the newly forming Manchester Groups.

Suddenly in 1957, now almost fifty years ago, Mr. Bennett and various other Ouspenskyites introduced us to one, Pak Subuh, of whom I had never heard before. Pak Subuh came from Indonesia and 'opened' the 400 or more pupils of Mr. Bennett to the exercise known as *latihan kejiwaan,* or the training of the soul.

Many others must have trod this same Stairway, in search of the Truth. The culmination for me was the arrival of Subud in England in 1957. Since I have added a lot of material to the original book, I have now called it "My Stairway to Subud."

Anthony Bright-Paul
March 22nd 2006

Part 1

Preface to Part One

Anyone who has the temerity to write a book must inevitably expect his own weaknesses and limitations to be exposed. This is doubtless true of my own book *Stairway to Subud*. It is particularly true because the subject of the book is the conundrum of life itself. Why am I alive? What purpose does my life serve? What is the Truth? What are the means by which Truth can be apprehended more fully?

These are questions over which man has pondered for centuries, and it would seem that all the answers that can be given have already been given and that the boundaries of the unknowable and the inscrutable have long been demarcated. If all that can be said about Truth has already been uttered, and if the great truths stand immutable and eternal, nevertheless, the drama of life consists in the fact that man's apprehension of these truths is something that can grow, can flare into a momentary brilliance—and also alas!—can diminish, subside and die away altogether.

Stairway to Subud then is not so much a search for the Truth as a search for the means by which Truth can be apprehended more fully. But what are the right means? What is the legitimate route to greater consciousness? What indeed is the 'royal path' of understanding?

In seeking to understand, I have inevitably portrayed the paucity of my own understanding. If this search had been entirely in the void, so to speak, I doubt whether I would be culpable in any way. But in fact my search lead me to question certain tenets of the Christian religion, to discover the Vedanta philosophy, to plunge headlong into the psychological exercises of Gurdjieff, and finally to become a practising member of the Brotherhood Subud. It is because of this, that I must emphasize that this book is a subjective account of my experiences. What I have written about Vedanta, for example, is what I was able to understand about that philosophy at a particular moment of time. Or more exactly, I should say that the vision that burgeoned within me at a certain time met with a correspondence in the Vedanta philosophy. The same must be said for Gurdjieff's ideas, which made explicit insights that had lain within me, dumb and inarticulate. What I want to make clear so as to avoid offense, if that is possible, is that my chapter on Gurdjieff is not a résumé of his system, but an entirely purposeful account of my subjective reaction to his ideas. Some of Gurdjieff's intuitions may be eternal truths for all I know, but as far as my book is concerned, his intuitions only mattered when they corresponded to my own. My chapter on Gurdjieff is biased; but then I believe it must necessarily be so.

As to Subud, most of the book was written in 1958, only a year after Pak Subuh first came to England. Though I have revised the whole book many times, the subject matter has remained stubbornly the same. I have not attempted to hide my lack of experience, so I need hardly say that I am not an authority on Subud. Indeed the very experiential nature of Subud itself precludes there being any authority on the subject.

When in 1958 I wrote to Pak Subuh telling him how I had already begun to write a book, he replied with a long letter of which I append a couple of paragraphs: *"In view of your wish to write a book—this, Bapak fully agrees. This indeed belongs to the field of your work. It is to be hoped that the book for which you are working will have the content which will be useful to our spiritual brotherhood Subud, in the hope that it can awaken one's inner feeling towards remembering the Glory and the Greatness of the One Almighty God.*

"This, of course, is rather difficult for you to write, but in your book you will be able to draw pictures from your own experiences, which have been obtained in receiving the Subud spiritual exercise of worship. You can also write about the possibilities in which a man, who is carrying out the exercises of the worship of Subud, can experience the change of the condition of the inner self, beyond the understanding of his mind and thinking brain."

I hope I have been able to take his advice in some small measure.

Anthony Bright-Paul
May 1964

Chapter 1

THE QUESTION OF GOD

The long dormitory contained fifteen beds. Though it was summer and still only dusk, the talking had stopped and most of the boys were asleep. But I could not sleep, for suddenly a question had come into my mind. Why was I living? Why was I lying there, fifteen years old with X number of years ahead of me? What was the purpose of my life? What was the purpose of living at all?

I sat bolt upright in bed, astonished to find that I could remember no answers to these questions, for the questions appeared so obvious to me that I was sure that we must have been taught the answers many times. I searched my memory but could remember nothing.

The dormitory prefect came in and began to undress by the bed opposite to mine. Risking his anger, since talking was forbidden, I called over to him: "Brooke-Little, what is the purpose of life? I have been thinking about this question and cannot remember the answer." A Roman Catholic, he answered without hesitation— "To worship God."

I lay on my bed and thought of his answer— "To worship God." But it was no answer. I had no question but that God should be worshipped, but that explained nothing. It did not explain why I was there at that moment, nor why my parents were far away in Africa. Nor did it explain the war which was drawing to a close and of which we, in the idyllic Dorset countryside, were but dimly conscious. I resolved to take my question to the Chaplain on the morrow.

The Chaplain's answer was just a variation of Brooke-Little's: "To Love God." There was more to his answer than the simple words. He laughed and little by little the implications of his laugh dawned on me. In an instant, I realized why I could not remember the answers to the question "What is the purpose of Life?" the question that had appeared to me the most obvious and basic of all questions. In fact, I had not asked myself this question before, nor indeed had I heard anyone else ask it. I had heard no one ask this question aloud for the simple reason that no one asked themselves this question. Life carried on, the athletes were preparing for Speech Day; the staff were quarrelling over the virtues of "H. M. S. Pinafore;" the English master, J. H. Appleby, was trying to define such indefinable words as "art" and "taste;" the boys were swotting for School Certificate. But nobody thought of this question.

A few miles away we could see the long shape of Hambledon Hill and the clear demarcations of the old Roman fortifications. In the south lawn, in the artificial pond, goldfish swam. Cypresses pointed to a cloudless sky. Horses wandered about the field that sloped down to the lake, fields yellow with kingcups and buttercups. But what it was all for, nobody had thought to ask.

There was yet more implicit in the Reverend Scadding's laugh. For if the question was new to me, it was not new to him, nor indeed to some of the other members of the staff. On the contrary, it was not only known but also so well known that it had become "academic." "Child," he seemed to say, "People have been arguing about this from the beginning of time. There are lots of answers, but there are really no answers. God alone knows the purpose of our existence, which it is not for us to question."

But I could not help it. I had begun to question and having once begun, I was forced to examine his answer more carefully. "To love God." But how to love God? I did not doubt the existence of God, but by definition His Existence was unknowable and incomprehensible and therefore unlovable, in any normal sense of the word. How could one possibly love or worship what was beyond conception?

The Chaplain's answers had not answered my question. He had seemed to imply that we could never know the meaning, the purpose, of life. In spite of this, in spite of the fact that nobody knew the answers or even cared to know them, I still could not help but feel that life was significant. I was sure that the span of life, the journey from birth, the process of experiencing and the arrival at death; the "three score years and ten" must have a meaning. If not, then better to kill off the babies before they had a chance to sin. *Reductio ad absurdum.*

My questioning had begun, but I don't believe that it was as urgent or condensed as it may appear in retrospect. The big issue was clouded, or rather postponed, because there was an immediate purpose, to prepare for the outside world. That, of course, meant passing exams. Besides which there were the immediate interests— playing tennis barefoot, running across the lawns to dive into the swimming pool, playing ice hockey when the lake was frozen, or tramping across the fields to have tea in Tarrant Gunville. But ev-

My Stairway to Subud

ery now and then, another question was triggered off.

A visiting preacher, the Rt. Reverend Bishop Walter Carey, formerly Bishop of Bloemfontein and now Chaplain at Eastbourne College, gave a sermon. Some people do not believe in God, he argued, but we have only to look at a leaf, at its exquisite construction and we can see that such a perfect creation could not come into existence without a Creator.

I followed his sermon with an essay that I never finished: "The observation of a certain order in the universe is supposed by some to indicate and even to prove conclusively the existence of God. But this is a *non sequitur*. The observation that laws exist indicates only the existence of laws and does not indicate a conscious Creator of laws. On the contrary, if I drop a penny, it drops to the ground. If I repeat this many times, I see that this is a law-conformable phenomenon. The fact that a penny always drops to the ground indicates the law of gravity, but hardly proves the existence of God."

The fact that I wrote this did not in any way interfere with my own feelings and beliefs. It just seemed absurd to me that people should have to argue from the sensible to the supra sensible. Probability was not proof, and even if it could have been proof, what exactly had been proven? Besides which, the preacher was only putting thoughts into our heads. We were much more concerned about the ethic, the code, the ideal of Christianity, than about the inscrutable Godhead. Unconsciously, we were behaviourists.

It was two years later, during a Scripture class that the next question was triggered off. What happened after death? Not just what happened, because in a sense we all had a simple answer to that—the good went to Heaven and the bad went to Hell and forever and ever, Amen. No, what happened to those who were not Christians? What happened to the Buddhists, the Muslims, and the Hindus? What happened to those who knew nothing of the Christian ideal, who were satisfied with their own faiths? (It says something for the Public School system, that I had only recently discovered that there were other Faiths.)

I asked the Chaplain out loud during a Scripture class. For some moments he was very grave and he did not answer. After what seemed to me a long pause he said something about the Buddhist conception of the after-life. Buddhists apparently conceived of life only as an endless wheel of suffering, the necessary result of existence itself. At death, they believed that the personality was annihilated and that man then entered into a state of oblivion, or Nirvana. Christians on the other hand believed in a personal redemption, believed that the after-life could be a state of bliss, made possible because Jesus Christ had taken upon himself our sins.

To the schoolboy mind, Heaven was obviously preferable to annihilation. For the moment, I did not remark that the Chaplain had not answered my question. I was not concerned about different conceptions. Very simply, were non-Christians inexorably bound for Hell? Or, if not bound for Hell, were they inexorably deprived of Heaven? Why had the Chaplain hesitated to answer my question?

I was then asked to prepare a lecture on Islam for the next Scripture lesson. The only "authority" that I could find in the school library was H.G.Wells in his *"Outline of History."* It is hardly surprising that I was not attracted to Islam, feeling it to be a fanatical bleak religion, founded by a proselytizing visionary. I preferred the dove of Christianity to the sword of Islam, celibacy to polygamy, and Heaven to Paradise. For the moment I was silenced, satisfied with the superiority of the Christian dogma. I don't think I gave a very good lecture!

My next question was not triggered off suddenly but gradually unfolded itself. In fact, it was never formulated explicitly because the real question, that lay behind my fumbling, has only recently began to emerge. At this time, it was more an attitude, than a question.

I was beaten somewhat savagely in my second term and became at once a violent opponent of corporal punishment. This led me into many arguments with boys and staff and inevitably, I was forced back to consider the question of discipline. About this time I read A. S. Neill's *That Dreadful School* and under its influence, I found myself rejecting all external discipline and all forms of punishment out of hand, and advocating self-discipline and a rather vague and wonderful love.

It is difficult to reconstruct the processes that took place in me over a period of five years. Certain emotional convictions simply arose in me and I was forced to justify my position. This led me to conclusions that I was quite unable to foresee.

In my first term, I had joined the Junior Training Corps and had marched about and practised drill with considerable pride, but by the time I was seventeen, field days and drill appeared to me both boring and a waste of time. I had much more interesting things to do, and I managed to engineer my way out of the ranks, a manoeuvre that was by no means easy at that time.

It was only subsequent to this defection from the ranks that the conclusions attendant upon my actions and opinions were pointed out to me. At an interview with the Warden, E. M. King, I was advised: "Either become a conscientious objector or go all out to become an officer." (This same E. M. King later became an MP for the Labour Party, whose every speech was cheered by the Conservatives, until he was persuaded to cross the floor of the House and become a Conservative himself.) There was then no question but that I would go all out to become an army officer.

In fact a few weeks later, I decided to become a conscientious objector, ironically enough, because such a step I had not even considered prior to my conversation with Mr. King. Exactly how I arrived at this position, I do not know. I had an instinctive horror of mobs, of cruelty and violence, and I had an emotional, vague, lofty and extreme idealism. Looking back, it seems to me that my arguments were largely rationalizations of feelings and processes that had already taken place within me.

It is certain that my ideas and principles were by no means clear, or rather that the various arguments that I used were based on quite separate sets of principles. Somewhat naively, my main difficulty in making up my mind about conscientious objection was its universal implications. I was not concerned simply to follow my own conscience; I was concerned with the feasibility of whole nations refusing to fight, and permitting themselves to be subjugated. I put my problem to my Housemaster, J. H. Appleby, who had encouraged myself and others to write verse. He replied that any action of consequence cannot be taken in *vacuo* and must necessarily have reverberations and involve other people. As an illustration, he pointed to the Crucifixion, an action in which Christ involved not Himself alone, but his disciples immediately, and subsequently, the succeeding generations of Christians. Though he did not know it, this argument finally clinched my decisions to become a pacifist, and I left his study with extraordinary feelings of relief.

On leaving school, I immediately joined the Friend's Ambulance Unit Post-War Service. My parents were in Africa, so I had no home to which to go. It was in this Unit that I first met the Friends and learned of the Quaker approach. This caused me considerable surprise.

Most of the young Friends were Pacifists by nature and by upbringing. They came from pacifist families and had gone to Quaker schools. I, on the other hand, had never met pacifists before and had only just arrived at my conclusions after some months of verbal dogfights with boys, staff and relations. I quickly found that there was a fundamental difference in our attitudes.

The Quakers were concerned with Peace. They wished to be in contact with the Inner Light and their pacifism was a natural external manifestation of the peace they hoped to achieve within. In consequence, they refused to kill or fight. At the same time, they were willing to concede that people with diametrically opposed convictions were also acting according to their lights.

I, on the contrary, was concerned with the problem of War. I was a pacifist because I hoped that sufficient numbers of people could be persuaded not to fight so that the vicious circle of wars could be broken. "Resist not evil" seemed to me a severely practical counsel, the disregarding of which had involved generation after generation in ever increasing wars and bloodshed. While "Resist not evil" meant for me the rejection of all forms of armaments, I was a vehement supporter of non-violent passive resistance on Gandhian lines. At that time, I could admit no dichotomy in my attitude.

I don't know what I had hoped from this Quaker Unit. There were about twenty of us, housed in some old farm buildings on the edge of Birmingham, and the main activity was taking one's turn in cooking and in doing plenty of long distance runs. I enjoyed the latter immensely. I had imagined that we were to do some practical work on the Continent of Europe, and that this would be linked with the dissemination of the pacifist ideal. In fact, after some 2 months of training, I found that the intention was to farm somewhere in Sussex for nominal wages. This hardly accorded with my own ill-defined fervour to put the world to rights. The whole idea smacked too much of monkishness and self-abnegation for my wayward spirit, so after some eight weeks of quasi-military discipline at the training camp, I took a hint and decided to leave.

Nevertheless, I liked the Friends very much and was grateful to them for their tolerance, not only of other Christian sects, but also of the other great religions of the world. I am also indebted to them for stimulating the growth of yet another question.

This arose simply from attending their meetings for worship. Described to me in cold blood by a Friend, the formlessness of the service seemed rather ludicrous after my own Anglican upbringing. The Friends simply sat on benches facing inwards in the form of a rectangle. Sometimes they would sit in complete silence for the hour of their meeting. Sometimes someone would be moved to speak, perhaps to comment on a problem or to reveal the humble questionings of the heart. Such earnestness, such humility and such an innate sense of order could command in me nothing but respect.

But what was it that proceeded in these silent Friends? As I sat quietly, I became conscious of the voice of my thoughts, of the turbulence of my feelings. If someone spoke my thoughts followed a certain direction for a while, but all too easily were deflected by a chance association. What was it that moved the Friends to speak? They strove to be in contact with the Inner Light, but what was that Inner Light? Was it of the same kind as aspiration, as noble thoughts, as idealism? And if not, how were the workings of the Light to be distinguished from the normal, albeit noble, impulses of the feelings?

Of course this question did not emerge at once, but it was the embryo of the question: "What is the Holy Spirit? What indeed is Conscience? Was the Inner Light any different from the light that one received via the experience of the senses?"

On leaving the Friends Ambulance Unit, I foisted myself upon my ancient Aunt Belle, my father's eldest sister, who lived in Leyton in the East End of London, and who was a devout Christian Scientist. It was then that I had the opportunity to attend lectures and rallies and to meet a wide variety of pacifists. There were Quakers, Jehovah's Witnesses, members of the Peace Pledge Union, vegetarians, Buddhists, anarchists, intellectuals, artists and simple rebels against authority. Somehow the voices that cried for Peace were too discordant, too strident with self-righteousness and facile condemnation. The ideal was right, but what about the idealists? Suddenly I began to feel that nothing was changing and that nothing could change that way. All my own talk, and all that of the others—pacifists, idealists and Utopian dreamers—really led to nothing. In truth, it was a form of the very "war" to which we were so bitterly and vehemently opposed.

About this time I revisited my old school, Claysmore, in the heart of Dorset. The Biology master, Humphrey Moore, remarked to me that if I was a pacifist, I was also the most militant one he had ever met. His words stung me greatly at the time, but somehow I was able to accept the essential truth of his observation.

Chapter 2

Vedanta: God within Man

Soon after parting from the Friends I met up with my friend John Eveleigh. Three years my senior, he had been to the same school, Clayesmore, had become a pacifist, joined the same Friends Ambulance Unit where he served both in Norway and Austria. He had just begun studying at the Slade where he had an Art Scholarship. I had not seen him for several years, since before his going abroad.

I had never formerly discussed ideas with him, since for a schoolboy three years is a truly venerable seniority. Now I found that our ideas and ideals had much in common. More than that, John put forward some new ideas, which were to have a profound effect on my thinking and which in fact immediately deflected me to a new and immensely rich path.

It transpired that in Austria he had met a monk belonging to the Sri Ramakrishna Vedanta Society. I cannot now remember the details but I believe this monk had been attending an international work camp in the Tyrol at Brixlegg. He had impressed John with his robust sense of humour, his absence of humbug and his fervour for the spiritual life. He had explained some of the fundamental ideas of the Vedanta philosophy and told John something of its great exemplar, Sri Ramakrishna. Chandra, who was in fact an Austrian, had spent some twelve years in India as a *sannyasin*, or wandering monk. He wandered from place to place, depending upon the generosity of people for his food and lodging, while devoting much of his time to meditation and ascetic practices. It was not only the ideas but also the man himself that had influenced John. Chandra flouted conventions with impish glee. Though at a work camp he did hardly a stroke while teasing others for their exertions. He displayed a remarkable fearlessness, often going off into the dark forest to meditate during the night; but above all he had a tremendous fervour for spirituality and a burning faith in his ideal.

This picture at once fired my imagination. Here apparently was a man who took literally the injunction, "Take neither scrip nor sandal for your journey" and was prepared to throw everything to the winds in his quest for enlightenment. The word 'meditation' was also new to me. I gathered that Chandra's meditation was no mere pondering but the definite practice of certain techniques.

John then went on to explain about the ideas of reincarnation. I still remember how we were walking along the cliffs at Folkestone on a warm summer night, and how I was almost transfixed by the beauty, the sublimity of the idea. It is some reflection upon our system of education that I had to live nineteen years before I even heard of the idea of reincarnation! At once, uncritically, I swallowed the idea in its entirety. The notion that the soul of man lives on the earth many times in different bodies, gradually progressing or degenerating according to the quality of the experiencing at once explained many things. A phenomenon like Mozart could be accounted for; indeed all the phenomena of precocity. For however it is sometimes declared that all men are born equal, experience forcibly declares the opposite; that there are extraordinary inequalities, differences and variations between them. They have different talents; they are born into different circumstances and they are impelled by different fates. All this could seem to point to a Divine Injustice or Divine Indifference. At least reincarnation did seem to explain both the ordinary and the genius.

Perhaps I am mistaken if I say that I swallowed the idea entirely uncritically. I was not particularly concerned with the question of former lives and memories of the same, as are most critics and protagonists of the idea. I was much more concerned with freeing myself from the toils of heredity. I needed some means to assert that what I felt as 'myself' was not merely a mathematical combination of my parents' genes; and moreover to explain my own precocious insight into experiences that I had not experienced.

My meeting with John Eveleigh led me very quickly to three books which taken together I consider as a milestone in my own reading: *The Perennial Philosophy* by Aldous Huxley; *Vedanta for the Western World* by Christopher Isherwood; and the *Life of Sri Ramakrishna.*

The theme of *The Perennial Philosophy* might be said to be the universality of religious experience, with the rider that all religions are ways to God. Huxley illustrated his theme with quotations from mystics and saints of East and West, supported by his own trenchant commentaries. The list of sources in the bibliography itself was fascinating reading; Eckhart, William Law, St. Thomas Aquinas were ranged alongside Jallal-Uddin Rumi, Shankara and Chuang Tze.

To read the book itself was more than fascinating. It was like the great blast of the trumpet whereat the walls of Jericho began to fall. This blast met with an immediate and kindred vibration in me.

I did not need to read the hundreds of quotations to be convinced that God is Merciful and that be He called Allah or Yahweh or Tao or Brahman, He is the One God whose Love is visited upon every creed and every race. I did not need to be convinced because already subconsciously I had rejected the idea that non-Christians are bound at worst for Hell and at best for Limbo. Something within me rang out its assent that the true worship of God is not the sole prerogative of the Christian Religion, and that Divine Love knows no frontiers and no creeds.

The Christian Churches, in particular the Fundamentalists, assert that the acceptance of Christ is the *sine qua non* of salvation. But just in what does "acceptance" consist? Jesus Himself had declared, "He loves Me that doest the Will of My Father that is in Heaven." If to accept Christ means to accept what He taught then what could be more wonderful? For then all follow Christ who love God and surrender to His Will. What Christ taught was all embracing. Yet it seems that many Christians understand that the acceptance of Christ is synonymous with the rejection of other Prophets.

Having found one clue a hundred others seemed to fall into my lap. I knew nothing of esoteric book shops, but stumbled on one and bought *Vedanta for the Western World*. If *The Perennial Philosophy* illustrated that mystical experience was not confined to one religion, *Vedanta for the Western World* went a stage further. It boldly and explicitly stated the fundamental unity of all the major religions and showed how their apparent differences could be reconciled.

In the admirable introduction Christopher Isherwood explained some of the fundamental concepts of Vedanta. These stem from the most ancient sacred writings of India, the Vedas. Vedanta proposes that all men have within them a spark of Divinity, which is called the Atman. This Atman is essentially and mysteriously the same as Brahman, which is God Transcendent. Man is seen to be in a state of *avidya* or ignorance. He is ignorant of his own essential Divine nature, his Atman. The aim of man's existence can be said to be the realization of this Atman, and if this realization can be achieved then man will see that Atman and Brahman are one.

Vedanta proposes that all religions are ways to God, and accepts many Prophets from different religions as being 'avatars' or incarnations of God, such as Krishna, Jesus and Mohammed.

The idea of reincarnation is usually associated with the law of

Karma. Christopher Isherwood himself and of course the great majority of Hindus and Buddhists tend to believe in the idea of successive lives on planet Earth. However the doctrine of Karma does not necessarily imply this. Certainly it asserts that every cause must have a result and that the Karma that a man had acquired must be worked out before he can be liberated. Indeed the idea implies a satisfying universal economy, but I feel that it is too rigid an interpretation of a great concept to confine this working out to the planet Earth. Besides which this evokes the whole problem of the personality. Is the 'person' himself sufficiently permanent to prevent his Karma flying apart at the shock of death? Or is the 'person' simply a composition of Karma, simply a bundle of causes on different levels? If the latter is the case the problem of memories of former lives dissolves, because there is no one to remember!

In the Vedanta philosophy the realization of the Atman is synonymous with the liberation from Karma. Indeed this is salvation from the pitiless circle of existence. The *Bhagavad-Gita* which is perhaps the central book of Hinduism, asserts both the inevitability of Karma and that there is a way of becoming free from it. Vedanta is altogether much taken up with asserting the inevitability, the inscrutability of certain laws and then demonstrating the means by which they can be defeated or avoided. Perhaps this apparent contradiction could be reconciled by the idea of different levels or Higher Dimensions, which would mean that the Atman is rather different from the somewhat cosy conception of a super-ego held by many would-be Vedantins. The Law of Karma, though doubtless understood imperfectly, at once produced a radical change in my thinking that earlier I had not been able to receive from the Quakers. I had begun to see how all my pacifist argumentation was without avail. Now I began to understand why. The opinions that people held were all the results of their own Karma. It was impossible to substitute a result that did not follow from a cause. My own opinions and views and actions, my own moods, were also the result of my own Karma, and as such they were inevitable. All around the processes of war were occurring through just this same inevitable action—there was an unutterably complicated mass of causes that inevitably called into being certain results.

The implications of the Law of Karma were indeed staggering. It seemed that not only was everything determined, but also that what was determined was an ever increasing absurd and muddled chaos. Yet Vedanta was not a philosophy of determinism. On the contrary the central theme is that of the Brahman, the Universal Con-

My Stairway to Subud

sciousness that is beyond causality. The aim of the Vedantin is to realize the Atman and in so doing to become free from his own Karma.

For the Vedantin this realization is not merely a philosophical postulate but a severely practical issue. There are a whole series of techniques called Yoga, by which the pupil strives to be non-identified with the causal sequences, and to be joined or "yoked" to the consciousness of the Atman. (There are five main Yogas: Hatha Yoga which deals primarily with the body, with postures and *pranayama* or breathing exercises, all of which need to be undertaken under the supervision of a guru; Bhakti Yoga which is lead through devotion and the cleansing of the emotions; Karma Yoga which is the yoga through work; Jnana yoga where the route is through the concentration of the mind; and finally Raja Yoga, which is known as the Royal Path which attempts to deal with the raising of the Consciousness.) This gave me a clue to the Quaker attitudes, which formerly I had found so incomprehensible. They wished to be in contact with the 'Inner Light', something that was beyond causality that was out of Time. Suddenly things began to slip into place. *Out of Time* was the key. The Law of Karma took place in Time. In Time, it was impossible to halt the inexorable effect of causes. *"Avidya"* was the ignorance that knows only Time, and the world seen from this point of view is an Illusion, Maya.

Yes, the Quakers were right in seeking first their Inner Light. This had seemed to me like Quietism, like running away from life, a spiritual "I'm all right, Jack" attitude. Now I felt that this apparent Quietism was intensely practical, whereas my own argumentation only added to the Karmic muddle. "Seek ye first the Kingdom of Heaven" is the practical counsel. "Make Utopia first" is the counsel of fools.

Vedanta gave me an aim in a way that the Church of England had not. I suppose that this was because apart from a few confirmation classes we were never taught much about the philosophy of Christianity. Besides which everything Christian was inextricably bound up with the Public School code: Don't tell lies, except white ones; "Play the game" particularly cricket; always behave with honour; do as you would be done by, but never, never sneak!

Even if this is to mock a little, nevertheless the whole emphasis lay in doing the right thing. In Vedanta it was not a question of "doing" but of "being," of "becoming." However, little conception of its real significance, there was an aim—to realize the Atman!

Inevitably it seems I was lead to read *The Life of Sri Ramakrishna* whom Christopher Isherwood described as one of the greatest exponents of Vedanta. This at once proved to be the most astonishing book that I had ever read. It was astonishing not so much for what was stated but what was taken for granted.

For example Khudiram, the father of Sri Ramakrishna, made a pilgrimage of some 2,000 miles on foot, and this was taken as a natural thing for an old man to do. It was not just that God was worshipped, but that it was natural for people to have their own *Ishta Deva,* or favourite aspect of God, on which to meditate. The young Gadadhar, later Sri Ramakrishna, on the *Shivaratri* day elected at the age of ten to fast all day and to spend the evening in meditation. That is astonishing enough, but his friends wished him to take the part of the God Shiva in a play, since the principal actor had fallen ill. Gadadhar was only persuaded to leave his meditations when it was argued that by playing Shiva the whole action would be worship. When he was finally dressed as the God, his body smeared with ashes, he had to be supported on to the stage where his body became rigid with ecstasy, tears streamed down his cheeks and a beatific expression lit his face. That is remarkable enough, but perhaps more remarkable is the fact that the audience not only took this in their stride but were also overcome with enthusiasm!

Sri Ramakrishna was born in 1836 in the village of Kamarpukur into a Brahmin family. Both his parents were already well known for their exceptional piety and had been blessed with many unusual experiences and religious graces. From an early age Sri Ramakrishna showed a great distaste for the more conventional ideas of education and a precocious appreciation of the *Puranas* and all the sacred writings, legends and songs of Hinduism. He delighted in fashioning images of the Gods and in taking a leading part in religious plays, and even as a boy frequently fell into a trance-like state of ecstasy.

When he was seventeen, his father having died, Sri Ramakrishna went to join his brother Ramkunar, as a priest in the temple of Mother Kali at Dakshineswar, four miles to the north of Calcutta on the banks of the Ganges. At once, Sri Ramakrishna distinguished himself by the extreme manner of performing his duties. Instead of hurrying through the service, he would become so absorbed in his worship that he would often remain seated motionless for hours in front of the image of Mother Kali. The nights he would spend in meditation, sitting naked in a ghostly part of the garden. At other times he would rapturously sing devotional songs in praise of Mother Kali. This was his period of *Sadhana,* of self-discipline, when his one desire was to realize God! So intense was his desire to be completely purified of his own egoism that the whole quality of his consciousness was transformed, and he constantly saw visions and experienced phenomena. All these he also surrendered, not knowing whether they were indeed signs of spiritual progress, praying only that Mother would guide him in everything.

His experiences were so extraordinary that there is no human standard by which they can be judged. For example: "Sri Ramakrishna also saw the Ultimate Cause of the Universe as a large luminous triangle which was giving birth every moment to an infinite number of universes. He often heard the *Anahata,* a great solemn sound like the *Om,* produced by the conglomeration of the infinite variety of sounds in the Universe." I cannot presume to comment on such an experience, and even less so when it is related that he attained to *Bhava Samadhi* and later to *Nirvikalpa Samadhi.* The astonishing thing is that the Hindus actually have a psychological language to describe these rare and subtle states.

Sri Ramakrishna attained the highest realizations following the orthodox Brahmin modes of worship. One day a monk called Totapuri stopped at the temple and noticing his unusual signs, offered to teach Sri Ramakrishna the methods of *Advaita Vedanta.* These differed from his former practices where he had worshipped God in the form of Mother Kali. *Advaita Vedanta* teaches that the formless Brahman is the one Reality, and the pupil is taught methods to raise his consciousness to the unconditioned state. Sri Ramakrishna realized this *Samadh*i at his first attempt.

After this he submitted himself to many different disciplines. Orthodox Brahmin that he was, he sat at the feet of an Imam and repeated the name of Allah like a Moslem. Later still he had the Bible read to him and he saw visions of Christ.

At length this period of self-discipline and austerity came to an end. At first people had been alarmed at the extremity of his devotions, but now a group began to form around him who looked on him as their Guru, and indeed as an Incarnation of God.

Sri Ramakrishna then began to show his disciples methods best suited to their own temperaments, at the same time declaring that there is one God, though He is sometimes called Allah, Brahman or Yahweh. It is perhaps for this syncretistic message that he is

My Stairway to Subud

best known. He always encouraged his disciples in the form that was natural to them. "Do you believe in God with form or without form?" If a disciple favoured the formless Brahman, Sri Ramakrishna would also strive to help them understand the rapturous devotions of those who worshipped images.

As more and more pupils gathered round Sri Ramakrishna the description of his conversations with them convey a feeling of extraordinary joy and merriment. Everything to do with the worship of God was shown to be exciting and full of bliss, while the world of those attached to material things seemed increasingly dull and void. How much in contrast was this to the impressions I had received from Christendom. Somehow every thing in our education tends to show virtue as something dull and sombre, whereas vice is both cavalier and seductive. Luther and Loyola, Calvin and Bunyan, convey an agony of the spirit in their fights against the lusts of the flesh. All the Saints seemed overcome with a sense of Sin, and are spurned, buffeted and tortured by the worldly-wise.

I welcomed this shift of emphasis, which seemed to me psychologically right. Religion that is true cannot be a gloomy puritanical thing. If it is true it makes man free, and it is the man who is inwardly free who is full of joy. The man who is not free is the slave of care. Sri Ramakrishna, towards the end of his life, was a supreme exemplar of the joyousness of spirit, which is illustrated in hundreds of his conversations, such as these:

Sri Ramakrishna smiling, "One cannot know Him through scholarship and reasoning." He then burst into a song full of enthusiasm, Who knows how Mother is! After this song, he said to Vidyasagar, "Did you notice? The whole Universe lies in the womb of the Mother. And even the six systems of philosophy cannot reach Her. You must have faith and devotion. They say that Hanuman had so much faith in Rama's name that he could cross the ocean at a bound. But Rama himself had to build a bridge."

On another occasion a disciple asks how to get devotion. "I have already told you. You must have yearning. If one weeps for Him with the intense yearning of a child for its mother, one can realize Him. What will you gain by swimming on the surface? You must dive deep. The gems lie deep under the water, so what's the good of keeping on the surface? A real gem has weight—it doesn't float, it goes to the bottom. If you want to collect the right gem you must dive deep."

My Stairway to Subud

Disciple: "Sir, what can we do? We are tied to a cork which prevents us from diving."

Sri Ramakrishna: "Well, all sins vanish if one remembers Him. His name breaks the fetters of death. You must dive deep."

Sri Ramakrishna died in 1886, but not before he had fired a number of young men with the ideals of renunciation and the desire to realize God. So strong was this desire that some of them at once gave up the world and became monks, living together in an ashram or wandering over India with the traditional begging bowl.

Some years after his death one of his young disciples, Swami Vivekananda, travelled to America to attend the Parliament of Religions. His contribution there aroused such enthusiasm that he was invited to lecture all over the States and he also visited England. Thus the Western World was enabled to hear of the great ideals of Vedanta.

It is impossible to describe in a few words the impact of this life on my thinking. I did not fully realize the extent of it myself at the time. A number of things stood out however. Firstly, it was possible to "realize God" and that this was also possible in this very life. Secondly, there were states of consciousness that it was not only possible but also desirable to reach. Thirdly, the most favourable conditions were those of a monk, one who has renounced "Woman and Gold;" and fourthly, it was necessary to have a Guru or Teacher, who understood the techniques by which man could be liberated from his selfhood and joined to his Atman.

Incidentally, my life at the time of reading these books had become rather complicated. I had left the Friends and gone to live with my Aunt Belle in the East End of London. Shortly after going to stay with her, I had to face a Tribunal to determine whether my conscientious objection was genuine. This Tribunal asked me questions based on a written statement of my beliefs, and they seemed to be satisfied with my answers. However, they did not give me the unconditional discharge that I had hoped for, but ordered me to work on the land or in the building trade. In the event I could not live on my aged Aunt and was forced to go to the Labour Exchange to seek employment. Seeing my papers, they at once sent me to work with a big building contractor, Wates, on a vast site in Loughton. I was put with the labourer's gang under a fierce peg-legged foreman, whose physical strength was renowned throughout the site. For three months, I had to work as I had never worked in my life, digging trenches, unloading tiles and humping sacks of cement. In the evenings I wrote verse till about eight, sitting in the kitchen with my Aunt Belle and a lodger. She still had a coal-fired range in those days and gas lighting, and with the range permanently on the kitchen was the only warm place in the house. I would be in bed by eight, only to rise by six in the morning to walk to Leyton Underground. There I caught the tube to Chigwell, in those days the end of the line, where I boarded a lorry for Loughton with a host of other labourers swinging about in the back.

After three months, I got the sack, greatly to my amusement, and having been out of work for a week or two, my Aunt sent me packing, which is hardly surprising as I must have been a sore strain on her meagre resources. Before this happened, I had been to an Appeal Tribunal. As my conscientious objection had already been accepted as genuine, I was appealing against the direction of labour, arguing that this interfered with a fundamental liberty of man. At this Tribunal, I was not asked any questions but was summarily struck off the register. This meant that in due course, I would be called up for National Service.

When I left my Aunt I went to stay with my younger sister for a few days. She was an art student and had a bed-sitter in Bayswater, and I slept on the floor. One evening, she remonstrated with me, as my aunt had done and my parents also. My nerves were fully stretched and I burst into tears as I answered her with some vehemence. I think that this showed her the depth of my convictions, for after this, she never remonstrated with me again.

The very next day, I had a letter out of the blue from a schoolmaster and his wife, whom I knew only vaguely, inviting me to their Dorset cottage. I set out at once hitchhiking the 100 odd miles since I was quite broke. Kate and John Halls then kept me and fed me and also bought me some clothes of which I was in dire need. In return for which I did precious little but dig in the garden. I read and wrote a good deal. If I am grateful for the fact that they kept me for some months, I am even more grateful because they encouraged me in the ideas that I held, at a time when I felt rather severely on my own.

Then one day, quite by chance, I met a young farmer, and having helped him capture some pigs, I offered to go to work with him. He accepted my offer and I moved from the Halls' cottage up to the lonely farmhouse near the top of Iwerne Hill and a mile from the nearest road. Bruce was also an idealist!! He was a devout believer in compost and worms and he utterly rejected the plough. I also had to read *Ploughman's Folly*, which greatly interested me. Bruce was not only an unorthodox farmer, but he also had a natural flair for living in an unorthodox way. He used to arise late and eat his breakfast of soaked corn with chopsticks while reading the letters of Disraeli. Afterwards, he would set me on a tractor to disc harrow a field, while he disappeared in a lorry to Salisbury or somewhere. When I had finished my field I would return to the farmhouse and finding nothing to eat, I would slake my thirst out of an enormous barrel of rough cider and afterwards fall asleep in a furrow. When he eventually returned, he would make himself a meal of Jerusalem artichokes and dandelion leaves, while I would cook an enormous omelette and fry up some old potatoes. He considered that I had an uneducated taste! Sometimes we would roar off into the night on some extraordinary excursion of which I could not see the point. Nevertheless, it was all very romantic. I have never heard such nightingales as sang in the copses near the farm. Nor have I since enjoyed so much the glory of the stars at night as when we whirled madly through the Dorset countryside in a crazy old Canadian truck.

Eventually, this part of my life came to an end with the arrival of a summons to appear at a court in Salisbury. My mother, by this time had come home from Mombassa, and she and my sister came down to the courthouse. It really is quite an experience to appear in court. I was charged with failing to appear for a medical examination, and was summarily ordered to have that examination that same afternoon. I spent a couple of hours in the cells looking at the window high on the wall before I was marched between two policemen through the streets of Salisbury, with my mother and sister following some twenty yards behind, weeping. The doctors then tried to bluff me into having an examination, but I knew that if I once did this, I would come under military law and I refused. I was taken back to court and fined £50 with the alternative of three months jail. I was quite prepared for the prison sentence, but to my great surprise, my mother gave me the money for the fine. It was not that I doubted her generosity; I was merely surprised that she had the money.

Soon after this, I applied for and obtained a job as a teacher in a Preparatory School near Wokingham. I think that the events in this period of my life did stimulate me to a great deal of thought and one thing I learnt for sure, the meaning of the expression "fair-weather friends."

My Stairway to Subud

Shortly after becoming a schoolmaster, I became aware of the existence of the Sri Ramakrishna Vedanta Society in London, and soon I began to attend lectures given by Swami Ghananda. Subsequently, I learned from him my first spiritual exercise, though events prevented me from going far with him.

At his meetings, I did meet two kindred spirits in Arend Vos and Lewis Parker. The former was very interested in Yoga postures and later we began to practice them together. They were both vegetarians and avoided smoking and alcohol. I joined them in this, which at that time was hardly difficult. During the war years, we had been starved of fruit and what could be more delightful than to breakfast off dates and grapefruit and to refuse the tasteless flesh served at the school lunches. I never became a vegetarian from a moral point of view, but rather because I thought it would hasten my progress in the practice of Yoga. Some time later, I did give up these disciplines as such. It was, in fact, much harder to stop than to begin, and it was only when I had stopped that I saw how much they had involved me in feelings of self-righteousness.

Lewis Parker was several years my senior, a tall and striking young man of Jewish family. He was extremely well read in occult literature and knew a great deal about the theory and practice of Yoga. He was very reticent about himself, however, and what lead him to these interests. It was only after knowing him for a considerable time that one day, walking in the hills near Guildford, I got him to tell me. At the age of fourteen, he had quite spontaneously begun to have strange experiences. His chest became flushed and feelings of religiousness arose within him. He felt the need to be alone and went off for long cycle rides in the country. Often he would be impelled to his knees. At this time he also experienced a strange force rising from the base of his spine, which filled him with a great energy. It was these experiences that led him to search for explanations in books, and at length in books such as The Life of Sri Ramakrisha he encountered phenomena similar to his own experiences. In books on Yoga he found mention of a great power called Kundalini, situated at the base of the spine. It is said that higher states of consciousness depend upon the availability of certain fine psychic energies, of which Kundalini is the most powerful. It claimed that Yogis who are adept experience this force rising up the spine, passing the various chakras or psychic centres and that if this arises to the "thousand petalled lotus" at the top of the head they achieve Enlightenment.

Lewis certainly experienced some such force. At the age of sixteen, these experiences were repeated, though this time with the aid of a breathing exercise, based on the Pranayama of Yoga, but with a personal variation that he hit upon by chance. The force travelled half way up his spine, turning the chakras alternately hot and cold, a small detail that I have not read elsewhere. He was filled with such energy that he did not sleep for a week. He could see his own aura, but not those of other people.

From that time on, while carrying on with his job in the City, he had maintained a quite remarkable self-discipline. Every day he arose early, had a cold bath and spent some time in meditation. He used to walk from Earls Court to the City, eat grated carrots for lunch, walk home and spend the evening in meditation. This meditation consisted in recalling the events of the day and in analysing what had disturbed him. Though young he had quickly risen to a position of some responsibility within his firm.

His whole mode of life was in complete contrast to those of his brothers, who would often be going out to the Hammersmith Palais for dancing, while Lewis would remain at home. They knew nothing of his experiences, but it is a fact of some significance that there was a good relation between them. Interest in esoteric ideas too often goes hand in hand with a proselytizing zeal that can have disastrous effect within the family.

Lewis' experiences were added confirmation for me that there was an inner world to which the key was hidden. I began to copy some of his practices, though I never overcame my own sloth and deep-rooted aversion to cold water.

Arend, Lewis and I shared the view that it was necessary to find a Guru, or Teacher. To this end we went to many meetings of different societies: Theosophical, Anthroposophical, Spiritualist, Vedanta, Buddhist and so on. We met people who taught Yoga postures. We visited a Muslim mosque, and disputed with the Imam. Everywhere we met nice people, often learned, with great tolerance and breadth of vision. In some cases they taught techniques, but rarely claimed to be more than seekers like ourselves. Of course we had no precise picture of what we were looking for, but by this time we could easily recognise ideas and methods that we could glean for ourselves from books. I spoke to Swami Ghananda about going to India to join the Ramakrishna Order. He was inclined to discourage me and I did not press the point. By that time I had acquired a number of Indian friends and had become intensely interested in their art, music and dancing. I did want to go to India but did not feel impelled to make any immediate moves. In any case I had no money, and something told me to wait.

After two terms at the Prep. School at Wokingham I left and took another job at a school in Sheffield. I did not enjoy either job, and found cause to be thankful that I had been sent to an enlightened school, whose staffs still inspires in me respect and affection. Appleby, in particular, had encouraged me in my efforts to write verse, so it was natural that I should wish to communicate to him and to the Chaplain, the Reverend Scadding, some of my own world-shaking discoveries.

A correspondence ensued. My Housemaster was very far from sharing my new enthusiasms. On the contrary, he told me bluntly that I had not grasped the fundamentals of Christianity; that I was emotionally in agreement with parts of the Sermon on the Mount; that other Religions contained Truth, but Christianity was The Truth; that the core of Christianity was contained in the sayings, "I and the Father are One" and "I am the Way, the Truth and the Life." When in reply I equated "Atman and Brahman are One" with "I and the Father are One," I was told that my interpretation was ingenious, but not that of the Church.

Once again I was faced with the problem, "Am I to reject my own understanding of Truth if it conflicts with that of the Established Church?" I had faced the same problem with Pacifism. How could my attitude be right when ranged against it were the views of my parents, my teachers, indeed the greater part of the society in which I lived? But the problem was not a real one since it was incapable of any other resolution than the one that had to occur. When I became a Pacifist I was only acknowledging aloud a process that was already complete. And when my Housemaster pointed out the errors of my thoughts it could make no difference. Though it was with feelings of some awe that I realized I was a heretic!

Chapter 3

GURDJIEFF: MAN AS MACHINE

For the summer of 1950, I had to go north for a temporary job in a school in Sheffield. I was so desperately short of cash that I had to ask an unwilling Headmaster for a small advance of £10. Since my total salary for the term was £70, he only agreed as he wished me to get a haircut! My impecunious position restricted my movements and in any case all my friends were in the south of England. I therefore spent a lot of time after school in my room on my own trying to achieve the celebrated lotus posture of Hatha Yoga. In spite of my long legs, I could only get into it with difficulty and remain in it with acute discomfort. I don't believe these efforts served a particularly useful purpose.

My correspondence with my former Housemaster had piqued me and I set myself the task of reading and comparing the Gospels in order to find out just exactly what it was that Jesus Christ had taught. Was it really true that I was in "emotional agreement" with parts of the Sermon on the Mount, but in truth, understood nothing of the fundamentals of Christianity? Appleby had stressed the uniqueness and divinity of Christ and the authority of the Church. But which Church? Within Christendom alone there were a hundred different Churches. If he meant the Anglican Church, did he not realize that the Roman Catholic Church to this day still prays for them as heretics? And then there were some who saw Jesus as the first Socialist, and others who opined that Communism was the practice of primitive Christianity. Yet others saw Christ as the first Scientist, or again as a Master-Yogi. What was the truth?

My study of the Gospels resulted in bewilderment rather than clarity. In the first place I found it difficult to read the texts with attention because of the associations of false sanctity and sentimentality with which the Bible has become invested; a difficulty that I did not experience with the sacred scriptures of other religions. Secondly, I was bewildered by the lack of system. I could not really find a teaching. Certainly there was teaching, but it was in isolated bits and pieces. My Housemaster had said that I was in emotional agreement with the Sermon on the Mount, but while I felt its grandeur, I could not "agree" with it for the simple reason that it was quite beyond my comprehension. Even the answer given to the direct question, "What must I do to inherit eternal life?" I could not understand. Familiarity with the texts from years of daily school Chapel, had made the answer seem simple, but a little study made it far from so.

In fact I had to concede points to Appleby. The Apostles were not so much concerned with giving answers to the great philosophical riddles as to demonstrating in a hundred and one ways the Power, the Authority and the Divinity of Christ. I found this difficult to reconcile with Christ's own teaching, "The Kingdom of Heaven is within you," and I was inclined to select those texts that affirmed the divinity inherent in every man and put aside those that made special claims for Christ himself.

One thing only became clearer and that was the character of Jesus the man. Gentle Jesus, meek and mild, was dispelled forever. Indeed how mild is the following: The Pharisees and Sadducees asked for a sign from Heaven, and Jesus replied: *"When it is evening you say it will be fair weather for the sky is red. And in the morning, that it will be foul weather for the sky is red and lowering. O you hypocrites, you can discern the face of the sky but can you not discern the signs of the times? A wicked and adulterous nation seeketh after a sign and there shall be no sign given unto it, save the sign of the Prophet Jonas."*

I soon found that there was no one on the School staff who shared my interests, so I took to attending Quaker Meetings on Sundays and joined in the outings with the Young Friends. Many of them had an admiration for Gandhi and were prepared to discuss sympathetically such things as Vedanta. My apparent interest in such things resulted in the proffered loan of a book, *In Search of the Miraculous* by P. D. Ouspensky. This book interested me so much that in spite of its length and the profundity of its ideas—and in spite of the agitation of the Speech Day weekend—I read the whole of it in four days.

Ouspensky recounted that, having returned to Russia in 1914 after a long journey through the East, in search of the "miraculous" that he was convinced existed, he was taken somewhat unwillingly to meet a certain Gurdjieff, who was reputed to be directing the Work of an esoteric group. His first meeting at once eliminated his skeptical attitude and convinced him that Gurdjieff was a man of exceptional knowledge.

Gurdjieff's main thesis was that man was a machine, that a man could not "do." He stated this in an extraordinarily direct, startling and unqualified manner. Man is a machine that reacts to external influences. The passages in which this thesis is stated are so striking that I will quote them at some length.

Gurdjieff: *"...Have you ever thought about the fact that all peoples themselves are machines?"*

"Yes," I said, "from the strictly scientific point of view, people are machines governed by external influences. But the question is, can the scientific point of view be wholly accepted?"

"Scientific or not scientific is all the same to me," said G. *"I want you to understand what I am saying. Look, all these people that you see—"* he pointed along the street, *"—are simply machines, nothing more."*

"I think I understand what you mean," I said. "And I have often thought how little there is in this world that can stand against this form of mechanization and choose its own path."

"This is just where you make your greatest mistake," said G. *"You think that there is something that chooses its own path, something that can stand against mechanization; you think that not everything is equally mechanical."*

"Why of course not!" I said. "Art, poetry, thought are phenomena of quite a different order."

"Of exactly the same order," said G. *"These activities are just as mechanical as everything else. Men are machines and nothing but mechanical actions can be expected of machines."*

"Very well," I said. "But are there no people who are not machines?"

"It may be that there are," said G., *"only not these people that you see. And you do not know them. That is what I want you to understand."*

"People are so unlike one another," I said. "I do not think it would be possible to bring them all under the same heading. There are savages, there are mechanized people, there are intellectual people, and there are geniuses."

"Quite right," said G., *"people are very unlike one another, but the real difference between people you do not know and cannot see. The difference of which you speak simply does not exist. All the people you see, all the people you know, all the people you may get to know, are machines, actual machines working solely under*

the power of external influences, as you yourself said. Machines they are born and machines they die. How do savages and intellectuals come into this? Even now, at this very moment, while we are talking, several millions of machines are trying to eliminate one another. What is the difference between them? Where are the savages and where are the intellectuals? They are all alike...

"But there is a possibility of ceasing to be a machine. It is of this that we must think and not about the different kinds of machines that exist. Of course there are different machines; a motorcar is a machine, a gramophone is a machine, and a gun is a machine. But what of it? It is the same thing—they are all machines."

"Can one stop being a machine?" I asked.

"Ah! That is the question," said G. *"If you had asked such questions more often we might perhaps have got somewhere in our talks. It is possible to stop being a machine, but for that it is necessary first of all to know the machine. A machine, a real machine, does not know itself and cannot know itself. When a machine knows itself it is then no longer a machine, at least not such a machine as it was before. It already begins to be responsible for its actions."*

"This means, according to you, that a man is not responsible for his actions?" I asked.

"A man" (he emphasized the word) *"is responsible. A machine is not responsible."*

****

I asked Gurdjieff what a man had to do to assimilate his teaching.

"What to do?" asked G. (Gurdjieff), as though surprised. *"It is impossible to do anything. A man must first of all understand certain things. He has thousands of false ideas and false conceptions, chiefly about himself, and he must get rid of some of them before beginning to acquire anything new. Otherwise the new will be built on a wrong foundation and the result will be worse than before."*

"How can one get rid of false ideas?" I asked. "We depend on the forms of our perceptions. False ideas are produced by the forms of our perceptions."

G. (Gurdjieff) shook his head: *"Again you speak of something different,"* he said. *"You speak of errors rising from perceptions but I am not speaking of these. Within the limits of given perceptions man can err more or less. As I have said before, man's chief delusion is the conviction that he can do. All people think they can do, all people want to do, and the first question all people ask is what they are to do. But actually nobody does anything and nobody can do anything. This is the first thing that must be understood. Everything happens. All that befalls a man, all that is done by him, all that comes from him—all this happens. And it happens in exactly the same way that rain falls as a result of a change in the temperature in the higher regions of the atmosphere or the surrounding clouds, as snow melts under the rays of the sun, as dust rises with the wind.*

"Man is a machine. All his deeds, actions, words, thoughts, feelings, convictions, opinions and habits are the result of external influences, external impressions. Out of himself man cannot produce a single thought, a single action... Everything he does, says, thinks, feels – all this happens. Man cannot discover anything, invent anything. It all happens.

"To establish this fact for oneself, to understand it, to be convinced of its truth, means getting rid of a thousand illusions about man, about his being creative, and consciously organizing his life, and so on. There is nothing of this kind. Everything happens—popular movements, wars, revolutions, changes of governments, all this happens. And it happens in the same way as everything happens in the life of the individual man. Man is born, lives, dies, builds houses, writes books, not as he wants to, but as it happens. Everything happens. Man does not love, hate, desire—all this happens.

"But no one will ever believe you if you tell him he can do nothing. That is the most offensive and unpleasant thing you can tell people. It is particularly unpleasant and offensive because it is the truth and nobody wants to know the truth."

I must confess that something in me responded at once to these ideas. Bleak as they were, there was about them the ring of truth. I read on avidly to find the answers to the question that Ouspensky had posed—"Can man stop being a machine?"

There was yet more in Gurdjieff's analysis of the situation. The reader can avail himself of the book and thus see for himself the development and connectedness of the ideas. For the purposes of this chapter, I will attempt to summarize some of the major premises on which Gurdjieff's system is based.

Man is under a delusion in thinking that he has Will. On the contrary what people generally understand as strong or weak will is merely the reflection of strong or weak desires, themselves the results of external stimuli.

Man thinks he is a conscious being. On the contrary, man is an automaton, and lives in "sleep" with but rare flashes of consciousness. Further he has no "being;" he simply has functions.

Man is deluded in thinking that he knows himself. In fact he lives mostly in imagination, in dreams.

Man has no "I" in the sense of a single, permanent conscious centre of initiative.

Gurdjieff held that it was necessary for man to rid himself of these delusions, in order to appreciate the tremendous possibilities latent in him. He maintained that it was possible for man to have his own "I," to have Will, to be a conscious individual and to be "master of himself." But all this could only be attained at great cost, and as the result of a certain prolonged and arduous "work on oneself."

Gurdjieff's views of every aspect of the life of men flowed from his basic premises, but the conclusions were nonetheless startling and unlike anything that I had heard before. I was particularly struck by his views on immortality. I already knew three beliefs: one, that man ceases to exist after the death of the physical body; two, that the soul of man is immortal and that according to the deeds committed on earth would be consigned to the joys of Heaven or the torments of Hell; and three, that the soul of man is reincarnated in various bodies until it achieves final liberation from the circle of life and death.

Gurdjieff held that immortality was conditional. For the man who was simply a machine, there could be no life after death. What was dust must return to dust. If however, during his life, something had begun to form in a man that could withstand the pressure of external events, then that something might survive death. But he asserted that there were very different types of immortality possible according to the degree of man's evolution. If, as a result of "work on himself" an astral body had been formed, then that could exist after death, but only for a time. True immortality belonged only to the complete or perfect man who had his own imperishable "I." And Gurdjieff said that in their origins all religions were ways to this same immortality.

His teaching on war was somewhat more complicated. The real causes were remote from man; they were the results of planetary influences; perhaps of tension between two planets. Under these influences man imagines that he hates, then fights, kills, commits atrocities. Nevertheless war was not inevitable. Man could become free from these influences, but only as the result of training, of "work on oneself." Moreover Gurdjieff implied that these periods of tension between the planets were in reality most propitious for this "work on oneself;" that during these times this Work could take place acceleratedly. War was the negative response to the demand of which the positive would be evolution.

As might be expected, Gurdjieff had an equally unusual view of the word "Christian." For him no-one could seriously be called a Christian unless they were able to and did in fact live according to the precepts of Christ. With his premises, it is manifestly absurd for people to call themselves Christians. A machine simply does not have the ability to live according to a high ideal. A machine reacts. The aim to be a Christian is a very high goal. Man's first aim should be to acquire "being," to acquire a certain inner coherence that can withstand external pressures. Only subsequent to and consequent on the growth of his "being" has man the ability to follow the commandments of Christ, and moreover understand the true significance of just those very commandments.

For many people the idea that man has no Will is so absurd as to be vaguely amusing. The freedom of man's will is made evident by the visible act of choice. "I had the choice of buying a new fridge or a new TV, and having thought about it, I decided to buy the fridge. Why? Because I reckoned that very soon there would be coloured television and I preferred to wait for that. You see, I used my reason and I made my choice."

At first glance, this seems pretty watertight. It seems that the man has exercised his will and chosen. While the fact is that he has been acted upon by two external stimuli and has seceded to the more powerful one. That these two stimuli have set off a process of ratiocination and perhaps aroused successive emotions may be psychologically interesting, but is not relevant. What is relevant is that he has been acted upon by two inanimate objects *external to himself.* And one object has proven stronger than the other. What is demonstrated is the power of material things, not the freedom of the Will.

If people are often sure of their freedom to manifest, they are less often sure of their freedom to choose their states. It is relatively easy to demonstrate how a harsh word can produce resentment, how a long dull Sunday can induce boredom, how the sight of a new-born baby can induce tenderness; in short, that all our states and moods are produced by external stimuli and not by an act of choice. But it is sometimes argued that people respond differently; one man delights in oysters, while another experiences distaste. This of course is perfectly true. People do respond differently, but that does not alter the fact of response.

However, in respect of what I shall call "qualities," there are many people who are fully convinced that not only can they change their qualities, but that everybody else should do so too. They are the Puritans, the self-righteous of this world. And they can in fact very often demonstrate that by some self-discipline or other they have overcome laziness, or fear of the dark, or by some technique they have overcome shyness and developed self-confidence. What they rarely see is that the elimination of one quality is invariably, by law, and immediately, counter-balanced by the production of another quality—by pride, or greed or boastfulness. Such people are nearly always impossible to live with. And what they never see is the stimulus that provokes these efforts. Because, whether they succeed or not, it can equally well be demonstrated that these disciplines receive their motivation from external influences.

But while there are many such types, there are yet more ordinary common or garden people who have a much shrewder evaluation of human nature. They may know no philosophy, but they understand very well the weaknesses of their friends and neighbours. They know their "form" and expect no other. For all their money, a man may be able to choose to be different but they can only expect him to remain the same; the gossip to gossip; the snob to ride his high horse; the querulous to complain. Such predictability hardly demonstrates choice and poorly illustrates the freedom of the Will.

In recent years I have had occasion to meet with many scientific men, particularly industrial chemists in the course of my work. Such has been their training that in one sense they have no difficulty in seeing man as a machine, and can illustrate this with a plethora of examples inaccessible to the unlearned layman. They have no difficulty in seeing man as a complex of systems, vascular, digestive, and nervous; they can explain goose pimples as a natural reflex of the body, likewise the reason for man going pale in the face of danger or the sudden secretion of adrenalin from the glands. All these are clearly reflexes. But when I have demanded of them the outcome of their own scientific observations with such questions as: "Where in this complex is that which can be called 'I'?" or, "If man reacts to stimuli in the way you describe, then can he be said to have Will?" I have been met with the classical objections already enumerated. Man has Will because he can choose. "I" is the sum total of the functions lumped together. People can respond differently if they want to. And so on and so forth, to such and extent that I have begun to lose faith in their celebrated scientific method.

It is curious that men of religion are often likewise certain of the freedom of their own wills and urge on their flocks the all-mighty power of choice. And I have talked to priests, bishops, and monks, Protestants, Catholics, Baptists, Quakers, Seventh Day Adventists, Evangelists and Jehovah's Witnesses. Almost invariably they have taken for granted the freedom of their own wills. If and when they have admitted their own sins and shortcomings, they have explained these by wrong choice. And yet they spend much of their time exhorting others to follow a behaviour pattern in which, sometimes at least, they are confessed failures.

If they are asked why it is that man makes the wrong choice, that is chooses "evil" instead of "good," they refer to the seductions and enticements of this world, the weakness of the flesh and the power of the Devil. But this is tantamount to admitting that man is not free. One cannot admit power to the Devil and then with the same breath claim that man has free will. If the will of man were free, that fact alone would deprive the satanic forces of their power.

Frankly speaking, the assumption of free will must lead to a logically indefensible position. For if the will of man were completely free, why do not men choose to be like Christ, and, moreover succeed? And if a man's ideal is the Buddha why then does he not follow the Eightfold Path? Or if he is a Muslim, why does he not demonstrate to the world the precepts of Compassion?

In a word, why does not man always choose to be good and to do good? To be happy and to make others happy? Why in Heaven's name should a man choose to be a sexual pervert? Or the dementia of self-pity? Does a man freely choose to be fearful, to be malicious, to be endlessly critical? Does a man freely choose to become an alcoholic? To puncture himself with drugs and ruin his own health? Why do not all men freely choose to live harmonious creative lives in amity and concord? Finally do men really choose to murder, to go to war, to torture others in indescribable ways, to commit genocide, to abuse, to slander and to misunderstand each other in every conceivable way?

No, surely not. In fact it must be the opposite. The horrors, the cruelties, the absurdities and the futility of men's lives can only be accounted for precisely by the lack of Will.

All this must lead to the question: Can man choose at all? Can man acquire Will? What must be the nature of Will? And in what sphere or through what medium must Will operate?

Gurdjieff was no nihilistic determinist. On the contrary, in the foregoing quotations he had already made clear that man need not, even should not, be a machine; that man can acquire his own "I," and that life could be directed by a Conscious Will. And that must lead us to the question—How?

All these ideas had a very immediate impact upon me. All at once I felt they were the key to the absurd contradictions in my own nature. I had written numerous idealistic poems, and yet I felt disgust, contempt and fear for many people around me. I believed in Pacifism, yet was famed for my militancy. I hungered for peace, yet my inner world was a turbulent whirlpool of elation, depression, sexual hunger and a sometimes-desperate feeling of isolation and oddity.

The idea of the mechanization of man at once explained these contradictions. That man has many "I's" made up of the random succession of experiencings fitted the facts of my experience. And as for the question of Will, I knew that I was like I was, precisely because I had no choice in the matter.

Some people think that such arguments are dangerous because they relieve man of responsibility. But surely the opposite is true. To see that men are irresponsible is to bear to acknowledge a fact, but not to condone it. And as this book proceeds the reader perhaps will see in illustration that it is just those people who see this most clearly who also see the need for a way out.

Once I had begun to grasp even some of Gurdjieff's theory, I found that all the former ideas that I had studied were illumined by it. Initially it seemed to me that Gurdjieff was the first philosopher ever to have seen that man does not possess free will. But on reflection, I realized that that every religion is based precisely on this premise. For example in Vedanta, what is the Law of Karma if not another way of repudiating the freedom of man's will? How could a law of causality be compatible with freedom of action? And what is the realization of the Atman other than the acquiring of a permanent conscious centre of initiative?

It is the same with Christianity. One has only to think of a few random texts: "He that doeth the Will of the Father…" "The World, the Flesh and the Devil…" "Man cannot serve both God and Mammon." There is no suggestion of freedom; on the contrary, the whole burden of the scriptures is that man is in bondage. And it is because he is in bondage, that the Gospels are the good news.

Gurdjieff likewise hammered home the point that man is not free. But while he made this point forcibly, he did not make it absolutely. On the contrary, Gurdjieff emphasized the reality of slavery so that people should not be satisfied with an illusory freedom.

In any case, in his system, everything is relative. Man is shown to be under a certain number of laws. Gurdjieff asserted that it is possible for man to fall under "higher laws" and in so doing to become free from lower ones. What is most notable is that after having denied man Will, Gurdjieff admits the possibility of choosing between influences. *"Humanity, or more correctly, organic life on this earth, is acted upon simultaneously by influences proceeding from various sources and different worlds: influences from the planets, influences from the moon, influences from the sun, influences from the stars. All these influences act simultaneously; one influence predominates at one moment, and another at another moment. And for many there is a certain possibility of making a choice of influences; in other words of passing from one influence to another."*

"To explain how, would need a very long talk. At this moment I want you to understand one thing: it is impossible to become free from one influence without becoming subject to another. The whole thing, all work on oneself consists in choosing the influence to which you wish to subject yourself and actually falling under this influence."

I think it very important to establish this point. Many people are horrified at the thought of being a machine. Of course there are many who dismiss the notion since they cannot bear to think about it, as the very idea constitutes an attack upon their egotism. But there are also many others who are prompted by an inner voice that cries out and will not be denied, that life is not completely determined, that choice must exist somewhere. So it is important that Gurdjieff did not say that man is absolutely a machine. Far from it, because he constantly emphasized the immense possibilities latent in man. But it was necessary to establish clearly where those possibilities lay, and where they did not. It was particularly important to establish just where it is that man has choice and where he has not. If the foregoing arguments are conceded it is clear that man has little or no choice in respect of manifestation, of states or of qualities, but that he does have *a certain possibility of choosing influences.*

This leads us back to the question of "work on oneself." I shall attempt to put down here some of the principles as I understand them, but it cannot be overemphasized that this Work was subtle, and was given out piecemeal to people who were themselves moving, evolving, gaining in understanding and who to some extent already felt their powerlessness in the face of the external world.

The principles of this work cannot be taken apart from the psychological teaching. Gurdjieff attributed to man four possible states of consciousness. The first was normal sleep. The second was the state of automatic functioning which is usually called the "waking state," but which Gurdjieff called "sleep." The third state of consciousness of one's being, he called "self-remembering." The fourth state he called the "objective state of consciousness." He asserted that the third state should be the normal heritage of every man, but is in fact a rarity that can be made permanent only by a special training. Moreover he said that self-remembering was the only right way to objective consciousness. This last was the state in which man could see reality, a state that is perhaps referred to in various descriptions of mystical experiences, and under such religious terms as *"samadhi"* or "enlightenment." I say *perhaps* because there is a tendency to lump together all supra-sensory experience under one heading, experiences that may have arisen from vastly different origins.

Why is it that Gurdjieff called the normal waking state "sleep?"

*"Only one thing is true in what you have said: that you **can know** consciousness only in yourself. Observe that I say you can know*

for you can know it only when you have got it. And when you have not got it, you can know you have not got it not at that very moment but afterwards. I mean that when it comes again you can see that it has been absent for a long time, and you can find or remember the moment that it disappeared and when it reappeared. You can also define the moments when you are nearer to consciousness and farther away from consciousness. But by observing in yourself the appearance and disappearance of consciousness you will inevitably see one fact which you neither see or acknowledge now, and that is that the moments of consciousness are very short and are separated by long intervals of unconscious mechanical workings of the machine..."

It is just these long intervals of unconscious mechanical working of the machine that Gurdjieff called sleep. Such a statement issues a challenge and it is a challenge that can be accepted by anyone who so wishes. All that is necessary is to make a decision to remain conscious of this same mechanical working, and this will inevitably show whether it is or is not a fact that the moments of consciousness are short and separated by long intervals of automatic functioning.

Gurdjieff never expected his pupils to accept his statements, but urged them to experiment and to verify for themselves. Ouspensky related his own attempts to remain conscious of himself, to "remember himself." This at once demonstrated for him the truth of the assertions. He saw that memory is connected to moments of consciousness. We remember so little because we are so rarely conscious. Another fact that he encountered was his own resistance, his own inertia, and above all his sheer inability to remain awake in spite of the most ferocious efforts. Nevertheless, he did get tastes of this state, and these tastes alone convinced him of the central position of self-remembering in Gurdjieff's method.

By the time we read of these experiments a small group of people had been formed who were not only studying the ideas, but were making experiments under Gurdjieff's direction. This group Work was based on the idea that man does not know himself, and that self-study is the first step necessary for a man who wishes to enter the Way. The chief means for self-study was self-observation; Gurdjieff explicitly repudiated self-analysis. He said that observations had simply to be registered dispassionately without changing anything. Further, he said that self-observation must be undertaken according to definite principles; the first being to relate the phenomenon to a definite centre.

The idea of the centres alone is very interesting. He said that there were five lower centres, the thinking, feeling, moving, instinctive and sex centres. The distinction between intellectual activity and feeling responses is not too difficult to understand. The regulation of the respiratory, vascular and digestive systems, together with all forms of sensations belonged to the instinctive centre. And all postures and movements that could be learned or imitated belonged to the moving centre. The classical example of moving centre Work is driving a car. At first the learner is clumsy because his thinking centre directs his movements. Then moving centre learns, and a mass of complicated movements can be done while thoughts are engaged on other things. Incidentally, speech was also shown to be largely a function of the moving centre.

The idea of the thinking centre, which at first sight seems ordinary enough, proves on examination to be a strange idea. Gurdjieff showed that the thinking centre is largely an apparatus for association and comparison. Such a conception goes counter to the elevated position that is normally accorded to the mind. Contemporary education and environmental associations tend to make man think that his brain is the seat of his "I," that his thoughts are the conveyances of his Will and the means of expressing himself. Even religious people write in newspapers that thought is the thing that distinguishes man from the animals, and suggest that the cranium is the seat of the conscience.

The division of the centres might be of academic interest to psychologists only, were it not that these distinctions throw light on and support Gurdjieff's original contentions. For if a man begins to observe his associations it gradually becomes clear that "he" is not his thoughts. If he observes his emotions he sees that they are responses to external stimuli. And that normally he identifies himself with the processes of his functions. Gurdjieff's pupils began to observe themselves, and this led them from a purely theoretical notion of man's mechanization to a practical understanding of the same.

There are a number of other things that must be noted about the centres. According to Gurdjieff, one centre could usurp the work of another, and this resulted in absurd wrong functioning. He also said that each centre worked with a different fuel or energy, and that they worked at different speeds, the thinking centre being the slowest, then the moving centre. The emotional centre should be much quicker but rarely worked at its proper speed. In theory it was necessary for the centres to do their own work and moreover to work together.

It is also important to note that the centres were not only mechanisms but also receiving apparatuses, designed to connect man to the visible, tangible, external world; that is the world that we can know via the evidence of the senses.

If this is indeed so we can appreciate even more the significance of the Higher Centres. For Gurdjieff asserted that there were in man two higher centres, the "higher emotional" and the "higher mental" centres. These centres, he said, were already fully functioning and did not need to be developed. On the other hand, they worked with yet higher energies and at much greater speeds than the lower centres. Self-remembering and objective consciousness were connected to the functioning of these higher centres. According to Gurdjieff, it was the lower centres that needed to be put in order and made to work together, so that a connection could be established in the consciousness of man between the higher and lower centres.

If the lower centres are "receiving apparatuses" and connect man to the sensible world, then the higher centres must also be receiving apparatuses and connect man ...but to what? It is at this point that we depart from the visible, the verifiable, the utterly empirical, to the mysterious, to the numenal, to the supra sensory.

For many people it is not too difficult to accept Gurdjieff's analysis of man's situation here on the earth. Indeed of recent years there has been a growing, if inarticulate concession of Gurdjieff's major premises. We are creatures of circumstance. But if we cannot do, what then precisely is "doing?" If the external world does push me and everyone else around, what can be the meaning of having one's own "I?" If it is true that man is asleep in the sense that he functions automatically, what can be the meaning of being awake? If I pose the questions here it is only to highlight that the questions belonged to the natural world, whereas the solutions evidently belong to the supernatural.

Let us here briefly recapitulate some of the principles of the Work. First is self-observation, a practice that soon brought his pupils from a philosophical acceptance of his ideas to a real and perhaps terrible realization of their helplessness in the face of the forces around them. Gurdjieff demanded of his pupils that they struggle with their habits, that they make efforts to remember themselves, but he emphasized that these *efforts were for the sake of self-observation and specifically denied that man could change through efforts.*.

This principle is one of the most difficult for anyone interested in self-perfecting to understand. Be they Christian or Buddhists, and further be they even students of Gurdjieff's system, it is incredibly difficult to accept that the transformation of man's nature cannot be accomplished by effort, cannot be accomplished by the strength of a man's will, however strong. Because if that were so indeed, the implication must be that man is sufficient unto himself; which is the unconscious blasphemy that the entire system of Gurdjieff repudiates. What else is the meaning of "Man cannot do"?

If there is a principle that is central to the system as a means of development, then without question that means must be said to be "self-remembering." Even self-observation was impossible without "self-remembering." The study of "identification," of "considering," of the "stop exercise," all hinged on this same "self-remembering."

At first glance this "self-remembering," as described by Ouspensky seems simple enough. He drew a single-headed arrow. This is the direction of man's attention towards the external world. He then drew a double-headed arrow. This represented a division of attention; one part drawn to the world and the other is retained on a feeling of my self. On the one hand, I read a newspaper; on the other I have an awareness of myself reading the newspaper. I walk and remain aware of my walking. I talk and am conscious of my voice.

It is not difficult for anyone outside of groups to make experiments in self-remembering, as indeed I did myself. And it is likewise certain that they will encounter just those same difficulties that Ouspensky described, and that subsequently I have heard hundreds of others describe. First of all, it is no easy thing to divide attention. Secondly, it is difficult to maintain this division once achieved. Any serious such effort must convince a man of the power of the forces that suck him out of himself. Thirdly, he will be unable to remember himself, to be conscious of himself for any length of time. Inevitably he will fall asleep without realizing it, and wake up much later. As long as he does not deceive himself, as he tries again and again the same thing will happened again and again.

Such efforts may convince a man not only of the power of sleep, but also of the necessity of studying just how it is possible to wake up. And further they may give a man, even for a few moments, such a taste of consciousness of his Self that he becomes sure that this is the right road and the key to the mysteries.

Gurdjieff made clear that the state of self-remembering was dependent on the elaboration of a certain fine energy; and that once this energy was used up self-remembering inevitably came to a stop. And so he brought attention to all the needless and useless activities on which people waste their energies, daydreaming, unnecessary muscle tensions, and most particularly the expression of negative emotions. The study of energies alone occupied a large part of the system, and Gurdjieff made many extraordinary psychological distinctions in respect of them. These the reader can read for himself. I want here only to emphasize that the point of working to avoid unnecessary talking, or the non-expression of negative emotions, was to save energy for the central idea, which is self-remembering. Gurdjieff also said that each centre had its own accumulator for energy. Also available to man was what he called the big accumulator, which contained vast reserves of energy. It is noteworthy that he said that a connection with the big accumulator could come about neither through the intellectual nor the instinctive centres, but only through the development of the emotions.

In order to come to as all-round an understanding as is possible in a short chapter on the principles of the Work, I must refer to another aspect of Gurdjieff's theory. He made a remarkable distinction between personality and essence. In brief, essence is what a man really is. A baby is all essence, and its characteristics, its likes and dislikes, all belong to essence. However, family and teachers, education and environment, all promote the growth of something false, the personality. Gurdjieff said that very often the essence stops growing around the age of six. The personality may develop so that a man appears cultured and highly educated, while the essence remains primitive, savage or stupid.

The point to which I wish to draw the reader's attention is this. *"A man's real 'I,' his individuality, can grow only from his essence."* The idea of self-remembering came to be connected with this growth of essence, and with the lessening of the pressure of personality, which prevented this growth.

In order to try to understand the position better here is a diagram of how man should be:

I
Will
Conscience
Mental Body
Higher Mental Centre
Astral Body
Body of Consciousness
Higher Emotional Centre
Physical Body
Five Lower Centres
External World – Material Forces
Received through the five senses

What is illustrated here is that the "I" of man, his Conscience, His Will, should be the controlling factor. It is sometimes illustrated by the coachman and his horses with the passenger inside. The passenger should be the "I," who gives the orders to the coachman, who drives the horses, the feelings, which pulls the carriage, the body. That is the way that should be, that is the way that religions originally lead man to, as did the Sufi disciplines or the true Yogas.

But, of course, what we actually observe is the complete opposite. Men are entirely dominated by the material or satanic forces. The Higher Centres are not connected to the ordinary consciousness and to all intents and purposes man has no "I," no Will and no Conscience.

The significance of self-remembering becomes clearer. Self-remembering is the link with the higher worlds. It should also be remembered that self-remembering is connected to the functioning of the Higher Emotional Centre. Gurdjieff also said that there was a relation between the Higher Emotional Centre and the Astral Body. If they were not the same, yet the one could not be conceived without the other.

The wrong functions of the centres might be called the maladjustments of the soma. The adjustment of man's soma, or the regulation of the soma, can only be brought about by the psyche. The psyche, which we may here call the "individuality," can only grow in the essence of man. Because of the absence of his psyche, man cannot even be sure that he has a soul, let alone follow the directions of the soul.

Self-remembering as a means has many ends in view and produces simultaneously many results; namely, the lessening of the pressure of personality on essence, the prevention of energy waste, the harmonious working of the lower centres; but above all, these have as end view the creation of the psyche; that is the creation of the link between the visible and the invisible, between the sensible and the supra-sensible. In theory, the practice of self-remembering should bring about the crystallization of the psyche. And this should in turn provide the link between the true "I" of man and his functions.

Here something must be said of Gurdjieff's attitude towards the body. In contemporary thought, there is current a certain dualism, namely that of the "body" and the "mind." There is an inclination to elevate the mind and denigrate the body, and people often boast of the power of the mind over the body. Also some authors write disparagingly of Hatha Yoga, because it pertains to the physical exercises of the body, while emphasizing the superiority of Raja Yoga, which pertains supposedly to the development of the mind. In Gurdjieff's system such an attitude is *per se* inadmissible. For the mind is seen to be but part of the body, simply a function of the body. The thinking centre, the feeling and moving centres, the instinctive and sex centres are all equally body. But more than that, Gurdjieff demonstrated that thoughts, attitudes of mind and mental associations are largely subordinate to the moving and instinctive parts. It is for this reason that a great part of the practical study of Gurdjieff's system was taken up with the study of dances and ritual movements and postures, and with the sensing of the parts of the body.

In fact, from the point of view of the system, people lived too much in their minds. That is to say that the attention is too often preoccupied with idle thoughts of past events and future longings. All this was called living in dreams. Work on postures and Movements could bring man more into the present, more into contact with his body, with his own self, in a word, with his essence.

In the system what people often call "mind" was called the mechanical part of the thinking centre, or the formatory apparatus. It was also sometimes said that this was the one centre of the personality. On the other hand, it was made clear that the instinctive and moving mechanisms were nearer to the essence.

In attempting to outline the principles of Gurdjieff's methods, I have had to condense and select from a vast amount of material in

In Search of the Miraculous. Having accepted the idea of the man-machine as a working hypothesis, I have tried to put together the principles of the Work in the belief that if these principles are valid for Gurdjieff's "Fourth Way," then they must also be valid for any and all ways, and be a criterion (or yardstick) by which we may measure them.

What I am trying to say here is very difficult to express, so I shall repeat it in another form. If the principles of the Work that Gurdjieff enunciated are true, then they cannot be true *in vacuo*. If they are true, they must be universals. And this is important to establish. Because if they are universals, then they are the means to distinguish a true Way from a false one, to distinguish a heresy from a true doctrine. For example, if it is true that "Man cannot do," then any doctrine that says that man can change his own nature by the strength of his own will is a heresy. If it is true that the possibilities of man are connected to the growth of his essence, then any Way that is based purely on the development of mental powers is open to doubt, and is likely to be an imaginary way. In all of this, I say "if." Of course, it is up to the reader to make his own judgment as to whether the principles are valid or not.

The conversations and the methods of Work that Ouspensky recorded took place during the first Great War and the years immediately following. The vicissitudes of the groups at this time in themselves make interesting reading. Both Gurdjieff and Ouspensky left Russia in the midst of the Revolution. Ouspensky eventually made his way to London, while Gurdjieff after periods in Tiflis and Constantinople, finally set up his "Institute for the Harmonious Development of Man" in the Chateau du Prieuré, Fontainebleau, France. By this time, Ouspensky had become inexplicably estranged from Gurdjieff, and began to teach the system separately in England.

****

The system of Gurdjieff appeared in some ways to contradict my beloved Vedanta, but I felt nevertheless that the fundamentals were the same. In truth Gurdjieff amplified much that is obscure in Vedanta. But if the aims could be squared, it was not quite the same with the methods.

Sri Ramakrishna had advocated renunciation, most particularly of "Woman and Gold." His pupils left the world and became monks. Gurdjieff, on the other hand, demanded of his pupils that they remain in life, since their very life circumstances reflected what they were, and provided the obstacles necessary for the Work. With Gurdjieff, the emphasis was on inner freedom, rather than on outer renunciation.

Plunged into the world after the sheltered existence of a Public School, I had found responsibilities irksome and the life of a monk had some appeal for me. I had a rather naïve and wishful conception of renunciation!

But Gurdjieff's system, which he called the Fourth Way, required connection to life. In spite of the novel form of his ideas, I had no doubt that they were fundamentally religious, while official religion seemed to have departed far from its origins. Again Gurdjieff's Law of the Octave explained how, in the course of time, everything is inclined to become its own opposite. How else could the Religion of Divine Love produce the Inquisition or in our own day the "Troubles" in Northern Ireland?

In these days, religion has become divorced from life, and little or no attempt is made to answer the fundamental questions, such as posed in the first chapter of this book. The relation of man to his Creator is considered a private affair, but the exigencies of this world are considered to be a matter between man and man. It is unconsciously assumed that wars and strikes and crime and class distinction will fade away if only man would be reasonable. But Gurdjieff made clear that man without "religion" could only be considered a machine, helpless and irresponsible. I say "without religion" in the sense of neither having a connection to his Higher Self, nor connection with the supernatural. And he made it clear that the only way to lead a becoming life on this earth and not "to die like a dog" was to find a way to a connection with this same supernatural.

****

At the end of the summer term, I left the school in Sheffield and took a job working in the kitchen of a Hotel in the Isle of Wight. When I had earned sufficient money, I at once bought Gurdjieff's own book, *All and Everything.*

Gurdjieff's book, as the title implies, is about all and everything. It is a vast tome of some 1200 pages. Beelzebub, returning on a space ship to the place of his birth after a long exile on the planet Mars, undertakes the education of his grandson Hassein, and for this purpose describes the life of the planet Earth. With such an extra-mundane and supra-temporal status, Beelzebub is able to describe the life of man from centuries ago to the present day, and in fact does not hesitate to range over archaeology, the migration of races, the laws of vibrations, perpetual motion, the founders of religions, the questions of the soul and the possibilities inherent in man.

In *"In Search of the Miraculous,"* Gurdjieff is presented through the eyes of Ouspensky. G, as he is referred to, speaks precisely, economically, even clinically. Unwittingly, Ouspensky garbs him with the austerity and integrity of his own thought. Gurdjieff, in his own writings, presents himself as a far more rumbustious figure with a gleeful sense of humour and a somewhat involved Asiatic form of narration. But above all he distinguishes himself by his compassion for mankind and by his reverence for Our Common Creator.

If *All and Everything* is about all and everything, nevertheless, it is still about one thing. It is about the situation of man on this earth, about the possibilities of what man could become.

On his vast canvas, Gurdjieff paints a truly extraordinary picture. It is of a Universe in which everything is related and interdependent, a universe that is alive, organic and moving. The earth, far from being at the centre of the Universe, is shown to be in a remote corner; but the evolution of the earth is connected to the whole process of energy exchange throughout the whole universe. Humanity is shown to have a particular role in this evolutionary process, so that the "becomingness" of the life of man is of concern not only to the Conscious Individuals, but also to the Creator Himself.

The whole universe is shown to be under laws, a conception of tremendous significance, because the Creator Himself cannot contravene the laws of His own making. It is a dramatic universe. From time to time, Messengers-from-Above are sent to the Earth in order to give a new orientation to the life of man, in order to help man to fall under higher laws. It is implied that the evolution of man is synonymous with the diminution of the number of laws under which he lives. At the centre of the Universe there is but one law, the Will of the Creator.

Perhaps the central message for mankind is contained in the chapters on the *Very Saintly Ashiata Shiemash*, a *Messenger from Above*. Ashiata Shiemash meditates on the way to save mankind from their unbecoming existence and comes to this conclusion: that all the other Messengers-from-Above have always made use of one or other of the Sacred Impulses—Faith, Love or Hope; but that these same Impulses have now become so atrophied, so mixed with other impulses, that they are no longer perceptible, no longer available as a means of self-perfecting. But there is one Sacred Impulse still in its primordial state, and this is so because it had become embedded in the subconscious of man. He therefore concludes:

"When all the above-mentioned was completely transubstantiated in me, I decided to consecrate the whole of myself from that time on to the creation here of such conditions that the functioning of the 'sacred-conscience' still surviving in their subconscious, might gradually pass into the functioning of their ordinary consciousness.

"May the blessing of OUR ALMIGHTY OMNI-LOVING COMMON FATHER UNI-BEING CREATOR ENDLESSNESS be upon my decision. Amen."

There is one very curious factor about the life of the mythical Ashiata Shiemash. He is presented as having lived a long time ago. Again it is said that he taught nothing, unlike the other Messengers-from-Above. The result however of his labours was the introduction of the Golden Age, of the thousand years of Peace. Not only did wars cease, but also different nations and hostile governments disappeared, as did castes and classes of people. Everywhere on Earth, men strove to manifest according to Conscience and to the objective impulse of Divine-Love.

But when the analysis of man's situation, according to Ashiata Shiemash, is studied, it becomes clear that the conditions described are not those of the distant past, but on the contrary, those of the present day. Who are the Prophets of Faith, Love and Hope if not Abraham and Jesus and Mohammed? What then is the Golden Age other than a time that we can look forward to? And who shall be its Prophet? At least, he will not be a Teacher. But if we can take this as prophetic, then He must be someone who is able to bridge the gap, so that Conscience can begin to function in the ordinary consciousness of man.

I have heard that Gurdjieff attached great importance to the chapters on Ashiata Shiemash, and that shortly before his death in Paris in October 1949, he himself hinted that they contained an "intentional inexactitude" which if perceived would provide the key for their understanding.

Chapter 4

J. G. Bennett
Life at Coombe Springs

The young man who had loaned me *"In Search of the Miraculous"* did more; he gave me the address of a certain J. G. Bennett who had apparently gathered around him a number of pupils studying the Gurdjieff methods. He told me that he had been to London to see a demonstration of some temple dances and complicated Movements performed by these same pupils as part of Gurdjieff's training. After that his interest had lapsed.

Mine on the contrary had been fired, and while still on the Isle of Wight I wrote to J. G. Bennett explaining my interest in the Work-ideas and asking him to clarify certain difficult notions. I was particularly puzzled by Gurdjieff's references to Kundalini. In Yoga, Kundalini is the "coiled serpent power" at the base of the spine. The development of higher states of consciousness is said to depend upon the release of fine psychic energies. Kundalini was said to be the most powerful of these energies, and one aim of Yoga can be said to be the raising of this force through the psychic centres or *chakras* to the "thousand petalled lotus" at the top of the head. Just about everything seemed to be dependent on this power. It was claimed that through this power miracles could be performed; that a Yogi could be in two places at once; could levitate; could produce bodily warmth in icy mountains, could go without food; could be buried alive and so on and so forth. Gurdjieff, on the contrary said that Kundalini was the power of imagination and *All And Everything* is full of "the maleficent consequences of the organ Kundabuffer," an organ that made everyone see everything upside down.

This bewilderment would have been academic had it not been for the experiences of my friend Lewis Parker, the truth of which I could not doubt. I asked Mr. Bennett to explain this anomaly.

He replied, saying that Coombe Springs was the headquarters of a number of Gurdjieff students; that I could pay a visit by arrangement on Sunday; and that if I was impatient I could contact a Miss Rina Hands, who lived in Chelsea. As to my question about Kundalini, I could ask that at open meetings at Denison House, Victoria.

I returned to London in the middle of September and at once contacted Miss Rina Hands by phone, and was invited round to tea at the flat in Chelsea. I gathered that she had studied personally both with Gurdjieff and Ouspensky.

When I arrived, she took me upstairs to her flat and at once made me feel at ease. I saw many familiar books on the shelves, Aldous Huxley and T.S.Eliot among others, and my interest in them provided an opening for conversation. She went along easily with my enthusiasm for these authors and I was relieved to find that she did not disparage those who followed different systems. Every now and then she made some slight qualification to one of my remarks. Later she answered many questions about Gurdjieff and Ouspensky in a perfectly natural and indeed humorous manner. In no sense did she try to teach me anything and it was not until I had departed that I realized the impression she had made upon me.

For with all her naturalness there was a certain authority. The qualifications she made, and made without a hint of superiority, made me feel she understood far more than she said. There had been nothing extraordinary about her, as about some of the Yogis and Swamis I had met. On the contrary she dressed normally, wore make-up and smoked a great deal. And yet withal I had the impression that she knew and understood many things that I wished to understand.

I soon rang Mr. Bennett and arranged to visit Coombe Springs the following Sunday, with three friends. With Lewis Parker and Arend Vos I shared an interest in Yoga, but had not prevailed upon them to read Ouspensky. Charles Higham I had known briefly at Claysmore. He was a most remarkable poet, since his verses were written almost straight off, as if dictated to him. He was later to become a well-known author.

Through an error with trains we did not arrive until noon. We walked up the gravel drive, were met at the door by a charming lady, a Mrs. Eve Wilkinson, and at once were ushered upstairs to Mr. Bennett's study. Sunlight streamed in through the bay window on to the pale green walls, where there were prints of dancing dervishes, coloured pictures of Sufi Saints, and two remarkable frames with Arabic writing written diagonally. All round the walls were bookcases crammed but not tidy. On the large table in the window there was a mass of papers, open books and an assortment of photos under a large sheet of glass.

We waited for some minutes seated in armchairs when an enormous man in carpet slippers entered suddenly, and without introduction took his seat in another armchair. For some moments he sat quite still, then uttered the one word, "Well?"

Such an entrance was hardly calculated to put one at one's ease, but my reading of Gurdjieff had prepared me for this. Overcoming my initial embarrassment I asked Mr. Bennett whether the aims of the system were the same as those of Yoga.

"If you understand the aims of Yoga then it might be said that the aims are the same. Only you must understand that the methods are different." He elaborated a little.

Lewis then asked whether breathing exercises or *pranayama* had any place in the system. Mr. Bennett at once turned to him. "But what do you understand as the meaning of the word *Prana*?" he asked.

Lewis replied, "The yogis say that *Prana* is a substance in the atmosphere which they can extract by means of their breathing techniques, or *pranayama*."

"But can you do that?" Mr. Bennett asked.

Lewis flushed, considered the question, but did not answer. Since I knew of his experiences related at the beginning of Chapter 2, I was not surprised at that. I guessed that he felt that he could do just that. But as for me, I knew that I knew nothing about contact with or control of psychic energies, and there was something in Mr. Bennett's manner that suggested that he did.

I asked another question about the Movements and sacred dances of Gurdjieff and Mr. Bennett explained the important role they played in the system. There is much now that I am unable to remember of his answers because certain things he said—for example, about the role of attention—were quite meaningless to me at that time. I listened and heard the words all right, but just what the words referred to I could not grasp. Later on I began to understand the reason for this.

When my questions dried up Mr. Bennett did not prolong the conversation. We were handed over to a certain Pierre Eliot, who took us across the lawns, then down a wooded brambly area to the old spring house at the bottom of the garden, to draw water. (In fact, Cardinal Wolsey had built this Spring House in order to lead water

My Stairway to Subud

Cardinal Wolsey's spring house, Coombe Springs

under the Thames to Hampton Court Palace.)

At once we could not help but be struck by Pierre's manner. When asked direct questions about the nature of the Work, he was slow to reply and evasive. There was certainly nothing glib or slick about his explanations, in fact so much the contrary that I was aggravated by his hesitancy.

Owing to our late arrival, the lunch bell sounded before we could join one of the working parties and we returned to the dining room in the house. About sixty sat down to lunch at bare wooden trestle tables. There were a surprising number of young men in a great variety of working clothes, and a preponderance of athletic rather than intellectual types. But it was the variety of types that surprised me at once. They were neither "arty" nor "respectable-conventional" nor "mustily-clairvoyant" nor "worthily homespun." On the contrary, they could not be fitted easily into any convenient category.

The conversation at lunch table was somewhat one-sided. My friends and I compared and equated ideas from different systems and asked the opinions of those we were sitting with. But they either pleaded quite unaccountable ignorance or hung their heads and took an unconscionable time to produce an absurdly simple answer. All this produced a very strange impression. At one moment I thought that these students were either stupid or ill informed, or that they were posing unnecessarily. Yet on the other hand, his or her very restraint commanded in me an unwilling respect, and I could not doubt the essential good will of everyone around me. Subsequent experience gave me an entirely different view of that first lunch.

Later I saw that we had bandied about big ideas without any hesitation or restraint; indeed as if we understood the principles of the ideas to which we referred. These Gurdjieff students put upon themselves a demand always to relate the words they used to the facts of their own experience. It was this inner discipline that produced what seemed to us awkward and strange manifestations.

At the end of lunch the cooks and waiters brought in chairs, the conversation stopped and a somewhat embarrassed silence ensued. Mr. Bennett was in his place in a large red chair at the top table. He sat quite still and his features were impassive, but his presence could be felt most powerfully throughout the room. In the face of it what little conversation there was withered away.

At length someone made an observation, which clearly related to a particular exercise. Since we did not know what that was we could only observe that the speaker seemed to make a painful and unnecessary exaggeration of his inabilities. He had hardly remembered the task, and had only worked for a few seconds. Mr. Bennett asked what he had seen from this and whether he had been able to return. I was unable to follow the conversation, noting only Mr. Bennett's precise and powerful manner of speech and the unusual care for the meaning of words. After a number of observations and commentaries, we left the table and everyone returned to their tasks in the garden.

My friends and I joined in with a gang of young men cutting up logs. Some were swinging axes, while others worked in pairs on long woodsmen's saws. Already by the time we joined the party, work was in full swing and conversation was practically nil. We were allocated various jobs, after which an earnest young American drew us aside and explained the task for the day. While we worked we were to try to divide attention so that one part remained rooted in the sensation of our left foot while the other half was to be applied to the work in hand.

My friends, who had not had my advantage of reading about the "Work," had not been prepared for the eventuality of manual labour, so the situation was not without comedy. Formerly we had together visited the headquarters of various movements, where the enthusiastic adherents had usually entertained us to tea and readily explained their ideas, while here we had to Work and with people about as communicative as Trappist monks. In spite of this my friends continued their philosophising—not even sawing up logs could stop that. Eventually the young American drew us aside to enquire what we had made of the task. My friend Charles, the poet, who had not even removed his jacket, and whose tall thin body seemed especially ill equipped for manual labour, looked pained. He had never ceased from conversation. How absurd a question! He had never lost contact with his foot! My other friends, Lewis and Arend, had not tried, because frankly they were used to meditating on such high themes as "I am Brahman" and so the suggested exercise must have seemed to them faintly ridiculous.

This simple exercise, however, quickly showed me many things. Following my reading of *In Search of the Miraculous* I had already made many attempts to "remember myself," most often when walking back to my room at night. But just exactly what should be remembered? I tried to remember myself looking at the green glow of the street lamps, listening to my own footfalls and the noise of the traffic, feeling the sensation of the frosty air on my face, smelling the London air redolent with odours from Olympia—but all these attempts had only filled me with perplexity. There was too

My Stairway to Subud

great a multiplicity of impressions—and what exactly should be remembered to constitute "self-remembering?" I began to be sure that the essence of the matter was not in the book at all.

But this exercise was a clue. Though the reason for it had not been explained to us, I felt that there was some significance behind it. Very quickly my efforts showed me how unrelated I was to my own body, how difficult it was to place my attention in the way required, particularly without the work in hand suffering; and finally, how very soon I forgot what I was trying to do. But at least it was something that could be returned to. Soon, however the interest of the experiment wore off and I let my attention roam unfettered and unbridled.

Eventually the tea-bell rang, and as we drank tea in the hall the dining room was cleared of chairs and tables for the Movements class. In the middle of the *mêlée,* Mr. Bennett suddenly entered and called "Stop" and everyone froze in the positions they were in. My unfortunate friend Charles told me, many years later that at that moment, he was pouring tea from a heavy brown pot. The "Stop" caused him to drop the pot and to receive a glare from Mr. Bennett!

We wanted to watch the Movements class, but were told that we would better understand the significance of working at Movements if we took part. We therefore took our places in rows. At first we were shown a simple marching rhythm, by our guide of the morning, Pierre Elliot. This was easy enough to accomplish, accompanied as we were by brisk rhythms on the piano. Then we were shown an arm movement to be done on a certain count, then another movement for the other arm. Finally on top of these separate arm and foot movements, we were to add in a head movement. This was quite bewildering and I found it quite impossible to add in even one arm. But some of the older pupils were able to put everything together, even with a superb and beautiful precision. Other movements quickly followed, and again some of the people learned them with extraordinary speed. At the same time Pierre constantly enjoined everyone to keep a connection with their bodies, a feature that puzzled me at the time.

After the Movements class there was a long reading from *All And Everything* followed by dinner. At dinner the atmosphere was very different from lunch. For one thing Mr. Bennett left early and people began to converse and dispute with us. We expressed surprise on finding that nearly everyone ate meat and many also smoked. We had formed a conception of what people who followed a Way should be like, and this was mostly based on what we had read about Yogis. My two friends and I were strict vegetarians, teetotallers and non-smokers, and attached some importance to these disciplines. But the Gurdjieff pupils merely smiled at our arguments.

After dinner we returned to London. We had been together the whole day and certainly at all the important conversations. I was therefore surprised at the reactions of my friends. Not only were our evaluations different, but also we had evidently seen and heard quite differently. Charles thought that Mr. Bennett was concerned with his personal appearance, whereas I thought that he had been quite careless, and nothing in my later experience led me to change such a view! Lewis considered him an intellectual; yet it seemed to me that he had discouraged all talk not related to experience.

I think we were encumbered by our conceptions of what a Teacher or Guru should be like. Nevertheless I had seen enough to be very interested, and I had already decided to go again. There were indications that these people had knowledge of methods, and that was what I wished to learn. To my friends the exercise had appeared trivial and the people pleasant but ordinary.

Although at this time I was much enamoured by the ideas of Gurdjieff, I was still strongly influenced by the life and teachings of Sri Ramakrishna. But there was one very important difference in their approaches. Ramakrishna urged detachment from "Woman and Gold," and it is notable that his chief pupils became monks, while others chafed at the responsibility of householders, wishing to devote themselves entirely to the spiritual life. Gurdjieff, however, said that while retirement from life was necessary in the Ways of the Fakir, the Way of the Monk and the Way of the Yogi, yet in the Fourth Way the very opposite was necessary. The conditions of a man's life reflected what he was and at the same time provided the obstacles necessary for inner Work. Gurdjieff encouraged his pupils to be efficient, versatile and clever at their work. The emphasis lay, not in retiring from life, but on guarding the inner life while manifesting externally.

During the next few weeks I visited Coombe Springs again, went to Question Meetings at Denison House, and attended readings of *All and Everything* and of the second series of Gurdjieff's writings. I was still uncommitted and thought of going to India to become a monk. I think I was fascinated by the idea of having no responsibility and no work. Gurdjieff's method was the very antithesis of this.

I soon found that every activity that Gurdjieff students undertook was used as a means of Work. This produced very striking impressions in spite of the prior readings of Ouspensky's book. For example the readings of *All and Everything* were taken very seriously and would often continue for near on two hours. At my first reading, I distinguished myself by falling fast asleep, which made me feel rather sheepish.

When I telephoned Miss Rina Hands she reassured me gaily, "Oh everyone falls asleep during readings of Beelzebub." Why can't I read it to myself at home? Because listening in this way is an excellent Work of attention. Many of the pupils would sit cross-legged completely immobile during the whole reading.

The second series of Gurdjieff's writings at this time used to be read on Wednesdays at a large house in Colet Gardens. This book had not been published then, but formed an extraordinary contrast to *All and Everything*. Whereas the latter is written in an involved prosody with sentences of great length and with fantastic invented names such as HEPTAPARAPARSHINOKH, *Meetings with Remarkable Men* is written in a vivid, lucid, easily understandable style. Moreover, the adventures of Gurdjieff's youth were remarkable in the extreme.

At these readings, as indeed everywhere that Gurdjieff students met together, one saw evidences of a discipline. While waiting for the reading to begin most people would sit quite still and there was no chat. For the newcomer, the silence was awe-inspiring if not forbidding. Naturally, I wondered what precisely these students were doing.

Very soon, through the agency of Miss Hands, I joined one of the Movements classes at Colet Gardens. Here for the first time, I saw some of Gurdjieff's own Movements and heard the special music composed by Thomas E. Hartmann. I shall never forget watching the lowest class performing the Obligatories. These were the simplest exercises but seemed to me incredibly complex and utterly beautiful. The Eastern music, the precision of the Movements and the quality of the gestures called forth my admiration. I did not realize then that this was the lowest class and that their standard was far from perfect.

When I joined the class myself I soon began to understand the strange silences and immobility of the other pupils. Everyone used this time to practice self-remembering and self-observation—right from the moment of entering the room we were encouraged to regard this time as an opportunity for "Work." For a period of an hour and a half, we attempted to permit no mechanical manifestations, but to do everything as consciously as possible.

First we sat cross-legged and relaxed, but even then keeping our eyes steady on a spot, not permitting our eyes to wander or the attention to be distracted from the business of deepening the relaxation. Then it was explained that when we learned the Movements each gesture and position should be taken with the maximum economy; that we should Work to visualise in advance with our heads the gestures we were to take, that we should constantly return to the relaxation of all unnecessary muscular tensions; that we should watch the inner state of our feelings as if "carrying a glass of water."

The Movements were so complicated that they were impossible to perform unless one's feelings were sufficiently quiet to permit one's head to Work in advance. Not only were the arms and head moved on different counts while the feet performed various rhythms, but sometimes one had to count aloud in various contrived and complicated ways. One, two, three, four; four, three, two, one; two, three, four, five; five, four, three, two; three, four, five, six; six, five, four, three—and so on while performing an exercise. Or sometimes, 1 100; 2 99; 3 98; 4 97; and so on. It was not for nothing that one Movement was called the *"Arche-difficile."*

My own first attempts to do Movements made me very miserable. I was quite unable to master the complicated rhythms. As I worked at the back of the class, everything in me cried out against the absurdity of performing these impossible tricks. This was one of my first tastes of what was called the "denying force," a taste that soon became all too familiar.

I almost gave up. Then one day, we were doing a simple marching rhythm, four with the left and four with the right. A Frenchman, Alfred Etievan-Etieval, who had been with Mr. Gurdjieff in Paris, was instructing us. He said, "Every time you bring your foot down, affirm your presence." This I tried to do, bringing my attention back again and again to this affirmation. At the end of the class I found that my inner state had completely changed and I understood then for the first time the sense and aim of these Movements. I experienced a great quietness in my feelings, a warm glow in the breast, and I could sense my presence all around my body. All at once I began to see why the other students sat so still and why there was the strange insistence upon connection with the body. And this was a pointer also to the real significance of "self-remembering." A general heightening of the sensibilities accompanied this state. I could hear my own voice and even simple objects appeared to me immensely rich and variegated in colour and shape. This state did not last long and I did not notice the moment of its passing. But at least I knew now that the Work could produce a definite change of state. Only some time later did I awake and remember the state I had been in.

As suggested by Mr. Bennett in his letter to me, I soon began to attend "Questions and Answers" meetings at Denison House. These meetings were open to new people who could be readily distinguished from the regular Gurdjieff students. At eight o'clock precisely Mr. Bennett would appear from behind a screen and mount the rostrum. There he would sit perfectly still, with impassive features. Sometimes he would glance at someone, smile and then return into himself again. His entrance always caused an instant silence—sometimes ten minutes passed before anyone asked a question. Indeed in such an atmosphere it wasn't easy to speak.

With my friends I had formerly been to many public meetings and delighted in such teasers as "How can free-will be reconciled with fate?" "Can you explain the change of personality affected by leucotomy in terms of the Karmic Laws?" The atmosphere at Denison House, however, precluded any such clever-clever questions. When at last a question was forthcoming, Mr. Bennett would consider it a long time before answering. If the question was sincere and related to a wish to understand the Work, then the forthcoming answer often contained more than the questioner had requested. But philosophising, or wiseacring, or equating ideas from different systems was severely discouraged.

Questioners were also apt to have their questions fired back at them, which could be very disconcerting. So that when someone asked how to work against day-dreaming, they were asked, "But what have you tried?" What seemed a brilliant question and observation met with short shrift; "Why have you made such a tale of this?" On the other hand, Mr. Bennett seemed often to hear and to answer the true question that lay behind an embarrassing formulation. I shall never forget one such meeting when a tall fair-haired young man said, "I want to ask you a question and I do not want to ask you a question. My question is: Why am I speaking?" Such a question appeared nonsensical to me. Mr. Bennett however answered with great force and gravity, "Because you were created to be free."

I soon began to understand that it was necessary to have made a study, to have observed closely, to have gathered material, before asking a question. Mr. Bennett would sometimes chide people for their passivity: "I could tell you things, but without your Work, it would be like dry peas rattling round."

At the beginning, I gathered very little from these meetings and new people often complained that things were not said clearly, or were put in some sort of secret language. Actually, everything was said as plainly as possible, but it was only much later that I saw that this was so, and understood why at first I simply could not *"hear."*

In spite of all these new activities and the fact that I soon found many kindred spirits among the other students, I began to feel very dissatisfied. I had been to Coombe Springs on a few more Sundays, cut logs, dug trenches, and washed mountains of pots and pans in the back kitchen. I had tried the psychological exercises but they had eluded me, and after lunch I could understand neither the observations nor the explanations. I felt that I was getting nowhere. I had heard bits and pieces about the Work, but they seemed unrelated and there was nothing I could get my teeth into. Then early in November, I had a notice giving me the opportunity of a private interview with Mr. Bennett. I was not very much inclined to go, as I was a bit sore after having been "shot down in flames" at one of the Question Meetings. I appealed to Miss Rina Hands. She said simply, "You should go along."

A number of others were waiting at the flat in Kensington so I had to wait my turn. When at last I went in, Mr. Bennett asked me gently how I was getting on. At this simple question all my discontent seemed to flow over. I was very satisfied with the ideas of the Work, but did not feel that I had got to grips with work on myself. I complained that many students at Coombe Springs seemed to think that this was the only way, and asked whether criticism was forbidden.

"On the contrary," Mr. Bennett replied. "Mr. Gurdjieff even had written up over the door of the study-house words to the effect that 'He who has no critical power might just as well go away from here.'" He went on to say that I now knew something of the ideas of the Work, but nothing of the techniques. I could not help interrupting him to say that was indeed the case and was for me, personally, exasperating. He then said that if I wished, I could join a study group, which would have its first meeting that Saturday. At this my heart sank a little. I had arranged a birthday party, but I knew that Mr. Gurdjieff had expected his pupils to put the "Work" before everything. Hesitantly then, I explained that I was twenty-one on that day, and that I had already arranged a birthday party for that day, but which nevertheless, I would put off. Mr. Bennett smiled and said that on no account should I do that, but simply to learn about the meeting and come a fortnight later. He said that I was very fortunate to find the Work so young, and that he himself had not met it until he was twenty-three. Further, he said, that it was a very good omen for me to take such a decision on my birthday—Mr. Gurdjieff always used to put his own birthday aside for taking major decisions.

This interview gave me a new view of Mr. Bennett. Up to that moment, I had still thought of going to India to find a Guru. Although I had been impressed from the start, I was nevertheless wary. Had not Gurdjieff warned of pupils who had "set up their shacher-macher workshop booths with crumbs from his ideas table?" This interview, however, dispelled any lingering suspicions. Normally Mr. Bennett had seemed to me severely aloof, as if he wished everyone to evaluate the ideas for their own sake, without any personal consideration. At this interview I felt a warmth, a human sympathy. In fact this turned out to be a turning point of my life—and it was not the last time that I almost missed a great opportunity because of my vexed feelings

In the last chapter, I described very briefly some of the major ideas of Gurdjieff. For example, that men are machines, that they have no "I" or no Will, but at the same time they have the possibility, through a process called "work on oneself" to acquire an "I," a conscious individuality, something that could be both Master in this life and could pass through the jaws of death to exist in the next.

So much I felt, rather than understood, to be true. But why did I personally wish to undertake this "work on myself"? At this distance in time, I find it difficult to answer in all honesty. For one thing, others very rapidly replaced the reasons I gave myself at the time, once I began to understand the nature of the Work itself.

Certainly for quite a long time something had compelled me to search for a discipline. But not any discipline would do. Any discipline that required Faith as a first step was for me impossible. I believe that many young people feel as I do on this point—that they need a discipline, but it must be based on a teaching that fits the facts of their experience. In this sense Gurdjieff's system appealed to me immensely. Gurdjieff constantly admonished his pupils to accept nothing he said, but to test, to experiment, to verify for themselves. Under his methods, everything that was pseudo, sentimental and false was cauterised away. This permitted the growth of new tissue, of a different sort of Faith that was nurtured on experience. But I am getting ahead of myself. Why did I personally wish for such a discipline?

I have already said something of my idealistic pacifism, how I wished to put the world to rights, and later how the Vedanta philosophy and particularly the Law of Karma helped me to see why it was that things could not be changed. Since then I had become gradually more aware not just of the faults in the social system and other people, but also of the weaknesses and failings in my own character. Pacifist that I was, I once struck a boy so hard with a book, that he got concussion. Gradually I was becoming able to admit in myself vanities and jealousies and black moods quite incompatible with my own ideals. Mr. Gurdjieff was reputed to have said, "Nothing can change until a man changes himself."

Though perhaps I would not have formulated it to myself at the time, I knew that my outer manifestations were related to the quality of my inner experiencing, and that it was really the inner life that needed to be changed. It was just the methods of transformation that I hoped to learn from group Work. My experience did not lead me to think that this would be easy. Work, however it be named, can never be easy. It may indeed be simple, but it is also subtle, and our consciousness is usually too coarse to apprehend it. Quite apart from the intrinsic difficulties, I did not expect knowledge of methods to be handed out on platter, and indeed my expectations were amply fulfilled in this respect.

The new group consisted of about thirty people, a few of whom I had met before at Coombe, but most of whom were quite unknown to me. It was at once apparent that we were a group of widely differing types, and I suppose that the others like myself must have wondered how they came to be thrown together in a common enterprise. We had seated ourselves in Mr. Bennett's study and we awaited his entry. At length, he came in and took what I later knew to be a characteristic pose, with his left arm lying limp along the arm of the chair.

He asked the people to say whether they had made any attempts to remember themselves. In spite of the fact that everyone must have read the books, or at least be acquainted with the basic ideas, this request at once brought forth a number of strange observations.

A lady, Irene Whiffen, explained how she had tried and how "for a time the sun had shone more brightly." A man, Trevor Gawen, sitting cross-legged on the floor, in calm and measured tones said that he had remembered himself for half a day and moreover that he was remembering himself at that moment, even while speaking. Mr. Bennett leant forward and gazed at him with penetrating eyes, while I was almost transfixed with embarrassment. Another man said that he found it easier to remember himself while looking straight into another's eyes. "As you are looking into mine now?" Mr. Bennett asked.

Even from these preliminaries, I could see that Group Work was going to be a very different matter from practising Yoga with a few friends, or writing verse with a crowd of mutually admiring poets. Already I had approved some of the members, and others I had written off as sentimental or utter fools. So much for my own arrogance!!

After a few minutes Mr. Bennett began to make comments and to give an outline of our study. The first comment was that all the attempts at self-remembering had been made with the head, and it was just the head that was the least reliable instrument and the most prone to imagination. I need hardly add that in the course of his dissertation most of the efforts described above were shown to be manifestly imagination. What was necessary was to establish connection with the body.

As a first step he suggested, even while we sat there, that we should alter our postures and choose and affirm a more erect position. He then suggested a form of relaxation which would enable us to be more related to our bodies, and which we were to practice for some ten minutes every morning. He ended by saying that now we had the opportunity to learn something of the Work. If we took this exercise seriously and brought our observations to the next meeting, a further step would be shown. But if we only wanted to talk then nothing could result. Finally we were admonished to keep this study to ourselves, neither to talk of our Work to other people or to other members of the group, since this in itself was a very good way of going counter to our mechanical manifestations.

One group meeting showed me without doubt that here there was to be Work in earnest. Once again there was this talk of "connection with the body." Later I came to realize that this was the hallmark of Gurdjieff's Work. So many "spiritual exercises" that are taught either by monastic or esoteric schools can easily become a means of self-deception. People can imagine that they are doing a mental exercise when in fact they have fallen asleep. There is no means of checking where the attention has gone. All the authentic Gurdjieff Work emphasizes this connection with the body. So it was said that, "Work with one centre is deception; Work with two centres is semi-deception; only Work with three centres can lead to reality."

The daily task at once made a whole difference to my feeling of life. This Work had one important difference from any former self-imposed discipline—the fact that in a fortnight, we had to produce our own formulated results.

For anybody who joins in such a Work, the first group meetings must produce an unusual gamut of emotions, as even the memory of them does in me now, some twelve years later. First it was an ordeal simply to speak in front of the group. I don't mean in the sense of a public confession of sins such as is practiced by some bodies. Happily there was none of that, because we were all making observations on experiments that each one of us had carried out. But in speaking in front of such a group, deception became, if not impossible, at least very difficult. In the beginning people made observations, and claimed to have achieved things that were manifestly impossible. But it was patently clear to other members when people were deceiving themselves. By means of Mr. Bennett's questions and the parallel observations of other members, what was really possible and what was real, began to reveal itself.

One of the first things we began to understand about was the role of attention. It soon became clear that we could not remember ourselves for hours, or even minutes, because we had not sufficient power of attention. Repeated experiments showed that we could direct our attention for very short periods of time, and more alarmingly could not tell at what moment the attention was broken. On the contrary the effort could only be remembered when one had woken up again.

Very rapidly as meeting followed meeting more was demanded of the members. So that they would themselves look to their postures when they came to the meeting, and would prepare beforehand their state and their observations. And Mr. Bennett, who at that time could be severely aloof, would also be caustic with those who had made no efforts, or those whose comments were "purely formatory." "Purely formatory" was just about the most damning comment that could be made. I remember once asking a question and Mr. Bennett replying, "That is a purely formatory question. If you had listened to the previous answer, you had no need to ask this question."

As Mr. Bennett had promised he gave us further experiments when we showed that we had worked at the first tasks. Though I must say that "experiments" is a very inadequate description of what we had to do. Most of these experiments required carrying our Work into life, and in a curious way was a source of amusement to me. At one time, we were set a task of remembering ourselves on the hour of every hour. At that time I had begun to teach at Eaton House School, just off Sloane Square, and for me these points often coincided with the ringing of the school bell. There was I attempting to collect myself, while all hell was let loose around me.

The tasks were very varied in their nature. Sometime we would work to observe our thinking associations. Even now I do not know if this is possible. It is one thing to daydream, it is quite another to watch or to able to watch those thought associations.

Another task that we were set was to provide each day with one single and simple act of decision. Such a task must seem incredible to those who believe that their whole day is made up of a series of decisions. But this exercise showed with devastating clarity the utter mechanization of men's lives. Whatever we had read, we were still human beings and felt that our lives were full of "decisions." But our experiments showed conclusively the falsity of such a picture. Even today, I groan inwardly when I think about "tasks of decision."

These tasks of decision took many different forms. Sometimes we had to prepare a single sentence that was to be projected into the day. We always used to prepare for these decisions at the time of doing our morning relaxation exercise. Even that is a misnomer, because in reality it was a *"sensing"* exercise. When we had completed this exercise it was then that we decided what we were going to say, to whom and when. Much later when I had left school mastering and become a salesman in the North of England, I used to do this exercise while making my calls. I would choose a particularly difficult buyer, perhaps one who always made me feel uncomfortable. I still remember one such call that I made on the buyer of a very large paint manufacturer in Darwen. When the buyer, a Mr. Nightingale, entered the room I swung round on him and uttered this one sentence. I had taken this task very seriously, and this sentence was so charged that it sounded to me like a rifle shot. One immediate effect was that he acceded to my request for a sample of his Hansa Yellow, which gave me a chance to match it with the possibility of a large contract. He had never been amenable formerly, since he belonged to the old school of buyers who did not readily disclose the source of the materials he used.

However, I do not want to emphasize the success side of this story, as if such a task could be used as a means of making bigger sales! This simple task showed clearly the fact that everything is normally done without decision at all. That one act decided upon stood out in contrast to all the other events of the day. This demonstrated forcibly the truth of Gurdjieff's contention that everything happened.

As the weeks went by my attitude towards Mr. Bennett and indeed towards all the other people in the groups and connected with Coombe Springs, underwent a profound change. No longer could I concern myself as to whether Mr. Bennett had authority from Gurdjieff to be a Teacher. Such a question now seemed naive and laughable. It was soon manifest that what we had learned simply could not be got out of books. The Work that was passed on was something organic, and Mr. Bennett could pass it on only in so far as he understood how to "work on himself." Certainly we all came to have a profound respect for him, but not because he taught. Rather the tasks were means by which we were able to recognize our own truths, and it was truly marvellous how much they were one's own yet shared by all the others in the group. We knew that alone we could never put ourselves under the demand that we believed necessary. In any case, he was not half as severe with us, as he was with himself.

This closer acquaintance cleared up many of the mysteries and the curious first impressions. For example, the talks at Denison House became more and more intelligible for one simple reason. The terms of reference lay in the experiments that we were doing. Without doing the experiments oneself it was impossible to recognize the processes and substances referred to. Everything was said as plainly and as accurately as possible, yet the newcomer felt that everything was being made purposely mysterious and unnecessarily complicated.

I also began to see why people often spoke of their failures in what seemed extravagant terms. They were trying to align their observations with the facts of their experience. They were trying not to "lie."

As time went on people in the group began to speak with greater frankness. There were types whom I never got to like—I believe it was mutual—but for whom the Group Work made me have a profound respect. One had evidence that everyone at least wished to be free from their exasperating weaknesses. And it was salutary to reflect that what one regarded as a playful foible in oneself was a similar cause of exasperation for others. Respect and tolerance were the least results. With the majority there was forged an indissoluble bond of friendship and understanding.

Throughout the whole of Gurdjieff's Work a tremendous emphasis was placed on "payment." This word was understood on many different levels. "We must learn to pay the debt of our arising" was almost a favourite theme of Mr. Bennett's. The idea that we had a debt to pay was quite contrary to my opinions at that time. Without much consideration I held the view that I had not asked to be born, and therefore life owed me a living, and leisure and freedom of expression and so on - a view that is held by many young people today.

Mr. Bennett however spoke of life as a gift, which put us in debt. Obligation—we were under an obligation to pay the debt of our arising. We came to expect to pay for everything. Gurdjieff had taught that what a man does not pay for, he does not value. So we paid, as we understood with efforts and pertinacity, and also with cash. One paid a subscription for Group Work and also for Movements classes. Of course, many could not pay, and on the contrary were helped. But still it was implicit that Group Work was more valuable than the odd packet of cigarettes.

During this time I myself was somewhat poor, and while teaching during the day, I had to return at night to a bleak room behind Olympia, where my fat landlady was almost always in a state of vocal inebriation. Not that that mattered much to me. Indeed neither did my teaching work. That was a drab world compared to this other, where everything was always changing and exciting, imbued with a sort of Eastern or Arabian Nights atmosphere.

I then began to cast about in order to live at Coombe Springs. Just as formerly no-one had told me that Groups existed, so also there was no advertised way for going to live at Coombe Springs. Through the good offices of some of the ladies, who had mercy on my tender years, my desire was made known to Mr. Bennett who intimated that I should ask to see him one Sunday. This I did and explained my wish simply. But it was not so simple. Why did I wish that, he asked. Stumblingly I explained, and was told that I could come if I was prepared to work, in every sense of the word, and that I would have to consider myself merely on probation. In fact, I was on probation for the next three years!

Group Work had drawn together the scattered threads of the psychological Work, and unified and made comprehensible such different activities as the readings, manual work and the Movements classes. Going to live at Coombe Springs at once accelerated many processes and gave me a much more intimate picture of the Work and those engaged in it.

Coombe Springs is a large house set in some eight acres of grounds. Its pink walls and green shutters gave it a rather unusual appearance. There are a number of buildings containing garages, laundry and sleeping quarters. One of these, constructed during the war for research laboratories, was called the "fish bowl." (I don't know whether this reflected on the plentiful glass or the state of the residents!) To the south and the west of the house there is a rose-garden surrounded by a yew hedge, and this in turn is surrounded on both sides by large lawns. Further to the west the ground slopes down through a wooded glade with many brambles to the old spring house built by Cardinal Wolsey, from where water was piped under the Thames to Hampton Court Palace. On the north side was a large kitchen garden.

[Alas all this was true at the time of writing in 1960. A few years later the whole estate was given away to one Idries Shah, who promptly sold it all for its land value. An old oak and the Spring House are all that remains.]

When I went to Coombe Springs about thirty people were living there, some of whom were working full-time as cooks and gardeners, but most like myself went out to work. Mr. Bennett was engaged most of the time in writing his book *"The Dramatic Universe."* During this time Mrs. Bennett, who was some 20 years older than her husband, had been seriously ill and expected to die. However, by the time that I arrived at Coombe, she had recovered sufficiently to grace our meals with her presence and to assume her accustomed direction of the household affairs.

Living at Coombe perforce gave me a more realistic attitude towards my fellow students. Meeting only on Sundays or at Group Meetings it was easy to get the impression that everyone was immensely earnest in their endeavours. On the whole they were, but I had seen this to the exclusion of their personal *faiblesses,* their personality characteristics. In the family it was impossible to conceal anything. Everybody's personal weaknesses were simply household jokes. But the very seeing of this was a salutary process. We were all in the same boat. We all had personalities that masqueraded absurdly, but which nevertheless dominated the entombed and struggling seed of being.

One of my personal weaknesses was very quickly spotlighted—*instinctive imagination.* This took the form of extreme fussiness over food, a dislike of cold water, set hours for sleep, and so on and so forth. Concerning food, I had always liked plain fare. At Coombe Springs, however, there were many people with quite recent memories of eating in Mr. Gurdjieff's flat (he died in October 1949) and moreover, Mr. Gurdjieff's niece, Luba Gurdjieff, was one of the cooks.

It is strange now to think that I had a struggle to accustom myself to dishes even the names of which make my mouth water today: Shashlik, goulash, ragout, Borsch and Piroshki and wonderful beet root soups, and extraordinary Russian salads, and cheeses from Lapland, and even on occasion that rarest of delicacies Khaisarian Bastourma. Delicious as they now sound, at that time, they caused me considerable difficulty and embarrassment.

At one lunch I was served with Vienna Sausages and Sauerkraut. I whispered to the waiter that I was not hungry, and to my aggravation he fussed about while I repeated murderously, "I'm not hungry. I want nothing." But nothing escaped Mr. Bennett. "What is it, Tony?" he called in ringing tones.

"Nothing, Sir. I'm not hungry."

After lunch he passed me in the hall and said simply "This is slavery." I was indignant. Slavery? Just because I did not eat Sauerkraut? The man's a maniac. But it was no good. Justifying associations got you nowhere at Coombe. In ordinary life, "I am always right." At Coombe, we observed ourselves—we were always wrong!!

I well remember a number of occasions for fighting against that particular form of slavery. Who could forget those huge and glutinous pigs' trotters? I regret to say that I managed to evade them! This however was only one aspect of Work in regard to food. Mr. Bennett as indeed Mr. Gurdjieff before him often drew our attention to the careless and bestial way in which we ate. The process of eating was fundamentally a sacred process. Food was not merely food for the body, but also contained *the food of impressions.* So mealtimes at Coombe were regarded as an opportunity for Work, and people prepared their inner states so as to eat and taste as consciously as possible.

This attitude towards food, perhaps more than anything else, used to produce a profound effect upon newcomers. It was strange indeed to sit down in a dining room with perhaps a hundred people, none of who spoke and all of whom were intent upon their inner Work. Great importance was also attached to the cooking and serving of food.

Even this example of eating in silence illustrates how much we were between Scylla and Charybdis, and how truly the path of Work is called a Razor's edge. We had no sooner avoided the Scylla of automatic manifestations than we were sucked into the whirlpool of Charybdis— identification with our inner state. Many of us found great difficulty in understanding this, and Mr. Bennett's attempts to help us often filled me with fury. On the one hand he drew our attention to our carelessness for our inner state, how it was necessary to relax our bodies, to *be present*; on the other hand he had no sooner urged this with great effect and seriousness than he would mock us for doing this very thing. If he found us sitting silently he was sure to initiate a loud and merry conversation; or he would ask us what we imagined we were doing, and he would pick the one most obviously dispersed person and say that she was the only one awake in the room. How difficult it was to understand even the necessity of achieving a balance between the outer and the inner worlds.

Since people went to Coombe Springs with the intention of working on themselves, every activity was used as a means toward that end. There was then no question of people doing jobs for which they were best fitted by nature, or for which they had been trained. On the contrary, it was typical that I was asked to look after two infernal machines, since I had an utter loathing for anything mechanical. The first was the central heating boiler. Simple enough that it seems now, at that time I regarded it with horror. I still remember being taken down into the dank pit where it was housed, where one, John Penseney, tapped the wretched thing intimately with a crooked poker while explaining the mysteries of the worm-screw feed and the absurdly friable cotter pins. Though I regarded this task with horror it turned out to be quite easy. Having an aversion to cold, it gave me some pleasure to keep the house warm. Some of my happiest moments occurred when barrowing anthracite from a large heap, tipping it into the pit and then shovelling it into the hopper. We were often faced with tasks, which seemed loathsome and impossible, but whose difficulties evaporated once the burden was shouldered.

I was also asked to mow the lawns and had to look after a very temperamental Rotoscythe. How many Sunday mornings was I filled with helpless vexation because the thing would not start? And then aggravation when, with a sneaking hope that it had really bust, the wretched thing roared into life. Mr. Bennett was sure to pass at that moment and cry "Stop!" and we froze and took snapshots of our inner state. That was bad enough, but who could forgive the weeding women who deliberately planted boulders in my path?

Another little task that I was given for a few weeks was to cook breakfast for the Bennett's in the top kitchen, while Margaret Wichmann was away on holiday in Germany. Since I also had to do the central heating boiler and attend the practice Movements' class before breakfast, this was manifestly impossible. But we had to be clever; we had to find a way. What did we expect? Had we not come to work on ourselves?

I must not overdraw the picture as if we spent the whole time dealing with unpleasantness and obstacles—this was far from the case. There was a tremendous spirit of camaraderie, and there were plenty of times that we had outings, say to the gardens at Wisley, or a picnic on Leith Hill. But of course the greatest fun was the Work itself. It may have been difficult and at times unpleasant, it may have forced us to see our weaknesses in sharp relief, but nevertheless it gave a point and direction to existence, as well as providing us with any amount of humorous situations.

This attitude towards physical work was very much influenced by the stories Mr. Gurdjieff had told of his early life in the second series of his writings. His father had made him learn one skill after another; he had no sooner learnt carpentry than he would be put on to metal work, and so on. As a result he became extremely versatile. His father had never let him lay a-bed, but forced him to rise early and to wash naked under a pump. We tried to follow this example, to be more connected, more at home in our bodies, at the same time not to be slave of the body but to make body work. Mr. Gurdjieff laid great stress upon this, explaining how the body will get up to all sorts of tricks to avoid work—it will even feign headaches and sickness. From accounts of life at the Prieuré, Fontainebleau, it seemed that Mr. Gurdjieff made it the first aim for people that they should become masters of their bodies and for that it was necessary to make the body work enormously hard.

In this Mr. Bennett set a disheartening example. He was wont to arise early, stalk across the lawn in his yellow dressing gown, and go for a dip in the springs. Naturally the young men, and many of the women also, followed this example. I did not continue this practice for long myself. After the dip in this lead lined basin sunk into the floor of the ancient Springs house, we assembled in the Fishbowl in a bitterly cold room with a concrete floor to practice the Movements we were learning. Since there may be some twenty of us who were in different classes, we would all be practicing different Movements, so it was incredibly difficult to attend to one's own Work.

Mr. Bennett used to work to a terrifying schedule. Sometimes he would appear in the garden and take part with a gang doing the heaviest work, and often after a hard day he would drive up to London to give a lecture, then return to Coombe Springs, go straight to his study and dictate his book, *The Dramatic Universe,* till two or three in the morning.

Naturally we all began to take a pride in becoming as versatile as possible, in learning new jobs quickly and in overcoming obstacles. I fear that my own body must have been conspicuously inert however. At one summer seminar we had to drink toasts to each other at dinner. I had the honour of being toasted by Mr. Bennett himself: "May Tony be freed from instinctive imagination which is for him an unnecessary obstacle in Work!"

The weekends were always times of great activity at Coombe Springs. On Saturday afternoons right into the evenings the groups would meet and perhaps some two hundred people would pass through the house. Many who came from distances would stay for the night.

Sunday was the day par excellence for physical work of all kinds.

My Stairway to Subud

Many people came down from London and around, and would find their names on a list for cutting wood, repair work, cooking, looking after children or the sick, washing-up and waiting at tables. At ten-thirty everyone would have met in the hall and be sitting, silent and motionless, when Mr. Bennett descended the stairs. He would then discourse upon one particular aspect of the Work and suggest some line of study, after which we would go about our tasks.

These Sunday experiments were very varied in nature. It is impossible, alas, to represent their true sense and aim without giving the discourses in full, and even then that would only be an apology. To really understand the essence it was necessary to take part in the Work.

However here are a few examples. Sometimes we worked to make the thinking, feeling and moving centres work together. This experiment made for a great difference in attitude towards all sorts of tasks. I mostly regarded Work as something to be got through and liked to have my mind free to think its own thoughts. But in attempting three centre work, any work whatsoever could become alive and interesting, as well as being done with maximum efficiency. I can still remember working at this task while washing a mountain of dishes and saucepans in the back-kitchen for close on two hours and the extraordinary satisfaction that I felt. Not my normal reaction to this task!

Sometimes we worked to be free from day-dreams and while doing our tasks we would learn lists of words; perhaps the Tibetan years—*Shing-chiwa-lo, Shing-lang-lo.* Or count inwardly One, A Hundred; Two, Ninety-Nine; Three, Ninety-Eight; Four, Ninety-Seven. My readers may imagine doing this for a period of two to three hours while shovelling anthracite or barrowing heavy wheelbarrows of sloppy concrete mix. At other times we worked to maintain the relaxation of our bodies and to avoid all unnecessary speech and Movements.

Every single exercise went against automatism, required decision, effort and persistence, and created the conditions for self-observation. If undertaken with sufficient intensity they could bring about a remarkable change in the inner state. After lunch people volunteered their observations.

Movements after tea were also a regular feature of Sundays. At the Movements' classes in Colet Gardens, London, we all learnt the Movements devised by Mr. Gurdjieff himself with the music of

Thomas de Hartman, which were complicated but also aesthetically satisfying. Sunday Movements however were improvisations usually made up by Pierre Elliot or Mr. Bennett himself. They were not only hideously difficult, but often barbarically ugly as well. As time went on the usefulness of these Movements became more and more apparent. They were a unique means for learning how both to achieve an inner state and manifest outwardly at the same time.

One Sunday in 1951 the most expert of the Movements classes from London were to be filmed outside on the lawns. It was a glorious midsummer's day and I had arranged to cut the long grass under the old oak in order to have a good view. The experts from many groups had gathered and were to perform in their white costumes with coloured sashes and gold headbands. However, I had reckoned without Mr. Bennett's Sunday morning talk. He suggested that we all make it a task not to let our interest be drawn to the Movements class, but to attend religiously to the work in hand. I joined a gang at the bottom of the garden clearing brambles and bamboos in a swampy patch. All day long we could hear the piano playing a Kurdish melody, but nobody went near or watched the class. Even those who had to cross the lawn never raised their eyes, much to the surprise of the class, who knew nothing of our task. At the end of that Sunday's Work everyone understood in a very real way the meaning of the "force of interest". I loathed that Sunday.

Since I am writing in retrospect it is impossible to portray the gradual unfolding of ideas. Many things that are clear now were bewildering at that time. One of the most bewildering was the attitude of some of the older pupils, who were always declaring that they did not understand this or that, and continued to ask simple questions about such things as self-observation. I confess that I was much deceived by this at first, and wondered how such people came to be chosen as group leaders. There were other precipitate devils that thought that they understood much more than they did. May the Good Lord deal mercifully with them!!

I think it must have been my second Sunday at Coombe Springs when Mr. Bennett asked the assembled company how they understood "self-remembering". A long and for me incomprehensible silence followed. At last one of the women mumbled something about having a connection with her body. I felt somewhat sorry for Mr. Bennett that he should have so many dull and inarticulate pupils, and was about to give a glib answer from my "formatory apparatus," based simply on my reading. Happily for me on that occasion I desisted. Much later I began to see that I did not understand at all in what self-remembering consisted. Of course many people who have read Ouspensky make the same mistake, and even go so far as to write about experiencing of manifestly different qualities and lump them all together under the heading of "self-remembering."

It was only after a long period that it became clear that self-remembering was not one thing, but was composed of innumerable facets and gradations. It related to "being" and depended upon the availability and blending of certain energies. Even a little experience helped to make clear the tremendous variety and richness of inner experiences, and incidentally to show that what is sometimes called "mystical" can derive from different origins.

While those who lived in London often complained of the difficulty of remembering the Work, for those who lived at Coombe Springs it was impossible to forget. One lunchtime on a weekday shortly after I had gone to live there, Mr. Bennett came in when what we called a "dispersed atmosphere" prevailed. In other words we were chattering like monkeys. He asked us all with what aim we were living at Coombe Springs. Mr. Gurdjieff had laid great stress upon the necessity of having a personal aim, an idea that I had never really understood. I spoke up and said that while I wished to follow the various exercises and activities I could in no way formulate for myself a satisfactory personal aim. I don't remember how the discussion proceeded, but on many similar occasions Mr. Bennett would remind us of the futility of living together if it were not for the sake of the Work.

On this particular occasion I ran after him up to his study after lunch and asked him to help me formulate an aim. He said, "Make it your aim to understand what is 'work on yourself.'" I felt very disappointed at this. What else was I doing, living at Coombe Springs, attending Groups and Movements' classes, sitting immobile through long readings of *"All and Everything,"* working like a navvy on Sundays, were it not for just that "work on myself?" It was only very much later that I came to understand that merely taking part in no way constituted work on oneself. It was not until the interest and the novelty had worn off that I began even to wish to understand.

Like many people I had mistaken my affirmation for my Work. At Coombe Springs, however, I became aware gradually of the reality of the denying force. When once I spoke to Mr. Bennett of certain difficulties, he replied, "Now you can Work. When you

My Stairway to Subud

first came all was affirmation without negation and that made an unreal triad." At that time, I had no idea what he was talking about.

In our group many people began to say that they did not want to Work. "Why are you here then?" I thought. I knew my own laziness, but never doubted my fundamental desire for the Work and felt impatient with my failing brethren. Later I saw that these people had observed more deeply than I. They already saw what I can now but dimly grasp—how really fundamentally our natures are opposed to change.

In the summer seminar of 1953 a woman from Germany said she was not able to understand what was said about not wanting to Work. As soon as she had heard of the Work she felt a great joy, and she wanted nothing more in the world than the Work. Many people hung their heads with embarrassment. This made clear how nothing could be explained. She did not see and therefore she did not and could not understand explanations. Later she would understand and then again explanations would be unnecessary. Such talks as we had were really "symbols" in the sense that they could only confirm what one had already understood.

People have often complained of the mysteries of Gurdjieff's system, as if it was deliberately obscurantist. But in reality it was not the Work that was a mystery but that all Work, however it is called, is always a mystery. And it must always be so because of a defect inherent in our natures—blindness that makes man believe in his own strivings towards the good, and inability to understand the significance of Grace. Gurdjieff's methods helped one to see gradually what was meant by "Man cannot do." Indeed it was constantly reiterated that we must come to see our own nothingness. And little by little our complacency was chipped away and we were brought to our knees. But, I must emphasize, I did not understand this at the time.

Certainly the area of impossibility became clearer. Curiously, it was just "effort," which showed so clearly that man, cannot do. Effort always highlighted our inadequacies rather than our achievements. But I did not think that it was always to be like that. I felt that Mr. Bennett had some master-joker up his sleeve, and that some day we would be taught a highly esoteric trick and would plug into the vast energy resources of the "big accumulator" and be able to remember ourselves for the rest of our living days!

One aspect of the life at Coombe Springs that is difficult to convey was the continual flux in the population. When I first arrived the "family" was really quite small. There was Olga de Nottbeck, Marjorie Wilmshurst, Sally Jenkins, Kate Woodward, Bryn Thring, Eve Wilkinson and Joan Cox. The men were quite few and mostly very young: John Wilkinson, Saxon Aldred, John Penseney, Patrick Wilson and Sidney Jenkins. Later, following the publication of Ouspensky's *In Search of the Miraculous* and Gurdjieff's *All and Everything,* there was a constant stream of new people. Perhaps the most remarkable feature was that they were mostly young men. Mr. Bennett also gave some lectures at Denison House in Victoria, London, but that was as much publicity as Coombe Springs ever got. The way so many arrived at Coombe Springs was full of coincidences so that one could not doubt the workings of some invisible force. People arrived not only from all parts of England, but also from South Africa, Australia, Canada, the States, Norway, Holland and so on.

One thing that is worthy of comment and yet which we all took for granted, was the complete absence of colour bar and racial discrimination of any kind at Coombe. Nor was there any question of being artificially friendly to foreigners. In general there was no concern as to where people had come from—everyone was accepted simply as a brother in the Work. This was a matter of great satisfaction to me personally, since I had a number of Indian friends. I was always confident that I could introduce them to people in the Work and be sure that they would be delighted by the complete ease and friendliness of their reception.

This same attitude could also be said to apply to religions. I think that everybody at Coombe was interested in all religions and there was never any question but that everybody had tolerance of other faiths. More than that, many people had a particular interest in one religion or part of their scriptures. The favourite reading of my friend, John Penseney, was the *Mathnawi* of Jallal Uddin Rumi. Another friend who had lived in India discovered the *Upanishads* while living at Coombe! My own favourite was the Life of Sri Ramakrishna, I used to read to Mrs. Bennett while she was ill in bed. Very occasionally, she used to read to me from the Gospels— she knew the whole of St. Matthew by heart. Mr. Bennett's knowledge of the sacred books was likewise prodigious—he could quote equally well from Greek or Pali texts, from Old and New Testaments. Sometimes people at Denison House would ask questions to be met with a reply like, "But how do you understand *neempsis* which is generally translated as *sobriety*?"

This open attitude was extended to many other things other than race or religion. Medicine and music at once come to mind. While there was a natural respect for orthodox medicine, there was also an interest in homeopathy, and in de la Warr's methods of diagnosis. At Coombe one could meet osteopaths and teachers of the Matthias Alexander techniques, and in more recent times Dr. Rolf from the USA has given demonstrations in "postural dynamics."In music too one could rely on everyone to be catholic in their appreciation, or at least to be ready to listen to all types of music. Many a Sunday evening after a long day's work we would gather in the music room and Donald Neill, our resident Australian, would play for us. Mr. Gurdjieff was a Georgian and his music combined many influences—Greek, Kurdish, Russian, Arabic, European, Semitic and Asiatic. At other times we would listen to classical music, or Turkish or Indian records.

Apart from those interested directly in the Work, there were many distinguished visitors. One day we had to demonstrate the movements before the famous Japanese Zen Master, Professor D.T.Suzuki. Rumour had it afterwards that he had said that Coombe Springs was the nearest thing to a Zen monastery in the occident. Another time a music professor from Vienna interested the household in the twelve-tone scale of music, almost to the point of infatuation, till Mrs. Bennett had him banished suddenly.

Frank Lloyd Wright, the celebrated American architect, paid a visit to inspect the nine-sided hall that was built later. He was heard to remark, "Mr. Bennett, you have the ugliest house that ever I saw— it just hates its environment."

Apart from these, there were many of the older pupils of Gurdjieff or Ouspensky, who had been at Fontainebleau or Gadsden. These pupils mostly distinguished themselves by their modesty, simply joining quietly in the routine. Mrs. Bennett would perhaps give me a tip and I would discover that the new person had been six years at the Prieuré or had been chauffeur to Ouspensky. However, they were not all so modest. To tell the truth, some liked to teach and thought that they had the right to administer shocks. For example, a German lady once read accounts of conversations with Mr. Gurdjieff in his Paris flat. Afterwards I innocently told her how much I had enjoyed the reading. "Enjoy?" she said witheringly. "Enjoy is masturbator word."

The people who lived in the house had many unusual opportunities. One evening after dinner one of the older women pupils asked why it was that Mr. Gurdjieff had laid such emphasis upon the necessity of loving one's parents. She had a particular difficulty in that she had lost her parents while young and hardly knew them. Mr. Bennett answered this question with great gravity. He said that many people in the Work made great efforts and just because they were never reconciled to their parents everything came to nothing. He spoke of the mysterious connection of blood, of how it was necessary to love one's parents whether one had known them or not. (Miss Rina Hands had also told me that Mr. Gurdjieff had said that a child must love his father so that a place could be prepared from which later he could love God.)

This talk had a profound effect since many people had family difficulties. I was among them, and as Mr. Bennett left the room I sprang impetuously up the stairs after him and asked whether I could speak to him at once. I explained my difficulties. My parents were colonials whose views and ideas were quite incompatible with my liberal views, particularly on matters of colour and religion. I simply did not see how it was possible to love one's parents when there was such a lack of communication.

Mr. Bennett said that he did not mean that I should become blind to their weaknesses, just as I must become cognizant of my own. "Your own state is not free in relation to them," he continued. "You must be able to love them consciously, because you choose to." I asked him how I could remedy the situation and he suggested what seemed to be a simple task. When I wrote to them I was to hold within myself a certain attitude, but on no account to attempt to explain anything of my own ideas and views to them.

This simple task proved to be far from easy, but the fact remains that from that date my relationship with my parents grew better. They even remarked upon the sudden change in my letters. Inevitably I began to see things about myself, how I was connected to my parents in a way that formerly I had denied. Certainly it remained true that there is a part of man that is not related to anybody but is connected solely and directly to God. But I began to concede how very like I was to my parents, being a compound of their faults and virtues.

As my confidence in Mr. Bennett increased, I consulted him about all sorts of personal matters. I might say that interviews with him were never an easy matter, for in spite of being in the family the relationship of pupil and Teacher never changed. Though Mr. Bennett joined us for meals and for various social occasions, such as picnics and cocktail parties, there was never any question but that these were simply opportunities for a particular type of Work, which was called "playing roles." We had to remember ourselves in all conditions, and what better than a party for self-observation? On these occasions, Mr. Bennett would hold forth on a variety of topics—flowering shrubs or the price of steaks in America—but I never heard him gossip about other people or scandalmonger in any form. The relationship never became on a casual footing so that one could ask for advice in a normal way.

The degree of confidence is exemplified by the fact that people began to make observations about sex, notoriously the most difficult subject for discussion with any degree of freedom. Odette Hedgcock once asked about Work during periods of menstruation, while another asked what should be done during pregnancy. I never ceased to admire these pupils for whom it was a real struggle to speak. Mr. Bennett always replied in a natural manner, with great sensitivity and care for the feelings of the questioner.

Throughout *All And Everything,* Mr. Gurdjieff referred to the sexual act as a sacred process, and Mr. Bennett also spoke of the misuse that was made of sexual energy. I once asked him in private what Gurdjieff had meant by "normal sex." "First let us get the principles clear," he replied. "There is masturbation; that releases a tension temporarily, only to be created again. There is mutual masturbation, which does the same thing for two people. Finally, there is sexual intercourse, which if done properly makes room for one's own 'I.' It is not a question of morality—even Bernard Shaw observed that there was as much immorality inside marriage as outside it. It is a question of energies. What is harmful is sexual imagination."

Once again he said much that I could not understand immediately. I thought to myself that since joining the group I had been free from the sexual thoughts and imaginings that I had had as a schoolboy. Only later did I see that sexual imagination could be in all centres, and how many apparently innocent activities are really "abuse of sex." Ordinary morality related only to external behaviour. The "right use of sexual energy" at once did away with the hypocrisy that is so often connected to conventional morality, and implied an Objective Morality, because like all Work, it was connected to the invisible inner condition. The chastity that is beholden upon the religious, or the *"brahmacharya"* of the Yogi could then be seen to be not merely a brake on outward behaviour that is so commonly understood, but to refer more truly to a discipline of the psychic energies.

As time went on, I began to see more and more how sex entered into activities and how often people were unaware that this was happening. Failure to understand this resulted not only in the nullifying of creative activities, but also in the dissipation of that force on which depended the creation of one's own being.

****

Mrs. Bennett occupied a unique place at Coombe Springs, as she did in my life and in the life of many others. She formed a complete contrast to her husband and was an ideal complement to him. If he was a huge man, she was short; if he was careless about his appearance and wore shirts and ties that clashed excruciatingly, she on the other hand would dress with great taste and delicacy. Mr. Bennett had the untidiness and the clumsiness of the exceptionally vigorous. Mrs. Bennett was neat in everything. In fact, she was not only neat, but—one has to say it—she was chic.

When I first went to Coombe Springs in 1950 at the age of 20, Mrs. Bennett was so ill that she was expected to die at any minute. Visitors had to tiptoe about the house and Mr. Bennett was apt to leave his group meetings abruptly to visit Mrs. Bennett in her bedroom next door. By the time I went to live there in the Easter holiday of 1951, she had so far recovered as to grace our meals and meetings with her presence.

Mrs. Bennett "graced" our meals in her own inimitable way. She used to sit at the top table from where she surveyed everything, and there was very little that she missed. She was utterly fearless about the opinions of other people—or in Gurdjieff's language, she was singularly free from "considering." She had a clear ringing voice that could be heard at great distance and which she was not afraid to use. Her fearlessness and perspicacity, combined with her utter contempt of all that was small minded, pompous or vain, made her at times a quite terrifying person. She would mock mercilessly, which was hilarious except for the victims of her sallies. Sometimes it was not even funny, because she was so devastatingly accurate. One of the older women, Margaret Wichmann, who served her with the utmost faithfulness till the day of her death, she used to tease, raising her hands and rolling her eyes to heaven in mock German piety. After which, to add insult to injury, she ordered her to her knees and whacked her with a newspaper.

My Stairway to Subud

This was one side of Mrs. Bennett that many people saw. I myself soon became her victim. At one lunch, Mr. Bennett asked that someone should cut off the protruding tops of the yew hedges bordering the rose-garden. Knowing my own penchant for putting things off (the disease of "tomorrow") I set about the task immediately after lunch. The next day, when Mr. Bennett had left the dining room and the tables were being cleared, Mrs. B. asked who had mutilated the hedges. "I did." "Who told you to?" "Mr. B." "Mr. B. says this, Mr. B. says that, and you all run hither and thither. Don't you know there is a Mrs. B. in the house?"

By this time she had advanced upon me and biffed me once or twice on the chest for emphasis. Gurdjieff had taught that one should not justify even when wrongfully accused. I stood silently; albeit with an inner state of indescribable fury, while the onslaught rapidly increased in intensity. Then she left the room on the arm of her doctor, Dr. Bernard Courtenay-Mayers. I heard later that he had said to her, "Why were you so angry with the boy?" At once she smiled all her anger gone. "Angry with him? What? Have you never heard of playing a role? I was not angry with him. Don't you know he is my son?"

On another occasion, I had cut my friend Peter Kermode's hair out on the lawn. Mrs. Bennett heard of this and led me to the spot by the ear, and made me get down on my knees and pick up the hair, almost invisible in the grass. I was fuming. As she walked back to the house, leaning on my arm, she stopped suddenly. "Cross as two sticks you are!" she said.

Many people saw this side of Mrs. B. to the exclusion of everything else and they would sometimes ask, "Is Mrs. Bennett in the Work?" But if Mrs. Bennett had a terrible contempt for all that was sham, she had also a complete reverence for all that was real. One of her most marvellous traits, and one which bound a number of people to her with complete devotion, was her instantaneous perception of suffering. Even though still very ill, Mrs. Bennett used often to sit through four consecutive group meetings on a Saturday afternoon. Perhaps she would pick someone out and ask them to tea in her room afterwards. Then she would talk gently of this and that. Afterwards, she sometimes asked me what I had thought of them. "Can't you see that they have suffered?" It was typical for her that she was rarely direct about the suffering itself, preferring the language of gesture. She told me how once she had found a picture of a young man with flames all around his head. This exactly corresponded for her to the state of someone she knew. She bought this picture and gave it to him. This was a typical gesture.

She also had an uncanny knack of simply picking people out and taking them for a walk in the garden. In my experience, if the person was in trouble, she rarely enquired the cause. Rather she would admire the flowers or more likely make some hilariously diverting remarks at the expense of some wretched self-conscious newcomer, but however she manifested one could always feel the delicacy of her sympathy, and troubles often evaporated in her presence. At the same time, one had to have real troubles. With these, she showed sympathy, but on self-pity she hurled the thunderbolts of her scorn.

During my three years at Coombe Springs Mrs. B. was never really well. Again and again, she had relapses and was confined to her bed. Very often, I used to visit her in her room, where the atmosphere was so much in contrast to the rest of Coombe. There everything was bustle and activity and austerity. But Mrs. B.'s bedroom was both beautiful and still. On the wall were two of her own paintings, one of a monk in his study and another of steps leading down to a Church. On the east wall hung a magnificent standing Buddha in a black case. Windows looked out to the south on to the rose-gardens and the lawns, so that the room was often filled with sunlight.

Mrs. B. often asked me to go to her room at night and read her the Life of Sri Ramakrishna. When by her breathing I judged that she was asleep, I would tiptoe to the door. How often then she would call out, "Go on!" and I would have to begin all over again. At least she slept well after these readings, which proved them more efficacious than her sleeping draughts. On occasions Mrs. B. read to me, nearly always from the Bible. When she read about Our Lord her voice would sink to an intense whisper, "...and she touched the hem of His garment." and I would leave her feeling only shame, shame, shame.

She gave me this prayer taken from Don Quixote;

"Hold it for certain, Sancho, that if it be given us, at last, as they promise thee, to behold the beatific vision of God, that vision will be a labour, a continuous and never completed conquest of the Truth Supreme and Infinite, a submergence deeper and deeper in the bottomless gulf of Life Eternal. Some will go to this glorious absorption sooner than others, and farther and more blissfully, but all will go, all will be swallowed up in it, forever and ever. If we are all on our way to infinitude, if all are becoming more and

more infinitised, so to speak, the difference between us will consist in our various rates of progression, of growth, but all are advancing, and continuously growing and nearing the unattainable end, at which none will ever arrive. It is the consolation and joy of each of us to know that he will sometime reach a point attained by some other, and no one will ever rest at the goal. And it is better not to rest there, in that stillness, for if there shall be no man see God and live, as the Scriptures say, he that fully attains to the Life Supreme is completely absorbed in it and ceases to be.

"O Lord, give work to Sancho, and to us all poor mortals, give us the lash, let it always cost us effort to attain unto Thee, save by losing, dissolving ourselves in Thy bosom. Admit us unto Thy Paradise, O Lord, that we may work therein, and care for it, but not to sleep there; grant it to us that we may spend eternity in submergence more and more profound in the boundless deeps of Thine infinite bosom."

But when Mrs. B. was well there was no containing her. She ruled the household and the cooks had to report to her every morning. This was always an ordeal, because at best Mrs. B. would be sweetly unreasonable. At other times, she would be a cruel tyrant, calling for Kate Woodward on her day off to drive her up to town and mocking her discomfiture with "Holy Thursday!"

Everything about Mrs. B. was feminine. On my twenty-second birthday, she treated me out to a show in the West End and afterwards we went to a Greek restaurant in Soho. She dressed up so smartly with a perky little *toque* on her white curls and was so gay and responsive to everything, that one could not help but be proud and delighted—and she was then almost eighty.

Incidentally, Mr. Bennett himself would as often as anybody have to suffer her shafts. "Why are you behaving like a great Panjandrum?" she would ask him in ringing tones in the dining room. On the other hand, every day when she was well, she would herself go and make Mr. Bennett's bed and arrange the things in his bedroom. She often urged me to be ready to serve him and go anywhere.

Mrs. Bennett was an artist and loved colour and beauty in everything. She seemed to love the colour pink particularly—the walls of the house and the dining-room were both in that colour. One of the girls who came to Coombe on Sundays, Marie King's daughter Pat, had a glorious pink and white complexion and Mrs. B. used to speak to me ecstatically about it. I once found her looking at a pin-up in a magazine and tracing the outline of the long legs with her fingers. She spoke in bated breath of her beauty. It was Marilyn Monroe.

She also had a great love of birds. Every day she used to break toast into tiny pieces to feed the doves. I always used to think that there was something very bird-like about Mrs. B. herself. On the other hand, she detested cats and many's the young man who was instructed by her to throw stones or even shoot at the numerous strays, who regarded Coombe Springs as a haven. For the sake of cat-lovers, let me assure them that we all knew this particular foible and while we threw vigorously, we also threw wide.

It was impossible to be near Mrs. B. without learning something. If Mr. Bennett taught you the principles of self-observation, Mrs. B. deftly put you in such a spot that you could not help but see yourself. Of course with people who did not really wish to see, she was hardly popular. "My dear," she used to say, "How wonderful you are!" with such an emphasis as was hardly calculated to win friends. Small wonder if her victims asked if she was in the Work. But with people who were close to her she was equally merciless.

I once asked a question about Kundalini in the dining-room. My friends laughed as if to say "Haven't you got that one out of your system yet?" Mr. Bennett did not answer then, but Mrs. B. took me later to her study. She lay on the couch and began to speak to me in very serious tones. As she was talking I interrupted her. "Fool! Fool!" she said, "now go." I pleaded with her to continue, but it was no good and I was dismissed. I was never able to get her to speak of this again.

Mrs. Bennett had had a very adventurous life, though I never succeeded in establishing the exact chronological order. Her childhood had been spent in India. She had studied painting in Belgium. She had once run away to Mexico with only £10 in her pocket. She had lived by herself in the mountains of Greece, painting. With a Turkish lady, she had started the first girl's school in Turkey. In Constantinople, she had met both Ouspensky and Gurdjieff. And it was there that she had met Mr. Bennett at the palace of Prince Sabaheddin. Later in England, she studied with the Ouspenskys and, after the war, visited Gurdjieff in his Paris flat with Mr. Bennett.

In 1954, Mrs. Bennett suffered another series of such severe strokes that she lay in a coma for weeks. Eventually she recovered sufficiently to be got out of bed and dressed, but she was no longer able to direct the household. People had to be in attendance on her all the time, as she could do nothing for herself. Her mind often wandered and she began to fail to recognize people around her. In spite of her terrible and continuous suffering, she had moments of great lucidity when she gave brilliant illustrations of her own inimitable wit. One young man, Robin Mitchell, who was spending an hour with her, had lain down on the bed as she had fallen asleep. Mrs. B. was later heard to say "Do you know what, Mr. B.? I fell asleep and when I woke up, there was a handsome young man in bed beside me!" She was still unerring in her detection of sycophancy, which she treated with her usual pungent scorn. "What a bore you are!" Even when she was bad tempered, and truly she was often demanding and tyrannical to those around her, she gave evidence of her tremendous vitality.

In July 1958 she died at last. I was happy to be able to attend her funeral. And indeed what a strange and grave and indefinable happiness there was among the hundreds who came to the service and her grave. I am sure that the prayer for Sancho is the prayer she would have wished— *"Admit her unto Thy Paradise, O Lord, that she may work therein, and care for it, but not to sleep there; grant it that she may spend eternity in submergence more and more profound in the boundless depths of Thine infinite bosom."*

****

The life at Coombe Springs was one of change, of continual movement. The form kept changing, the demands were different, as I believe it always must be where real possibilities of inner development exist. It is interesting to look at the life of Mr. Gurdjieff in this respect. The emphasis kept changing. Sometimes he worked with many people, who were encouraged to make super-efforts in regard to their bodies. Then suddenly everything would be changed, his groups dispersed and in despair, and he would work with just a handful of people on a particular psychological work. The form of the Work at his Paris flat was different from Fontainebleau and this again was different from the earlier Work in Moscow and St. Petersburg. So much is obvious just from reading.

In 1951 at Coombe Springs, there was a very intimate atmosphere about the groups and many of us came to rely on the individual help we received from Mr. Bennett. But as the numbers of people increased, the sheer physical demands upon him magnified, and not only in England. He was invited to lecture in America and was away for some time. When he returned, many of us expected things to be the same as before. In fact, they never were and it frequently took us a long time to accept that things were different. This was particularly marked in relation to group Work. Whereas at one time all the groups were directly under his direction, gradually he made other leaders. Though we all had great respect for these group leaders, none of them pretended to be able to help us in the same way as Mr. Bennett. Many of us looked forward to again having his undivided attention—but the time had passed and gradually we awoke to the increased urgency of understanding for ourselves the principles of the Work.

Each year, often in conjunction with the summer seminars, major schemes were brought into operation. The glasshouse and the pottery were rebuilt, the rockery rearranged, the brambles cleared and the ground levelled. Then came a really much bigger scheme when a dormitory block of fifteen bedrooms and a Finnish Bath were constructed. This was completed in the space of a few months and was a matter of considerable pride to the men who worked together on it.

The biggest enterprise was the construction of the nine-sided hall, later called the Djamichoonatra, a name borrowed from *All and Everything*. This was designed according to certain principles by a team of architects, amongst whom were Robert Whiffen, Richard Bigwood, John Donat and James Leask. The lower part of the walls were made from reinforced concrete, and by the sort of coincidence that we came to accept simply, a concrete expert, van Sommers, had come from Australia to study at Coombe. A great part of the construction work was under his direction. Bob Prestie was prominent and Stuart Gray-Thompson. Dan Cahill, an American with the merchant navy, after 2 days instruction from an expert, somehow learned how to work with copper in order to work on the roof. And all the men who visited from the Provinces, from Manchester, Liverpool, Bournemouth, Bristol all helped on this great project. It was designed, constructed and built entirely by the people at Coombe without any outside help.

One man had the task of constructing the portal frames, in itself a major operation. Someone else welded the frames for the stained glass windows. And again it so happened that a member of the group was experienced in stained glass! This hall took a year and a half to build, entirely the work of students of the Gurdjieff methods.Every summer there was a seminar for three weeks, when many people came to stay for a period of intensive study. Some-

Djamichoonatra, the nine-sided building at Coombe Springs (now demolished)

what naively at first, I looked forward to these seminars—to what better use could one put a summer holiday? But as year followed year, I came to look forward to them with increasing foreboding. As on Sundays, we did a lot of physical work, psychological studies and Movements together, but to a terrifying, exhausting schedule, best calculated to make one realize the reality of the "denying force." For many visitors from overseas, this was their first taste of the Work. One can hardly blame the young Dutchman, who, after an exercise we had been studying which contained the words "I WISH TO BE," had rushed up to Mr. Bennett's study shouting out, "I do NOT wish to be. I do NOT wish to be."

My Stairway to Subud

Sometimes we experimented with fasting. How thrilling it was to read about these sorts of efforts in Ouspensky's *In Search of the Miraculous* and how I had been fired to put myself under the severest of disciplines. But practice was a very different matter to theory. In practice, I was already convinced of the absurdity of not eating by eleven o'clock— in the morning! By noon, I could see no sense in any of the ideas of the Work and just could not remember how I had come to live at Coombe Springs at all. By one o'clock I wanted only to be warm and go to sleep. And by two not only did I hate Bennett, but I thoroughly despised the sheepish frauds so sanctimoniously working around me.

In theory, we were a band of brothers united by a common aim, whose very wish for understanding and good relations should have automatically brought these about. Such proved to be a very naïve expectation. In practice, some people loathed each other so cordially that they would have to make it a task to sit down at the same table. One cook would be jealous of another. Two women would quarrel over who was to arrange the flowers. And one mild little man (Charles Sprague) surprised me with a gift of two books in a brave effort to work on the feelings produced in him by my bossy manifestations when we did a mammoth washing up in the back kitchen together.

I was once so struck by the endless clash of personalities and had such a feeling of our general unworthiness—how could we sincerely imagine that we were working to become men?—that I asked Mr. Bennett on impulse in a crowded dining-room whether the pupils who worked with Mr. Gurdjieff at Fontainebleau had displayed the same negative manifestations. I had in mind a saying attributed to Mr. Gurdjieff— "Here there is no place for personality." I pictured a group of people rising early, making super-efforts against the inertia of their bodies, existing on a frugal diet of beet root soup, and displaying a strict economy of speech and movement. Mr. Bennett answered after a long pause: "There was more negativity per square yard at the Prieuré than anywhere else on the earth."

In spite of our personalities, there grew between us a very wonderful and real bond. There was nothing sentimental about it because we had few illusions about each other. It was a unity that existed beyond like and dislike. This could most strongly be sensed at those times we worked together as at seminars.

In 1954, Mr. Bennett undertook a long journey in Turkey and Asia

Minor. None of us in the house knew the purpose of this journey. He sent back a series of long letters to Mrs. Bennett, extracts of which were read aloud to us. The accounts of the visit to Tesephon, Baalbek and Babylon were fascinating, and the encounters with various sheikhs and Dervish Orders were fabulous; but more interesting to me was the revelation of the struggles that took place within Mr. Bennett himself. This was really the first time that I had a glimpse of his inner world, which normally he did not reveal at all.

The return from Turkey marked the beginning of a new phase. There was a renewed feeling of the urgency and seriousness of our endeavours. Everyone in the house had to see Mr. Bennett individually and discuss their aims and Work. Personally I could not understand what he wanted from us and I was dismissed abruptly. But very soon near impossible demands were put upon us all so that we had to show the seriousness of our intentions. It was clear that Mr. Bennett was preparing for something, but none of us knew what it was. And only seven weeks after his return, my life circumstances changed and I had to leave Coombe Springs.

My Stairway to Subud

Chapter 5

Further Studies with J.G.Bennett

Formation of the Manchester Group

In 1953, I left school mastering, and since I had no money, I began casting about for a job that would both pay and train me at the same time. The only openings of this kind that I could find in the advertisement columns were for salesmen or Representatives. After making numerous applications over a period of three months, I at length landed a job with Thomas Edison selling dictating machines.

Pretty well all my life up to that point had been concerned with schools. Both the Preparatory and the Public Schools that I had attended as a pupil I had loved very much, though one had been almost Victorian in its strictness and ideals, whereas the other had been extremely liberal and free. Perhaps there was one common denominator, consisting in the fact that at both schools there were dedicated teachers who loved their jobs, who were fond of boys and who were concerned with the ideals of education.

I had taught in three different preparatory schools. They were all sadly in contrast to the schools I had attended in my boyhood. I can only remember one man to whom school mastering seemed to mean something and who had at least one cultural interest—music. Most of the others appeared to hate their jobs and to be indifferent to the boys. One man knew quite a lot about cricket, but I cannot remember a single one who evinced any interest in literature, art, drama, languages, philosophy—in fact, I was never able to find out what interested them.

Nevertheless it was with some foreboding that I exchanged my accustomed corduroys for a dark suit and a stiff collar, and joined the crowd of office workers on the eight o'clock train for the City. By this time however I had worked at Coombe Springs for two years, and regarded the difficulties from the point of view of the Work, as a challenge, as an obstacle to be overcome.

I was very fortunate in having as my first Sales Manager a dignified and kindly man, who was about as different from the popular image of the aggressive sales manager as is possible to imagine. Later I was to see him in action, and I can vouch for his abilities as a salesman.

My first task was to learn something of the principles of recording and to learn how to give practical demonstrations on the machine. It seemed to me somewhat ironical that I had to study some principles of physics, a subject that I had completely neglected at Clayesmore. In fact, I had even once been beaten because the physics teacher caught me reading *Wuthering Heights* under the desk. I was sent out of the class and had to report to the Head.

My first practical demonstration might have ended in disaster. It was based on an old-fashioned type of machine, which used wax cylinders, and I was unable to get the cylinder on the machine. Luckily there was another salesman accompanying me and he deftly flicked a lever to the neutral position. After that, I quickly became familiar with the workings of the Ediphone, and learnt a certain patter to demonstrate its capabilities. I soon lost my initial nervousness as I came to see that most companies treated salesmen courteously and had a genuine desire to see for themselves whether the product offered them any advantages. Besides which I remarked a certain *faiblesse* of my clients—they were often willing to come out of their offices for a smoke and chat, and the chance of warming their bottoms on a convenient radiator.

That is not to say that I did not have embarrassing moments. I was once demonstrating one of the latest disc models to a party of eminent scientists. Having delivered myself of a little speech, extolling the virtues of this super up-to-date model, I switched over to playback and nothing happened. My mechanic had to undo the lid and examine the works, while I made apologies for the delay. The eminent scientists slipped off one by one, and when at length I was ready to resume, the house was almost bare.

After ten months I changed over to another company, Brunsviga, selling calculating machines. There were about twelve young salesmen all starting at the same time and we had to go to school for a fortnight. Our teacher was an old bald headed Scotsman, one of the few people I have ever met with a passion for mathematics. He had an almost maternal affection for this particular hand calculator and knew any amount of tricks by which one could produce astonishingly quick results. At school, I had never applied myself to mathematics, but this time I really set myself to understand the problems and to master the tricks. The tricks were really very simple. One had only to understand the problem and to determine the constants, and then mark them on the machine in a decimalised form. One could then do any amount of multiplications against this constant, and produce a stream of results to the astonishment of the customer. I think I became the old Scotsman's favourite, and was given E.C.3, the heart of the City of London, as my territory. Much to his joy and mine, I sold my first machine on my very first call. (The company was an Air Freight company, who had to change pounds into kilos and French Francs into £'s sterling. I asked for their books, which it normally took them the best part of 4 days to do, and I rattled the whole lot off in the space of one hour!) Only once did he tell me off—for working too hard! I had made eighteen cold calls and given five demonstrations in one day.

Certainly the training at Coombe Springs was of great practical assistance to me. I doubt that I could ever have learnt about machines without it, and moreover with zest. Also, I often used to prearrange with myself the rate at which I would work, but how could I explain that to my superiors?

I soon began to acquire a spurious reputation as a good salesman; spurious, because most of my friends had no idea of the extent, or rather the limit of my successes. Nevertheless, this spurious reputation served me in good stead. On one memorable day, four different companies offering me jobs approached me. It was a particularly memorable day since it was January 13th 1954, Mr. Gurdjieff's birthday and the first day of the New Year, according to the Muslim calendar.

The Gurdjieff groups used to meet *en masse* on this anniversary for a grand party at the house in Colet Gardens where we did the Movements. I say groups, because there were other Gurdjieff groups quite distinct from those of Mr. Bennett. The most notable were those of Dr. Nicholl, Kenneth Walker, Miss Jane Heap, Miss Crowdie, and Madame Lannes, the last name being in direct contact with Madame de Salzmann and the Paris groups. Such parties were the sole occasions when one could see the massed ranks of the Gurdjieff disciples. Apart from that there was no other communication; certainly one never discussed the Work with members of other Groups, since to talk about the Work was considered to be mechanical, and as to discussing group tasks that was especially forbidden. Of course, these parties must not be compared with those of another genre. They were always the occasion for a lot of people working together, preparing the food, serving and washing-up, and usually of long readings from Gurdjieff's writings and a piano recital of his compositions.

Returning to my life experiences, one of the jobs that I was urged to apply for interested me considerably since it offered better remuneration, a large territory and a motorcar. (Actually £400 per annum, plus a car without a heater or radio, plus expenses and a 1% commission on new business!) That I should apply for this post was put to me by W. G. Wade, also one of Mr. Bennett's pupils, a much older man than me from the Bristol area.

However, the post necessitated a move to the North of England. I applied halfheartedly. Only after I had written did I consult Mr. Bennett. He advised me to go all out to get this job, saying that while I must surely do nothing dishonest, I should make it a task for myself to succeed in life.

This advice put an end to my procrastination. Having lived at Coombe Springs for some three years, I had naturally become attached to the place. I had thrown myself wholeheartedly into the activities to such an extent as to have almost severed connections with my former friends; nearly all the people I knew were connected with the Work. So it was quite a step to contemplate moving to the North, away from friends, the Group meetings, Movement classes and the Turkish lessons I had just begun with Mr. Bennett.

Nevertheless, I was in need of a change. Life was lived under constant pressure at Coombe Springs and latterly the tempo had quickened rather than slackened. I had no doubts about the Work, but my feelings for it had dried up and everything had become stale.

Mr. Bennett's advice helped me to get through a difficult interview with a Mr. C. M. Beavis, Managing Director of Golden Valley Colours, and to land a job for which I had no technical qualifications. Happily Wade had given me a small book on paint, oil and colour technology to read before this interview took place. Undoubtedly Mr. Beavis was impressed by this fact and the interview swung in my favour!

Incidentally, the advice that Mr. Bennett gave me was not peculiar to me but was for him a principle. Some years later, at an Easter seminar for people under thirty, I heard him enunciate this principle in such a way as to engrave it on my memory. A young man (Ron Dicker) had asked a question about bringing his work into life. He was an engine tester and he often had long periods of enforced idleness because there were no engines to test. Mr. Bennett looked sharply at him and, having first asked his qualifications, asked whether he was studying to get any higher. He answered no.

Mr. Bennett then observed that many people make a great mistake and imagine that their success in life does not matter as long as they have the opportunities of working in a group. But the contrary was true. It was an integral part of the Work to work well at one's job, to be active about it, to seek advancement and to take on greater responsibilities.

In March 1954, I left Coombe Springs to take up my new job. In the first place I had to go to Bristol for a month's training at the factory at Wick, Bristol. If I had known little mathematics and less physics, my lack of chemistry could only be described as abysmal. During my training period, I was hard put to it to disguise my ignorance and to learn as quickly as possible the properties of a vast range of pigments and their applications in the surface coatings industries.

After this month of training, I went north to lodge at first with the retiring representative at his house in Wilmslow. He was a kindly man with a degree in chemistry, who was surprised to have such an unqualified person as his successor. He then drove me all over the North of England from Liverpool to Hull, to Ripon, Aycliffe, Gateshead and Newcastle, introducing me to all his existing customers. While he was evidently knowledgeable, he made no pretence at being a salesman.

Once this training period was over the outward character of my existence changed abruptly, and I was thrown back very much on my own resources. This served to show just how limited those resources were. I took a small room where I did my own cooking, but was often oppressed by my solitude, and to my chagrin found myself an easy prey to self-pity. Within the multifarious activities at Coombe Springs I had begun to think that I was free from such moodiness, but I was clearly shown to be mistaken.

[The pattern of a rep's life in those days, before any motorways existed in England, was very different to today. If I went to Hull, I would stay in the Station Hotel for several days. I would spend a whole week going from Ripon, to Darlington, to Newcastle, across to Lancaster and then back to Manchester. So a great deal of my time was spent alone in hotels after my day's work. In those days, there was no television. Then again when I returned to my room in Manchester, I was again on my own. This was in great contrast to life at Coombe, where I was in a large house with beautiful grounds and with the constant companionship of other seekers of the truth.]

There was a small group of people in Manchester, who met once a fortnight for a reading of *All and Everything*. They were inclined to be despondent, since their former group leader from the South of England, and had suffered in health and was rarely able to visit them. I felt that they needed to be more active and to demonstrate their seriousness in regard to the Work, but it was hardly my business as a newcomer to say so. Perhaps I did drop a hint or two.

Though this group was cordial towards me, some even inviting me to their homes for meals, there were none of my own age and inclinations. I therefore spent more and more of my free time with some Indians that I met by chance. They invited me to the British Council, where I played table tennis with them, and we soon formed a little group. One of them, Ghosh, was a Bengali with a remarkable voice and it gave me great pleasure to hear him sing. Then there was Shiva Shankar Shukla from Nepal, Ganesh who was a Tamil from South India, who had also lived in Malaya, and Indu Bhave, from Bombay, who also used to sing in Mahrati. These last two also featured in the next stage of my life.

Ghosh explained to me some of the principles of Indian music and the construction of the *Ragas*. We often met together on Sundays for lunch, while Ganesh would cook such curries as can be obtained in no restaurant. We would sit cross-legged on the floor and I was shown how to eat with my fingers. The curries were often so hot in every sense of the word, that I would not only scald the tips of my fingers, but my lips would smart, my bowels burn and I would break into a deeply satisfying perspiration. The meal was accompanied by jokes of such verbosity, as I believe only Indians are capable.

Nevertheless, free time was frequently a problem for me. During the day I had my job, which both interested me and occupied me because of its inherent difficulties. Besides which Work was more easily applicable to working conditions. This is worth remarking because many people think that they need free time in order to cultivate the inner life. All the observations that I heard from Coombe Springs served to convince me that everything connected with keeping one's state, with self-remembering, was more applicable to working conditions. Free time and especially holidays provided much greater difficulties.

At the end of one seminar, I asked Mr. Bennett how best to use my free time, and in particular whether I might write. "It is impossible to work all the time," he replied. "Now you must be reconciled to

My Stairway to Subud

enjoying your work and suffering your pleasures. As to writing, I advise not. You need your energy for doing your job, and writing would be too much the same sort of thing. You have to relax, and you must be reconciled to doing such things as going to the cinema. Only you must be active about it. You must decide when you will work; you must decide when you will relax."

Though living in Manchester, I went to Coombe Springs every other weekend to be sure not to miss my group meeting. Indeed, I was determined not to lose contact with the Work, and practiced our various tasks and exercises assiduously.

The Groups had been reshuffled and mine consisted of some forty people, mostly in their twenties and early thirties. Over the passage of time a great sense of unity had grown up between us, as well might be, since through the medium of the group we knew each other's personal problems and difficulties in a way that is quite rare. In a curious way, we were beginning to march in step! That is, very often we found ourselves confronted with the same problem, or had come upon a similar realization at the same time. Sometimes only four or five people spoke and Mr. Bennett commented, and yet it was as if everyone had spoken and all had received answers.

By this time, the whole character of the meetings had altered. At first there had been the interest and novelty of new techniques. We had learned numerous different ways of working with the attention and relaxing the body; we had begun to recognise the "taste" of certain different energies. We had learnt in a great variety of ways to arrive at a state of self-observation; and we had been given hints, though always grudgingly, of the way that the laws, such as that of the Octave, could be linked with our practical work.

At first everything had been new and exciting, but by this time a subtle change had taken place. Certainly, it did not take place all at once. It was a progressive action that continued over a long period.

This change cannot be put simply in two words. But it was something like this: The experiments we had done had given us "tastes": tastes of self-remembering, tastes of self-observation, tastes of the "collected state," tastes of decision, and tastes of our own denying forces. By this time, we understood more or less that we could not remember ourselves with our thoughts, and we knew a variety of techniques by which we could become "present" and more connected with our bodies. Perhaps the change that was taking place was the gradual realization that we could not keep these states. We could no longer doubt their essential efficacy, and yet not only could we not keep these states, we could not even wish to work for them.

It was indeed a curious dilemma that we were in, which I will try to illustrate with some personal examples. Shortly before leaving Coombe Springs, certain matters were causing me a good deal of distress. To speak frankly, I was infatuated, mad with jealousy and desirous of revenge. In all, I was in a pretty low state. Mr. Bennett happened to see me and he suggested— which was a rarity—that I speak to him. He suggested a line of work that consisted in returning to the sensation of my body every time my revengeful associations arose.

I think that I shall never forget the next day. I went out to work as usual. Every time these thoughts arose, I did as he suggested. At first, I felt quite physically sick, but I persisted. By evening my state had undergone a complete transformation. I even felt as if I was a foot taller and exceedingly happy emotions welled up inside me. When I entered the hall at Coombe Springs, Mr. Bennett was there. He looked at me piercingly and asked, "How is it, Tony?" I blabbered something incoherently, for in truth, I was overcome with feelings of gratitude and elation. Mr. Bennett then said, "It will pass." This vexed me and I was determined to prove him wrong. I was determined to try to keep this state.

A week later, I went to see him somewhat sheepishly to say that everything had evaporated just as he had forecast. He then told me how his own daughter, Ann, had once asked to be introduced to a dervish friend of his, and he had been curious to know what she would ask. She said something like this: "In Mr. Gurdjieff's system, I have learned a way to change my state. Do you dervishes know how to keep your state?" The dervish replied: "Even the Holy Prophet Mohammed could not keep his state."

My example does illustrate the first triad of Work: My revengeful associations constituted the denial of my body; against this I had brought the affirmation of the Work; and the reconciling force had appeared as a change of state in my feelings. We began to see that it was the presence of the denying force that created the possibilities of Work. Sometimes, as in my example, life itself created the denying force. We began to see the necessity of denying ourselves, of deliberately creating our own denying force. But it was one thing to see this in theory; it was quite another to accomplish it in fact.

It seemed rather that the more we understood this principle, the more difficult it became to apply it. We had all had tastes of a different world. We all knew that if we could bring affirmation and denial together, however feebly, the results in terms of a change of state were excessive in proportion to the efforts made. Yet everything began to cry out, to flinch at the very idea of making such efforts.

One day, while still living at Coombe, I was discussing my Work with Mr. Bennett. He asked me rather typically, "What is it you find difficult?" That was easy to answer—Friday night. This was known as men's night and had been instituted in the summer of 1953. All the men in the household worked together between seven and nine and had their evening meal at ten. To start with this had been a bit of a bore, since it demolished my one free evening. Nevertheless we did get something from working together and there were certain definite tasks to be accomplished. However, men's nights carried on into the winter. The work then took on an altogether artificial aspect. It almost seemed that work was invented and the tasks seemed absurd. I remember working outside in the garden tying canes together with frozen fingers in the pouring rain. Many times we dug enormous pits, with the aid of specially rigged electric lights. There were always too many people digging in the same pit, and my mood became more and more rebellious. In any case, I was always something of an *"enfant terrible,"* so my wretched companions had to suffer also my bantering and querulous manifestations. Besides which, I made all sorts of excuses to "play hooky." All this I explained to Mr. Bennett.

"Then," he said, "set yourself a task that you will arrive on time, that you will work to the end, and above all that you will not permit yourself these particular manifestations." I gulped, but at once decided on the task, and arranged that I would do the back-kitchen wash-up alone, if I failed. Came Friday night, and I was put on another absurd task—making *cloches* from panes of glass with wire that had no rigidity. Nevertheless, I worked conscientiously and in silence, and gradually I began to sense my presence.

Later I saw Mr. Bennett. "Yes," he said, "you set yourself the tasks but with my force. Could you set such tasks for yourself?" I considered his question for some time, while he sat waiting for an answer. "No, Sir," I replied. He nodded. "But you see that sometime you must come to that."

Again one Easter Sunday we worked together at a simple task. This consisted in eating at mealtimes solely what was necessary and not a mouthful more. I was surprised to find how little was necessary, and this discipline at once gave me an unusual sense of well-being. Since that was so it might be imagined that I have practiced this ever since. But I have never again been able to put myself under such a demand. This may well seem incomprehensible to those who have never tried. But in fact, all this Work constituted a threat to the personality. It was not just that we had weaknesses, but that these weaknesses had behind them the force of Monsieur Self-Love and Madame Vanity. I began to glimpse the division of "I" and "Bright-Paul," and Bright-Paul was always the stronger and devoured everything.

In Manchester the small group continued to meet for readings. Those who wished to continue group Work were advised to contact the Bradford Group, which Miss Rina Hands visited as leader. One or two like myself chose to remain directly in contact with Coombe Springs.

In 1955, Mr. Bennett received an enquiry from a couple in Manchester, John and Gwen Tyrer. This couple at once evinced a strong interest in the Work and brought along a number of friends, including John and Marjorie Fletcher and Alan Popplewell. Mr. Bennett then asked me to read them the typescripts of some lectures he was then giving in London. A few more people contacted Mr. Bennett independently, and soon there was a group of some fifteen people who were interested to hear not just the theory, but to undertake some of the practical aspects of group Work.

Mr. Bennett then asked me to sit in on a new group at Coombe Springs and to pass on the course of study to the people in Manchester. At the same time, he made it abundantly clear that I was in no wise to think of myself as group leader. Nevertheless, in the North I was faced with the simple facts of the situation and little by little I began to comment on the observations.

This development brought a certain new factor into my life. Previously nothing had depended on my work; it was entirely up to me whether I worked or not. But with the formation of this new group, I had to work whether I liked it or not. In fact, I found it necessary to do the exercises of both my own group and of this new group.

This proved of great interest because I had myself worked at some of these exercises some years before but had entirely forgotten their significance. Worked at again, my own observations seemed to me so new that I had to repeat them again and again for the sake of verification.

For example, we worked at an exercise to confront thoughts and feelings, at certain intervals during the day, and to put to ourselves the question: "Am I thinking what I am feeling; am I feeling what I am thinking?" With a little knowledge of the psychological ideas one might well have expected to have found a disparity between the two functions. The thing that I believe surprised everyone was that they could not observe feelings at all, and were then compelled reluctantly to the conclusion that they simply did not have feelings; or at best that their feelings were dormant. This was the more surprising since everyone knew that they experienced a succession of emotional reactions. What gradually became clear was that life in the feelings could only be experienced if given a certain substance or energy. That energy could only be elaborated by work itself, by a certain intensity of friction between the affirming and denying forces.

Later I discussed my findings with Mr. Bennett one evening while we were taking a Finnish Bath in the new building. He confirmed them. Not that I was in need of confirmation. But what impressed me forcibly at the time was the need to verify in such a way that one would be forced to conclusions, which would form the basis of understanding. In such an understanding there could be no division; there could not possibly be a difference of opinion. With understanding there could only be unity.

In Manchester, I was in such a position that when in doubt I had to verify. There was simply no-one with more experience to turn to, as at Coombe Springs. Little by little I began to have confidence that I could rely on my own observations.

Most of the members off the Manchester Group soon proved themselves to be active. Some of them made the journey south to spend a weekend at Coombe Springs. Back in the North we began to organise work parties for manual work to work on the same lines as the Sunday work at Coombe. And we met once a week, alternately for readings and group meetings. Later on, early in 1957, I arranged with Pierre and Vivien Elliot to come North in order to teach Mr. Gurdjieff's Movements. We were very fortunate in this since they both had long experience of the Work and had both studied with Mr. Gurdjieff in Paris.

In the beginning of 1957 Mr. Bennett gave a series of lectures in London entitled *"Man and the Universe."* These were intended partly to serve as an introduction to his own book, *The Dramatic Universe,* which had just been published. I asked him whether he would agree to lecture in Manchester. He consented to do this in March, immediately on his return from a brief visit to the United States. The Manchester Group meanwhile gave itself the task of preparing the way. Normally people were forbidden to talk about the Work, but during this period everyone was encouraged to make contacts and to get notices of the lectures displayed on notice boards.

The result was that two hundred and fifty people turned up at the Onward Hall. Mr. Bennett then proceeded to give a lecture the like of which I had never heard before. The thing that surprised me chiefly was the way he spoke about Will; perhaps because, at that time, the centre of gravity of my thinking was on change of state.

First he constructed a framework so that the facts of experience, or science, could be considered as a whole. Then he spoke about value, and all that belongs to the field of religion. Finally he spoke about his own beliefs of how fact and value could be reconciled.

"I believe that man has three independent patterns. Firstly, his body: not only his flesh, but the living body with all its functions, its power of thought, its capacity for feeling, sensation, memory and reactions of all kinds. Secondly, his essence: this carries his unique pattern that makes him just what he is. It is the sum total of possibilities. But there is nothing in it, which guarantees that those possibilities will be fulfilled. The possibility of fulfilment depends upon the third part, that I call his Will.

"In ordinary people the Will is asleep; they live only with their bodies and their functions. They mistake their thoughts and feelings for volition. They do not realise that there is sleeping within them something quite different—their own Will. As long as a man is in that state he has no soul. His essence can remain just what it is—just a pattern of possibilities. His body can die and be disintegrated, but his Will can remain asleep. By soul, I understand that which is formed in a man when his Will awakens and he chooses to fulfil this pattern of his own existence. When the Will takes possession of the essence and the body, then man becomes a living soul, but only if the process is accomplished in him.

"And lastly I believe that there is a Higher Power, a Higher Will, that is the friend of the Will in each one of us. This is the Will that

helps the process of the awakening of the Will in all separate beings, but that Higher Power or Will I call the 'Essence Individuality.' It is one everywhere. It is the one awake Will."

After the lecture there were a number of questions that stuck me as being clever-clever or irrelevant. At last, however, a woman rose to her feet and said with great sincerity, "If it is true as you say that the Will of man is not free, then how can his Will be freed?" There was at once such a murmur of approbation from the audience that one could not doubt that she had been able to formulate the question, indeed the burning question that was of the greatest importance for many of them.

Mr. Bennett replied simply that those who wished to study just that question should leave their names and addresses.

About fifty people did so, and shortly after this, meetings were arranged where I read some former lecture of Mr. Bennett's, dealing specifically with the life and ideas of Mr. Gurdjieff. By the end of April some twenty people showed that they wished to study further and a second Manchester group was formed.

This period was one of pretty intense activity. In addition to my own group meetings at Coombe Springs, I had two group meetings on separate evenings in Manchester, readings from *All and Everything* and the Movements classes with Pierre Elliot. However these new activities were hardly under way when an event occurred that was to have profound repercussions on us all.

The first hint that there was something extraordinary in the wind was in the middle of May. One Saturday morning I was travelling down to London by train with Pierre Elliot. "A distinguished visitor will be at Coombe Springs," he said. I guessed at the various group leaders and people whom I knew had been associated with Mr. Gurdjieff in France. I could not guess right and had to contain my curiosity since I knew from past experience that he had not the slightest intention of satisfying it. I began to talk of other things and referred to my interest in Indian music. He evinced no enthusiasm, then quite suddenly declared an interest in Indonesian music. I thought this rather strange, but said nothing; I already knew his penchant for the enigmatic.

Before I describe this event, I will describe a little of my own evaluation of the Work at that time, and the stage the group had reached. By May 1957, I had been working with Mr. Bennett for almost seven years. Where had I got to? Where did I imagine that I was going? What was the point of all these efforts, of all these meetings? Of what consequence was the collected state? And what did I expect from endless self-observation?

It is difficult to answer these questions in all honesty. While we were constantly admonished to remember our aim, it was also made clear that such an aim as to be "Master of oneself" was too far away. At any one time, we studied aspects of the Work, and we had more immediate, limited aims.

We were discouraged from theorising, from wiseacring, from talking about anything not personally experienced. Even Mr. Bennett rarely referred to the theory. In all the time I was at Coombe Springs I never heard him speak of the Astral Body. On the other hand, he often used to say that something had not yet formed in us from where we could remember ourselves.

For a long time I felt that Mr. Bennett had some other methods that he had not yet revealed to us. I once expressed this view, to be met with the sarcastic rejoinder: "What do you imagine? That I have some special exercises in a little red book, and that you are now on No. 53?" The group roared with laughter.

Nevertheless, I did feel that constant effort of certain intensity would distill a *"body of consciousness."* As to self-observation, I had begun to feel that it was a practise valid in itself, that it inevitably brought people to a different self-evaluation, and just as inevitably, though indirectly, affected their manifestations. I had begun to think that *"seeing"* was the same as *"doing."* At that time, I had also formed a conception of *Conscience,* not as something that distinguished between right and wrong, but as the prime impulse for "work on oneself."

Some time in the future, I hoped to become a Conscious Man. I had formed a conception of the "Conscious Man," largely as a result of the various exercises and Movements that we did. For me the Conscious Man was the very opposite of spontaneous. Everything he did, he did deliberately. He did not speak without first deciding what he would say. If he displayed anger, he did so on purpose for a purpose. If he moved, he saw in advance where he was going. If he relaxed and permitted his associations to wander, he did so because he chose to.

How this sublime state was to be arrived at exactly, I did not know.

At that time I think that Mr. Bennett was for many of us the model of the Conscious Man. Certainly his long pauses before answering questions fitted the picture. Indeed many people used to ape this characteristic with people who were not in the Work, much to their astonishment and aggravation. I used to feel that Mr. Bennett's sarcasm, his indifference, his words of praise, were equally deliberate. One evening at supper, I remember him saying, "Truly, I must tell you, that I have not my own 'I'." I think that most of us were inclined to be incredulous.

In the group it seemed that we were all arriving at the same point, which can be illustrated by some example of the observations. A young journalist, Bill Aitken, described the history of his Work. He said that first of all, he had come to the group with interest and enthusiasm. Even when he had come to see that part of his nature was opposed to the Work, still the original force had carried him along. But now that force seemed to have spent itself, he no longer felt interest or hope and didn't know why he still came. In reply, Mr. Bennett quoted from the Gospels concerning the young man "who sold all that he had to buy a pearl of great price." He commented, "When you first came to the group all that you had was the force of interest. That carried you along even for some years. But now you have spent that force. With it you have bought a pearl. Maybe it is only a tiny pearl, but at least it is your own. That pearl is your understanding. Formerly your Work was based on interest. But now you cannot Work from there any more. Now you will have to Work from your own understanding."

Another time a medical student (John Musgrove) described how he had failed in certain efforts that he was making. "But why did you fail?" asked Mr. Bennett. "Because I did not make enough effort," the student replied. "Why then did you not make enough effort?" "I suppose I should have tried harder." Mr. Bennett replied,"Is it really like that? No, you made the efforts that you could. If you could have made more efforts you would have. What you could not, you could not. What you must see is that this is your measure."

Another man, a doctor, said that he had a cold and that he felt too ill to Work. "But how do you understand the term 'work'?" Mr. Bennett asked. "I think you have a very narrow understanding of it, as if it was something apart from life. By now you should have understood more; your Work should be adapting itself to life conditions. For example, Miss E. (Edith later Margaret Wichmann) is in bed with a skin complaint and all the time she has a terrible desire to scratch. She does not have to set herself tasks; it is quite enough that she lies still. Someone else has started a new job. Their Work is to master it as quickly as possible."

I think that it was at this meeting that Mr. Bennett said that he would no longer suggest any programme of Work, and that we must become more flexible and adapt our work to the conditions we met in life.

At one meeting I explained my own difficulties. I saw the necessity of putting myself under a demand, but I could not do so. I had tried now sufficiently often, over a long period of time, to feel that I never would be able to do so. In the simplest terms, I could not work. Mr. Bennett turned on me almost ferociously, as he said with great emphasis: "Of course you cannot work. What else is the meaning of 'Man cannot do'?" I was exultant.

To return now to the day in May 1957 when I travelled with Pierre Elliot to London. I went as normal to my group in the study at three in the afternoon. It was a superb sunlit day, warm and mellow. Mr. Bennett asked us to speak, and one after another put forward their observations—"I must.— but I cannot—" The meeting began to take a familiar course. But Mr. Bennett made no comments, simply asking for the next person to speak. At length he interrupted.

He said that we had all arrived at the same point, but that we could not go forward without help. He then indicated that there was a certain new development, a new possibility of help that could be for us of the utmost importance. He then left the room abruptly, saying that Mrs. Elizabeth Howard would explain.

Mrs. Howard then said that before Mr. Gurdjieff had died, he had given indications to those close to him that after his death, someone else would come who could supply something that was missing in his work. He had said, "Even now, he is preparing himself." He also evinced an interest in India: *"But not your India,"* he said to the English, *"but their India,"* indicating the Dutch. He encouraged Mr. Bennett to maintain contacts in Holland and later a group was formed there.

In consequence of these hints, Mr. Bennett had been on the lookout for some time, and it was on this account he had made his recent journeys to Turkey, Syria and Persia. Then one day he had received a letter from a man in Japan, expressing interest in the

My Stairway to Subud

writings of Gurdjieff and Ouspensky, because they corresponded to, and in part, explained a mysterious *something* that he had received from a man in Java called Pak Subuh. This aroused Mr. Bennett's interest. Some while later, a certain Husein Rofé, an Englishman, who had worked for several years with Pak Subuh, came to England. Mr. Bennett and a number of the older pupils of Gurdjieff, some of whom were no longer Working in groups, met this Rofé, who claimed to be able to transmit a certain "exercise" that he had received from Pak Subuh himself. In fact, Pak Subuh had already been in England for some days, and was arriving that very afternoon with his entourage to stay at Coombe Springs.

I cannot recollect exactly what was said at that meeting about the nature of the exercise, for immediately afterwards, I attended another meeting and heard Mr. Bennett himself speak. I remember that self-remembering, for the first time in my experience, was related to the idea of purification. And there was some talk of making a contact with the Higher Emotional Centre. It was also said that this exercise could supply us with the force for Work, of which we felt in need. We were told a little of how Pak Subuh himself had received the exercise and a consequent series of revelations. Later he received indications that he should pass on this exercise to whoever sincerely asked for it. The exercise was open to everybody of any faith and not merely to the Gurdjieff groups. Pak Subuh himself had been brought up in the Muslim faith.

And indeed that afternoon Pak Subuh arrived with his wife Ibu, and his daughter, Rahayu. Also in the party were Battara Pane, and Icksan and his wife, Ismana.

My Stairway to Subud

Chapter 6

The Arrival of Subud

When Mrs. Howard had first told us of the arrival of Pak Subuh, I got to my feet at the rear of the group. I was both astonished and incredulous. The announcement had an immediate and quite extraordinary effect. Some people at once made touching declarations of their fidelity to Mr. Bennett—he was their teacher and they wanted none other. Others declared that Subud must be all right simply because Mr. Bennett had recommended it.

For my own part I felt it was absurd to accept something on Mr. Bennett's say-so; this was itself contrary to everything that we had been taught. We had never been encouraged to accept ideas without first testing and verifying for ourselves, so that we could arrive at an objective understanding. On the contrary, we had always been advised to accept nothing, an advice that still held good for me. To do otherwise was to thrust an unfair onus of responsibility on Mr. Bennett.

Those who wished to undertake the new exercise had to inform one of the senior members of the group. It is notable that in spite of the widely varying attitudes of people, the great majority elected to be "opened" and to receive the Subud *latihan*. (Incidentally I shall use the Indonesian term *"latihan"* fairly often. It can be translated as training or exercise, but it has a particular connotation for members of Subud, as can be seen by reading on.)

That first evening Mr. Bennett had dinner upstairs in his study, together with a few guests, amongst whom was Icksan Ahmed, one of the newly arrived Indonesians. I was asked to wait upon this party, a task that I did willingly, if only in part to satisfy my curiosity. Pak Subuh and the other Indonesians ate alone in the West Wing.

Icksan Ahmed was a young, thickset Indonesian, with a wonderful flashing smile. During the meal there was a great deal of hilarity as Mr. Bennett explained to Icksan how upset people were at the thought of having a new teacher. Mr. Bennett was so full of mirth as to be almost giggling with it. This did impress me greatly at the time. We had for so long looked upon Mr. B. as our teacher and leader that it was difficult to see him sitting at another's feet. And in any case, his ordinary accomplishments, as a scientist and linguist, were such that I wondered what kind of man he would accept to follow.

My Stairway to Subud

Icksan Ahmed was a young, thickset Indonesian, with a wonderful flashing smile

From left to right: Sjafrudin, Ismana, Ibu, Pak Subuh, John Bennett, Mrs. Sheila Ross, Rahayu and Asikin at Coombe Springs, 1957

My Stairway to Subud
Chapter 6

The Arrival of Subud

When Mrs. Howard had first told us of the arrival of Pak Subuh, I got to my feet at the rear of the group. I was both astonished and incredulous. The announcement had an immediate and quite extraordinary effect. Some people at once made touching declarations of their fidelity to Mr. Bennett—he was their teacher and they wanted none other. Others declared that Subud must be all right simply because Mr. Bennett had recommended it.

For my own part I felt it was absurd to accept something on Mr. Bennett's say-so; this was itself contrary to everything that we had been taught. We had never been encouraged to accept ideas without first testing and verifying for ourselves, so that we could arrive at an objective understanding. On the contrary, we had always been advised to accept nothing, an advice that still held good for me. To do otherwise was to thrust an unfair onus of responsibility on Mr. Bennett.

Those who wished to undertake the new exercise had to inform one of the senior members of the group. It is notable that in spite of the widely varying attitudes of people, the great majority elected to be "opened" and to receive the Subud *latihan*. (Incidentally I shall use the Indonesian term *"latihan"* fairly often. It can be translated as training or exercise, but it has a particular connotation for members of Subud, as can be seen by reading on.)

That first evening Mr. Bennett had dinner upstairs in his study, together with a few guests, amongst whom was Icksan Ahmed, one of the newly arrived Indonesians. I was asked to wait upon this party, a task that I did willingly, if only in part to satisfy my curiosity. Pak Subuh and the other Indonesians ate alone in the West Wing.

Icksan Ahmed was a young, thickset Indonesian, with a wonderful flashing smile. During the meal there was a great deal of hilarity as Mr. Bennett explained to Icksan how upset people were at the thought of having a new teacher. Mr. Bennett was so full of mirth as to be almost giggling with it. This did impress me greatly at the time. We had for so long looked upon Mr. B. as our teacher and leader that it was difficult to see him sitting at another's feet. And in any case, his ordinary accomplishments, as a scientist and linguist, were such that I wondered what kind of man he would accept to follow.

Icksan Ahmed was a young, thickset Indonesian, with a wonderful flashing smile

From left to right: Sjafrudin, Ismana, Ibu, Pak Subuh, John Bennett, Mrs. Sheila Ross, Rahayu and Asikin at Coombe Springs, 1957

On the weekend of his arrival I saw Pak Subuh once as he was ascending the stairs. He was dressed neatly in a fawn coloured tropical suit. Nothing impressed me much except his particular manner of walking. Indeed there was a certain neutrality in his appearance.

It was only later that I saw the womenfolk. They were at once remarkable for their quiet dignity, their lovely clothes, their grace and their essential femininity.

The arrival of Pak Subuh and his entourage at once created a great commotion. The news of his arrival was shattering enough. We had hardly time to ask ourselves the relationship of Gurdjieff's ideas to Subud (of which we knew so little) before the household had to cope with the physical presence of Bapak and his people—Pak Subuh is frequently referred to as Bapak.

The people at Coombe Springs had long been trained to cope. After all they had been brought up on the tradition of *tout est changé* at a moments notice. Visitors were fairly common, and the household was used to working together for big occasions, such as a visit by Madame de Salzmann, or for the wedding of Mr. Bennett's daughter, Ann.

Formerly, however, the household had met all eventualities on their own terms. Almost all former visitors were either high in the Gurdjieff hierarchy, and therefore understood and respected the *raison d'etre* for Coombe Springs, or were people who were at least interested in and sympathetic towards the system.

Pak Subuh and his people were entirely different. Firstly, they evinced not the slightest interest in the system of Gurdjieff then or later. Secondly, they did not join us for meals in the dining room, as was the custom with most visitors, but ate alone in the West Wing. Thirdly, they ate Indonesian food, and so the kitchen workers had to prepare two different sets of meals (mostly done in the top kitchen later). Also, while they as Muslims drank no alcohol, they did drink vast quantities of Coca-cola, which had to be brought in by the crate. Fourthly, Pak Subuh did everything as the spirit moved him, with a disarming disregard for the clock.

Mr. Bennett was almost pedantically punctual. I remember his once lambasting a hapless Marjorie (Marjorie Wilmshurst) for being late for a meeting, and when she protested that she was in fact on time, he had replied that if she was only on time she was already late, because she had not given herself time to prepare.

The Indonesians in Pak Subuh's party always ate after Pak Subuh and Ibu had eaten; they could sometimes be seen trailing around the garden late in the afternoon, hoping that Bapak would soon be moved to eat. However, I don't want to imply that Bapak was late for lectures. He was quick to adapt to Western ways and when punctuality was required, as later during the Congress in '59, he was notably on time.

Apart from the Indonesians, a host of people began to descend upon Coombe Springs, who were interested solely in Subud, and who often had a condescending and amused attitude towards the disciplined Gurdjieff forces, who prepared the meals, catered, washed up, wrote letters, prepared accounts, and did a hundred and one things regarding the organisation. But, of course, the greatest dislocation of the routine was caused by the *latihan* itself, as I will explain shortly.

I remember that on this first day of Pak Subuh's arrival, Mrs. Howard remarked gaily to me that this latest development was "right up my street." She referred to my well-known liking for Asiatic peoples, to my enthusiasm for Indian music and dancing, and to my interest in the great sacred writings of the East. I responded sombrely to her gaiety. I had cultivated many friends from the East, only to find that they were mostly interested in Western technology, and that they often ridiculed their own cultural heritage, if they were not abysmally ignorant of it. They seemed even less inclined to an interest in things of the spirit than Westerners, and I had begun to doubt that anything existed in the East other than fragments of a past knowledge, the essence of which the Easterners themselves did not understand.

I say all this in order to convey something of my jaundiced and unexcited attitude at that time. Subsequently, in talking over these early days with my friends, I found that many of them were immediately moved by the advent of Subud, that they felt instinctively its sacred character, and that even before they were opened, they experienced a certain inner excitement or strange dreams and premonitions. [Actually, there were at least two young men who had very striking experiences before they were officially opened. Only very much later did I realise that Mr. Bennett had already been opened some months before by Husein Rofé. This in part accounted for the electric atmosphere of the meeting at the Onward Hall in

My Stairway to Subud

Bennett, he had interpolated, "Quite wrong. You have given a quite wrong impression of our Work. I am my attention." But if she was mistaken in her view of attention as a "means," I think the majority of us shared this error.

However this may be, all Gurdjieff's methods and his movements had a character of control, of decision, of deliberation, whereas the Subud *latihan* seemed to be the very antithesis of this.

All these thoughts made me quite miserable. Coombe Springs and all that it stood for had become a part of my being. However hard were the tasks, however ridiculous they may sometimes have seemed, however inconvenient and expensive it had been to go there as often as I did—mattered nothing. It was an island of hope, a place where life had point and significance in the sea of absurdities, contradictions and chaos.

Now what had become of that island? Had Mr. Bennett taken leave of his senses? But what of the other independent followers of Gurdjieff—what of Bissing, and Wolton and Hoare? They had all been students of Gurdjieff, companions of Ouspensky, who had been above all the arch-enemies of self-deception—had they all together been duped?

I could not answer my own questions, and when I got to bed in the early hours of the morning, I found myself faced with the scarcely credible proposition that I might have to sever my connection with J. G. Bennett and Coombe Springs.

My thoughts on the morrow were rather less dramatic and heroic. The people in Manchester had heard a little about Subud by then, but I determined to add nothing further, and in this case I was helped by the Gurdjieff discipline of not talking about one's work. In any case, I did not wish to influence the people in Manchester. And within a week, I found myself once more at Coombe Springs.

This time my fear in the *latihan* did not recur. There was relatively little noise and my state of fear was replaced by boredom. I simply shifted from one foot to another and nothing happened. This mood was followed by skepticism, which engendered further mood of querulousness and aggressiveness.

That Sunday morning Pak Subuh gave a talk to the men who had been opened. Those who had not yet been opened were not permitted to attend. This was the first time that many of us had seen Pak

Subuh closely and heard him speak. Husein Rofé, the Englishman who had studied with Pak Subuh in Indonesia and who had opened Mr. Bennett and the other seniors, translated.

Pak Subuh's voice was musical and his enunciation clear. This was most important to me, since I had read that a "true Yogi" always has a beautiful voice, and I held a conviction that no man of inner development could possibly speak sloppily. The Indonesian language, at least to my ears, was also very charming.

I was at once impressed by Pak Subuh's complete relaxation, which seemed easy and uncalculated. At any rate it was of a different brand from that which we had been used to practice. As to the talk itself, it was completely different from anything that I had heard before. It was certainly a far cry from the sort of thing we heard from Mr. Bennett, which was above all psychological and full of fine distinctions. Pak Subuh gave explanations but they were not explanations at all. For one thing they were delivered ex cathedra—they could more truly be described as pronouncements.

For example, explaining that the word Subud is itself a contraction of three Sanskrit words, Susila, Budhi and Dharma he said: "Susila means right living according to the Will of God, Budhi is the force residing in the inner nature of man. Dharma means surrender and sincere acceptance of the Will of God."

But such statements did not explain to me that the *latihan* was the action of this force, nor that surrender to it was submission to God's Will. When he said such things as "Material objects are enveloped with a life force that can influence the heart of men," I felt, Yes! We are mechanisms that react to our environment and maybe material objects are enveloped with a life force, but that I do not know. Pak Subuh also said that the action of the *latihan* could only be experienced when the heart, the mind and desires had come to a stop, and urged those who had experience not to be proud of themselves, and those who had not to have patience. He said that the true significance of the exercise we could not see now, but this would be revealed as we made progress.

In the question time that followed, someone asked the question that had worried me. "We have our attention. What are we to do with our attention in the exercise? I understand already that we should not direct it or meditate but that still leaves the question, what are we to do with our attention?" This was translated and Pak Subuh replied that he should not worry about this, but simply fol-

Manchester. Also, there was a group of young men in the household who were doing a special morning exercise with Mr. B. and quite possibly these young men had effectively already been opened by him.]

Such was far from the case with me. I doubt if anyone can read the preceding chapters without seeing how deeply I was touched by Gurdjieff's ideas, and how devoted I had become to Mr. and Mrs. Bennett personally. In retrospect, it is easy to see certain things. It is easy to write that many of us were at a spiritual impasse; that we had come to acknowledge the necessity of the Work; yet we had come more and more to see that we could not work—and that we needed help. All that is clear now. But at that time I was far from conscious of this impasse.

On the contrary, I found the whole system of Gurdjieff's ideas deeply satisfying, and the work of the groups was for me the centre of my existence. If I had begun to see that I could not work, could not remember myself, I did not doubt that there were others who had the key. Frankly, I felt that Mr. Bennett had an ace card up his sleeve that would only be produced when we had made the necessary efforts. Only much later did I begin to comprehend the spiritual anguish of just those whom we regarded as leaders, and who had the humility to acknowledge that they could go no further with the strength and knowledge they presently possessed.

I was scornful of the host of people who suddenly found themselves at the end of their tether. I was mystified by the sudden revelation that Gurdjieff had declared that someone would come after him. Why had we not heard of this before? And I was affronted when I heard one of Ouspensky's own pupils say that Ouspensky had declared that the system was a failure "—unless we can find a way to the opening of the Higher Emotional Centre, and we have not found that way."

All that I heard about Subud made me suspicious. It had been hinted that the *"latihan"* might connect one to the Higher Emotional Centre. This was against all theory that stated that the three lower centres must first work together. And after seven years of study and efforts I found it hard to stomach the idea that spiritual grace could be transmitted as a gift. This seemed to me not only extraordinary, but also unlikely and even impossible.

I had to return to Manchester on the Sunday night, but was advised to say nothing for the present to the Manchester group. I had by

My Stairway to Subud

then heard Mr. Bennett's explanations to a number of groups. Later on, I was given permission to speak to the people in Manchester and also to play a tape-recording of an introductory talk that Mr. Bennett gave to the groups in Holland. As talk followed talk, there was a noticeable development of ideas.

In spite of my own feelings of suspicion, there were many aspects of these talks to which I was attracted. Mr. Bennett said much about the problems of Will and Self-Will, and suggested that much that we liked to call "Work," and many of our efforts, in reality arose from our self-will. Of course, this was not anything really new to us, but his language of that time highlighted the famous spiritual dilemma. "How can I surrender my will with the force of my own will?" It is an obvious contradiction in terms.

I was also attracted by the honesty of Mr. Bennett's appraisal of the situation. His ability to acknowledge that we were not really getting anywhere and that we were fooling ourselves if we imagined we were making progress impressed me. He said that there was no doubt for him about the rightness of the principles and direction of Gurdjieff's work, but that an additional shock was needed. There was no doubt that the way of *self-remembering* was necessary, but none of us could *remember* ourselves. We were in need of help and, furthermore, help from a Higher Source. In Mr. Bennett's opinions, the "opening" in Subud was just that opening to a Higher Source. It was represented, at least to the Gurdjieff people, that the Subud exercise would be of help in their work, and that there could be no better preparation for this exercise than the studies we had all been engaged in.

I could not fail but be impressed by these arguments. I think that all of us, more or less, knew that we needed help. And presented in that way, I somehow got the erroneous idea that Pak Subuh was going to teach us a highly esoteric exercise; in fact that he was going to produce that trump card which I had long imagined to be held up Mr. Bennett's sleeve.

Things turned out somewhat differently from my expectations. I received a letter from Mr. Bennett to say that he had spoken to Pak Subuh about me, and he suggested that I should be present at Coombe Springs for the Whit weekend, and as many Monday and Thursday evenings as possible, so that I could become established in this new exercise.

The whole of that Whit weekend, except for its culmination on the

My Stairway to Subud

Monday evening, has now been blotted from my memory. I can only remember that sometime on Monday afternoon about fifteen men gathered upstairs in Mr. Bennett's study, prior to being "opened." He gave us a very brief introductory talk. We were to take off our shoes, our ties and our watches. We were simply to stand and to be open in our feelings. If we experienced the spontaneous arising of movements within our bodies we were not to resist, but simply to follow. We were not to make any effort to control our mental associations, but were to let them wander freely, constraining nothing.

We then filed downstairs to the dining room, the floor of which had been covered by a number of new carpets, and the curtains had been drawn. We were placed in a rough sort of circle in the room. Pak Subuh was already in the room, with a number of Indonesians. I recall a very fine exquisite odour, such as I had never smelt before.

Pak Subuh then said a few words in Indonesian that were translated haltingly by one of the Indonesian helpers. He said something about coming to the true worship of God, and that in the way of Subud, we should not use our thoughts for meditation but simply receive. Then, "Close your eyes and we begin."

Almost at once a number of people began a very strange singing. They sang independently, though it did blend in a curious way. The singers also seemed to be moving about the room. Someone else began to pray in a loud voice in a language that I presumed to be Arabic. The words "*Akbar Allah*" were repeated a great number of times. But if I simply say prayer in a loud voice, such as one has heard from a priest or a *muezzin*, that would give entirely the wrong impression. This prayer seemed to be heaved from the very depths of his being, as if he was in an agony of remorse, sorrow and supplication. It had a strong effect upon my feelings and I began to feel very small and utterly unworthy. At the same time, I began to be afraid and tensed up. I heard a friend on my left crash to the ground. At the other end of the room someone began to weep as if he would burst in two. Yet another began to laugh, as if at the greatest joke in the world. And still others were moving about quite rapidly, to judge from the panting and the feet padding on the floor.

The longer the exercise lasted the more I tensed up, till I was holding on to myself, determined to resist anything that might come. Suddenly one word was called out—"Finish!"—and the pandemonium stopped. I opened my eyes and saw that six or seven of my friends were still standing as I was, while the rest had obviously been moving about. A half-hour had passed.

I went next door to put on my shoes and jacket. A friend tried to catch my eye with a questioning look, but I avoided him. I quickly gathered my things together and went down to the station to catch the train to London. Four of us shared a compartment who had been to the exercise, but not one of us spoke a word.

I arrived in London and caught a late train for Manchester from Euston, where I had a compartment to myself and time to appraise my feelings. They were in a tumult. I could not doubt that I had been present at something very exceptional. I could not doubt that there was present a very strong force, but my feelings about this force were mixed and incoherent. On the surface of my mind, a host of questions raged. Why had there been singing? What accounted for the prayers in Arabic? Why did people move about? And what caused them to move? What was the force to which we were opening ourselves? What was it we were receiving?

All through the night these questions reiterated themselves in my brain. My feelings were so confused that I don't know what most alarmed me. But one thing I could not get over. The whole exercise seemed contrary to all that we had been taught in Gurdjieff's methods.

How often had we struggled with our attention, sitting cross-legged on the ground, gazing at one point, not letting our eyes wander, not permitting an involuntary movement. Somehow I had been sure that the Subud experience must be an exercise of attention, but clearly it was not.

Attention! Attention! Attention! I cannot describe just how often this word was used in the Gurdjieff system. We attempted to divide attention, to refine attention. We observed ourselves by means of the question, "Where is my attention now?" We asked how to increase the power of attention. We put a tremendous emphasis upon this power for one simple reason: It was considered the prime and eminent means for Work.

Incidentally, I may have been mistaken in this, but my understanding was shared by many others, as is illustrated by the following. A young girl friend of mine (Dinah Day) had been to India and met a guru who had enquired, "What means do you use for Work?" She had replied, "Our attention." When she recounted this to Mr.

low the action of the exercise. I think that neither Rofé nor Pak Subuh really understood the question; or rather, they were not interested in the psychological role of attention, but only in creating the attitude of mind that would help people be receptive in the *latihan*.

I spoke up and said that quite frankly I had found my first exercise quite terrifying. How could one be sure that one was opening oneself to higher and not to lower forces? When the first part of my question was translated, Pak Subuh looked over at me and chuckled, whereat the assembled company roared with laughter, and to this day I cannot remember what he said after that. [Actually I have in my possession a tape of this very first talk, which is especially interesting as one can hear Husein Rofé's immediate translations.] I could not help but be affected by Pak Subuh's humour. In fact there were many humorous touches that would take too long to relate. But while I was charmed and wanted to laugh, another half of me was vexed and complained, "He did not answer the questions. He did not answer the questions."

During the rest of that day I had conversations with many of my friends, only to discover that an enormous change had taken place in one short week. "What did you think of the talk, Victor?" (Victor Stephenson.) He cut me short and strode away. "But have you experienced in the *latihan*?" asked another. "The same as all of you," I retorted quickly. A third friend I found to be in sympathy with me. Neither of us had experienced anything, and both of us were astonished to find that already half our friends seemed to have come under the influence of Subud, and to have accepted it. Had they already abandoned Gurdjieff? Could they so quickly have taken leave of their critical faculties? We were talking in this strain when Mrs. Howard (Elizabeth, later to be Mrs. Bennett) came into the room. "I know how you feel," she said. "I went to three *latihans* and after that I said to Mr. B., I really can't go on with this. 'Try once more,' he said. And then it worked." I pitied her.

I was never much good at dissembling, and by now my feelings of anguish and misery began willy-nilly to communicate themselves to the group in Manchester. I felt proud of them as a group. At least, I consoled myself, no one will be able to deceive these hardheaded northerners. In my discussions with them, I still said nothing about Subud, but I did encourage in them their native skepticism and fostered their independent and critical outlook. And when one of them, who practiced hypnotism, assured me that I would be a most difficult subject, I took some cold comfort from his words.

In spite of my mounting antagonism, I still went down to Coombe Springs on every possible occasion, often spending as much as five pounds for a flying visit to an evening *latihan*. My own mood became more and more rebellious and morose. At least formerly, I had got something for my money. Now I was attending a strange exercise, where I experienced nothing at all except boredom and exasperation. And, further, it seemed to me that I was witnessing the rapid dissolution of all that I had held most precious during the preceding seven years.

For everything had begun to move with astonishing rapidity. Within a few weeks over four hundred people had been opened; mostly Mr. Bennett's pupils, but also some of the older independent students of Gurdjieff and Ouspensky, as well as a number of other seekers of the truth. Some also came for reasons of health, having heard that the practice of the *latihan* sometimes effected physical cures.

The large nine-sided hall that was being built had not been completed, so a large hut was temporarily erected in another part of the grounds. This could accommodate about thirty people at a time. With such a number of people, however, the evening exercises often used to run from eight until midnight. At the same time, the work of the groups continued, and the working parties on Sundays also. Subud was simply added to the already heavy routine.

Within only a few weeks the general pattern of reactions to Subud began to be apparent. Some were deeply shocked and left quickly. Some were simply bewildered and looked to Mr. Bennett for explanations. Some, who had experienced nothing, stayed on doggedly, but were sometimes caustic and critical toward Subud. Whereas the vast majority of people had not only experienced, but regarded this experience as the most important of their lives. To say that they were happy is to say the least of it. Mr. Bennett himself seemed to be walking on air. His face was noticeably flushed, as if he was in a peculiarly excited inner state. In fact this was phenomenon that was common to many who had experienced. Once I heard Mr. Bennett say: "Today is my birthday. I thought that I would prepare people, but I never expected to see such a thing in my lifetime."

Once, as we walked out in the garden after a *latihan*, he asked me, "Did you feel anything?" I had hardly begun to explain before he walked off abruptly. How did one account for his increasing impatience? I began to feel angry with him, as if he personally was responsible for my misery. I could not resist telling him this, when he came into the pantry where a group of us were washing up. "Well," he replied, "when Christopher started (Christopher Baynes) he drove home perfectly convinced that I was round the bend." "And I still think you are," I said. He merely laughed.

And everyone laughed. I went round like an angry hornet, plunging my stings into my unfortunate friends. They laughed. Some of them began to tell me of their experiences. This, of course, could not fail to interest me, since we had known each other for many years. I remember particularly the account of a young engineer who had visited Coombe Springs from Norfolk, while still an officer in the Army. He was a quiet fellow (Stuart Gray-Thompson) with clipped speech, great mechanical ability and a quality of natural leadership. He had done a great deal of construction work on the nine-sided building, and many people liked to work under his direction.

I discovered that it was he, who had been weeping so piteously, at that same first *latihan* when we both were opened. I was especially interested in his account, because at that time I was very suspicious of anyone who had experienced movements, since I felt that they were probably phony or self-induced. I had determined that I would on no account move unless it was completely clear to me that the exercise moved me. This engineer told me how he had felt an inner push, first one way then another, until he had fallen to the ground. Then he began to weep, but "the weeping went through me." All the time he simply observed it happening, and it was quite clear to him that he had to permit it, and that he could stop the action at any time.

Such simple narratives from a number of my friends could not fail but impress me. The fact that there was an action of some powerful kind quickly became indisputable. It was the validity of this action that caused me more and more concern.

Pak Subuh gave more talks. He reiterated that the *latihan* was a "grace," a gift from God. He explained that a process of purification had been set in motion that would proceed by itself, and that gradually all faults would be eliminated. The whole tenor of everything he said seemed to run counter to my own beliefs.

How could faults be eliminated without great perseverance and continuing efforts? Pak Subuh spoke again and again about "sub-

My Stairway to Subud

mission" and "surrender" to God's Will; that we could not understand the exercise with the mind but that it would assuredly bring us in due course to the true worship of God. But, I asked myself, is submission in the *latihan* the same as submission to the Will of God?

I was not alone in my thoughts. Some people had already left, amongst whom were some of Mr. Bennett's closest lieutenants. As to my personal friends, who were mostly young men, they were divided.

I continued thus for some six weeks when my annual holiday became due. The arrival of Subud had upset all my plans for a continental holiday and so I intended to spend a week on the south coast. I was so unhappy about the turn events had taken that I was in no wise looking forward to my vacation.

I drove down to London and stopped off to see my great friends, John and Mollie Penseney, in their Hampstead flat. There were two others there, who had studied with Mr. Bennett in the same group. We knew each other rather exceptionally well. All of them had begun to experience something from the *latihan*.

I was in an aggressive sort of mood and soon launched into the attack. It went something like this: "Don't mistake me, I have no quarrel with religious terminology as such. It is easy enough to transpose the idea of having one's own 'I' or 'inner master' to 'submission to the Will of God.' But do you know what you are doing? Do you understand the force to which you are surrendering? How can you accept so easily that surrender in the *latihan* is submission to God's Will?" I went on and on in this vein.

My friends listened and laughed. They were so evidently full of good will towards me that I could not help but be impressed by their forbearance. While not concurring with my views, they made no attempt to correct me. At last I said, "The trouble is this—I am right and all of you are wrong. On the other hand, I am in a negative state and all of you are positive."

"Good for you, Tonio," Mollie replied. "At least, you are always honest."

John added something that, while I did not understand at the time, later proved to be of great help. "I find that if I try to be open my exercise begins to slow down. One must not even try anything."

Of course, I had tried to be open. After the initial shock, I had done all I could to be in the right state to receive. I did want to experience, and it had certainly hurt my pride to think that I was duller and less sensitive than the other people at Coombe.

That evening I went to the *latihan* determined that it would be my last. Subud might be of help to some people, but I doubted that it could ever be my way. I was in such a skeptical frame of mind that I determined that this time I would open my eyes and see what went on.

A few minutes after the *latihan* had commenced, I followed my intentions. One man opposite me was rotating his head and shoulders at great speed. Another knelt on the floor and made a series of arm gestures of great simplicity and beauty. As for Pak Subuh he simply walked about and smoked a cigar, stopping occasionally in front of someone. Suddenly Icksan Ahmed was in front of me. "Close your eyes," he said chidingly. As soon as I had closed them I heard him chanting, "Allah! Allah! Allah!" and at once a great force was rained down in and around me. My back was bent back and then forward and back again very quickly, so strongly that I lost my balance and fell to the floor. As I lay there I could feel this force surge and sway through my body. I believe that I laughed. All my former fears instantly evaporated.

When the *latihan* came to an end, I went up to the main house and joined some of the others for a cup of tea in the kitchen. I could still feel in myself the presence of vital energy and I felt elated and yet detached. But within I was deliriously happy.

The state that I was then in, far from being unfamiliar to me, was, on the contrary, well known. Even now I can remember the aroma of the tea I drank. I walked into the back kitchen and took a tomato, and it seems I can remember the taste of that tomato. All my senses had become sharply alive. And within myself, I felt very much at home and at ease.

The taste of this state was similar to what I had experienced on several occasions after making great efforts either at movements or at some psychological exercise. If there was any difference it was only in the intensity and the effortlessness with which this remained with me. But of course the main difference was in the origin. Normally, it required effort and time, the struggle between "yes" and "no," between affirmation and denial before the reconciling force appeared. In the *latihan* on the other hand, I had been moved by a mysterious force beyond my comprehension, and felt flooded by a vital energy.

My eyes must have shone and my face looked flushed, because when I went to chat with some of my friends and told them that I had experienced, they at once said, "Oh yes, we can see that."

The next day I delayed my departure to the south coast in the hope that I might see Icksan and talk with him. Shortly before noon I found him in the hall reading a newspaper. "Do you remember me?" I asked.

"Yes," he replied with a wide smile. We went into the rose garden and sat down on a bench. I asked him how it was that he had come over to me in the *latihan*, and he replied that he was drawn. I also asked why it was that I had experienced that night but not during the previous six weeks. He said simply that I was "open" at that time. I thought this rather strange in view of my extremely skeptical state of mind, but later I came to see that at this moment I did not care; and later on there were a number of occasions when I had experiences just when I was without care and without hope.

I don't remember the exact course of the conversation, because amongst other things, Icksan did not speak English well at all. He did say, " I say *Allah! Allah!* Same thing I say Lord! Lord!" and as I sat there I began to feel again the vibrations of the exercise within me. He also spoke about *pembersihan* or purification, and he did a number of tests. The essence of what he said was that the *latihan* would bring alive and to a state of purity a number of inner instruments and that there were many things we could comprehend directly, given this inner purification. How he did these tests I could not tell, but it appeared his sensitivity enabled him to know a wealth of things quite inaccessible to the senses and the intellect.

Icksan was a stocky, cheerful young man in his thirties, who liked kicking a ball about or listening to light music. Yet in this one short interview, I came to my own private conclusion that he was miles ahead of the most advanced Gurdjieff followers that I knew. There were many brilliant minds among them, but for all their attainments and Icksan's lack of them, Icksan had access to a source of knowledge that made even high intelligence seem pedestrian.

My holiday on the south coast was remarkable only for one thing; and that was the extraordinary pleasure I had in the use of my eyes.

My Stairway to Subud

I watched the sea, shimmering with sunlight for hours, and feasted on it.

After a week I returned to Coombe Springs, eager for another *latihan* and wondering whether I would experience again. This was the start of the second summer seminar. A great number of people had arrived from abroad and from the provinces, including many men and women from Manchester.

I did experience again in the *latihan*, but in a completely different form. This time my whole trunk was rotated to the right and then the left while my arms flung rapidly like flails for a few minutes, before I was put down on the floor.

These movements lasted only a short time, say ten minutes. But as I continued to go to the exercises there was each time a progression, a variation of the movements and an increase in the amount of time before I was, as it were, laid out on the floor and nothing more happened. More of this later.

I am bound to say that by this time my whole feelings towards Subud had changed. It was certain that I still had many questions. But then again, nearly all the answers and explanations that we had already received seemed quite irrelevant. Having experienced for myself, I was no longer concerned with making the experience square up with any words. I still did not know if this was "submission to God, purification" or the working of the higher emotional centre. Far from knowing, I was impatient with any verbal formulations. None of them could approximate to experience. This is likewise true of what I am writing. I can describe manifestations, hint at changes of states, but I can neither convey the experience by words nor the import of the experiences. I felt simply and deeply its rightness, and that it was something that I needed. But, of course, I also felt a lot more than that.

My hardheaded, independent, critical northerners did not disappoint me. Many of them experienced strongly at their first exercise, and most of them within the following week. There were, however, two friends who were shocked at the *latihan* and upset by some of the answers that Husein Rofé gave to questions. They felt that hypnotism was involved and that they were surrendering to the influence of Pak Subuh and his magic. Later on, I met one of them at odd intervals in Manchester. He seemed to think that Bennett and I were in some esoteric hierarchy and that we were using the astral blood of the others for some shocking purposes. And that

Pak Subuh tuned in to our exercises! In spite of these fantasies, I felt all along that he was searching for a formula to come back.

The other was shocked because Rofé had come out with some intriguing answers in relation to sexual purity. Amongst other things, he had warned against intercourse with promiscuous women, since the man would have to work off not only her faults, but also the imperfections of all the men with whom she had slept!

As far as I was concerned, Rofé was engagingly frank and straight from the shoulder. Anyway, the two friends mentioned left our group and continued to study Gurdjieff's ideas and methods independently. This was a matter of some regret to me, since I had felt that we had been brothers in an enterprise, and I had benefited from our association. It seemed to me that they had come to conclusions too quickly. But then, who was I to talk? Of one thing I am sure. We may fail the work, but the work never fails us. Mr. Bennett often said this, and I felt very strongly that they might follow a different road, but that what was valid in their past endeavours would and must be eternally valid.

The summer seminars of 1957 must have been the most extraordinary ever. Externally, there was the usual strenuous routine. I have already mentioned the building of the nine-sided hall. During these seminars, the building went on apace and with great enthusiasm. There was an added incentive to get the building operational with the advent of the *latihan*. The sides and the roof were being constructed, and all day long, people were scurrying up the tall scaffolding.

In these endeavours, there was a great feeling of unity. But regarding the psychological work, everything was in a state of flux. Mr. Bennett gave his usual talks and we understood that Pak Subuh had said that this work should continue. These talks were supposedly about the principles of work, and we were discouraged from asking questions about Subud, to avoid confusion. In spite of this, it was quite obvious that the majority of questions had a direct bearing on Subud, which was the event uppermost in our minds. There were also movements as formerly.

But the truth is that within those few short weeks the centre of interest had shifted to Subud. A lot of the London people had already been opened, and during these weeks the provincials groups from Bournemouth, Bristol, Liverpool, and Birmingham appeared *en masse*. Numerous people came from Norway, France, Holland,

and Germany, not to mention other far-off parts of the globe. In consequence of this there was a constant stream of new people experiencing their first *latihans,* while others had virtually become "old hands" within two months.

All this created a complex situation. Some people who had experienced strongly and who had been faithful followers of Mr. Bennett dramatically lost all interest in his expositions and attended no more of his talks. What they had received in the *latihan* was of prime importance to them. Talk and words only seemed heavy and confusing. For others such an attitude seemed lacking in gratitude. While yet others were shocked or confused and turned to Mr. Bennett for support. Some simply left altogether. The great majority of people were in the middle position. They continued to go to talks either because of interest or because of a sense of gratitude, but willy-nilly they were changing.

And they were changing by the force of one simple factor—the experience of the *latihan* itself. The immediacy of the experience, the oft repeated evidence that there was no intermediary and none needed, and the uniqueness and privacy of what was received, could have only one effect; to make everyone independent and to wean them from leaning on or seeking advice from any other man. This did not happen all at once. At this period of transition the people were divided; some having become quite independent, while others traditionally sought for guidance and advice.

Everything was turned topsy-turvy. Many people that I thought would be receptive and sensitive experienced nothing. Pak Subuh or Ibu designated others, who had been almost barred from Coombe Springs, as Helpers within two exercises! Even within this short time, some people were conspicuous for the changes that had taken place within them.

The occasional talks given by Pak Subuh were of tremendous interest to all. For a great many people his basic premises no longer afforded any difficulty; namely, that the *latihan* is a Gift from God and that a process of purification would take place. Because, however strange the form of the *latihan*, many had their own direct experience of its action both as grace and purification. The Indonesians themselves were astonished at the receptivity of the people and the rapidity of the progress.

The matter of his talks was very curious. Pak Subuh never set himself up as any sort of prophet. He spoke of things we might come

My Stairway to Subud

to experience and if he spoke *ex cathedra* there was always implicit that this was a temporary measure. He explained that the purificatory process started on the periphery—the body—and that subsequently the feelings, then consciousness, then understanding, would be purified.

Pak Subuh also demonstrated a number of "tests." He would pose a question, while everyone put himself or herself in the state of the *latihan* to receive an answer. The receptivity of individuals varied according to the degree of their purification. He also said that the whole body would be brought to life, and some of the tests concerned the life of the different organs of the body. For example, he would ask: "My eyes, how my eyes?" or "My lungs have I got lungs?" I personally received nothing at these tests. But others did, very obviously. In the case of the lungs, this was clearly audible for a small number of people. Pak Subuh also tested how one would feel in different situations. For example, "How do I feel in front of someone who is very rich?" or "How do I feel when near someone who is in need of help?" I mention here a few of the more simple things. Later, I heard of tests that must seem truly fantastic—"For a man who has a soul on the vegetable level, how fast can he travel round the world?" The answer to this was intriguing. It sometimes makes me think that the aeronautical people are wasting their times.

The burden of Pak Subuh's talks was that we should continue with the *latihan* and that in time our faults would be rectified and we would be brought to the true worship of God. We did not have to search for God, but only surrender. God was closer to us than we are to our own eyes. As we continued we would be led automatically more and more into the right path. This was something beyond our own willing. The operation of our thoughts and feelings, though necessary for this life, were inimical to the *latihan*. It was impossible to understand the *latihan* with the power of our thoughts. We should not attempt to comprehend the movements or interpret any experience, since the true significance would be revealed in due course.

These talks of Pak Subuh also caused a great deal of discussion, even dissension, as well may be imagined, as the words "efforts" and "super-efforts" were almost sacred at Coombe Springs. For my own part, this did not cause a great deal of difficulty; since Gurdjieff had been specific that self-knowledge could result from efforts, but not change. And it was perfectly true that many people had gained a very clear cognizance of the obstacles that confronted them because of these same efforts, as is recounted in the previous chapter. They were also in despair because they felt unable to surmount these obstacles—they were at a standstill. Gurdjieff had also said that man had a choice of influence and that one could fall under higher influences. It seemed to me that Pak Subuh said precisely the same thing but in a different language. According to him, we were under the influence of material, vegetable, animal and human forces. This seemed to me very similar to the idea that we are mechanisms reacting to the external world. Gurdjieff had also said that prolonged "work on oneself" was necessary, and Pak Subuh did not say other than that purification would be a long process. A lot of confusion arose because effort was taken to be synonymous with "work on oneself." But this particular misunderstanding had been present long before the advent of Subud.

During these seminars, I began to feel the people around me very differently. Without being told, I could sense those who were experiencing strongly and we seemed to be drawn together in a strange way. And I was likewise strongly aware of those who approached every problem mentally and intellectually, just as I had done myself. I began to see why some people had been impatient with me. The mental approach made me feel heavy and uncomfortable, and it was evident that many things in Subud needed to be approached through the feelings rather than the intellect. This was particularly the case with Pak Subuh's talks. Later I was to hear recordings of talks at which I had been present, and I realised then how poor the translations had been. At the time, although Pak Subuh spoke in Indonesian, I had felt directly the significance of what he was saying.

I was also fortunate in getting to know the young Indonesians—Icksan, Rahmad, Sjafruddin and Asikin—to whose sitting room, I was sometimes invited. Icksan was the most approachable and was of great help to many of the young men. They still took little part in the activities at Coombe, other than was directly concerned with Subud. Icksan was normally cheerful, but also had disconcerting changes of mood. On one occasion I was asking a lot of questions and Icksan became more and more discomfited. As a matter of fact, he belched a number of times. One of the other Indonesians explained, "All the time you ask questions you are throwing off." I was surprised to say the least. Mr. Bennett had always encouraged us to ask questions; even saying that if one worked, one was bound to have a question. And mine had been serious questions concerning the principles of Subud.

I knew by then that during the *latihan*, the trainees threw off their emanations to the discomfiture of the "helpers," who might have to exercise again later to clear themselves. (I should explain here that the term "helper" was the term used to designate those whom Pak Subuh had given permission to open others, to pass on the contact and generally assist in the *latihan*, and to look after probationers.) But I had not realised that I might be throwing off in the course of a normal conversation. I apologised to Icksan. "It does not matter," he replied, and then suddenly: "Exercise!"

To tell the truth I felt a little embarrassed as I had once, when as a boy of fourteen, a young Cambridge graduate had flopped suddenly to his knees and suggested that we pray! Still sitting in my chair, I closed my eyes. Gradually I relaxed, but could hardly let go my thoughts and felt upset at the discomfort that I must be causing Icksan. At length, my thoughts began to dissolve away and I could feel the miracle of the life-force vibrate within me. After a quarter of an hour we stopped. My forehead was covered with perspiration. Icksan laughed. "Coca-cola?" he asked.

Though we were supposed to attend the formal *latihan* only twice a week, Icksan demonstrated to many people how to exercise inwardly and how to remain close to their exercise. Sometimes he would sit on a sofa in the hall when the dinner gong had sounded and the hall was crowded with people and he would say to his neighbour, "Now exercise, but don't let anyone see." On many occasions, he gathered a number of us just to sit together for some twenty minutes before going into *latihan*. We would exercise inwardly, so that later our *latihan* went deeper. This was beneficial. But simply to sit and daydream is, in my opinion, worse than useless.

The return to Manchester at once brought an interesting new development. A number of men and women had been opened, about a dozen in all, who wished to continue with the *latihan*. Up to that time all the exercises had been held in London at which the Indonesians had always been present, or "helpers," who had been designated by Bapak. A few people had been authorized to exercise on their own. We now quickly made our own arrangements, for the women to exercise at the Tyrer's house and for the men to exercise in my flat. We had only to say "Begin," and to put ourselves in a state of surrender, and at once our exercises started by themselves, each one according to his individual receiving. We were soon to see that there was no diminution in the power; on the contrary, the exercises began to change and develop by themselves. This at once got rid of the misconception that the exercise would not work with-

My Stairway to Subud

out the presence of Pak Subuh himself, a misconception that was still current among many people at Coombe. I remember telling some of them that we were continuing to exercise on our own in Manchester, to be asked, "Who takes the exercise? Who starts it?" Before long other groups began to exercise on their own in Bournemouth, Bristol, Liverpool, Kensington and also in Holland.

It is impossible to talk about the developments that took place in September, October and November of 1957, except in a general way. There continued to be a great influx of people who wished to be opened. At first these had been mostly students of Gurdjieff's ideas, mostly those studying with Mr. Bennett. As I have mentioned before, there were a number of independent Gurdjieff groups. Some of these groups came en masse. But the main bodies, which were under the direction of Madame de Salzmann in Paris and London, did not. Later I heard that they were specifically forbidden to have anything to do with Subud if they wished to continue with group work. It was during these months that more and more people appeared who had no former connection with Coombe Springs. Many of these were relatives of those who had been opened. Very often they had had no former interest in things of the spirit, but having been impressed by the changes they had seen and sensed, they simply wished that they might have this something too. A great number came who were students of Theosophy, Rudolf Steiner's Anthroposophy, followers of Krishnamurti, students of Yoga, Spiritualists, to be followed later by Quakers, Catholics and indeed Christians of all denominations. [This included later, Catholic monks of the monastery of St. Wandrille in Northern France, where part of this book was written. They were Benedictines, following *la régle de St. Benoit.*]

This put a great burden on the organisation at Coombe Springs. Thousands of letters began to arrive that had to be answered. There were requests for accommodation and meals and interviews. Luckily the former groups had a strong financial structure. Pak Subuh was against any sort of tithing or per capita levy and insisted that all donations should be voluntary.

In the ensuing changeover, some people took everything for granted and others had to bear a considerable financial burden. It would be wrong to pretend that over the following months this did not cause some bad blood. Some people sacrificed a great deal in time and money to serve Subud at this time and simply because they were ready and available, responsibilities fell upon them. Later, their power and responsibility came to be resented. I think that many people may now be ashamed for their behaviour at this time. Still, I don't see how this could have been avoided. In the midst of the general elation, it was sobering to be shown so clearly how much we were in the preliminary stages of purification.

At the beginning of November 1957, I had occasion to discuss the situation of the Manchester Group with Mr. Bennett. The greater part of them were still meeting together, but had not been opened. Mr. Bennett agreed to speak to Pak Subuh for me. A few minutes later I was summoned to Pak Subuh's sitting room. I had never been there formerly, though Icksan had invited me once. I had refused to go, since I did not have a question! At once, when I came into Pak Subuh's presence, I smelt that wonderful sweet odour that I had smelt at my opening and I could literally feel the vibrations in the room, which seemed to flow against me like waves. To my surprise, Pak Subuh agreed to come to Manchester in five days time, together with Ibu his wife, his daughter Rahayu, Icksan and Ismana Ahmed, Mrs. Sheila Ross, Mrs. Elizabeth Howard and Mr. Bennett.

[I experienced this phenomenon of smell a number of times. On one occasion, the aroma from Mr. Bennett was so strong that I thought to myself that the Indonesians must have given him some exotic eastern after-shave. Later I was to smell this fragrance many times from Bapak and Sjafruddin particularly, and on rare occasions from other English members of the group. I realised then that it was connected to purification, and it used to produce in me an ecstatic quickening of the emotions.]

My request had met with such a swift response that I at once telephoned Manchester, so that the news would be passed around. I received a call from the Tyrers, offering to accommodate Bapak's immediate party. (Bapak is the more informal way that Subud members refer to Pak Subuh.) On Monday morning, I managed to book two different halls to cover the period from the Friday till the following Tuesday. In the evening I spoke to the group, appealed to them for funds, and asked them to permit me to make arrangements and dispose of the funds arbitrarily, since there was so little time. They all rose to the occasion. One man, Bob Paskin, took me aside and pressed fifty pound notes into my hand, and within a couple of days I had well over one hundred pounds. There were perhaps three or four people, who had money to spare. For the rest, I knew that even ten shillings was a sacrifice, so I was highly gratified at this response.

My Stairway to Subud

On the morning of Pak Subuh's arrival, there was such a severe frost and such a dense fog that I got lost in Victoria Park, where I lived. Luckily, the fog dispersed and gave way to bright sunshine just before the party arrived. A number of the group met them at the station and drove them to their respective quarters. We soon found that our nice neat plans had to be rearranged. We had quite reckoned without Ibu, who insisted that Sheila Ross should stay with her. So the Tyrers had rather more than they had bargained for. The Ahmeds stayed with the McLeods, and Mr. Bennett and Elizabeth with the Paskins.

That evening, most of the remaining members of the Manchester Group were opened, together with others who had come from Liverpool, Garstang, Sheffield and Hull. The *latihan* was characterised by a great feeling of rejoicing. By this time, many of those who had already been opened at Coombe, had begun to make noises and sing as well as move about. Even Mr. Bennett himself was rather concerned with the noise and it is true that we were just over a bus stop.

After the *latihan*, many of us returned to the Tyrer's house and crowded into the small sitting room. We were all a bit awkward, not knowing whether to depart or linger, and Mr. Bennett himself soon left, which was a sort of big hint to the rest of us that we should do likewise. However, Icksan soon put us at our ease, and Pak Subuh began to speak informally and to answer our questions. That evening brought about a complete change of atmosphere. At Coombe Springs we had only seen Pak Subuh at formal talks or briefly, when we entered the hall for the *latihan*. Very few people had personal contact with him or the other Indonesians, having a natural desire to respect their privacy. Then there was the language barrier. But at Coombe, there was more than just that. There was a tradition that one must not take up the time of spiritual leaders unless one had a serious question or problem.

In Manchester, all these feelings were at once dispelled. Within a few minutes, people were sitting on the floor, passing around drinks, laughing and smoking. Pak Subuh explained about the animal forces and he was not just amusing—his illustrations were killingly funny. At once, we all felt a new kind of relaxation. Many of us had been inclined to be intense. Pak Subuh said in English, "No more seriosity!" and behold, it was not.

The next few days were filled with many incidents, which produced a feeling of being in a supremely happy family. Pak Subuh and his family came out with us for drives or went shopping. In the evening there were formal *latihans,* after which Bapak gave talks. I can't remember the matter of them now, except for one thing. He said that we were not even like children in a classroom yet, but rather like children peering through the panes of glass at other pupils in the classroom. But if I cannot remember the matter, I can remember the atmosphere. Everything was very light and entertaining.

After these talks, many returned to the Tyrer's house. One evening, Mr. Bennett introduced two doctors to Bapak. Bapak explained to them that the practice of the *latihan* did very often relieve people of their illnesses, but this was not the aim of Subud but was purely incidental to the purifying process. Pak Subuh also said that as the doctors progressed, they might find in themselves capable of sympathetic diagnosis—of sensing in their own bodies, the ailments of their patients.

The truth of what Bapak said came to be demonstrated in due course. I know a number of people who have been cured of asthma. In the Manchester group, there was one woman who had suffered from pernicious anemia for ten years and consequently had to take injections every few weeks. After a few months of *latihan,* she felt she could carry on longer without injections, and later, on Bapak's advice, she dropped them altogether. Twelve months later, she had a check-up and her blood count was found to be normal. As to sympathetic diagnosis, I have myself had a number of striking experiences, which I shall recount later.

In the evening, Pak Subuh and Ibu often watched television. (The word Ibu means mother, just as Bapak means Father. Ibu was the very embodiment of motherliness.) I was surprised at the interest all the Indonesians shared in television, since at that time, I regarded it as an abomination. [These were the days of black and white—colour had not then arrived.] I can only say there was an unfeigned simplicity in their enjoyment of it.

One morning, I was smoking with Bapak and Icksan came into the Tyrer's lounge. I tried to explain through Icksan the sort of work we had been engaged in prior to the coming of Subud. I asked whether there was anything we could do in our ordinary lives to help the progress of the *latihan*. When Bapak understood my question, he made one emphatic gesture and said, "Tidak!" (nothing!). Many times after this, when I met Icksan he would smile, imitate Bapak's gesture and say *"Tidak!"* with great emphasis.

This was something that was not easy to accept. Earlier, I had heard someone ask Rofé what was the best preparation for the *latihan*. He replied that the *latihan* was the preparation. Icksan also used to insist that surrender was everything. Many people could not accept this either. This is hardly surprising. How many people had been able to accept the idea that "Man cannot do?"

Some people held strongly that they must make efforts and that they were personally responsible for a large area of their manifestations, while others declared that a compromise was impossible; that submission to a Higher Will could not be bettered by one's own ideas on the subject. Neither opinion seemed to matter greatly. They were after all only views; that is merely thoughts. The *latihan* acted upon people irrespective of their opinions and indeed made mock of them. How many of those who cried "submission" were remarkable for their efforts? How many of those who argued for efforts were remarkable for not doing anything at all? In spite of all shades of opinion, the *latihan,* willy-nilly brought about changes.

Or so it seemed to me. But then the subject of change is itself a difficult one. There are still many who declare that nothing has happened, that neither they nor anyone else has changed. There are others who make extravagant claims about the changes that have taken place in them, and at the same time exhibit only too clearly the weaknesses that remain. Perhaps this is because some of us have looked for change, where no change can really be expected, and have been disappointed, while others have mistaken a temporary amelioration of their state for a fundamental change in their character.

However that may be, I am personally convinced that a great many changes have in fact taken place and in a great many people. They are not always obvious. For example, a certain man confided in me, greatly to my surprise, that he had been an active homosexual. He told me in some detail about his affairs, how he recognised other homosexuals and how the urges came upon him. He went on to say that shortly after being opened, all these former urges dropped away from him to his great relief. Had I not been told this, I doubt whether I would have observed any change in him, since to all outward appearance to a casual observer, he remained a pleasant, humorous and conscientious type.

In Manchester, as in London, the form of the *latihan* affronted some of the group, who left immediately. Mostly people experienced strongly in those few days, but there were others who felt nothing at first, but who persisted in their attendance. How well I could appreciate their feelings!

One young fellow, a schoolmaster, attended the *latihan* for some months, all the while growing more and more bitter. His charming wife had experienced from the beginning, and he began to feel separated from her. Suddenly, he declared vehemently to the helpers that Subud was breaking up his marriage. It was not long after he gave vent to these pent-up feelings that he began to move strongly, indeed with a tigerishness that I believe surprised himself.

The experience of one of my closest friends was even more miserable. He was a tall American (Dan Cahill, later to found the Dharma Book Company and to be the publisher of this book) with shrewd intellect and the driest sense of humour. He was opened in May 1957 and attended *latihan* after *latihan*, experiencing nothing. His dry humour turned to solemnity; he became more and more solitary and morose. He kept putting off his departure for the States, and attended extra exercises. Finally he left, disappointed with Subud, and cynical at the hurly-burly of self-will being displayed by people supposedly in the process of purification.

Shortly after he returned to the States, Pak Subuh paid his first visit to California. Dan wrote to me to say that he was no longer interested in the *latihan*, and that he had got back his old job as a ship's officer in the merchant navy. Since the ship was delayed a couple of weeks, he took the opportunity to fly out to California, meaning to consult Bapak about his career. (By the way, he attended a *latihan* and suddenly and dramatically he began to experience. So strongly in fact, that he wrote to me to say that doing the *latihan* was the most enjoyable thing in his life.) His ship took him to Australia, conveniently arriving in time for Pak Subuh's first visit to that continent, where he played an active part. He later became one of the pillars of the New York group. He is remarkable for being a severe opponent of loose thinking, strongly refuting what he believes to be imaginary changes. Yet, I would dare say that he has changed greatly, as witness the pile of letters that I have kept.

This aspect of Subud—the anguish that can be caused by the lack of evidence of one's own experience—concerned me greatly in those days. I often wanted to ask Bapak why he never specifically helped those people who did not experience. It was cold comfort to be told, "—some corks were fitted tighter in their bottles and would take longer to shift."

I never did come to ask this question, because by the time that Bapak visited Manchester, I had already realised the answer. No such "help" could possibly be given. Indeed, if "help" could be given to people in this manner, then I, for one, would no longer be in Subud. For Subud would then be nothing but a form of hypnotism, just as I had feared in the beginning. In reality, nothing could be done, because nothing was being done anyway. Everyone was receiving. It is true that the helpers provided a medium, a conduit, through which people could receive initially, but what or whether they received was not in the helper's power. Pak Subuh did say that everyone did receive, some more subtly than others, and that not everything could be perceived consciously.

People could be opened at different levels, he said also, and that it was possible that a helper might open someone with a soul on a much higher level than his own, in which case, he would feel an intense state of happiness.

The term "helper" is a curious one, since it is evident that God alone can help, and Pak Subuh has been most explicit to the helpers themselves that any desire to help on their part is an obstacle. In practice, however, it is clear that some people are more easily able to let go their thoughts and therefore to submit, and it can then be seen why it is beneficial for people to exercise together. Those who let go their thoughts can do so more easily in a sympathetic atmosphere of submission. This is why it is initially difficult for a person to exercise on their own. Most people tend to intensify their mental processes, when they are solitary.

Before he left Manchester, Pak Subuh appointed a number of men and women as "helpers." namely the McLeods, the Tyrers, the Fletchers and myself, who were also given permission to open others. By this time, a number of men and women, including Mr. Bennett, had been made helpers in London. In spite of Pak Subuh's injunction to the contrary, many people looked upon this as a promotion. [When Bapak later went to America, just everyone wanted to be a helper, whereas in Indonesia, after say fifteen years in Subud, no one wanted to be one!] In every country, there were people who were upset if they were not made helpers, and only in the course of time has the helper's job come to be regarded as a duty.

We naturally wanted to know what was entailed in being a helper.

My Stairway to Subud

What were our duties? For at that time it had appeared to us that helpers were special people with supersensible powers. However, the advice given was more mundane; we were to keep the time, watch that people did not bump into one another, take care of those who got upset, and answer the questions of probationers. As to the *latihan* itself we were told, "Simply do your own exercise."

Simply. That was it. So utterly simple. Many of us imagined that the helpers did something, that their singing or chanting was like a mantra, that it was intoned to produce the state of the exercise. Now, at last, I understood my own baffling opening. The helpers who had sung were, purely and simply, doing their own exercise. The man who had cried, *"Akbar-Allah! Akbar-Allah!"* did so because that was how he was moved. The helpers did nothing; they simply received like everyone else.

The realisation that this was the fact of the matter removed my last doubts about Subud. Nevertheless, many could not accept this fact, nodding sagely in their conviction of some deeper mystery. In the course of time, many of the doubters were themselves made helpers, and only when they had experienced "opening" others were they convinced that there were no secret goings-on.

Pak Subuh also formed a committee in Manchester, just as he had done in London. I think that many of us did not attach much importance to these committees in those early days. I was made secretary, and one of the older men became Elder. It seemed that my position in relation was changed only in name. The helpers were supposed to look after the spiritual matters, while the committee's function was to arrange such things as the booking of halls, the purchase of carpets, the disposal of subscriptions and all such worldly matters.

It was not until Pak Subuh came to England two years later for the Subud Congress of 1959, that many of us understood the significance of these arrangements. Frankly, these committees seemed to be unwieldy apparatuses for making simple decisions and I was inclined to manipulate the Manchester committee as best as I could. I was not the only one to make this mistake and the committee soon manifested a marked independence and an unwillingness to be used as a rubber stamp. I believe now that something very fundamental to Subud was concerned with this structure, but at that time, it was difficult to conceive any other relationship than leaders and lead, to which our education and environment has conditioned us.

My Stairway to Subud

First Subud Congress, Coombe Springs, 1959

Within a few days of Pak Subuh's leaving Manchester, the national press was full of headlines concerning the well-known Hungarian actress, Eva Bartok. She had given birth to a baby girl and would not reveal the name of the father. This was sensational enough, but it also turned out that Eva had such grave internal complications that both her life and that of the baby had been in danger. She appealed to Mr. Bennett, under whom she had studied for some time, and he told her about Pak Subuh. The facts of this can be read in Eva's own book, *Worth Living For*. The result was that Eva was "opened," her health took a dramatic turn for the better, and she successfully gave birth to a baby girl.

That the birth was successful, Eva attributed directly to the miraculous action of the *latihan*. So, not only she, but Subud also, received a considerable amount of publicity, in England, the Continent, the States and Australia. Articles appeared in French, German, Swiss and Spanish magazines, with photographs of Eva, Pak Subuh, Ibu, Mr. Bennett and the nine-sided hall at Coombe Springs.

Eva had formerly studied Gurdjieff's ideas for some years and had frequently visited Coombe in the intervals of her film work. I still remember her first appearance, when she was put to work weeding with a gang of women in the kitchen garden. She took part in the Work, the Movements and the general studies with everyone else, even spending hours one day cutting up raw liver in the kitchen, a job I understand she did not relish. Many of the young men used to tease and joke with her, and I think she enjoyed being in a place where she was simply a sister in the Work.

This unsought publicity connected with Eva Bartok has a definite place in the historical development of Subud, in that many people on the continent of Europe were enabled to hear for the first time of the existence of Subud and of its aims, however garbled and inaccurate the newspaper articles might have been. The address of Coombe Springs was published and a flood of enquiries began to pour in. This soon led to the formation of new groups on the continent.

Mr. Bennett already had a remarkable series of contacts throughout the world, but apart from England, I think that only in Holland were there groups studying directly under him. I may be wrong in this. There were certain visitors from Scandinavia (Lilli Hellestinius) and Germany, who were frequent visitors at Coombe.

During the next few months, we were all to witness a remarkable proliferation of groups. In the latter part of 1957 Bapak and Ibu visited Holland and opened people already established in a Gurdjieff study group. This was followed by a visit to Germany, largely organised by Ruth Gruson. There the impact of the Eva Bartok publicity was felt in full force and some three hundred people were opened in a short time. For the first time in Europe, the majority of the people did not belong to any Gurdjieff group, and many came whose primary concern was one of health. Without any existing framework, the difficulties of organisation were terrific, and as may be expected, there was a large fall-out, though a very sturdy group evolved in due course.

When Pak Subuh returned from the Continent, he visited a number of towns in the provinces. Amongst them was Bristol, where my company had their works. Naturally, I found it necessary to consult my sales manager when Pak Subuh was in Bristol. Things worked out well for me. I had many meals with the Indonesians and took Bapak for some drives. I noticed that Bapak did not seem to be much interested in the gracious old Cotswold houses or the architectural glories of Bath, but he was extremely interested in the suspension bridge over the Avon, and the prospect of ships and railway cuttings. I tackled him with this, and he replied with a

My Stairway to Subud

chuckle that Bapak was interested in the future and not in the past. He had little tendency to hark back to things of the past in anything, unlike so many esoteric schools that are apt to compare the wisdom of the past very favourably with that of the present—they also look to the Orient rather than the Occident, a view that I had shared. For example, I had long considered Tibet to be one of the most spiritually advanced places in the world, a view shared by many students of the occult. Pak Subuh, however, did not share this opinion. The fact that Tibetan lamas could withstand extremes of heat and cold, he did not consider a great accomplishment, but rather a psychic ability to assume the property of stone.

In Bristol, I was instrumental in arranging a number of interviews, something I did before and later many times. These arranged interviews nearly always turned out badly. The conversation would be stilted, and questions would be asked such as, "I suppose movements have some meaning?" I would feel ill at ease for being the sponsor. Some people just naturally gravitated towards the Indonesians, and the Indonesians themselves always seemed more at ease with such persons. When there were fair numbers present, the conversation always seemed general, and the atmosphere heavy. It often seemed to me that the atmosphere got progressively lighter as more and more people dispersed. I know that I often felt my own state as too heavy and full of thoughts and I would hasten to vacate myself. Pak Subuh himself was always cheerful and patient, however many people there were, though his helpers often used to look distinctly ill.

On a number of occasions I was present for testing. Some of these tests were extraordinary, and I cannot pretend to understand them. "How big is the whole world for someone who has a soul on the vegetable level?" I felt nothing, but Mrs. Sheila Ross said it was like a pinprick on the end of the tongue. I complained to Bapak that I never got anything from the tests, and he got me to stand in front of him. I did make some gestures, but the responses did not satisfy me.

Reverting at this point to my own experience in the *latihan*, once I had begun to experience, I found no difficulty in entering into the state of the exercise. It is impossible to describe how this is done. I could say, "I make an inner movement of consent," or "I let go," but this conveys nothing to someone who has not already experienced the action. Most often my exercise would start with very deep breathing that was sucked in between my teeth and then my movements would begin.

After a month or two, my movements became very violent. I had had trouble with my shoulders and it seemed the exercise wanted to loosen them up. I was bent forward and then, in the movement of straightening up one arm was flung over my head to hit me with a painful thwack on the back of the thigh. So violent did this become that I used to stagger about and then fling myself over backwards. I picked myself up only to repeat the performance. Then suddenly one day I felt as if I was on a moving turntable. I began to spin rapidly on the spot, while my arms rose to shoulder level with the momentum. At the same time, from the base of my lungs, emerged a truly horrifying howl of such volume and duration as seemed impossible for human lungs. After spinning for a while, I crashed to the ground. The force of the exercise was very strong in me, and when the *latihan* came to a stop with the command "Finish," my exercise continue to pulsate through me and I confess that at times, I was frightened. It seemed as if my personality might dissolve away all at once. My feelings were so open that the slightest things made me want to weep or laugh with delight.

I have now experienced such a state many times, and this has impressed upon me not merely the necessity of spiritual training, but the almighty wisdom of the gradualness of the training itself. People often imagine that they would like to be spiritually advanced, that they would like to achieve the state of purity of the Prophets; but I wonder how many of us could bear to be in the requisite state of openness and sensitivity, and for how long. Even with the little that I have experienced, the sensation of being alive was almost too much. In such states, I have been convinced that God truly does send indications to man if he is open to receive them. Further, such indications can move man with much greater speed and subtlety than is possible to think. But it is clear that in my present condition, I could hardly bear to live at such a pitch for long.

I continued to whirl like a howling dervish for months. I often used to feel sick after spinning at great speed for half an hour, particularly if I held back at all. But a little later, I felt tremendously alive, as if a whole lot of dirt had been cleansed from my system. Many times, I felt as if my head was completely clear and devoid of any thoughts, while every form of sense perception was immeasurably heightened. Frequently then, I had the curious sense of feeling people's motives. Lying became impossible or, worse still, I could feel myself lying and I knew that others detected it. Not that I was telling untruths, in the course of expressing an opinion—and I was always wont to express my opinions strongly—I would feel a certain unease and embarrassment. Later, I came to recognise this feeling. It always came when my opinions were fabricated, when they did not correspond to my own inner condition. It is in this sense, that I was lying.

Suddenly my whirling period ceased, and I began to leap into the air with great cries of joy. This quickly changed to Indian dancing, complete with finger postures and intricate foot rhythms, and leaps in the air with my feet tucked underneath me. At this time, I also did the Yoga *asanas*. I had often tried them before (with my friend Arend Vos before even going to Coombe Springs) and could struggle into the lotus posture and remain in it only with acute discomfort. But now, laughing aloud, I would kneel on the floor with my knees apart, and my body would slide backwards to lie on the ground. I repeated this many times, with the greatest of ease and comfort, though it is one of the more difficult postures.

My cries had meanwhile become more articulate, till these gave way to speech one day. I believe that this was mostly in Hebrew or Arabic. A Jewish member came to me after an exercise and told me that I had been reciting the principal parts of a Hebrew verb. Another time, I spoke in Indian dialects. My friend Ganesh of my early Manchester days, who was a Tamil, had joined the RAF and been posted to Kuala Lumpur, Malaya. While there, he had flown to Singapore to be opened by Bapak himself. Now back in Manchester, apparently in the exercise, I rebuked him roundly in his own Tamil language!! I often used to think that I must have been saying mighty important or holy things, particularly as I often said "*Jiwa Allah.*" I knew that *jiwa* meant soul and Allah is the name of God. Much later, however, Pak Subuh's son Haryono came to Manchester and joined in the *latihan*. I gathered afterwards that I afforded him considerable amusement, as I said some shocking things in Javanese! Such as, "Scratch my armpit" and worse. Sometimes, I have suddenly realised that I was speaking French. Although, I can speak French badly, in the *latihan*, my accent was so much better as to be unrecognisable to me. On rare occasions, I have also spoken English. The whole experience is very strange. Words simply pour out, sometimes with a limpid clarity, sometimes with an awesome ferocity.

[There was another occasion when in the course of my exercise I yelled out in Arabic several times "It is absolutely forbidden by God. It is absolutely forbidden by God." Asikin rushed over to me after this exercise and said "Tony, what have you been doing? What have you been doing? And Bapak was there and Bapak could hear you." You may imagine how I felt.]

Just why I should speak in so many languages, I simply don't know. Perhaps, as Bapak has said, in due course we shall come to understand.

After a while I could not tell what to expect. Sometimes I was quiet; sometimes I would spend the whole evening in ritual prostrations. Often when I thought that nothing much had happened, I would experience the most extreme happiness for hours afterwards.

The manifestations in the *latihan* are peculiar to each individual. However, it is generally true to say that younger people move about more freely and vigorously than the older ones, and that the tendency is to get quieter, or at least more harmonious. However, there are some who have remained pretty vocal for a five-year period. Many people see visions during their exercises, and I have had some remarkable ones described to me, but personally I have never seen anything.

All these manifestations must seem odd or even mad to anyone outside Subud, to be entertained only by strange or mad people. Yet when I consider the Manchester group alone, they were a remarkably down to earth lot. For example, one of the young women (Gwen Tyrer) was a qualified nurse with a sharp tongue and nerves of steel, who often got round her friends to give blood to blood banks. Yet this same nurse woke up her husband one night because she saw an angel in the room! There were amongst us a number of teachers, two doctors, labourers, company directors, engineers, housewives, personnel managers, salesmen, hairdressers—in a word, ordinary people from every walk for life, with genuine Lancashire accents. And all these ordinary people had their own private and individual experiences of the phenomena of the purification process.

Familiarity with these phenomena led to their being put in their proper place. At first, it was all very exciting. After a while, people ceased to talk about their exercises, not only because Bapak advised it, but also because the manifestations and phenomena were not important. All this was purification, analogous to the casting out of devils. Without doubt many of the movements were therapeutic in character—they relieved muscle tensions and so relieved people of their complexes. But there was more than therapy. It was the source and origin of the action that was important.

I am not denying that the phenomena of the moment and the noises had not disturbed many people, as it had concerned me at first and will undoubtedly upset some people in the future. I am only recording that for those who continued, even more for those who were deep in their exercise, the movements of the others, the noises, the singing, ceased to disturb at all. The source was the important thing. Yet few of us could categorically assert what the source was. It was much more that we knew what the source was not. We knew clearly that the movements, the speaking in tongues, the singing of anthems, the dances of various types, were not of our willing, not of our construction.

The aim of Subud became clearer, more of a reality—submission. There were no longer arguments as to whether it was submission to God's Will—such a question was abstract. But there was an evolving sense of the meaning of submission, which entered more and more into the practical aspects of our lives.

Early in 1958 Pak Subuh left England for California, before which, within the space of a few months, hundreds of people had been opened in England and on the Continent. Many centres had been set up in the major cities. The proliferation of groups continued apace during 1958 in Great Britain, so that there were few people outside the range of one group or another.

This initial rapid expansion of Subud did make many of us feel that a miracle was a happening, that the whole world would be changed and that millions of people would be opened. I think that many of us had the sense of some impending big event, and this was in part fostered by the mysterious prophetic hints that Mr. Bennett was wont to give. However, if we were excited and full of enthusiasm, Pak Subuh and the Indonesians were quite unexcited and unmoved by the progress of Subud. Not that Pak Subuh was not interested, but he seemed to have what is sometimes called holy indifference. If progress were made, it was the Will of God.

In more personal terms, many people also felt that they had hit the jackpot. Subud would provide not only salvation, but would help them to a better career, solve their material problems, and relieve them of their angst. Such an attitude soon proved to be as naive as it sounds. I have no doubt that the Lord did provide, but we did not expect to be provided also with tests, like the trials of Job!

To be specific, there were many people whose health improved and some who experienced dramatic cures. A lady in South Africa was cured of an issue of blood that had plagued her for years, within a few weeks of being opened. Many people were relieved of rheumatism, asthmatic conditions, and insomniacs slept.

Furthermore, many people found that their marital relations improved, and that their sex relations in particular altered in character. Many people became noticeably happier, freer and more confident. And many others changed their jobs and had unusual success in business.

If many people enjoyed unusual good health and good luck, there were others who suffered misfortunes. One of my friends, Ron Brandreth, died from cancer only six months after getting married. During this period, his wife nursed him day and night, fully confident right to the end, that because both of them were in Subud, he would recover. In the event he died, whereupon his wife gave practical demonstration of submission. She was in fact so radiant and full of faith that I fancy it was hard for people outside of Subud to understand. The thing she found hardest to tolerate was the excessive condolences of friends.

Again, while many people became calmer and more relaxed, there were others who became noticeably assertive and critical. I well remember that after two years in Subud, my own sales manager, W.G. Wade, who was also a member from the beginning, said that as far as he was concerned my character had not improved! I must admit that at this time I was particularly irritable with him and inclined to sudden eruptions of wrath.

I think that all that can be understood fairly easily. As Icksan often said, "It will out." In the normal course of life, we are all trained and educated to behave in a certain manner and to keep our inner feelings hidden. The Subud training did not teach behaviour, but it did touch on the essence of man, and that essence was all too often in a savage, primeval state. So many people began to behave in a way that was more truly themselves, that was undoubtedly more sincere, but which could also be uncouth and childish. In many ways the changes were quite amusing; the easily swayed became obdurate, the meek became bellicose and vocal, and the retiring demanded attention—for a while at least. Many things had to come out in the process of purification, and many things did.

This catharsis had a great effect upon Subud affairs. For one thing, no one could bear authority any more, at least authority in spiritual matters. Those who had assumed the leadership of groups found that their leadership was questioned, and helpers often found their advice unheeded.

Mr. Bennett himself was in an invidious position. He had commanded our respect and admiration for sitting with his pupils at Bapak's feet. From being our teacher, he had become all within the space of a few months, our brother in Subud. However, he evidently found it difficult to give up the role of teacher and indeed there were many who still looked to him and leant upon him for advice. He continued to give lectures and talks in an unending stream, often explaining Bapak's explanations. It was this last that alienated him from many of his oldest pupils, particularly the groups of young men who had been proud to be called Bennett men. It also caused widespread argument. Many people became furious if they heard Mr. Bennett criticized, pointing out how much many of us owed to him.

It was not so much a matter of whether his doctrine or explanations were right or wrong, as that many people felt the need to be free of all explanations, so that they could await with patience the unfolding of the significance of their own experience, as Pak Subuh had said would happen. Many people even questioned in public on why he continued to speak, to lecture and to answer questions.

Mr. Bennett did not appear to accept the unequivocal attitude of the Indonesians over submission, which he always tempered with his own belief in Efforts. It may seem extraordinary, in view of the preceding chapters, that I was personally less and less able to accept his views and found myself quite unable to listen to his talks. I know many others in the same position as myself, who have retained their respect and good will for Mr. Bennett personally, yet are no longer able to follow him.

Many times on my visits to London, the Bennetts entertained me to dinner in the Lodge. (Incidentally, after the death of Mrs. "Polly" Bennett, Mr. Bennett had married again to the Mrs. Elizabeth Howard, mentioned at the beginning of this chapter.) I might say that I had openly disagreed with Mr B. on a number of occasions, and crossed swords at Council meetings—which prior to Subud, would have been unheard of—but I was always able to count on his good-will, and have often received practical assistance, such as references and letters of introduction.

When I spoke with him in his study, Mr. Bennett was far from disturbed at the rebellion. On the contrary, he recognised that people were growing up and of necessity growing independent. He even went further and said, "You know, all his life Mr Gurdjieff wanted to have around him people who were not sheep, but they always were. Now Subud has come and after three months, no one is a sheep."

There can be no question that after a short time, a great many people had become more self-reliant. I am reminded in this connection of two incidents with Pak Subuh. Someone said that they felt the exercise went better when certain helpers were near them. Pak Subuh replied in the negative, saying that if people depend on helpers, they would merely act as a weight on them and he made a characteristic gesture to this effect.

On another occasion I was with Pak Subuh, Mr. Bennett and a certain German. This German had been much attached to the well-known Indian sage, Krishnamurti. Bapak tested how this German had formerly regarded this sage and made gestures to indicate the feelings of reverence he had held towards him. Then he tested, "What is God's Will that your attitude should be?" He made two inward circling gestures with his hands and ended with the two forefingers pressed together and said in English the one: "Equal!" I could not help but feel that this demonstration, at least in part, had been for the benefit of Mr. Bennett and myself.

Early in 1958, shortly before Bapak left for California, some fifteen members of the Manchester Group went to Coombe for the weekend and I requested Bapak to see them all together. At 11 o'clock that Saturday morning, we all crowded into his sitting room. After a couple of questions, Bapak began spontaneously talking to us all. Typically, he spoke one moment with great gravity, and the next he had us in fits of laughter. I remember his making the Sign of the Cross and saying that this signified the conjunction of the male and female natures. He said further that Jesus Christ was the only man, who had ever had complete within him, both male and female natures, and therefore, had no need to marry. Then pointing suddenly to me, he said, "But as for Tony here, he must get married! Ha! Ha!" Everyone laughed.

After his talk, someone asked Bapak what we should do when someone came along to our group wishing to talk to us about Subud. The reason for this question was that a certain someone from Yorkshire paid us periodic visits. He considered himself a sort of superior helper and an authority on Subud. Bapak replied that we should sit quietly and listen, but meanwhile, let the *latihan* work quietly

My Stairway to Subud

within us. Then, he demonstrated, we might be moved to our feet, gesturing wildly, crying "No! No! No!" He was highly amusing and we all laughed. Much later, I was to see this in practice, with a friend of mine who was not in the Manchester Group, and with an embarrassing spontaneity.

In March 1958, Pak Subuh and his party left for California where they had been invited—Bapak only went anywhere in response to an invitation. Mr. Bennett accompanied him. Bob Prestie, who had spent some years at Coombe, also went ahead to prepare the way. Mr. Bennett had learned Indonesian in about six weeks (he was already a fair linguist, speaking Turkish, Russian, Italian and French), and had astonished us all one day when he sat down beside Pak Subuh to do the translation.

It will be remembered that Husein Rofé had done the translations initially, but he went abroad some weeks after Pak Subuh's arrival in England. It was Rofé, who had opened Bennett, and a number of other Ouspenskeyites (Aubrey Wolton, Reginald Hoare, Von Bissing) prior to the arrival of Pak Subuh. I believe that these original members had mixed feelings about Bennett. [In fact, it was only much later that I understood that the Ouspensky crowd regarded Bennett as a "loose cannon," a maverick; his principal crime being that he gave public lectures. They were not at all too happy that Pak Subuh moved to Coombe Springs, fearing Bennett's undue influence. Poor Husein Rofé was caught between the two parties. In the meanwhile, we at Coombe Springs, who were Bennett men, had no knowledge of this, being under the impression that it was Bennett, who had issued the original invitation to Pak Subuh, which was not the case.] Rofé had apparently laid great emphasis on the miraculous and curative side of Subud, and aspect that did not greatly appeal to those who were Gurdjieff students. Certainly Bennett and Rofé were markedly different in temperament.

I had only one occasion to speak with Rofé. I found him one day in the music room, playing the piano. He sensed that I wanted to talk to him and after a few short minutes stopped playing. Our conversation was short, but it did give me one overwhelming impression, and that was of frankness and clarity, of being straight from the shoulder. The books he later published, *The Path of Subud* and *Reflections on Subud* confirmed my first impressions. He did not gloss over anything. He criticized the adulatory attitude that some people had towards Pak Subuh, and he was not afraid to point out that Pak Subuh had been mistaken in some of his forecasts. His patent honesty gave an impression of strength, and the fact that he could criticise, rather than detracting from, only served to emphasize his underlying faith and respect for Subud.

Not all the Indonesians went back to Indonesia with Pak Subuh. Sjafruddin and Asikin remained in England, while Icksan Ahmed and Rahmad went to Ceylon, where once again there was the hard core of a Gurdjieff group. Within a short time, some hundreds of people were opened there and exercised happily together. Since Ismana Ahmed had remained with Pak Subuh, Mrs. Bulbul Arnold opened the women. This is a fact of some significance, since Bulbul herself had only been opened some months previously. The Ceylon group was perhaps the most mixed group of all, being composed of English, Singhalese, Tamils, Indians, Pakistanis—Jews, Christians, Muslims, Buddhists and Hindus. Perhaps only the Cyprus group could rival them, for during the height of the EOKA insurrection, Turks, Greeks, English and Americans; Muslim and Greek Orthodox joined together in the Subud *latihan*.

In California, a number of groups were quickly formed, the largest in Los Angeles and San Francisco. Here, the groups were formed from students of many different systems and churches, with hardly any Gurdjieff students, I believe. From California, Bapak was invited to Australia.

[As elsewhere, John and Elizabeth Bennett preceded Bapak to pave the way both with lectures and openings. The Eva Bartok story had broken at this time and the Australian press were doing their best to get into the *latihan* to take pictures! After an initial furore, it all died down. Dan Cahill also helped, his ship having arrived at Sidney fortuitously.]

Groups were started in many of the major cities, after which Pak Subuh returned to Indonesia. Icksan and Rahmad returned by way of Singapore, where yet another group was started.

By far, the greater numbers of those who came to Subud were those whom I shall call "Seekers after a Way," in contradistinction to members of a Church. By this, I mean that those whom the Church attracts are usually interested primarily in a code of behaviour. Whereas "Seekers after a Way," or "Seekers of the Truth," are not so much concerned with right behaviour as with becoming, with change, with inner development.

So then the greater part of those who came to Subud were already students of such things as Yoga, Vedanta, Sufism, Mysticism, Theosophy, Anthroposophy, Rosicruciansism, and the Gurdjieff methods. Perhaps this is hardly surprising, since such students had already a number of things in common, namely an acknowledgment of the fundamental unity of religions and the concept of inner development. This is not to say that Subud did not also attract members from the Churches. In fact, a number of priests and monks also have joined in different countries. In Manchester, there was a remarkably strong contingent of Roman Catholics, as well as Baptists, Plymouth Brethren and members of the Church of England. It was extremely interesting to see how these members of bodies that are usually inimical to one another came together, unified in their common experience of the *latihan*. Initially there was considerable difficulty for many of them in squaring their beliefs with the broad basis of the *latihan*. But this difficulty was only in the realm of ideas. The contact, the action of the Subud *latihan*, worked equally and indiscriminately no matter what the initial beliefs and convictions. In the course of time, the Subud *latihan* often revealed a deeper significance in beliefs already held; but it must also be said in fairness that it also brought a modified understanding of certain dogmas.

Ninteen-fifty-eight (1958) was a very exciting time for many of us. The impact and the experiences of the *latihan* were still fresh. We were witnessing a rapid expansion of Subud all over the world, and many were experiencing the first fruits of the *latihan* as Bapak had forecast.

Pak Subuh had said that some people might become capable of sympathetic diagnosis. My first experience of this came shortly after Bapak's first visit to Manchester. Mr. Bennett had told me that he had suffered on account of the vibrations in the house where he was staying. Since I had often been to this house and knew the people rather well, I was inclined to be skeptical. However, a few weeks later, I happened to call round unheralded. I was, at once, taken into the living room where the son of the house, a spastic boy of fifteen, was sitting on the sofa. Immediately on entering the room, it seemed as if a peculiar fluid or substance ran up and enveloped my legs. My chest felt constricted and small pellets seemed to be bombarding my head. I felt most uncomfortable, while the boy seemed happy enough and well disposed towards me. When I returned to my flat, I exercised for some minutes to clear myself.

I later told Pak Subuh of this experience and he tested and said that the inner condition of the boy was good, and that the affliction was all exterior. I understood that the boy could well have been helped by the exercise. At the same time, in the South of England, a spastic boy regularly did the *latihan*, accompanied by his father and helpers, and appeared to have made great progress.

Much later, I had another striking experience of sympathetic diagnosis. I was in Manchester, suffering a rather violent fit of depression, wondering to myself whether we were not in fact deceiving ourselves about Subud. I bumped into an acquaintance that was not in Subud, but was well known for his knowledge of esoteric ideas and who led a small group. We went into a café and began to discuss ideas. I asked him his views on the existence of the soul and the question of free will that had for so long absorbed me. Following his general answers, I asked him directly whether in his opinion his own will was free, and whether he had his own "I." Just in the instant that he declared to me that he did indeed have his own "I," the base of my lungs seemed to fill with about half an inch of water. I almost laughed aloud, because while he went on with his explanations about man's ability to choose, I knew that he had water in his lungs. My depression and doubts vanished suddenly. One curious factor in this incident is that the man had a bad leg, but I felt nothing in my legs. Later, I spoke about this to the Tyrers, who had formerly studied with this man. At once they said, "But you knew that he had something wrong with his lungs?" But, indeed, I did not know this beforehand.

On another occasion, I stopped at a hotel in the Midlands for lunch and went to the bar for a drink. As I was talking to the barmaid, I felt suddenly as if there was a long needle in my heart. I asked her if she had anything wrong with her heart? She was visibly astonished at my question. It transpired that she had been ill for a long time, but doctor after doctor had been unable to diagnose her complaint. Only a week before, at long last, a doctor had diagnosed that she had a lesion in her heart.

Latterly, this sort of thing has happened fairly often and I take little notice of it. Sometimes, I am unable to tell whether I am myself, ill or have picked up someone else's complaint. For example, when I was recently in California, I sometimes got acute sinusitis. Only later, did I find that my wife had been having a recurrence of her childhood sinus trouble, which disappeared just about the time that mine started. (Readers will observe here that I took Bapak's advice and got married in April 1962.)

My father, who was opened in South Africa, to whom I wrote of these experiences, often asked what was the use of them, since they could be both painful and inconvenient. I believe that the person who is sick is helped, if only by a temporary transference of suffering. There may be more than that, but I don't know. I do know that this has always occurred spontaneously, without any volition on my part. This sort of experience has also served to deepen my suspicion of spiritual healers and those who are obsessed with the idea of helping the sick with their spiritual powers. Not that I don't believe that there are some people who have genuine powers. But I am more and more convinced that those who help the sick must share their burdens and their sickness, even if temporarily. I think that anyone who has real experience of this cannot possibly want to help, though they may simply be called upon to do so. This may sound un-Christian, but I am inclined at the time of writing to avoid the sick if possible, and the negative and depressed as well.

This type of sympathetic awareness was not confined to the body alone. Many people reported experiencing feelings and thoughts for which they could account in no ordinary way. I remember that when Bapak first left England, I was so happy at the time that his departure made no difference. In fact, every time I thought of Bapak, I was overcome with the impulse to laugh with happiness. Shortly after his departure, I was with one of the young Indonesians (Asikin) who had remained in England and an acute feeling of sadness stole over me. This was so in contrast to my own general state at the time that I was sure I was feeling his state. Of course, one has to be careful not to attribute all one's states to other people. But in my experience, there is always a particular taste to a borrowed state, and a feeling of unaccustomedness and incomprehensibility.

One curious phenomenon must be mentioned in this regard, which was observed by a number of people. There was at Coombe Springs, a man (Sidney Jenkins) who indulged freely in criticism of Subud, Pak Subuh, Mr Bennett, the organization and everything. Above all, he denied that he, or anyone else, was changed by the exercise. He was so patently negative that I expected to feel uncomfortable in his presence, but on the contrary, I felt as if I was hearing a great joke and felt light and happy. It seemed to me that his inner state was much better than he would have us believe, and that his criticism was a mechanical habit and entirely lacking in venom. A friend of mine experienced the same sort of thing with Rofé— Rofé criticized, but nothing seemed to come away with his criticism.

Even stranger, was the sensing of a person's condition once removed, so to speak. I was once being consulted about the problems of a third party whom I had never met. Abruptly my state changed, and I interrupted my friend and began to describe the situation of this third person, to which he replied with some astonishment, "Exactly! Exactly!"

On another occasion, I was speaking to Gwen Tyrer about a man who lived in another city. Something seem to be niggling her, while I was speaking, and suddenly she interrupted and said, "He is a bit queer, isn't he?" I felt very angry, because this man had many admirable qualities. But she was dead right.

Sometimes, I experienced feelings that seemed quite unaccountable at the time. For example, I often used to eat in the Seven Circles Café, one of the first Subud enterprises, above which we had our *latihan* halls, which was run by members of the Manchester Group. There was a certain waiter there, who used to produce in me quite uncalled-for feelings of anger. Whenever he approached the table where my friends and I were sitting, I found myself quite unable to speak. These feeling were so marked that I could not understand what possessed me to be so obviously rude and churlish to this man. Only later did it transpire that a great deal of money was regularly missing from the till, and cartons of cigarettes kept disappearing. It was later proved conclusively that this waiter was the thief.

Some of these examples illustrate what I might call the awakening of Conscience, though of a conscience quite different from the normal conception of it. Normally, one has a sort of preconceived idea of the duties demanded by conscience. But this Conscience was demonstrably quicker than one's thoughts, and was often contrary to one's own sense of "ought." When I ought to have spoken, my tongue swelled in my mouth and I was compelled to be silent; when I ought to have been friendly, I found myself moved to wrath; when I ought to have wanted to help, I found myself indifferent. In fact, it seems to me that the sense of "ought" is purely a product of thinking.

As I have already mentioned, Mr. Bennett and a few others in London were given permission to open people within a few weeks of Pak Subuh's arrival. Before Pak Subuh left for California early in 1958, many of the provincial groups had their appointed helpers. It was not long before these new helpers had to deal with enquiries about Subud, look after the probationers, and after a three-month probationary period, to open them.

My Stairway to Subud

In spite of Pak Subuh's warnings, it was difficult for most helpers not to feel a certain rank, however, much they protested to the contrary. I say this in no derogatory sense. No matter how honestly and intelligently a man may declare that he is nothing, it is still well-nigh impossible for him not to feel that he is something, particularly if he is given a position, be it only that of a servant. Nevertheless, however, impure the feelings of my fellow helpers and myself, I doubt whether anyone felt pride when they came to open others.

Mr. Bennett had written about openings in his book *Concerning Subud,* stressing that the helpers do nothing and are there simply as witnesses. That is an objective way of speaking of the openings. Subjectively, I shall never forget my own feelings at the first openings that were performed by the helper's group in Manchester. Never was it more borne in on me that I could do nothing, let alone that I should do anything. Like many others, I felt concern only that I could not surrender enough, that I was too conscious of the occasion, and that my thoughts would not stop. It is just because of the utter impossibility of the opening that it is most miraculous. Never is it shown more clearly that "I can't surrender," but that "God's mercy yields me." And never is it more clear to the helpers that they do nothing, except to follow their own receiving, their own *latihan.*

With all our youth, our pride, our inexperience, it was really extraordinary to be present at these openings. I think it really surprised us all to see how strongly people were often moved in their very first exercise. The absurd thing was that those who were opened frequently used to thank those who opened them profusely, while the helpers themselves denied all knowledge and credit.

Some people opened very easily and made many movements at their openings. Usually this would produce in them very deep emotions of joy and gratitude. In such cases, the helpers also would feel light and happy.

By the summer of 1958, many helpers in England already had considerable experience in opening others. This lead to a remarkable development. Up to this time all groups had been initiated by Pak Subuh, or by such an experienced man as Husein Rofé. But Pak Subuh was back in Indonesia and Coombe Springs was receiving enquiries from all over the world, but principally Europe. The result was that helpers from England, with but one year's experience of Subud, were called upon to start groups in other countries. The very fact that this was possible is, in my opinion, one of the more extraordinary aspects of Subud. Without claiming proper chronology, the Elliots and Olga de Nottbeck went to Paris where John Bennett joined them and gave a lecture in French. The Whiffens went to Norway, Pierre Elliot to the South of France; Bruin Brown went to New York, where later Bennett lectured to some 600 people. And I, and later the Fletchers from Manchester with me, went to Madrid. Mr. Bennett was not idle, having accompanied or gone ahead of Pak Subuh on many of his journeys to Holland and Germany, to California and Australia. And this was only the beginning of the pattern. Soon the European helpers began in turn to initiate new groups, and the American helpers instituted a vast network of groups all over the States. Later, other groups were started in South Africa and New Zealand by people, who themselves had only a few months experience of the *latihan*.

My first visit to Spain occurred fortuitously. When planning my summer vacation to stay on a yacht in the South of France, one of the secretaries at Coombe Springs (Patrick Wilson) mentioned that there were three enquiries from Madrid and suggested that I go there. I flew first to the South of France, where I stayed on a yacht belonging to the American family of Charles Parsons. They had a house in St. Paul de Vence and Robin Mitchell and I exercised there with them. I think that the Parsons were a trifle alarmed as both Robin and I had vigorous and noisy *latihans!* After a week in France, I flew on to Madrid. The reception I was met with was truly astonishing. I was met at the airport by three young men and at once, offered accommodation in the apartment of a Madame Milly Pinna, a French lady and a milliner, in the centre of Madrid, Conde de Aranda 22.

One of these young men, Eugenio Pastor Freixa, had a great number of contacts, many of whom were already students of esoteric ideas. Luckily he spoke English, for at that time, I knew no Spanish, except a few phrases that I had hastily learned from a Daily Express course, on the old-fashioned 78-rpm discs. He organised meetings and within two days I had spoken with over thirty people. Apart from these meetings, I was again and again introduced to people in cafés, who at once evinced an interest in Subud. [It must be remembered that in 1958, Franco was still alive and meetings were quite dangerous. Also the meetings in cafés took place mostly around 10 o'clock at night. Spanish people then still took a siesta in the afternoon, but stayed up very late in the evenings.]

Frequently I was asked such questions as, "What is the difference between the practice of Yoga and Subud?" I gave explanations as best as I could, and found that in spite of the language difficulty, the Spaniards were quick to appreciate distinctions, and many times requested there and then to be opened. This was in marked contrast to the hesitant and cautious approach of most English people.

So keen were these people to be opened that I was in a bit of a quandary. I telephoned to Coombe Springs in order to speak with Sjafruddin, to ask for his advice on what I should do. Sjafruddin said simply, "You open them, Tony." I therefore opened eight men, all together at one time in the apartment where I was staying. Not one of them had any connection with the Gurdjieff work, or with Coombe Springs. With only two of them, could I speak English. Five out of the eight reacted very strongly to the *latihan*. One of them had a remarkable vision at his opening, and he was surprised when I told him that I had never had a vision.

Four months later I returned to Madrid with Lionel and Herina Fletcher. We passed through Paris, where we met up briefly with Bennett and Pierre Elliot in the process of forming the Paris Group, and then took the train to Bordeaux in the company of a French

Spanish group in Madrid

lady who had been to Mr Bennett's lecture. She kindly put us all up for the night, before we caught the train, crowded with Spaniards returning to Spain for Christmas, to the frontier and then on to Madrid, arriving at about six o'clock in the morning. This time, a group of sixty people met us at the station, all of whom were opened in the next twelve days. Herina Fletcher opened over thirty ladies by herself.

The Spanish people I found to be spontaneous, frank, generous, and proud. I felt more at home among them than among my own people. They even called me gitano (gypsy) like the Spanish dancers. I loved their tremendous voluble enthusiasm, and spent one of my happiest Christmases among them. And how the Madrileños see the New Year in!

I heard late from my friends the Whiffens (Robert and Constance) that they felt towards the Norwegians much as we felt towards the Spaniards—more at home with the Norwegians than among their own people. Perhaps this was *à cause de* Subud. Who knows?

I have referred to the proliferation of centres in England and their emancipation from Coombe Springs. I want to make clear that this was a gradual process. Some of the larger groups like Manchester and Bournemouth quickly became autonomous. That is they had their own Committee and their own Helper's Group, and felt entirely capable of running their own affairs. Formerly, when studying the Gurdjieff methods, the provincial groups' activities were entirely directed by Mr. Bennett.

During 1958 and 1959 there were a great many meetings of the various groups at Coombe Springs, at which there were discussions of financial and various practical problems.

It was at these meetings that one could most clearly see the growth of the new spirit. The representatives certainly expressed the growing feeling of independence in the provinces. There were some quarrels and acrimony over administration, and "organization" became a bogey word. But while there were difficulties and recriminations, the most important thing was that the formerly timid now boldly stated their views, the pliable stood firm, and the forceful retreated and gave way.

Bapak left behind him in 1958, two young Indonesians, Sjafruddin and Asikin; the first being in his early thirties and the latter in his early twenties. To many people, they were a great help as they were living examples of what could be hoped for from Subud. Their unfailing politeness, courtly manners, innate dignity, together with their scrupulous cleanliness and neatness of dress made a great impression.

My Stairway to Subud

I became friends with both of them and with a small group used to visit them in their rooms frequently. Initially, when Bapak left, they travelled to a number of the provincial groups to assist with the openings and give general advice and help. They both came north at frequent intervals and often stayed at Garstang, in the large country house belonging to Eric and Maria Bradford.

In many ways, they were curious guests. They were so unassertive and yet so compelling. I never heard Sjafruddin or Asikin gossip about anybody. If we began to discuss critically the actions of a fellow member, Sjaf, as we called him, was sure to be silent. It was a silence that caused many of us shame.

Though they were full of fun, and Sjaf was certainly fond of teasing Asikin, I never heard either of them talk lightly of the exercise or conjecture about it or wiseacre. Their simplicity was remarkable, as was their sensitivity. They seemed to suffer physically from uncharitableness. On one occasion, when I was in Bapak's company visiting a group, a rather pompous man enquired, "Has Bapak given permission for you to be here?" I was irritated by this remark, but poor Asikin told me later that he felt as if he had been kicked in the stomach.

Sjaf seemed to live by his "indications," which made him perplexingly unpredictable. Sometimes, he would be invited to a group and suddenly he would begin to talk and give general advice. Then he would go to another, who would be waiting for his counsels, and he would say nothing. Once an older man had encouraged him with some jocular words, like, "Don't be shy, young man," —Sjaf smiled as he related this to me—he had been quite unable to speak. It just happened that way.

People looked upon him as Bapak's representative in England and many went to him for advice about important questions. Those with a real need always got to see him. But for those with imaginary worries, it was more difficult. Sjaf told me once that some people were so confused that they really did not have a question, and they merely left Sjaf with a headache.

He seemed to like best to have a group of young people around him in his room, who were serious about Subud but did not talk seriously about it. He would play his guitar and sing, there would be a lot of leg pulling and laughter and a light atmosphere. Frequently, quite late at night, Sjaf would say, "Shall we exercise?" and we would go off and *latihan*.

Once, after I had been exercising for a couple of years, having just driven down from Manchester, Sjaf asked whether I would like to exercise. I was very tired, in a dry period, and felt reluctant. Nevertheless, I agreed, and we went to Mrs. Bennett's old bedroom, now completely cleared of furniture, to exercise. My exercise became very deep and I felt that overwhelming feeling of joy and gratitude that so many have felt as a result of the *latihan*. Afterwards, as we sat silently on the floor, Sjaf said, "Now you exercise when your exercise calls you to exercise. That is not so at the beginning. Then you must do as the Helpers say and exercise twice a week for half an hour. But now you respond, you exercise when your 'inner' calls you."

When Sjaf made such statements there would be no further talk. Abruptly, he would change from serious matters and go and make tea.

The extraordinary accomplishment of this young man was that all respected him and he offended no one. He was way above warring factions, who heeded him equally. He was impartial and absolutely indifferent to what others thought of him.

Many people tended to think of him as an oracle, but he discouraged this more and more. For example, my friend Peter Kermode was a sculptor, well known in the London groups. Like so many artists he was hopelessly impecunious—now in, now out, of work, sometimes working at picture frames, sometimes tending petrol pumps. One day, being at his wit's end, he decided to go to the Scilly Isles to pick flowers. However, before setting off, he tried to find some other helpers to "test" the correctness of his decision. One helper disagreed with testing on principle, while others were unavailable. So he phoned Robert Whiffen, who said simply that he had a guest to dinner. So Peter set of on his motorbike and decided to stay the night with his mother in a Sussex village. In the morning, on an impulse, he returned to Coombe Springs and went to find Sjaf, who greeted him with, "Did you find a Helper, Peter? I was the guest at the Whiffens!"

Peter sat down to explain his situation. He was jobless, he had no money, and he did not know what to do with his life, he did not know which way to turn. Sjaf replied, "You ask me, but I have the same problem too—I don't know."

"Well then, Sjaf," Peter said desperately, "what on earth shall we do?"

After a minute of silence, Sjaf said, "Let's go to the cinema, Peter!"

In 1959, Pak Subuh undertook a series of journeys that took him round the world. He visited Hong Kong and Japan, Ceylon and Malaya, Australia and New Zealand. Then he came to America, travelling extensively in both the Southern and Northern continents, starting groups, mainly in the principal cities. The list of places he visited is formidable, from Lima to Buenos Aires, from Los Angeles to New York.

Finally in midsummer, Pak Subuh came to England for the long heralded Subud

Congress. The programme that had been drawn up was so ambitious in scope that it was a natural target for Subud wags. Everything was to be discussed, Subud and Religion, Subud and Education, Subud and the State—in fact Subud in relation to the whole field of human endeavour.

In Manchester, we held weekly discussions so that the elected delegates would be acquainted with the views of the group. These discussions brought into the open the many ideas that had been brewing in secret. One thing that interested everybody was the form of the organization of the group. We had heard recently that Bapak wished that the helpers should not have anything to do with the organization, which was to be left to the committee. At that time, I was a helper and also had been secretary of the group for two years. I was opposed to the separation of helpers and committee on the grounds that most of the active and capable organizers had already been made helpers. It seemed to me then, that many groups depended on a handful of active people.

When Pak Subuh finally arrived at Coombe Springs there were some hundreds gathered to meet him from all parts of the world. There were delegates from England, France, Holland, Norway, Germany, the United States, Brazil, Peru, Cyprus, Ceylon, South Africa, New Zealand and so on.

The Congress lasted for some three weeks. In the morning meetings, the delegates discussed the subject for the day and the chairman made a list of questions. These were read aloud to Pak Subuh at the plenary sessions, when he gave his guidance upon them.

It would take too long to give the substance of the replies—in any case it is unnecessary, since a full report of the Congress has been published. I wish only to give some general impressions.

After two years, it may be imagined that there were many questions to be cleared up. Can children be opened? Why must men and women exercise separately? Why does the wife have to ask the husband's permission to be opened, and not *vice versa?* How can parents help a child with a higher soul? What is the right role for helpers? What are the duties of the committee? Should Subud people be vegetarians? How should a Subud teacher behave? Should a dying man be opened without his consent?

Many of these questions were loaded. Pak Subuh's answers can only be called inspired. If there were a hundred traps, he was sublimely unaware of them and never fell into them. His answers always went straight to the principle and were so worded as to cause no offense.

His advice had a great unifying effect and there was a wonderful sense of brotherhood amongst delegates of different nationalities and different religions. This Congress had a direct effect on the organization of the groups. Pak Subuh himself had in the first place appointed the Secretaries and Elders of the original committees. Now he advised that a new Committee should be appointed each year, a measure to which I had personally been opposed. However, the wisdom of this soon became clear.

It is a curious fact that many of the founders of groups, the most active people, had become unpopular. This phenomenon occurred in London, Birmingham, Manchester, Bournemouth, Paris and Los Angeles, to name just a few places. Subud is by nature essentially democratic, and the groups were inclined to resent any form of "dictatorship," however mild or well intentioned. The result was that many leaders retired, and the organization passed on to others.

I discussed this with Tarzie (later Varindra) Vittachi, of Ceylon. He also had shared my feelings, but as soon as the new committees got going, it was evident that they could handle the business quite as efficiently as their predecessors. In the event, many of the very active originators of the groups retired into the background; and this gave others the chance to come forward. The net result was the prevention of an abuse of power.

There were so many delegates—over three hundred—at the Congress that it was impossible for Pak Subuh to give private interviews as formerly. I was very fortunate therefore in helping to organize his visits to the northern cities. Since there were far fewer people the atmosphere was altogether more informal. Pak Subuh was driven north in a motorcade, and stayed for some days at Garstang, visiting Manchester, Liverpool and Sheffield.

One question that has baffled many people is how far to be active in Subud. Pak Subuh certainly discouraged publicity, but he gave his blessing to some authors to write books. He discouraged proselytising, yet seemed pleased when a large number of people wished to be opened—and it must be admitted that this was often the result of the activity of someone passing the word around in a circle of friends. Certainly, Bapak was very pleased with the fact that Manchester had so organised their affairs that they had their own rooms for *latihan* and offices, and that they had provided themselves adequately with carpets and radiators.

On this visit, Pak Subuh did everything to encourage co-operation between members in everything regarding material affairs. Indeed a number of enterprises were started immediately followings his visit. One of the most notable was the formation of a Community at Whatcombe House in Dorset, especially for children, who were unable to adapt themselves to the social order. Patrick Harding founded this community and staffed it with Subud members.

To return to Bapak's visit to the north, the most memorable thing for me was his talk one Sunday at Garstang. There, Bapak complained of the triviality of questions so often put to him. Someone experienced "Ouch" and then came to Bapak for an explanation of this Ouch. Others wanted to know whether such and such a woman would make an ideal partner for them. Pak Subuh said that some people expected him to be some sort of fortune-teller, whereas in reality they should become self-reliant and patient and receive their own indications. Pak Subuh also said that when he had undergone his own purification he had had to face many tests. He emphasized that love towards God should come before our own interests, and he said that he had been prepared to sacrifice his inner state, even his own soul, in order to come to the true worship of God.

On this trip, we all made a new friend in the person of Dr. Anwar Zakir—I should also say of his wife, Ratna, but I saw very little of the ladies—including Rochanawati, Bapak's daughter, or Rahayu, as on the previous visit. Of the ladies, I only got to know Ibu and Ismana. Anwar was a plump jovial fellow, from whom we learned many interesting things. He was not nearly as contained as Sjafruddin, whom he considered to be on a higher level than himself. Here are some of the things he said.

"I once asked Bapak, 'How old is my soul?' to which Bapak replied, 'Two years.' Some years later I asked Bapak again and Bapak said 'Two and a half years.' After that, I never asked Bapak again."

Anwar declared that he had only got a soul on the material level. "In South America," he said, "one woman reached the human level after one exercise. My wife also, she is on the human level—I can't understand this—she seems more attached to material things than ever before!"

One of us asked him, "If you are on the material level, what then is below the material level?" "Oh yes," replied Anwar, "There are seven levels below the material level."

Asked whether he had any doubts about Subud, he replied with great emphasis, "Of course, I have doubts!!"

He reminded us much of Icksan, who had been of such great help to us, and who had founded the groups in Ceylon and Singapore. Icksan had died of a heart attack in Singapore in 1959. I once said that it was much easier to talk to Icksan than to Sjafruddin. Anwar replied, "That is because he (Sjafruddin) is higher. Icksan was not considered very highly in Indonesia before he left. But when he travelled with Bapak, he made tremendous spiritual progress. Afterward he died. I hope I don't have to die!" I wish I could convey his lugubrious expression, his emphatic voice and his rich humour.

I told Anwar that recently, far from being refreshed by the exercise, I came away often exhausted and feeling ill. "That is because you are helper," he replied.

If Anwar delighted us with his roguish buffoonery, he was also very percipient. At the Congress at Coombe Springs there had been present a teacher from New Zealand. Apart from his taciturnity, I had noticed nothing about him, though we stayed in the same hotel. Anwar had at once spotted that this man was in a state of crisis. For three days, this teacher was struck dumb! He moved about among the delegates quite normally—I wonder how many delegates knew that he was going through something. This same man had a remarkable cure as a result of the Subud exercise.

The days that Bapak spent at Garstang were certainly very happy days for us. When I search my memory for events I can remember nothing; there is simply a glow left behind of a festive occasion. Everything was more personal there, and Bapak was wont to join the small party in the house at the end of supper. Sitting at the head of the table, he would talk of quite mundane things, such as forming an architects' group, but at the end of the evening I would want to run and shout like a schoolboy. I felt so absurdly happy and full of love towards everybody there.

During this visit Sjafruddin did the translating. On one occasion in Manchester, Sjafruddin so excelled himself in the middle of a talk that Bapak turned to him and said, "That's very good, but I have not said that yet!"

Bapak did some testing with the helper's group. One woman asked if she could help her dead father. Bapak replied that we should all test this. The answer was, "No." Then Bapak said that her husband would be able to help through his exercise. We tested again, and received that man is like a vertical line, and woman a horizontal. Bapak said he did not know why it was like that; he just knew it was so. Some time earlier he had said to me, "As the soul of the son goes up, so does the soul of the father, even if he is dead." I understood that this could reach back seven generations. This seemed to me to be related to the idea of prayers for one's forefathers.

**Harjono, Anthony Bright-Paul seated beside Ismana.
extreme foreground, the McLeods**

After this visit, I saw Bapak once again in Edinburgh and later, at Newcastle. Ibu and Rochanawati were also there. Ibu derived great amusement from seeing me hang out clothes on a line in the garden. Indonesian men did no such thing!

Pak Subuh continued his journey across Europe, visiting Germany, France, Austria, Greece, then on to India, Malaya and home. It was truly a fabulous journey.

In 1960, Harjono, Bapak's son, an engineer, married Icksan's widow, Ismana. They visited England on their honeymoon. I was fortunate in making Harjono's acquaintance very early, and quickly achieved a delightful relationship with him. I was quite fond of teasing people and Harjono said that he also teased others in Indonesia. I know that I was at once able to laugh and joke with him. Sjaf said that Harjono reflected the condition of the person he was with.

Pak Subuh had advised the various helpers' groups that they should practice testing. Following his departure this advice has been followed, but in a somewhat literal fashion. Simple questions were put to the test, many of which required only simple common sense. So whenever any question arose, Harjono would say to me, in mock seriousness, "Shall we test that, Tony?"

Ismana, who was famed for her receptivity, told me that once she had exercised with the ladies at Coombe, after which they sat on the floor and a heavy, heavy silence descended. Then someone posed a question and she realised that they were testing. Eventually one of the women said, "I don't feel it is right to test that question." Ismana found herself agreeing, "Yes, yes, that's right."

The question of testing is still somewhat of an issue. Ismana told me, "Some people can receive tests easily, but that is not necessarily a sign of advancement. Some people's inner is so strong that it refuses of itself to give answers."

There can be no question but that testing fell into disrepute with some of the helpers, who felt a natural distaste for questions of mere curiosity. But if there were some things that were frivolous and relatively harmless, there were other questions that were serious indeed. For example, some members approached their helper's group with questions related to their careers, their choice of university, to the acquisition of property, or to change their life altogether and to go to another country. [It is interesting here to note that Pak Subuh told me directly, "*Pergi ke* California!" Now that could be translated as an imperative, "Go to California!" or simply "You will go to California in the fullness of time" or simply that "California is a good idea." It can be imagined that it put me in ferment. However, when I asked Bapak what I should do about this statement, *Pergi ke* California, he told me to do nothing. In the event in 1961, I flew to California on my own volition because I was in love with the girl who was to become my wife in 1962! And when later, I decided to return to England after some two years selling Real Estate in the San Fernando Valley, I wrote to Bapak telling him of my decision, and he wrote back with his approval. The fact is that I made the decisions in both cases, and I believe that that is what Bapak wanted of us—to stand on our own two feet—whether one made the right decision, or no.]

It is small wonder that many helpers refused to test such questions, doubting their own powers to receive answers to such weighty questions.

In any case what is testing? It would be very rash if I pretended to know the answer to that. But I have had some experience, albeit very small, so I will venture something on it.

First of all, testing, as I understand it, is "receiving;" testing is not thinking or opining. When Pak Subuh first tested with us, I could not understand what we were supposed to do, or what we could possibly receive. We had simply to put ourselves in the state of the *latihan*. It was evident that when Bapak was there, some people did receive, and moreover all were in accord on what they received, while others had no experience at all.

From what Pak Subuh said, it appears that there is a special sense in which our bodies can be brought alive. For example, I remember Icksan testing with me, saying that my ears were becoming alive, but my eyes were not purified yet. I heard Pak Subuh say of one of the better known women helpers, after about three years in the *latihan*, that the trunk of her body was alive, but she had no legs or arms as yet. The degree of aliveness, the state of purification, affects one's ability to receive and therefore to test.

I complained to Pak Subuh once or twice that I received nothing in the tests, and I guessed that I could not have made much spiritual progress. Once or twice he got me to test, standing in front of him, but nothing conclusive resulted as far as I was concerned.

After about two years, I mentioned this subject to Sjafruddin one weekend when I was at Coombe, and he invited me up to Bapak's sitting room in the West wing. Asikin was also there. I had an appalling cold, and as Sjaf and Asikin sat there swaying slightly, I felt most uncomfortable. Two or three times, I tried to put aside my thoughts and just when I had given up, my exercise began to flow. Though I was sitting in an armchair, I began to be brought forward and have my head thrown between my knees, while great shouts were sucked out of me to shatter the stillness of the night. After a long time Sjaf told me to calm myself, though I was then scarce able. The truth is that I was so open in my feelings that everything in me seemed to be rejoicing, and I was near to tears with gladness. Then Sjaf did some tests asking aloud the questions. This did produce in me strong reactions and for the first time I began to see what testing could be like. But if I experienced strongly, I still could not understand its meaning. Curiously the questions themselves are quite wiped from my memory.

In 1959, when Pak Subuh was still in England, I was present on several occasions when there were tests, but again experienced nothing conclusive. In November 1960 however, there was a reunion of the Northern Groups at the beautiful stately home of the Widdringtons in Northumberland. John and Elizabeth Bennett came up for the day. Special interviews were arranged, Mr Bennett gave a talk, and some fifty enjoyed a superb buffet lunch, and late in the afternoon we did a *latihan*. A new man was being opened, so the man had an unusually long time to prepare, and the subsequent exercise was very free. Afterwards Mr. Bennett saw the men and women helpers—I think there were eight of us in all.

One of the women put forward some problems and Mr. Bennett suggested that we test. I remember very well my mood of that day. I had enjoyed the reunion very much, but by then I was very tired and frankly was wishing that Mr. Bennett would make an end. I was far from being interested in the testing. In the event I received quite suddenly, and with indisputable clarity, the answer to the question posed.

Mr. Bennett, who had earlier given a talk concerned with the question of "receiving," suggested that we each test for ourselves the question, "What is my chief obstacle in receiving?" Once again I was hoisted out of my chair and received a convincing and shattering response. In all there were some five tests, the answers to which I received in rather a dramatic fashion.

For some time after this, I was in a somewhat emotional and sensitive state, and there were many things that I understood at that time, of which I have now only a vague recollection. Subsequently, I don't think that I have experienced anything like in so convincing a manner. I think there are a number of reasons for this. First of all, it appears to me that formal testing requires a relatively deep state of the exercise. If there are a number of helpers present, they all need to be in such a state, otherwise response is affected by too much "thought." One characteristic of true testing seems that it always produces unanimity.

Secondly, I have noticed again and again that a certain type of apparently simple question, which often requires an answer merely of "yes" or "no," often elicits a mixed response, some feeling one way and some another, and testing then degenerates into voting. This frequently happens when there is some question as to whether a probationer should be opened.

On one occasion, when this question was posed, the helpers were divided. Then it was suggested that we test the condition of this probationer's head. This would appear to be something much more difficult, even arrogant to attempt. Nevertheless, the helpers were unanimous in feeling that the person in question was very confused, if not actually mental. It turned out that they were right. The helper, Dick Holland, who had proposed the man, had purposely not mentioned his condition, so as not to prejudice the case.

One thing that has increased of itself is what I shall call "spontaneous testing," as against formal testing. By this I mean that in the ordinary course of life, a person senses directly what to do, often in opposition to their reason. For example, a wife was nursing her sick husband and would set out to cook a certain meal. She would then find that she began to cook something else, or prepare it in quite a different way to the original intention. Whenever this happened, the husband would invariably declare that the meal was exactly what was wanted.

Or again, someone I visited without warning once told me, that they had cooked an extra portion of everything without quite knowing why. Later, when I was in the San Fernando Valley in California selling Real Estate, I once sold a house—or as the Americans say—a home—to a Subud member. He was in such an awful position that he had to have a house for himself, his wife and three children within one week! When I had shown him the only vacant houses that were available, I became somewhat impatient with him. However, quite by chance, we were put on to another house, with four bedrooms and a high existing loan. He was not a helper and did not know about testing. But, in my opinion, what he did was to test. In spite of his situation, he was perfectly calm. He seemed to sense the place, and then said simply that this was the house. I then picked up his wife in order to shown it to her. She also responded immediately. When I got back with her, her husband Roy was playing on his Hammond Organ. The only one who was really agitated was I—I had some three hundred dollars of commission at stake!

* * * * * * * * *

Now over five years have passed since Pak Subuh first came to England. There are groups established in Algeria, Argentina, Austria, Australia, Belgium, Brazil, British Honduras, Canada in five major cities, Germany in seven cities, Ceylon, Chile, Cyprus, Denmark, Ecuador, Finland, Formosa, France in eight cities, Germany in seven cities, Ghana, England with ten major centres and many sub-centres, Greece, Hong-Kong, India in three major cities, Indonesia in eight major cities, Iran, Iraq, Ireland, Italy, Japan, Kenya, Lebanon, Malaya, Malta, Mexico, Morocco, Holland in four major cities, New Guinea, New Zealand, Nigeria, Norway, Nyasaland, West Pakistan, Peru, Portugal, Rhodesia, Singapore, South Africa, Spain, Sweden, Switzerland in five cities, Thailand, Trinidad, Turkey, Uganda and the United States in about thirty major cities. This in itself is quite a formidable list.

But it still begs the question that is asked by almost every probationer: "What have you got out of it?" "Have you changed?" Is it really true, as Pak Subuh has said, that "a purification process has been set in motion and will proceed by itself?"

These questions are very difficult to answer, as Subud members tend to disagree among themselves. As I have said before, some people deny that they have changed. Others are unwilling to talk about effects, feeling that it is impossible to describe the significance of the *latihan*, or even saying that it is "purposeless activity."

Again, there are quite a number of people who experienced strongly at one time and have now apparently left and stopped exercising. There are some who would say that they have left Subud. That may or may not be so. I know that one of my personal friends ceased to attend *latihan* and returned to the family business—agricultural contractors—in Lincolnshire. I visited him from time to time. One day, when instructing a new hand on one of his mechanical excavators, the grab swung round and his foot was crushed. Apparently, he had fallen to the ground in great agony, only to find himself exercising and crying, "Allah! Allah! Allah!" no doubt to the astonishment of the locals.

When some time later someone remarked to me that this friend had left Subud, since he no longer exercised, I confess that I was pained. If there can be said to be an aim of Subud, it is surrender to God's Will. I think that we must be careful not to prejudge the form that this surrender might take.

Has success attended the steps of Subud members? There are hundreds of examples that would confirm this, just as there are hundreds that would appear to deny it. I think that there has come about a realisation that submission is unconditional. That is to say, that some may have to suffer all sorts of difficulties, and have done so with no diminution of their faith.

Without doubt there has been an overall change in the membership of Subud, in many ways more striking than the numerous personal changes.

This is evidenced by a number of small things. When Bapak first chose helpers, there was a certain amount of jealousy. Some people looked upon this as a promotion, and the helpers were not always remarkable for modesty. I know now that most helpers regard their office merely as a duty. Many of them deny that they are helpers at all, and laugh to scorn the suggestion. What I am trying to make clear is that this is not humility of the mind, but the humility of someone who has been spontaneously impressed with their own nothingness.

Another thing that has grown up is a non-suggestibility. There is just something in the *latihan* that makes people reject persuasion or pressure of any kind. Similarly, many Subud people are loath to use pressure on other people. That is to say some impulse arises to "let alone." For example, I have often seen Subud members smile and say nothing when perhaps someone is manifesting in a negative way. In this way the person has come to see his negativity for himself.

Pak Subuh was always very careful about people's feelings and never set out to shock. Before Subud, many people in the Gurdjieff work thought that they had the right to tell "the truth" in no uncertain way, wrongly in my opinion. I think that in Dianetics this is called invalidating. Within a short time, Subud people became exceptionally careful not to offend other people or offend their susceptibilities.

None of these things may seem remarkable to the casual reader. That is because it is so difficult to describe freedom except in negative terms. My own feeling is that the *latihan* has produced a succession of releases and that they are much freer. On the other hand, if one was to ask, "Are Subud people free from self-will?" I think that the answer to that is, "Steady on! Do you know what you are asking? That really is a very big question."

[Surely however the big difference is that Subud people are happy. They are happy and are enterprising; they are delighted to meet each other.Their friendship extends around the world. A Subud member can be sure of help from another, and friendships are forged with people one has never met. Contrast this with our society riddled with its drug culture, drowning in AIDS and in sexual scandals and depravity of every kind. The great majority of people are miserable, having no aim other than to enjoy themselves—life without purpose. Subud brings people to life, it brings everything to life, even one's nafsu, as Ibu Rahayu has made clear. So some people may have left the organization, but they are indelibly marked, they can never leave the Spiritual Brotherhood, as Bapak pointed out. And in fact, those that have supposedly left make a remarkable story in themselves. So often they have then devoted themselves to their Church, or become Buddhists or Sufis.]

There is a common realisation that there is a long, long way to go. And that God alone can guide our truly faltering feet.

Chapter 7

Who am I?

There are a number of questions that are frequently asked about the *latihan* by enquirers after Subud. They must be acknowledged as legitimate and the basis of genuine intellectual difficulty, though they are far from easy to answer.

The first question is the one that I myself posed to Pak Subuh: "What is the force to which one is opening oneself in the *latihan?* How can one be sure that one is opening oneself to higher and not to lower satanic powers?" The naturally corollary to this is: "How does this *latihan* differ from hypnosis, or auto-hypnosis? Are the trainees possessed by spirits or psychic forces?"

The second question concerns the manifestations: "Why do the trainees make movements and uncouth noises, and sing and speak in strange languages?"

Lastly, "If the power of God is everywhere, why do people have to be opened? Why does a helper have to be present?"

While these questions are no doubt valid and legitimate, they are virtually impossible to answer conclusively. Many people in Subud feel that it is useless to talk about the *latihan* at all without first experiencing its action; because the distinctive taste of the *latihan* will leave no doubt about its rightness and validity. With this view I am bound to agree. No amount of argument, no descriptions of changed lives or improved health can make avail without experience of the *latihan* itself.

But if it is not possible to make judgments about Subud without experience of the *latihan,* nevertheless going over general principles might dispel some difficulties

All through the life of man he is subject to the action of forces. He is subject to the force of gravity, to light and colour, to warmth and cold, to dryness and dampness. The food that he eats has a force that acts upon him. The dollar bill and the pound note have a force. The salesman and the politician wield influence. A car arouses desire, and jewellery positively seduces. The silken garment, the satin furnishing, the multicoloured carpet all have force. The newspaper creates interest. Even a mundane hamburger and French fries have a tremendous force.

My Stairway to Subud

It is clear then that man is subject to a multiplicity of forces. All the time these forces are producing in him actions, thoughts, feelings, and sensations. In the subjective consciousness of man, however, he is not aware of them as forces, but rather he is aware of the results of these forces in himself as his experience. I am cold. I would like a banana. I love red curtains. I dislike loud voices.

In fact the forces that man receives through his senses constantly arouse his desires, form his thoughts and opinions, and compel him to action, without any volition on his own part. We are back to the thesis of Gurdjieff; that man is a machine that reacts to his environment. Pak Subuh says that we are under the dominion of lower forces, our *nafsu,* which he divides into the material or satanic, the vegetable, the animal and the human. To quote his words:

"for man, from generation to generation, has been under the rule and influence of sub-human forces, so that his true inner essence, capable of awakening the human soul, has long been encrusted by his own thoughts and passions."

If it is true that man is a complicated apparatus through which forces flow, then one thing is clear: Man is already hypnotised. He is constantly under pressure of immensely strong hypnotic influences. He has no need to fear the surrender of his own will, since he is already happy to surrender his will to any number of influences, to such an extent that he even considers it to be normal. The freedom that man imagines he has is entirely spurious. His will is already surrendered and it must be so: that is to say his will must be surrendered either to the forces of the visible or of the invisible world; either to Mammon or to God.

Some readers may think that this is begging the question. They may object that the sense in which I am here using the word "hypnotised" is a philosophical sense, and not at all that of common usage. When they ask whether Subud is a form of hypnosis, they mean, "Is Pak Subuh a latter-day Svengali who has a lot of gullible cranks in thrall?" Many people have said to me, in effect, "those Easterners are terribly clever, and are quite capable of mass hypnosis."

In order to answer this, I have to return to my theme: Men are not free, they react to influences, they respond to forces. There is a sense in which everyone is in thrall. The whole question then is this: Are there different kinds of subjection? Are all influences of the same quality? Are there some forces that are higher and some that are lower? And are there some that are maleficent for man, and others that are beneficial?

There can be no doubt that influences can be of vastly different qualities. For example, the Prophet Moses was subject to the injunctions of the Lord Jehovah. The sort of compulsion under which he laboured was far removed from the compulsion of a drug addict. We can more or less grade influences in a purely subjective way according to the states that are produced in us, and from the manifestations that follow.

It should be clear that we never see forces—we can only observe the manifestations that are derived from them. We do not see electricity, but we can observe that a light bulb is switched on. We cannot see gravity, but we can observe, as Newton did, an apple fall to the ground. We don't see the force of the Sunday dinner, but we can clearly observe the fact that we salivate, that our mouths water.

So we do not think in terms of forces, which are foreign to our normal way of thinking, but we do think in terms of our subjective states. We do not say to ourselves that the "newspaper produces in me feelings of curiosity and makes me pick it up and read it." On the contrary, we think, "I am interested in the news." Because of this ingrained habit of ours, we make subjective judgments about the forces that act upon us in terms of our own states. If we hazard a judgment of others, we judge them in terms of their manifestations.

As an example, let us take the force of the hop plant. If I drink too much beer, I begin to feel sick and woolly headed. I therefore consider an excess of this influence to be bad. An observer would not experience my state, but he would see that my speech was slurred and my feet unsteady. From this he would come to the conclusion that I was drunk, or, as is so rightly said in common parlance, I was "under the influence of drink."

In fact, we all come to subjective conclusions about the forces that act on us. Those that produce in us anxiety, fear, hatred, greed, lasciviousness, dullness and boredom, we consider to be bad forces. If a gang of youths beat up a night watchman, we judge from this manifestation that they were under bad influences. On the other hand, the forces that produce in us compassion, forbearance, patience, calmness, courage, mercy and pity, we consider to be good or better forces.

Returning to the question of hypnosis as is commonly understood, what is it that everyone associates with hypnosis? Surely it is the surrender of initiative to the influence of another person, and above all suggestibility. It is difficult to see how such a thing could possibly be ascribed to the Subud *latihan*. In the first place, there are no suggestions made, and the manifestations of those in the *latihan* are entirely individual. In the second place, one has only to observe a number of members of the Subud brotherhood to see whether or not they are under the influence of another man. Not only are they remarkably free from adulation of any kind, but also a great many people now have not met either Pak Subuh himself or any of the Indonesians.

There are many who will not even read any of the Subud journals that are published. And furthermore, in every single group that I have been acquainted with, one has witnessed the eclipse of the former leaders, the extraordinary wane of their personal influence. In fact all the evidence points to Subud being a de-hypnotising force, the very opposite of hypnotic.

Then what is the force in the *latihan*? Pak Subuh himself dealt with this question in one of the talks that he gave in Australia. He posed the question: *"What is the origin of the force in the latihan?"* Laughing aloud, Pak Subuh answered himself, *"We don't know that!"*

This was for me very significant. For what we can know must belong to the lower worlds, and must be apprehended through the channels of the senses. Strictly speaking, a trainee is unable to assert that the *latihan* arises from God or the Devil. What he can assert is that the action is quite different, and uses a manifestly different channel, from those in which experience is normally produced. In other words that it is an action that is beyond his own thinking, desiring, passions and willing. If that is the case then it does not really matter what one calls this force, or where from it is derived, providing that it is empirically supra-sensible.

Why is it that people make movements and sometimes uncouth noises, and sometimes truly beautiful singing, and speak in strange languages? I simply don't know. One can surmise all sorts of thing about the origins of language, but I don't know. As for the movements, I have already said that the character of the *latihan* is partly therapeutic, and it is well known that the release of muscle tensions can also resolve complexes. In this regard one can refer to the experiences of the trainees. The *latihan* is supposed to be purifying. I believe that most Subud trainees do experience the exercise more and more as a purifying process, at the end of which they feel that they have cast something off and become clear.

I have spoken a great deal about "forces." Here I would remind the reader of something I quoted in Chapter 3: "For many there is a certain possibility of making a choice of influence." Gurdjieff enumerated a number of different influences and went on to say, *"All work on oneself consists in choosing the influence to which you wish to subject yourself and actually falling under this influence."* It is curious, but this could be a most accurate description of the Subud *latihan*.

In his book, *Susila Budhi Dharma,* Pak Subuh speaks a great deal about forces, enumerating and distinguishing between the material, the vegetable, the animal and the human forces. (In this regard Husein Rofé wrote within his book *Reflections on Subud,* commentaries on *Susila Budhi Dharma, The Way of Submission to the Will of God,* by Muhammad Subuh Sumohadiwidjojo. I can only recommend these to the reader.) While this is intensely interesting to read how the various forces affect us, for the purposes of this chapter, we are concerned only with the fact that the whole philosophical basis of Subud is the idea of forces.

The problem of personality is intimately connected to this same idea. The forces that act on me produce in me experience—and who am I, if not my experience? If that is so, then the quality of my life, the quality of my experience, depends on the force that is flowing through me. What is evident is that the body has no power of itself. And yet though this is evident it is rarely acknowledged. The illusion of power is the fundamental heresy of man, no matter to what religion or creed he belongs.

If the lower forces act on man and produce experience, this means in effect that the lower forces usurp the place of the Self. All religions assert that it is only by submission to the Divine Will that man can be liberated from the dominion of the lower forces, that only by the entry of Divine Life can man be rid of the burden of his sins. Thus it can be seen that what man should subjectively experience as "I" should be the force of the Divine Will, and that the realisation of the Self cannot be other than submission to God.

Finally, if the power of God is everywhere, why does one have to be opened? I know of quite a number of persons who, having heard

My Stairway to Subud

a recording of one of Mr. Bennett's explanatory talks, have declared that they have no need to be opened, because they are open already! Again I'm afraid I don't really know how to answer this question. Theoretically, I suppose that there is no need for a helper to assist at the opening, but in practice most people do not know how to let go of their thoughts and passions and open themselves to the vibrations of life force, except in the sympathetic presence of those who can let go and surrender to this same life force. *(Hidup jang besar.)* That this is so is confirmed by the fact that the first experience of the action of the *latihan* is for most people like a miracle, quite unlike anything that they have formerly experienced. (Pak Subuh has said, however, that the children of Subud couples do not need to be opened, since they are open already.)

The experience of the latihan is so unique that many people who have come to Subud, who have been interested in spiritual things throughout their lives and who have already tried different techniques and methods, have asked, "How is it that I have now been able to receive this? Why is it that Subud has appeared at this particular moment of history?"

It is interesting to note that the idea of channels is not foreign to Christianity. Indeed the confirmation service, the laying on of hands, is based on the idea that the Bishop is the channel for the Holy Ghost. This aspect of Christianity is little commented on these days, since the Churches seem almost wholly concerned with questions of ethics and morality. This is strange, since it is just this that is the distinguishing mark of Christianity.

For Jesus did not bring a new God-concept into the world; on the contrary, He acknowledged as God the same God of Abraham and Isaac. Nor did He bring a new ethic; Jesus himself declared that He came only to fulfill the law. So if God was the same God, and the Law was the same Law, wherein lies the uniqueness of Christianity? In fact, if the Jews already knew the rules of conduct and the God to worship, what more was needed?

The situation of the Jews at the time of Christ was very like our own today. We are all too apt to think of the days of the New Testament as olden times, when in reality, from the point of view of the history of the earth, they were very modern times. We are apt to think of the Jews as illiterate nomads, and picture the Romans as they appear in so many Cinemascope productions. In fact, the Jews were already a very cultured people at the time of Christ. The Romans, the Greeks, the Persians and the peoples of India already had their ancient cultures too. Their philosophers had already grappled with the great problems of ethics and their sages had had profound metaphysical insights. The ideas of selflessness and brotherhood were not foreign to them. They had speculated on the nature of Divinity, had probed into the mystery of death, and had constructed elaborate codes of behaviour, hardly differing from our own today.

Doubtless, as with us, they had their cynics, their crooks, their politicians, their pleasure lovers and their stoics. And perhaps they were also like us today. Blind! Blind to the fact that they were acted upon by the forces of the natural world, while vainly imagining that they were manipulating these same forces. Perhaps, in spite of their learning, they were full of *avidya,* of ignorance, having the illusion that they were masters of their own fates, masters of nature, and masters of their own natures.

Surely then Christianity is unique not because it created a new conception of Godhead, a new code of ethics, but because there was a new dispensation of Grace in the person of our Lord Jesus Christ. Perhaps, like many of us, the disciples felt the contradictions in their own natures, the futilities and frustrations of existence, and the need for purification; in a word, the sense of sin. Why was it that they could not find their salvation in the orthodoxy of the time, in Judaism?

The real transformation of the disciples seems to have taken place after the death of Christ, at the time of Pentecost, when the Holy Ghost came upon them. "Then Peter said unto them, Repent, and be baptized everyone of you in the name of Jesus Christ, for the remission of sins and ye shall receive the gift of the Holy Ghost." The formation of the early Christian Church was intimately connected with the passing on of this gift of the Holy Ghost. In one passage in Acts there is a very clear distinction made between those who believed, and those on whom the Holy Ghost had come. Remarkable also is the passage in Chapter Ten: "While Peter yet spake these words, the Holy Ghost fell on them which heard the word. And they of the circumcision that believed were astonished, as many as came with Peter, because on the Gentiles also was poured out the gift of the Holy Ghost. For they heard them speak with tongues and magnify God."

The early Christian Church must have been extremely interesting. It was founded by a man who was crucified like a criminal and who had scornfully criticised his own generation and lambasted the orthodox church of the time. It was perpetuated by men who believed that the same man, who was crucified, had power from God; by men on whom a strange power came that made them stagger like drunken men and speak in strange languages; by men who insisted upon passing on this strange influence. Somehow I feel that these early Christians might be considered crazy and hardly respectable, if they were alive today.

It is only in the light of Pentecost and the passing on of the Holy Ghost that one can understand something of the incredible courage of the early Christians. "Being led by the spirit" can be seen to be no mere phrase. "Bearing witness" was not testifying to an abstraction that strained the credulity, but was a stand taken upon experience that could not be denied. The Holy Ghost was not a theological riddle, but a force of which they had direct experience.

Why it appears that the Holy Ghost had to be passed on through the agency of the Apostles and those that followed them, I do not know. In the same way, in Subud, I don't know why there has to be an "opener."

Pak Subuh has always insisted that everyone in Subud received directly, and this accords with experience. It is evident that the helpers do nothing; they are but conduits. It is notable that Pak Subuh has also said that there are no senior and no junior helpers, but that all are equal, because the force itself is ageless and has no regard for the channel. Pak Subuh has always laid emphasis not on the channel but on the greatness of the Power of God.

Two days before Pak Subuh left England, in October 1959, he gave a talk in Newcastle. He said then that the action of the latihan takes place when the thoughts and the feelings have come to a stop. But, he continued, when people normally try to separate themselves from their thoughts and feelings, it is as impossible as trying to separate sugar and sweetness. It is only at death that this separation takes place. And he added: *"It is sometimes said that at his opening, a man experiences his own death."*

Part 2

The Awakening of the Soul

You, the child, are already fortunate in your life, because you have found a way that is able to awaken the soul, so that it is awake and can act according to your condition and strength. Little by little your soul will grow stronger and will eventually be able to fulfill your needs.

From *Susila Budhi Dharma*
by Muhammad Subuh Sumohadiwidjojo.

Now that 45 years have elapsed since Subud arrived in England, now that John Bennett is dead and Pak Subuh died in 1987; now that Coombe Springs no longer exists and now that my publisher and friend Dan Cahill, the founder and owner of the Dharma Book company in New York, has also passed away, I feel constrained to attempt once again to have my book republished. I have been encouraged greatly in this endeavour by the publication of *The History of Subud, Part 2* a monumental labour on the part of Harlinah Longcroft. Within this *History* are numerous quotations from my own book, and this has made me realise that *STAIRWAY TO SUBUD* is, in at least one sense, unique.

While there are several accounts of life at the *Prieuré* with Mr. Gurdjieff, I believe that at this moment in time my book is the only one that relates in some detail the life and the kind of work that we did under John Bennett at Coombe Springs. And while there are several books about Subud, such as Bennett's own *Concerning Subud* and two books by Husein Rofé, *The Path of Subud* and *Reflections on Subud* (books which are far more erudite than mine could ever hope to be) nevertheless, I believe that mine is the only book that recounts the arrival of Subud in England in 1957 and the extraordinary impact of the same for many hundreds, nay thousands of people, throughout England, Europe and the World.

So I have typed the whole of my book once again, but this time no longer on a tiny Oliver portable typewriter that I carried with me from England to California and back, but on this miracle of modern science, a computer. In doing this, I have as best as I could kept to the original text, only changing the syntax when I, myself, found the meaning unclear, or where the phraseology, once acceptable, is no longer *politically correct.* I have, however, added in some names in brackets, since I believe that these are to some small degree of historical interest, and furthermore I am hoping by chance to jog some people's memories so that I can find out the whereabouts of friends long departed from my ken.

I am, however, adding Part 2 and Part 3, since this will give some new material to those who read the original version of my book, and hopefully encourage them to buy it once again. There are several excellent books that have been published in the intervening years, but to the best of my knowledge, all these books have been published privately. To my mind, this is a great pity. The rapid expansion of Subud and the world journeys of Pak Subuh and his entourage coincided with the publication of the books mentioned above, together with *Worth Living For* by Eva Bartok, *A Fool in Love* by Kitty Trevelyan and my own *Stairway to Subud.* Also there were a number of books by Varindra Tarzie Vittachi, *A Reporter in Subud* and *Assignment Subud* which were published early on, and like my own book, were published by the now defunct Dharma Book Company.

SPI or Subud Publications International Limited has published a great number of books in the intervening years, and a list of these books can be seen on the web at http://www.subud.org or www.subud.org under links. This list gives the impression that these are the only books on Subud, which is a pity. Though John Bennett, after some years in Subud resigned as a Helper, a resignation that was accepted by Pak Subuh, it must not be forgotten that his book *Concerning Subud,* which was published by Hodder & Stoughton, was available to the general public, and was for many people their first introduction to Subud. Furthermore, it was hastily translated into German, French and Spanish to my knowledge. Later still another very remarkable book called *Witness* was also published by the same author. This contained the most remarkable accounts of John Bennett's experiences in Subud. Later editions of this same book, of which the culmination were the Subud chapters, were bowdlerised and the most significant chapters were cut out. Happily, I still have one of the original copies, as well as a great many letters from JGB, as we were wont to call him.

Now Bennett came under a cloud when he, so to speak, defected from the ranks, wishing as he did to continue teaching his own Systematics. Like many others, I disagreed with what he did in various ways, but that does not prevent me and many others who studied with him at Coombe Springs from being eternally grateful to him for leading us first in the Work and then later leading us all into Subud. Nor does it make any of his writings, when he was at the height of his enthusiasm for Subud, any less readable and enlightening.

Husein Rofé's two books are also not mentioned in the Subud website, which gives the impression that they never existed. Husein was the first Westerner opened by Pak Subuh, was a genius as a linguist, and could converse directly and correspond with Pak Subuh in his own language. He played a part in opening both John Bennett and von Bissing and the other Ouspenskeyites, Reginald Hoare and Aubrey Wolton. He also was part of the group that invited Pak Subuh to the West in the first place and surely his books should be known and available. While the *Path of Subud* is the story of his own search for the Truth, his second book, *Reflections on Subud* gives one of the clearest ever expositions of the principles of Subud. In particular, his commentaries on Pak Subuh's own book contain a very clear description of the role of the material, vegetable, animal and human forces. At the time of writing this, in the beginning of November 2002, I have just re-read this book, and I can recommend it to everyone in Subud and without, who wishes to increase their understanding.

Both of these men were intellectual giants and both were excellent linguists, although Bennett was not in the same league as Rofé as far as languages were concerned. But there the similarity ended. I think that from the beginning, Bennett never really liked Husein Rofé, and Husein, in turn, has never forgiven Bennett for usurping his position with Bapak, and for putting him in an impossible position vis-á-vis the other Ouspenskeyites.

While adding additional material to my book, I shall nevertheless not stray from the early years, say 1957 to 1963. It is not my intention to write history which I gladly leave to my esteemed Subud sister, Harlinah Longcroft. Even when I put in a Chapter on the philosophy of Subud, I will be quoting from the talks that Pak Subuh gave in those early years and which I was fortunate enough to hear in person.

I also intend to put in extracts from a very remarkable book by Arend, now Oliver Vos, for which I have his permission; some letters from Victor Rainier Gebers, who alas died two years ago; Rofé's own account of the composition of the group who actually invited Pak Subuh to England; and an account of his experiences by Bill, now Ridwan, Aitken, which appeared in one of the early Subud Chronicles, whose permission I shall seek!! Also my great friend Bob Prestie, who died suddenly earlier this year, entrusted me a book. I hope to add some parts of his story, as a fitting epitaph to him.

Chapter 8

The Philosophy of Subud

Is there such a thing as the Philosophy of Subud? One may well ask as Pak Subuh himself often repeated that Subud was not a teaching, but a receiving. In the Gurdjieff work that has been discussed and described in earlier chapters there is very clearly a philosophy.

One has only to read the first chapters of Ouspensky's *magnum opus, In Search of the Miraculous* to be struck, as by hammer blows, by the philosophy of Gurdjieff, by his basic view of life from which everything else is derived.

Man is a machine, Gurdjieff postulates. Man is a mechanism that reacts to external forces. Man has no "I;" or rather he says "I" to whatever happens to stimulate him at any given moment. He has no Will; but he is a slave to his desires, which he mistakes for Will. Man is "asleep," and he needs to wake up. I could go on and on, but the basic tenets of the Gurdjieffian philosophy, which were so new and startling in the forties and fifties, have now, some fifty years later, begun to sink into the collective consciousness.

It is no longer so strange to think that we are not Masters of our fates. Indeed the contrary; those people who are constantly trying to pick themselves up by their boot laces, who truly imagine that they can change themselves by their own efforts, by PMA or "positive mental attitudes" are themselves regarded as being slightly cranky, as being people who cannot "see themselves," who have little taste for reality.

The most striking and curious aspect of this is found in some of the former pupils of Gurdjieff and Ouspensky. Just those people whom one would expect above all to understand and to sense their own nothingness, that is to say to understand with all their being that Man cannot do, are the ones who still cling to the idea that salvation can only be achieved as the result of "efforts." And in some ways, in spite of the work in groups, it is not difficult to see how this has come about. The very words "work on oneself" seem to imply that man can bring about his own salvation; that is to say that he can eradicate the faults of his character, that he can by means of super efforts finally achieve having his own permanent "I," that he can have Will and direct his own life. And much of the Sufi writings, which were also popular with many Gurdjieff pupils, seemed to imply that spiritual progress could only be made after

My Stairway to Subud

years of discipline and asceticism.

Of course, in the normal way of things people do believe that they are responsible beings, in control of what they do. Normally people approve of themselves and blame everybody else. That is a normal or usual state of things, even with so-called religious people. But with students of the Work, that should not be. The whole aim of "efforts" was not to become some sort of super-person (though many of us doubtless imagined that that was the aim), but on the contrary those very efforts had to result in failure, had to result in our seeing that we could not work; that there was no way that by our own efforts we could succeed in changing our characters, in overcoming our faults or sins, that there was no way that by main force we could achieve that immortality that Gurdjieff stipulated belonged to Man Nos. 4, 5, 6 and 7, but not to Man 1,2 and 3.

Perhaps it was the cognizance of our own complete helplessness that made the Gurdjieff groups in general such a fertile ground for the coming of Subud. And indeed I would dare say that the more truly the Gurdjieff work was comprehended, the easier it was to understand also the sense and aim of Subud though the language and terminology is completely different.

It is interesting for me now, on the first day of Ramadan 1994, to read the very first talk that Pak Subuh gave at Coombe Springs on the 14th of June 1957. Now by that date, a great many people had been opened at Coombe Springs as has been described in the earlier chapters, but there was also a great influx of new people, and there were many who had not yet experienced the *latihan*.

..."*For those of you who are not yet opened it is not time for you to listen to this, for what Bapak is going to explain is more or less the direction and requirements of the spiritual way... According to Bapak's experience it is not Bapak who would be harmed, but those listeners who have not yet received the latihan, since they yet lack the inner strength to receive this. It might lead to unpleasant consequences, and if that happens they will certainly blame Bapak.*"

Bapak goes on the in the very next paragraph to ask for forgiveness in advance, lest he say anything that might offend or hurt feelings.

Now this is truly a remarkable beginning. Pak Subuh in no way wanted to persuade those who had not yet experienced anything. On the contrary, his explanations were directed entirely to those who had already some experience of the *latihan*.

Now this word "experience" is absolutely central to everything in Subud. There are no articles of faith; on the contrary, Bapak urged everyone not even to believe him or accept anything that was not their own experience. At the same time he pointed out, as the Spiritual Guide, the development and growth that could be expected in time.

...As regards the latihan that you have all received, this is in truth the worship of the One God by human beings, but not in a way that is familiar to you...

Perhaps the reader will better understand my bewilderment as a young man and why I wrote in earlier chapters that Bapak made statements *ex cathedra*. For in the first place in the Gurdjieff work we never used religious terminology, and in the second place Bapak did not say that we should worship God, but that the movements received in the latihan were indeed *"the worship of the One God."*

Modern man is used to thinking about everything; indeed in our universities and centres of thought we encourage discussion and logical analysis; and in this sort of dissection of ideas those of us in the Gurdjieff work were most particularly encouraged. Those who were pupils of J.G.Bennett (one has only to attempt "The Dramatic Universe" to see what I mean) even more were encouraged in us the   analytical processes So what were we to make of the following, and I quote from Bapak's very first talk again.

...It is not yet possible for you to truly think about what you have received; indeed it is not yet time for you to be able to really understand it, because it still arises and awakens in the most inner part of your inner being. But that power in there, the essence of God [sifat zat Tuhan], is itself spontaneously aware of what is happening.

No wonder many others and I found this so difficult at first, because we imagine that our thinking is the seat of our understanding. But that power is itself spontaneously aware of what is happening. That surely means that the inner can understand the inner and the outer, but the outer can by no means understand the inner.

...Human beings cannot possibly understand in a true way the touch of that all enveloping life-force, because that first requires that the life force that has begun to manifest in there should push outwards,

piercing the first barrier, which is called the physical body. This has the effect of bringing about movements in the inner feelings. So the movements that you have received are movements that arise due to the Great Power from God, which is pushing outwards.

And Pak Subuh went on to say that only when that cleansing has taken place could a man truly receive and understand the content of his inner feeling. And that is only the first barrier. The second barrier is called the "body of feeling" which is disturbed and filled by desires and day-dreams enveloped by the material forces, which also needs to be cleaned out.

Now in this very first talk to all of us at Coombe Springs the structure was emerging. For Pak Subuh goes on to talk about the third barrier, the barrier of Human understanding, which also needs to be purified. Only when that purification has been completed can the process go deeper to the fourth barrier, which is called the consciousness of the life of the inner self.

...This shows how deep within you is God's power, which you have all received in this latihan. That is why you cannot think about it, analyse it or understand where it comes from or where it leads... This was the overview you needed to hear. It is not Bapak's intention or wish that you should try to understand it, for you should never believe what Bapak tells you if you haven't yet experienced it for yourself...

Once again there is that word experience. No belief is necessary, only one's own experience. And Bapak stressed that the process would continue *"whenever you practice the latihan."*

Pak Subuh then continues to make a very curious point, which is that the obstacles in our natures are not only our own but are also inherited from our parents and indeed our ancestors, and that the purification that takes place means that *"...you are also purifying your forefathers and your own descendants."* (This is a truly wonderful idea; the idea that the practice of the *latihan kejiwaan* may not only help the individual but also his dead forebears. And there are those in Subud who have had some direct experience of the truth of this.)

...Apart from that, another benefit is that once your being has been purified and all the parts of your body have been awakened and brought to life, you will be able to find your way in life which fits with your jiwa, your human soul, meaning that everything within

your inner self will help you to find the direction in which you must go to make your life happy. It is clear from this that the worship of God is not only for our perfection after death, but also for the perfection of our life before we die.

As I re-read this talk myself, I am amazed at how condensed are the ideas contained therein. In the paragraph above alone there are so many things. Most striking for me is the idea of "happiness," because happiness is something that everyone pursues and strives for. Everybody wishes to be happy. But here it is abundantly evident that happiness only truly follows the awakening of the *jiwa*. But it is not only happiness in this world, but also happiness in the next. So now we are introduced to that theme, which is the preparation for the hereafter.

...It is certain that on your journey, or in the course of practising this training [latihan], which I have described as the worship of human beings towards God, Bapak cannot guarantee that you will all take the same amount of time...

Now what is interesting here again is that the awakening of the *jiwa* is taken as being synonymous with worship of God. Readers may possibly remember that in the very first chapter when I was a boy of fourteen I asked the dormitory prefect in a whisper "What is the purpose of life?" and he had answered without hesitation "To worship God." Now the way that Bapak talked of the worship of God was totally different from my boyhood concepts, which revolved around the outer manifestations of singing hymns and reciting psalms and intoning the Collects and the articles of belief. All these were performed in a prescribed form by one's outer; but the *latihan* was the spontaneous working of the *jiwa* from within.

If one may make the distinction between "I" and "Bright-Paul" that Ouspensky made in *"In Search of the Miraculous;"* there is the distinction between the "I" that belongs to the essence, to the inner being of man; and the numerous "I's" that belong to the outside, that is to say the functions of man. What is clear is that the realisation of the Self is synonymous with Worship of God. In fact it is only the soul or the *jiwa* that can truly worship; while the mind and thought processes, to which we often give an undue elevation, are strictly limited, and indeed are completely perishable, and relate only to this visible world.

The idea that the realisation of the Atman is the same as the realisation of the Brahman (Atman and Brahman are one) is a cornerstone of Vedantin philosophy. But when I had read about Vedanta as a young man, the concepts were things barely grasped with the mind. In Subud, the philosophy is not a theoretical one, but the movements awakened by the *jiwa* are part of the experience of those who have been opened and take part in the *latihan kejiwaan*.

It is for this reason that people of all religions are able to take part in the *latihan,* whether they are Buddhist or Vedantin, or whether they come from the Judaic-Christian-Islamic streams. Equally well there are those who are agnostic, even atheist, who have been opened, and received the *latihan*. It makes no difference because belief, or lack of belief, and opinions belong to the functions, to the personality, to that part of a man that will surely perish. What is evident, to anyone who has experienced the *latihan,* is that a probationer may come who is agnostic, that is to say that he is agnostic with his mentation. But when he is opened he may spontaneously weep, or rejoice, and cry on God or Allah; because what his inner, his *jiwa,* understands is totally different from his personality, his thought processes.

In the Gurdjieff work the seat of associative thinking was called the "formatory apparatus," and the work of self-observation made clear how any notion, any idea, any daydream could hitch a ride on this wagon. Man constantly identifies with his "thinking," imagining that that is who he is. But when a man is opened, when one experiences the action of the *great life force* in the *latihan,* then it becomes clear that his "thinking" and his emotions (his heart) are precisely who he is not. In the *latihan kejiwaan* it is the *jiwa* that is active, and it is clear then that if a person is anybody at all he is his *jiwa*.

Those people who think that death is the end of everything, (and I have friends who are sincere churchgoing Christians who do not believe in an afterlife, but believe that death is dust to dust, ashes to ashes) are in some senses correct. That is to say that as the body disintegrates, so do the functions, and thinking and feeling are part of the functions. That is why the exercise of the *jiwa* in this life is so important, and so important for all those who have been opened and received this gift.

It is interesting to read again what Gurdjieff had to say on the future life or immortality. It is so different from the cosy belief that we all live on afterwards irrespective of how we have lived in this life. For him immortality was conditional upon a certain crystallization being formed during this life. What he had to say, people can read for themselves. But certainly Gurdjieff was out to shock, to help people awake from their slumbers.

Pak Subuh on the other hand never went out to shock, speaking to those who were prepared by their experience of the *latihan*. Nevertheless what he had to say was in some instances quite as stark as anything that Gurdjieff uttered.

...What Bapak has been saying is in line with the words, in the holy books, of the prophets. They said that death is the continuation of man's life. The prophets advised people to keep God's covenants and to do God's Will, so that they would be able to behave well in their life on this earth, and then, through their good behaviour and human kindness, their soul would awaken by itself. And people would be able to feel, in their inner self, something that might seem to be new, but which really came before the life of this coarse physical body, and will also go on after it.

However, death will not be a continuation of a person's life if he cannot find the something in his inner feeling that Bapak refers to. It really will be death. It really will be the final moment and the end of the life that is in him.

And then Bapak goes on to explain the significance of the *latihan*.

...The real use of your doing or receiving the latihan is that all of you, while still in your life here can become aware of how life will be later on, after death...

When you are asleep, for example, even though you may be extremely clever, in your sleep you forget everything. This is even more the case when later you face death. Before your death you will not remember a thing. Your memory and your thinking will go blank. You will not even be able to see your children and wife clearly when they come near you...Finally at the threshold of death, these ideas completely vanish from memory and awareness. And, at that point, if a person still has a voice to speak, he asks for a gift from God. He asks for help from the one God. He asks that he may be given the way, that he may be opened up and freed from his mind... Clearly what we have received is beyond our ability to understand. We cannot think about it, and we cannot readily understand the significance of the moving within us, which you have experienced and received. In truth it is this that will awake and live on. It is this that will admit our life from this world into the spiritual world.

This body is generally referred to as the coarse physical body, while the fine body is the body of the spirit. Thus, as we carry out our duties in life, even though we are still in this world, we begin to have two of us or a double I...

So Pak Subuh makes clear in these two quotations that death will be final indeed, unless a way is found to the awakening of the soul. That is as stark a message as anything that Gurdjieff said about immortality. But it is, as it were, hidden away, because the emphasis is on that which has been received. *"In truth it is this that will awake and live on. It is this that will admit our life from this world into the spiritual world..."*

And then finally, there comes that *echo*, we begin to have two of a double "I's" or us the *echo* of "I" and Ouspensky or "I" and Bright-Paul.

An echo it may be, but for those who have been opened and experienced the *latihan* this division becomes more and more clear with every exercise. It becomes clear how I normally walk, which is totally different to when the life force makes me walk. It is absolutely clear how I normally sing, and how singing arises in the *latihan*. It is patently clear that most actions and thought arise from my self will; it is likewise clear when thoughts and feelings arise spontaneously by themselves in the *latihan* or in life in the state of the *latihan,* from beyond the thought processes, from beyond the longings of the heart.

Subud is not a religion, as it has no form, no ritual, no teaching. And yet it is the essence of religion, because it is a practical way to submit to a Higher Will; it is a means of salvation. It is said by Colin Wilson in *"The Strange Life of P. D. Ouspensky"* that Ouspensky himself declared that intellectual processes could achieve nothing, and that the only hope was to find the way to work with the Higher Emotional Centre and *"we have not found that way."* What is certain is that nothing can be achieved by the intellect, as that is part of the functions and will die with the death of the body. Does the Subud *latihan* correspond to the opening of the Higher Emotional Centre? I used to think it may be, and indeed John Bennett in his original introductory talks seemed to infer that this was so. But now I do not know.

After all that Pak Subuh said in so many of his talks that *"the latihan that you have all received is in truth the worship of the One God by human beings..."* it is interesting to see the following extract from a talk given to a large audience in the Friend's Meeting House, Euston in August 1959.

We should make no claim that what we have received comes from God, but we should base everything upon the available evidence. That is the right and proper way; that we should not speak about anything for which there is no evidence. It is useless to speak in glowing terms of Subud, for what is needed is experience. That is the basis upon which to reach the conclusion that, in truth, that which we have received clearly comes from a stream that - although we are incapable of understanding it - is beyond the power of the thinking mind, our heart and desires. This means that it comes from beyond the reach of the lower forces, and from beyond all that is usually referred to as magic. For the same reason, it is pointless to say that we receive this from God, for none can know this save God alone. The manner of God's giving to man requires no gesture of the hand, nor does it require any thought or feeling as it would in man, but all is in His Power, which is beyond our knowledge. It will be enough if we say to other people that this comes from beyond our knowledge, our thinking mind and our hearts, and therefore it follows that it must come from a level that is really free from anything pertaining to our desires, our hearts and our thinking.

As for ourselves, we have already received evidence that we experience a gradual process of change in the content of our inner nature. The change that we begin to see and feel being brought about in us is incomprehensible and unknown to us. Indeed the action of the Power of God can bring about that which is beyond the expectation of man's thoughts and desires. We should therefore not give any high sounding explanations to those who wish to hear about it, and if as a result they ask what we have received in Subud, the answer is that they should come and experience for themselves...

So if I were to ask myself in this present time whether the *latihan* corresponds to the working of the Higher Emotional Centre, the answer is simple - that Tony Bright-Paul neither knows that nor comprehends that. If I were asked if the *latihan kejiwaan* comes from God, likewise Tony Bright-Paul does not know that either. Certainly Tony knows that the action of the *latihan* comes from beyond his thought processes and is utterly unrelated to what are normally called desires. On the other hand his *jiwa* may directly feel certain things, which Tony cannot comprehend.

But Pak Subuh in his infinite wisdom has surely said it all *"...and if as a result they ask what we have received in Subud, the answer is that they should come and experience for themselves..."*

And finally my favourite quotation, which is a reminder of all that has been said about man having no "I," but that he says "I" to whatever happens to ride him at a given moment.

Now the purpose of the latihan kejiwaan is to enable us to experience the separation of the "I," the "I" of the jiwa, the "I" of the pure inner feeling of the jiwa - from all the lower forces that manifest within us through our nafsu, our passions. The latihan kejiwaan trains us to constantly experience the separation of our real "I" from these lower forces...

My Stairway to Subud

Chapter 9 — **Extracts**

"Some things need to be rescued from oblivion."
Anthony Bright-Paul

My first extract comes from a wonderful little book by Mangoendjaja. *"Why do you do the latihan?" the voice persisted.* It is a question, surely, that we all need to ask.

"*My Inner Guidance*" by K. Mangoendjaja:

After latihans I used to pray, asking God for His protection, and to provide for our daily needs. One night the inner self corrected me. "Mangoen, don't ask God for anything. He knows your needs better than you do. He will give you what you need, not what you ask, because He knows what is good for you."

At the next latihan, the voice asked, "Mangoen, why do you do the latihan?" Startled, I confessed I didn't really know. "If you don't know the purpose of the latihan," the voice said, "then it has no meaning for you. Why do you do the latihan?" the voice persisted.

I couldn't answer, but the question was repeated over and over. Suddenly I thought it might be the devil, or some lower force, that was interrogating me. I was quickly disabused of this thought. "Now you are in doubt again," the voice observed. "I'll show you who I am."

Instantly my breathing stopped. I nearly choked before air entered my lungs again. This happened several times. I had no control over my respiratory organs. The voice continued to question me. "Why do you do the latihan?" I had to answer that I did not know, and each time my breathing was stopped. "Mangoen," the voice said, "the latihan has a purpose. The purpose of our latihan is to worship God."

Why couldn't you have said so in the first place? I thought, rather ruefully, still weak and shaking.

In the Subud Journal of June 1964 Tarzie (now Varindra) Vittachi wrote an article called *Corked* which not only tells us about Varindra, but also gives a wonderful picture of Prio Hartono. I think that many of us will be able to empathise with Varindra in this one—I certainly can!

My Stairway to Subud

"Corked" by Tarzie (Varindra) Vittachi

Flying back from Delhi to Kuala Lumpur early last year, I decided to spend a day or two in Calcutta, and found, to my surprise and pleasure, that Prio Hartono had also arrived in Calcutta on his way home from Africa. Prio suggested a latihan. It went on, and on, and on, till I felt tired and bored. I sensed that Prio was exercising beside me. My weariness and sense of boredom increased steadily till it became almost insupportable. Then I stopped and left the room. I remember sitting outside the room and wondering why the half hour spent in latihan seemed to drag inordinately. Later that evening Ian Arnold, Prio and I sat talking. Suddenly Prio turned to me and said:

"You have corked yourself."

"What do you mean?" I asked.

"You have put a cork in yourself like in a bottle," he said. "Difficult to let go now."

I told him what I'd been feeling lately. About the minutes dragging in the latihan and continuous sense of boredom and futility. Prio explained that this was what he had meant.

"When you are in good, open state, willing to surrender, the latihan is not long enough. When you are corked up, the latihan is very long."

I asked him what I could do about this. Prio said: "All anyone can tell you is that you must uncork yourself. It is you, not anyone else who put the cork in you. You must take the cork out yourself. The latihan goes on from stage to stage. When we come to the end of one stage sometimes we refuse to move on. We resist. I can say that you should surrender, but I cannot say—no one can say—how to surrender. If anyone can tell you how to surrender then it is not Subud, it is a system, a teaching.

Ian went to bed but Prio wanted to sit up longer. We went to his room, sat on the floor, talked a little, "received" frequently in quiet stretches, and laughed a lot swapping tales about Subud and Subud people. It was almost dawn when Prio said:

"Cork much looser now?"

And indeed it was. He had helped me by being companionable and by receiving with me, to make me willing to surrender once more.

Next day, when Prio said, "Finish" and told me it had gone on for fifty-five minutes, I realised that the cork had come out.

Here now is an excerpt from a wonderful little book, written by my old friend Arend Vos, later to be called Ivan and now he is Oliver Vos. This describes a visit to Cilandak and is particularly appropriate right now as it is Ramadan.

Ramadan at Cilandak by Oliver Vos

The Chartered plane was scheduled for December. Just before leaving for the airport Robert told me he had written to Bapak over a month previously for a name for their child which was due to be born in early January. He had not received a reply and asked me to look into it.

It was a very old plane we boarded; so old in fact that someone remarked it even had outside toilets! Anyway the journey was not too bad except that on the last lap, after we left Bombay, we ran out of food and water.

We had our dinner served at 3am Jakarta time when we were told that no more food could be served, as there was nothing left and we had also ran out of drinking water. Strangely this coincided with the last meal before the Ramadan fast at Cilandak. So we actually started our fast at the same time as our brothers and sisters there.

After arrival, we all gathered in the latihan hall and someone from the Jakarta group gave us a welcoming speech. After the speech everyone sat quietly on their benches. I thought we should say something but all stayed quiet. I eventually stood up and said something like this: "We praise Almighty God for the opportunity to be here in Wisma Subud and many thanks to you for being our host." As an afterthought, as I was near Bapak, I asked him how my name should be pronounced, Aivan, as the English called me, or Evan, the Dutch way. It was to be Evan.

Soon after the welcoming ceremony, I went to the office to see what had happened to Robert's reply to his letter. I found it had been sent three weeks earlier to the wrong address. It read: "If it is a boy, the name should be Howard, and if a girl, Halima."

When I read Howard it was just ordinary, but when I got to Halima the words seemed to dance in front of me and I immediately knew it would be a girl. It proved to be right. Halima was born in January.

Fasting did not seem difficult except for not smoking. I smoked three cigarettes during the next day. I felt very guilty about this and in the evening I went into the latihan hall and prayed for help and strength not to smoke the following day.

At first nothing happened and I wasn't at all convinced that I could be helped, so I persisted in my prayers. Then all of a sudden I heard a voice in my head, loud and clear, saying "Promise." I argued, "How can I promise? I am so weak I might not be able to keep my promise." This kept on for some time but the voice insisted, "Promise" and in the end I had to promise. As soon as I consented the voice stopped and the next day I no longer had any difficulty with smoking.

The first evening Bapak spoke about the real meaning of the latihan. It is the greatest gift that can be given to man, a gift so precious that it is very difficult to grasp. It must not be treated lightly. If we went to latihan with 100% faith, God would repay with 100% and we would have no worries about this earthly life because God would provide everything. If we came to the latihan with only 5% faith God would only repay 5%, and 95% of the burdens of life would have to be carried by ourselves. This to me was so clear at that moment that I seemed to understand all the problems in the world.

Bapak also made it clear that there were no rules in Subud. One can go to the latihan once a month, once a week, or five times a week. Bapak does not mind. But from experience Bapak advises that twice a week on average is best. Too many latihans usually produce unnecessary suffering and crisis cases, too few usually results in confusion. But we must do exactly as we please and take the consequences.

Bapak spoke on three different occasions about promising. Making a promise is like digging a hole. Many people dig lots of holes and are unable to fill them so that in the end they fall into them. In marriage a very serious promise is made, "To love and to cherish till death do us part." A few days later, or sometimes before this, there is a quarrel, the promise is broken and another hole dug. It is not surprising that there are so many unhappy marriages.

Bapak talked to us every evening from about 11pm until 2am and I shall never forget the inner experiences I had during the time I spent in Cilandak.

The same story recurs with a slight variation in *"The Life of Eagle John Fox"* by Oliver Vos. This has clearly been privately published—it deserves surely a wider audience.

Some years ago I received a remarkable little book by my friend Arend Vos, who had changed his name to Ivan Vos, as was the custom with many people in Subud.

Here now is an excerpt from his **Chapter 6:**

Within a week after I saw Joseph Benjamin, I received a telephone call from a friend of mine at Coombe Springs to say that many miracles had happened there and that a Master had arrived from the East. The "Work" was now going by itself without any effort on the part of the pupils.

The new "Work" was called Subud.

It sounded too fantastic to me and I had heard enough of Masters from any direction, so I forgot all about it. But not for long!

About a week later I received an invitation from Mr. Bennett for my two children to attend his birthday party at Coombe Springs. I had not attended any meeting for a year but was still classed as a member of the Institute. This seemed to me a good opportunity to find out what had really happened at Coombe Springs.

I accepted the invitation and took the children to the party.

While walking up the drive toward the house Mr. Bennett walked down to greet us. He stretched out both hands and said: "Vos, I have not seen you for so long. What has been happening to you?" I felt a warmth that was not there before. He had always been very friendly but there was always this teacher-pupil relationship, which kept us at a distance. He seemed completely changed. I looked at him and thought, "He has at last become human," and the words that came out of my mouth were: "I want to join Subud." From that moment onward I knew with absolute certainty that Subud was the answer to all my searching.

Mr. Bennett said that he thought it would be better to talk to other members before making up my mind.

It was nice to see old friends again. They seemed to have changed in some way. All of them were full of the experience they had when they received the Grace of God. Some said that they were filled by the Holy Spirit; others called it the opening of the soul.

When the party was over I collected my two boys and Mr. Bennett walked down the drive with us. I told him I still wanted to join and how soon could I be "opened," to which he replied: "Well, I regret to say that a waiting period of three months has been introduced to give the applicants a chance to find out a little more about the Latihan Kejiwaan." "I cannot see why I should wait!" I said impatiently. "No, maybe not, but wait till Bapak returns from Holland. We will drop you a line and if you are still interested you can join."

I had to be patient and waited three weeks before I received the following note:

"Please come to Coombe Springs on 27 February 1958 at 8.00pm when you can make a start in Subud if you so wish."

I arrived an hour early on that Thursday, which gave me time to meet the other applicants. There were thirteen of us and we were all apprehensive. Mr. Bennett gave us a short talk. He told us that when the "opening" time came, we should just relax and leave everything to Almighty God. If we felt movements in our arms or legs, or wanted to cry or sing, we must not stop it but go with it and let it all happen.

We would be completely conscious and able to stop the process any time we wished, but this would not be right if we wanted to surrender and have complete faith in God. This was our chance to be guided by the Power of God.

I cannot go into any detail of my first latihan, except that it was very strong, so strong in fact that it lasted well into the next day.

I remembered the state of Nirvana and my friend saying it was death. Nirvana was death! The Subud latihan was the opposite. I was conscious of everything that went on during my first latihan. I was also aware that my body was being moved by something other than my mind or feelings and I knew then that I had been looking for Life, not Death!

My next extract comes from a talk that Pak Subuh gave in 1959, if my memory serves me aright in the Friends Meeting House in Euston. This is of particular interest to those who are Christians and to those who would be Christians:

Bapak on Jesus

Tradition associates Jesus with the colour green. This means that worldly influences had no hold on his essence, so that He truly was beloved of God. You probably know that the colour green is the symbol of the state of childlike innocence, as yet free from desires, especially the desire for woman and the desire for the things that have come to be coveted by man.

And it is also recorded of Jesus, that he not only had power to heal the sick and to raise the dead, but he also had power to walk on water, and that it was the Will of God that finally He should face death on the cross.

Healing the sick and raising the dead mean, respectively, the rectification of faults and weaknesses within the being of man, and the awakening of his soul which is still dead in him; and the power to walk on water means the overcoming and purification of man's emotions.

This is essentially similar to what you have received in the spiritual exercises of Susila Budhi Dharma or Subud.

In these exercises you are being purified, and your faults and weaknesses—such as diseased conditions of human nature, or whatever man may call it—are being corrected, and your souls, which from your birth up to the present when you are adult people, have been shut in by your emotions, your thoughts and your desires, are being awakened.

And for you it is no longer anything strange that having done your exercise, you should feel within yourselves the stirring of a new life, different from what there was before.

This stirring of a new life means the awakening and liberation of the soul from the imprisonment and bondage of worldly pressure. In this, Subud in no way departs from that which was revealed to the Prophets of old, of whom Bapak has spoken before.

And facing death by crucifixion symbolizes that perfected man stands in the middle, between earth and heaven.

That is why tradition tells us that Jesus after passing through death remained the same as before. This means that it is the Will of God that the soul of man should protect the consciousness of one's individuality and cause it to permeate and encompass the entire physical body.

Thus in his life after death Jesus had lost nothing that had become part of his individuality; He was still able to see, hear, smell, speak, perceive; and all other powers within his being continued to function.

This tallies with what we experience in our spiritual exercises, where one by one, all our members and organs are brought to life, so that our seeing and hearing, and all our other senses will remain intact even after death.

This does not mean that our physical body will continue to exist after death; what we shall bring with us and which will have become part of our individuality will not be our eyes, but our power of seeing; not our ears, but our power of hearing; not our mouth, but our power of speech; not our nose, but our power of smelling; not our blood, but our emotions; not our brains, but our understanding; not our heart, but our power of reflection and our inner self.

This is indeed what we have wished for and what we asked from the One Almighty God; that we may become such a man as indeed it is the Will of God that we should become.

This is such a remarkable passage that it merits reading again and again. For not only does it throw a light on the Gospels, but also it incidentally explains why in Subud there has to be an "Opening."
"*...and your souls, which from your birth up to the present when you are adult people, have been shut in by your emotions, your thoughts and desires, are being awakened.*"

It is precisely because we are "shut in" that we have to be "opened up." This opening of the soul is quite a different matter from being "open," an expression that is often used to describe those who are catholic in their tastes, or who are liberal in their views. Being open in Subud is quite another matter, since it means that the soul has been awakened.

That is why it is said that once a person is opened in Subud, they can never leave the Spiritual Brotherhood of Subud. Because even though they may become inactive in the organisation, even though they may neglect the *latihan*, nevertheless once the soul is opened then the work in the soul is the work of God. We may not judge of that.

Nevertheless and here I quote from the talk by Ibu Rahayu in Wolfsburg in 2002: *"And that is why although it is God Who is in charge and is doing this, is taking us through this process, we are the ones who do the work. Because we have to make the effort to do the Latihan. We have to bring ourselves to the Latihan to actually do it. And this is not easy because there are many, many things that try to block us. Whether it is that we are depressed or we are lazy or we are too busy. There are many, many things that try to block us and stop us."*

Extract 7 - ***Stories Icksan Told Us*** by I. Gerson

I did not know what I should type tonight—I had various options. Then I came across the following: *Stories Icksan Told Us,* written by Isaac Gerson in Ceylon. I never met Isaac, I do not even know whether he is alive or dead. But he wrote with such a delicacy of touch that many others and I are indebted to him and wish him well, whatever realm he may be in.

As for Icksan himself, he was for me very special, since through him I was enabled to experience first of all, as related in the earlier chapters. Shortly after I had begun to experience, Icksan asked to try on a short camel coloured coat I had bought, and of which I was very proud. He really liked it a lot and I, I did not understand. He was testing me. I should have given him the coat on the spot.

Now Isaac Gerson wrote a wonderful article in the Subud Chronicle of March 1959, and I am taking just one of his stories, which I hardly dare to type.

BAPAK'S SON

"Bapak's son was a Doctor. His name is Harijadi. When he was twenty-three, he said: "Bapak, I want to die."

Bapak said: "Not yet."

A year later Bapak said: "Now you are ready."

So Harijadi bathed himself, like Muslim, repaired the radio aerial for Bapak, and went to his room.

Bapak was sitting here: Harijadi's room was next to him.

Suddenly Harijadi called: "Bapak."

Bapak went and took Harijadi in his arms. He was dead.

The next day was the funeral. Bapak's grandson was there. He said to me: "Icksan, isn't he beautiful?"

I was not long in Subud then. I thought he meant the corpse. I said: "Yes, he looks very beautiful."

"Not that!" said the grandson with scorn. "We're going to bury that. I mean Harijadi."

Harijadi was there with us. Bapak's grandson, only seven years old, saw him. You also will see him, all of you, when you are ready, when you need him. He is Bapak's Helper—He comes with the knife for the operation."

Extract 8 from the **Letters of Victor later Rainier Gebers**

I knew Victor well in the days that I lived at Coombe Springs and before I went to Manchester. He had come from South Africa and lived at Coombe Springs for some 2 years, before returning there. This now is his story of the start of Subud:

I missed the 1956 seminar but came to the one held in 1957. Before I left S. Africa I heard that a Mr. Subuh had arrived at Coombe, that he was doing the same sort of Work as G. and that you could choose with whom you wished to work. Being a loyal sort of character I would of course remain with JGB. When I arrived in London I was told that JGB was away and would return from Wales within a few days. In the meantime I was filled with stories of the marvels and the dangers of this thing called Subud. I was told of John Ross. Several of my old friends were eager to offer explanations and I remembered how during my earlier days at Coombe I had come to so many a wrong conclusion by listening to someone's explanations and ideas. Find out for yourself had become my rule and as politely as I could, I refused all manner of story and opinion.

The day came when I went to JGB in his study. It didn't take him more than a few minutes to tell me what Subud was about and he wound up with, "If you wish to be opened you must say." Fast thinking got me on the right track; I knew this man JGB, respected him and trusted him completely. Yes, I'd go for it. I'll ask Pak Subuh, came his rejoinder and with that he vanished out of the room. He was back after a brief interval with, Pak Subuh says, Tonight.

That evening Pierre Elliot ferreted me out from a crowd of people standing in the hall. I must confess I was rather taken aback when I found myself alone with Pierre making my way up the stairs. What, me by myself? I asked. All comfort I had from him was his laconic, Why not? We came to the landing outside the small room near the upper kitchen where I was introduced to Icksan. After a few minutes Pak Subuh came from his room also on the same floor. Laughter, mostly on the part of Icksan ceased abruptly, Pierre was asked to go to the main latihan, the rest of us went into that small room and the opening took place.

Three weeks went by and the time came for farewells. After my last latihan I found myself standing next to Varindra. Should we say goodbye? Yes, better we do this and together we went to say our farewells to Pak Subuh before the next latihan started. He was standing as he usually did between latihans, at the table with its array of glasses and Coca-Cola bottles. Strange, I thought, I had on many an occasion talked to JGB but to this quite extraordinary and enigmatic man, not a single word, only goodbye, but things had happened. Varindra, by then, had asked his famous 10 questions.

On the following morning I went to see JGB before my departure and I spent some time with him in his study. He was very chatty, by no means the restrained and formidable JGB of old. I remember how he said as I was leaving, "I am absolutely convinced about the latihan, this is what we have been waiting for." With this reassuring note of confidence lodged within me I went my way.

Back home I did my latihan, alone, twice a week for a year.

My Stairway to Subud

In March 1958, like a bolt from the blue, a letter came from JGB then in New York with Bapak. In it he suggested that I go to Indonesia to be with Bapak when he returned from his world tour. After that I could perhaps open interested people in South Africa. This was something beyond my wildest hopes and expectations. I wrote and said, Yes, I would go and back came the reply this time from Australia that Bapak had approved.

I set off for Indonesia in July. In Bombay I was entertained by Indu Bhave who introduced me to Pat Gillivray of the BOAC. We chatted about Coombe and as that last lingering doubt about Subud still remained with me, I asked him, "How do you know we are not being lead up the garden path?" His reply, "Well if we have been, it's been worth it."

I arrived in Indonesia and it was there that I caught the faint glimmerings and evidence of something quite beyond me and it was there that I could let go of my doubts. Two things went together, the experience and the kindness and love shown me by my Indonesian brothers and sisters. This sustained me and in the process was forged something like an anchor which would hold me in all sorts of life situations, even to this day.

That then is where I was brought to stand and where I stand today.

And that, very briefly, is my tale. To JGB I owe an enormous debt of gratitude and to Bapak I owe an even greater debt of gratitude.

I had a further letter from Victor Rainier Gebers on October 25th 1993.

You ask about my opening. Did I experience straight away? Yes I did. Not long after the ceremony started there was a miniature explosion, something like a pistol shot in the right side of the head. With that my head went into a violent nod. I also had a feeling of wanting to fall but I seemed to resist this. For the remainder of my 15 latihans I had nothing more than mild movements of the arms.

Here is an article written by W. S. Aitken, or Bill Aitken as we knew him at Coombe, but who now has the Subud name Ridwan. He worked in Fleet Street on the *Evening News* and the *Daily Express* as Editor of one department or another. I knew him well when we were both members of the same study group in the Gurdjieff work, but lost touch with him after the beginning of Subud and after we both got married. I met him again at a meeting at

Anugraha a couple of years ago, still the same except that both of us have white hair! I speak with him occasionally on the phone, as he now lives in central France.

His article *The First 400* appeared in the Subud Chronicle of July 1959 and mirrored very clearly the experience of my own opening recounted in Chapter 6.

The First 400

The house at Kingston belonged to the Gurdjieff movement. It stood back from the road in large, well-kept grounds. There were about 200 men there when I arrived, all, like myself, coming for the first time.

Men and women worship separately in Subud, so certain nights of the week had been set aside to receive each. This was a Thursday, a men's night. I knew many of the people there. Some were apprentices and students in their early twenties, some writers, architects and engineers in their thirties, others were business men in their forties and fifties. All, like myself, were nervous.

Only a few days had passed since Pak Subuh's arrival. There had been no time to prepare facilities to handle large numbers of people. We stood around in the garden or in the lounge of the house, smoking, chatting and joking about our fate in order to cover our apprehension. From time to time, in groups of fifteen, we were asked to go up to hear a short talk by John Bennett. If we arrived first we sat on chairs, and if not we simply squatted wherever there was space on the floor.

Bennett did not say much. In essence, he told us that in order to receive this power we had to do nothing. This was very difficult for people. All that was required was to stand quietly and ask inwardly for help from God. "Let your thoughts or your body act as they wish," he said.

The talk did not reveal much and lasted only a few minutes. We returned downstairs to the lounge to await the next move. When we had arrived earlier in the evening, our names had been written in order of arrival. Now someone was reading out the first fifteen names. We watched silently as their owners separated themselves from the crowd and threaded their way towards the biggest room of the house, the dining room.

Through the open door we could see that the tables and chairs had been cleared away and that carpets had been laid to cover the floor. Inside two or three Indonesians dressed in lightweight slacks and shirts chatted together, smoking and occasionally laughing.

Standing quietly with Bennett near the centre of the room was a middle-aged Indonesian of about five feet ten. He seemed slightly broader than the others and wore a well-cut fawn, gabardine-type suit, light shirt and pale-coloured tie. His hair was straight and grey, brushed back flatly. His face seemed tanned by the sunshine, and he wore heavier than usual glasses. There was nothing about him that would have caused anyone to look twice. Pak Subuh looked like what he once had been—an assistant bookkeeper in Java.

The fifteen people filed through the door pausing only to take off their shoes, ties and watches and to leave them on a chair outside. In stockinged feet they were ushered in with gentle hands and large smiles by the non-English speaking Indonesians.

The door was closed.

There was silence for a few moments, then the sound of a man singing, a mellow tenor voice, singing in a strange key. A quiet drumming of feet or hands, growing faster and louder. A kind of chant in a deeper voice, somehow harmonising with the singing and the drumming. Then a shrill, shiver provoking scream like that of a man falling to his death. Within seconds there was such a din as I had never heard but which I was to hear often that night. There was wailing, crying, singing, shouting, laughing and sometimes in the quiet moment a kind of sighing.

It sounded as though a hundred maniacs were running berserk behind that door. We stood outside, frightened because we too might soon go in, wishing in a way that we were not there, yet knowing we would not leave.

We waited, trying to picture impossibly what was happening to our friends behind that wall. The mad shouting, laughing, crying, the thumping, drumming and wailing went on. Then as suddenly as it had begun everything stopped. Just like that. Dead stop. Dead silence.

The door opened slowly. The Indonesians were standing casually together, smoking, chatting, and smiling. Pak Subuh stood in the centre of the room, his hands clasped behind his back, a quiet smile on his lips.

The people walked though the door silently, picking up their shoes and belongings as they came. Their faces were perfectly calm, their movements and gestures quiet and easy. They looked as though they had been relaxing thoughtfully to some good music and were filing out for the interval. There was though something different about them. They did not speak and somehow we outside did not ask them. At the most, by a smile or a gesture, they indicated to some anxious looking friend that everything was all right, not to worry. Then quietly they walked to their cars, motorbikes or down the driveway to the bus stops, and went home.

They had been inside that room half an hour exactly. As the last of their group came filing out, the next fifteen were filing in.

Three groups later I was laying my jacket on the floor and laying my tie, watch and shoes beside it. I went through the door with two friends, one a journalist I had known for seventeen years, another a lawyer with whom I had once shared a flat. As the door closed we were guided gently to take up positions roughly a circle. I stood between my two friends. I was taking as few chances as possible. I was scared stiff.

Inside the dining room the curtains of the large bay windows were drawn. The lights burned brightly in the ceiling. The fifteen men, whose ages, clothes and bearing revealed to some extent their different walks of life, stood uneasily as Pak Subuh moved to the centre of the floor. He clasped his hands behind his back, looked up momentarily at the ceiling, and uttered a few words, staccato yet somehow smooth, in an unintelligible tongue.

A short heavily built Indonesian with a round cheerful face, standing unobtrusively near Pak Subuh, said: "There is only one God." Pak Subuh's talk was over. The translator looked around, smiling softly. "Will you please stand as relaxed as you can and close your eyes." Someone switched off the lights. I closed my eyes and at the same time tried to loosen the stiffness that knotted my legs and shoulders. Then it began.

The thudding, the screaming, the drumming, the wailing, the crying, the laughing, the shouting, burst out all around me. I stood there full of fear, unable to move, trying with all my thoughts and wish to find God—exactly as I had been told not to do. But I felt in a way, if I must suffer this, if there is a God somehow amid all this madness, I must find Him. He could protect me.

I could feel and hear people moving in the room. Some people brushed past me, singing or chanting or sighing in that strange way I had heard before. Only now it was happening within inches of my body. And I was afraid.

I wanted to see what was going on but I was too terrified to open my eyes in case I met a sight I could not stand. But there was something else. Somehow I knew that this was right. I wanted to go on and I stood there, with my eyes shut tight.

I could hear the sound of the people rolling on the floor. One man was laughing in a stupid frightening way. And yet all through this came the sound of beautiful singing, several voices, obviously singing spontaneously, yet somehow harmonising in an undeniably— yes it was undeniably—sacred kind of music.

I wondered where were my friends. Was John rolling on the floor? Was Jack singing? Were they in fact on either side of me? My thoughts raced on. Time was impossible to calculate? Was I now standing there more easily, more relaxed, as they had asked us to? Those little muscles in my face and neck—they seemed to be moving, loosening? What was this warm sensation that seemed to be seeping through my limbs?

And the singing. It was louder. Everyone seemed to be singing now. Should I be singing too? I tried, but did not seem to know what noise to make. Someone trod lightly on my foot and passed on. I felt a body brushing by my shoulder. How long was it now?

Suddenly, quietly but firmly, a voice said: "Finish." I opened my eyes. John and Jack were still standing by my side. Almost everyone was in the same position as when it had begun. But at the top end of the room someone lay still, curled upon the floor. At the bottom an Indonesian gently helped another to his feet with a smile. Somehow it did not seem right to stare at these people and, almost hurriedly, yet reluctantly, we crowded towards the door.

Like the group before us we came out silently, looking at each other's faces with an inner puzzlement. Everyone was so obviously calm, even the men who had risen from the floor.
Who then had made all the din? Who had been running and rolling and screaming and wailing? Was it the Indonesians? Or was it us?

My Stairway to Subud

On the way home I asked John and Jack. They did not know. Nothing had happened to them either, they said. But like me they were asking themselves again and again: Had nothing happened?

I had my second exercise at Coombe Springs a week later. This time the apprehension was not so bad. After all 400 of us had gone through that door and 400 had come out. Perhaps something had happened to some, perhaps nothing to others. In either case everyone seemed surprisingly cheerful and friendly.

We were eager to get in. But this evening there appeared to be even more of us. Cars blocked the driveway and outside on the road cars stood one behind another in a long winding line. Organisation—thank God—had started in the form of a cup of tea. After your exercise you could ask for a cup of tea through the service hatch. I am afraid that most of us used to ask several times before our exercise.

Really it was slow. Only 15 people at a time could get into the dining room and as each 15 was there for half an hour it was quite usual for you to wait four hours if you were 120th on the list. As the exercise began at eight sometimes we would wait till midnight. Or later.

Only then did we realise that the Indonesians were in that dining room for four hours at a stretch. But despite the din and the running and rolling about, none looked in the least tired. At the end of the night they seemed as cheerful, relaxed and rested-looking as when they first went in.

By now we were beginning to talk a little among ourselves about what happened during the exercises. Some people told how their arms, or heads or bodies began to move without any intention on the part. Others told how they had wept or sung or—he must be queer—screamed. Some said they found themselves going into a sitting position on the floor or even—they must be queer—lying down. Everyone, who had had some experience like this, insisted they had not tried to do anything. They had simply been standing with their eyes shut when it just happened.

For those of us, like myself, to whom nothing had happened, this was inexplicable. We looked at, and listened to, these people with a certain inward awe. What was it that had happened to them? Why had it not happened to me? Then little by little the awful idea came: Was there something wrong with me? Guilty memories of past misdeeds seeped back into our minds. Perhaps because I did that, I am unable to make this connection with God—if that is what it is. It was like being sexually impotent, a haunting fear, completely hidden, never spoken of. We did not tell each other in those first days that nothing had happened to us. We just listened and nodded as though we too knew what the action of Subud was like.

When my name was called out an hour later I entered the dining room with a kind of hopelessness. I stood there. Someone said: "Begin." The lights went out. I closed my eyes.

I had forgotten how terrifying the sudden mad din could seem. I stood there. Thoughts seemed to fly through my head. Then I began to feel a kind of solid warmth, seeming somehow to radiate outwards from the core of my body and limbs. I felt a strange calmness and at the same time a feeling of wonder and surprise. I was doing nothing. Without warning, my head eased itself gently forwards. My chin lay on my chest. In the same movement, my shoulders, arms and back drooped and dropped smoothly towards the floor in such a way that, with my head tucked into my chest I literally rolled myself up. My knees slackened and—only a second could have passed—I was being laid, and I mean laid, gently on the carpet.

My body curled up like that of a happy child, seemed weightless yet at the same time, filled with this warm, comforting solidness. I lay there. I felt so very, so strangely happy. Something seemed to be oozing out of every part of me. I felt glad. I wanted only to lie there. Then I realised that the screaming and thudding and wailing was still going on, but now it did not disturb me. I was no longer afraid. What all this was I did not know, but I did know that it was right.

I realised too that despite everything I still possessed all my ordinary awareness and control. This strange experiencing was somehow an "extra." I lay there, never having felt such complete and utter relaxation, never before having known such gladness and peace.

Once again time was impossible to measure. I began to have thoughts as to whether it was doing right to simply lie there. Should I be getting up and singing, or waving my arms, or walking about? But my body had no desire to move, only to lie as it was. So there I allowed it to lie.

Suddenly, unexpectedly, a voice said: "Finish." I opened my eyes and found myself getting easily up off the floor. Most people were still standing. A few were rising as I was. Again I was astonished and puzzled at the complete and obviously genuine calmness of everyone in a room, which seconds before, had seemed to be full of uncontrollable madmen. But this time I was not so concerned with other people. Something had happened to me. What it was I did not know, but I did know it had to do with something in me and also perhaps, not in me. I was certain it had nothing to do with any other man in the room.

I drove home that night in a kind of quiet exhilaration. I felt that something of tremendous importance had happened in my life. In a way I had begun a new life.

But I could never have foreseen the changes that were to come, and which never stopped coming. The first small signs appeared within days.

Extract 10 **Bennett's Opening**

Having seen how my friend Bill now Ridwan Aitken reacted at his opening, and how my friend Victor, then Rainier, Gebers also reacted, and seeing that my own reactions are well chronicled in Chapter 6, it is of some interest I believe to see how two of the major players in this great drama also reacted.

John Godolphin Bennett led all of us into Subud. Just how did that come about when he was our avowed leader and Teacher of the Gurdjieff methods?

Here are his own words from Chapter 25, *A Prophecy Fulfilled,* from *"Witness,"* the original versions.

"It is hard to explain why I went to see Rofé a third and a fourth time. I had no inclination to change from the proven ideas and methods of Gurdjieff's System, which had so greatly helped me for thirty-five years. I was far too busy to examine Subud out of mere curiosity. Indeed, I was not curious about it. I had studied many systems, and had not found any so comprehensive or so realistic as that of Gurdjieff. Bissing's experiences might well turn out like so many others: striking and encouraging at first, but in the end disappointing. I was profoundly convinced that no spiritual way can be judged from any superficial contact. One must be wholly in it, and one must be in it for years. The apostolic advice, to try the

spirits whether they be of God, is easier given than taken. I felt no desire to try the spirit of Subud, and yet I was aware of some quality, beyond thought and feeling, that drew me back to Dartmouth Road. This quality was impersonal. At that time, the man Muhammad Subuh was to me no more than a typical Asiatic wonder-worker. Rofé had altogether failed to convey to me the significance of the "contact" of which Muhammad Subuh had been the initiator. I must also say that Rofé made no attempt to persuade me. He seemed to regard my coming into Subud as pre-ordained and inevitable, and did not care if he made a good impression or a bad one.

In September, I found that two or three other old friends of mine were investigating Subud. Two of them were the same men who had gone to Madame Ouspensky in 1948, and who had subsequently joined Gurdjieff and worked for a time in Madame de Salzmann's groups in London. Their approach to Subud was very different from mine. They had already reached the conclusion that without Gurdjieff in the flesh, his System lacked an essential element. They were awaiting something not only new but radically different from what we had before. Being convinced that Work in groups, as it was being attempted in London and elsewhere by the followers of Gurdjieff and Ouspensky, was condemned to stagnation and sterility, they had withdrawn from all active participation in them. They were thus quite free from commitments both outwardly and inwardly.

My own case was not at all like theirs. I had by no means lost my belief in the practical utility of Gurdjieff's ideas and methods—even without the presence of Gurdjieff himself. I was very deeply committed, with more than four hundred pupils who looked to me for guidance, and for whose sake I had to keep Coombe Springs going. Moreover I had publicly affirmed my belief in Gurdjieff. In the Preface of Volume 1 of The Dramatic Universe, I had referred to him as "a genius that I do not hesitate to describe as superhuman." Even when writing these words, I had questioned their wisdom, and when I saw them in print, I had asked myself if they would be misunderstood. Now, after two years, I felt no wish to go back on what I and written. If man can in this life attain to superhuman status, as I firmly believe, then Gurdjieff was such a man. If Subud could not be reconciled with all that I had come to regard as well-established conclusions of Gurdjieff's cosmo-psychology, Subud was not for me.

Rofé himself appeared a blend of contradictions. He had sacrificed his material welfare and his father's good will in order to search for spiritual values, and yet he was an out and out materialist in his attitude to life. He was at one moment arrogant and intolerant; and, at another, most reasonable and modest about himself. There were, in truth, two Rofés. The inner, spiritual Rofé was evidently the product of Subud, and as such was an excellent testimony to its action.

One day in October I was taking tea with him, and was glad to find myself speaking to the "inner" Rofé. Our conversation spontaneously broke off, and we sat together in silence in front of the gas fire. I was praying that I might be shown if Subud was right for me or not. Rofé began to chant, at first very gently and then louder, in a language that was not Arabic, though I could recognise Arabic words. I did not try to follow the meaning, but relaxed peacefully in my seat.

After some minutes he stopped chanting and said: "That was just an experiment. I wanted to confirm that you were sensitive. I am now sure that at some time you will come to Subud." I did not reply, because I had entered a state of such profound calm that I had no wish to speak or move. Rofé watched me with a sardonic look of satisfaction. Ordinarily, I might have been irritated by his air of superior wisdom, but I had no such reaction. For the first time, I felt towards him as a friend. When I got up to leave, I told him I was going to America, and that I would ponder over what he had said, and especially over what I had experienced that afternoon."

In the following pages Bennett describes how he went to stay at Franklin Farms in the USA with Madam Ouspensky as her guest, where he spent some six weeks writing his book, The Dramatic Universe. In New York he found that the Gurdjieff groups treated him coldly and suspiciously. On his return to England his wife had improved in health, but there was so much to do that he was unable to continue as he wished with his writing.

"...I had to describe the most truly concrete Reality in meagre, wretchedly abstract terms. But at least I could express something when I did write. Yet at Coombe Springs I was unable to write a line.

It is scarcely surprising that I should say to myself: "I can at least stay away from Rofé and do nothing more about Subud until the book is finished." Then to my surprise the very same inner voice *that I had come to trust interrupted me and said: "On the contrary, you must go now."*

I went and asked Rofé to perform the formal opening, or initiation, that gives contact with the Life Force that operates in the Subud latihan. It was on the 25th November 1956. Rofé explained the contact as being analogous to an electric current that can be switched on and off at will. He said that I would feel its presence as a thrill or vibration. He was entirely matter of fact, and seemed almost perfunctory in asking me to make a declaration of faith in God and of submission to God's Will. I was not aware of any change that could be described as a vibration, but I did observe that the restless movement of my thoughts ceased, and that I entered a state of consciousness that I had supposed to be attainable only by a long well-directed effort. Soon I ceased to think at all, but was aware of an almost unbroken consciousness, free from all mental activity and yet intensely alive and blissful. I have no idea how long this state endured, for I lost all sense of time. I heard Rofé say: "That is enough. You can stop now," and instantly, I was back in my usual state, fully aware of my surroundings. The numinous quality of my experience gave it more the character of what mystical writers call "the prayer of diffuse contemplation" than that of Gurdjieff's self-remembering.

I was deeply impressed. Rofé was delighted, telling me that he had been convinced from the first time that he had met me that I would quickly recognize the unique character of Subud. He invited me to go twice a week to practice the latihan with others whom he had initiated during my absence in America."

Fate and Destiny - Varindra Vittachi

Here is another extract, written by Varindra Vittachi, recording the words of Bapak. In one short paragraph we have the meaning of fasting, a comment on Ramadan, and a discourse on Fate and Destiny. In one short paragraph: -

That evening Bapak spoke to us about the "true meaning" of fasting. He began with an explanation, a parable of Fate and Destiny: - "God sends us his postmen to deliver what we need in this world—a suitable wife or husband, children, a house, a job appropriate to our talents, transport for ourselves and our children. The postman's bag contains all our needs and he is willing to deliver them on time. But, influenced by our hearts and minds, we are impatient and ask for this and that ceaselessly, and are dissatisfied all the time. So we thrash about, creating a dense fog of passion around us so that the postman cannot find his way to us. What God wills for us is our Destiny. Destiny is what should happen to us. Fate is what does happen to us because our hearts and minds, which are influenced by the lower forces, make it difficult for human beings to surrender to God's will for them to reach their destiny. So their lives are ruled by Fate rather than Destiny. Bapak advises Subud members to fast because when you are not ruled by your appetites, the fog around you becomes less dense and the postman may be able to find his way to you."

Extract 12 - **Rofé's emails**

Two years ago I was enjoying a happy relationship with Husein Rofé, which was sadly broken by an unfortunate occurrence, none of my doing, concerning my acting as a go-between for someone who wanted to get in touch with Husein regarding his ex-wife of 25 years before. For some years I had visited him at his house in Brighton (he only came in the summer months), and on two or three occasions I had met up with him in the South of France. I had also arranged a big luncheon at the Aurora Hotel, where Husein was the guest speaker, and many people were enabled to meet the first European to be opened in Subud and the first ambassador of Subud to many countries, including Japan, Hong Kong, Singapore, Cyprus and Morocco.

On one occasion he came over to the Hotel Ibis in Grasse where Eileen and I were staying, and we had a luncheon to which we also invited the Jameses, who at that time were in Marseilles. Eileen and I also drove Husein over the border into Italy where Husein treated us to lunch and to a display of his remarkable linguistic abilities. I have numerous photographs of these occasions, but more than that ever since I had a computer I have had a voluminous email correspondence with him, and stored all his emails.

One of the things that has always interested me from a historical point of view was the way that the invitation to Bapak and his party came about. In fact Husein had told me about this on several occasions, but I could not trust myself to remember everything exactly, and since Husein is almost pedantic in matters of memory, I wrote to him so that everything could be in his own words.

For those of us who were students of the Gurdjieff methods under John Bennett at the Institute for the Comparative Study of History, Philosophy and the Sciences, we were all under the misapprehen-

My Stairway to Subud

sion that it was Mr Bennett himself who had invited Pak Subuh to England. While we were well aware that there were other Gurdjieff Groups, such as those of Madame de Salzmann in France, and those of Kenneth Walker, Jane Heap and Maurice Nicholl in England, what none of us realised was that Bennett was regarded by these other groups as a "loose cannon," in a word as a "maverick."

What was Bennett's chief sin in their eyes? It appears that he gave public lectures and attracted a lot of people, and that he did everything possible to propagate and make available Gurdjieff's book *"All and Everything."*

Unless this is understood against the background of "esotericism" that was the hallmark of the Ouspensky work none of this is comprehensible. So here below is a reply that I had to one of my emails:

REPLY:

the invitation of Bapak to England - names of those concerned. Many of the Coombe people thought that it was Bennett who invited Bapak (because they had been programmed to do just that— science fiction), opened Meredith Starr in Cyprus about mid-October 1955, taught there for one year.

Please distinguish between the Cyprus and London groups. Ran away from the Starrs and settled in the Turkish quarter of Nicosia. While still a guest of the Starrs in Kyrenia (north coast, now Turkish sector), I independently came to know Sir Eric Hallinan, the Chief Justice (he had been involved in the Sir Harry Oakes case in the Bahamas when the Duke of Windsor was Governor there). Eric became a close friend and I introduced him to Subud. Later he introduced me to the Bissings, Ronnie was a prominent land developer there.

Ronnie could not be opened in Cyprus as his wife was pregnant. I visited my father at his office in Cairo (he owned the Royal Exchange Building and others) during the Xmas 1955 holidays. He put considerable pressure on me to remove to England at end of the school year and offered me an allowance to enable me to resume university studies after an 11-year interval. So I moved to England in about July 1956 for purely personal reasons and having finished my job with the Starrs - and created a small group in Cyprus. In my new Willesden lodgings, I had already created the first Subud group in England which included a Turkish Pasha, the Woking Mosque Imam, Roger Corless (who now publishes books on Buddhism), Michael Fox and a few others. There was no contact whatever with any Gurdjieff people up to this moment except for a social relationship from Cyprus with the Bissings.

Nobody ever seems to have heard of that group since it was all swept under the carpet when the Bennett Mafia decided to take over and supplant me by devious and secret manoeuvres, Press releases and so forth.

It so happened that the Bissings rented a farmhouse in Deal where the child was to be born - following which he was accepted as a Subud member for my London group. He joined this in theory but received independent attention at his private opening as he had to drive 90 miles each way from Deal to Willesden twice a week and spent the night each time at my Willesden flat before returning to Deal, (where I had also visited him).

You will understand that all this gave me the opportunity to get to know a great deal about him and his background in countless conversations... So you should start by realising that the Gurdjieff group member who helped to prepare everything initially for them to hear of Subud was Bissing. In fact, he never mentioned the name of Bennett to me - and later confessed that he had done everything possible to prevent his hearing of it because he had had a long history of troubles, serious mistakes, causing accidents by misuse of the Gurdjieff method, etc. There were four Gurdjieff groups in England and Bennett's was ostracized by the other three (thus Bissing).

Gradually Ronnie introduced me to his sister Toska and her husband Aubrey Wolton, Dr. Alexander King based in Paris, Basil Fenwick, Reginald Hoare and Russian wife, Irene. They would all come to Dartmouth Road and join the latihan, Bennett had never been heard of while we were all practising...

A 16-year old Turkish Cypriot - Gökalp Kâmil, a Lycée student of mine had given evidence leading to the conviction of an EOKA terrorist. They threatened to kill him and I invited him to stay in my home with three other Turkish boys who were taking care of my place. One evening we went to the cinema and a boy found me to report that Greeks had come to the house asking for him. I rang up Hallinan who told me to bring the boy without delay to stay in his home: "If anything happens to that boy we shall never get any more convictions." It was decided to send G to continue studies in Bournemouth and the Cyprus Govt in London was told to appoint me his guardian. Meanwhile he too was following Subud. It was decided that I should spend Xmas in Jersey and he should come over by boat from Bournemouth.

Meanwhile, I was phoned by Hugh Ripman, another UK Gurdjieffite in London about to return to his World Bank job in Washington. He visited me, wanted more news about Subud and left. But before doing so he reported secretly to Bennett on what he had learnt. A letter came inviting me to lunch at Coombe. I replied that it was more appropriate to visit ME if Bennett wanted to learn about Subud and he came. During the course of the conversation, he admitted I had put him in seconds into a condition that normally took him up to hours to reach. So he wanted to join.

I told him of my Jersey plan and suggested he come down over Xmas for a discussion at my hotel, the Dolphin, right under Gorey Castle. He came, with Elizabeth "Howard" for two days. We walked up and down the beach discussing matters, and then he joined Subud in London.

Meanwhile, the other five Gurdjieffites following Subud there had expressed the wish for direct contact with Bapak. I told them he would gladly come if the means for suitable travel and accommodation were available for himself and Ibu. We held a meeting in Willesden to discuss the possibility and I invited Bennett also, pointing out to all the need for proper visa sponsorship. They agreed to share costs among the six of them. Then Bennett ventured sponsorship by "My Council" and Hoare countered that in this case, the others would all immediately withdraw their participation and support. Bennett said he would "eat humble pie". There was a joint invitation by all six; he had no more leverage than any of the others, less in fact as he was the latest addition to the band.

Bennett next brought up the Eva Bartok medical case, she was on the way to England. It was agreed that before any operation, she would come to Willesden to meet Bapak and Ibu for the first time, in my flat. Bennett brought her. I was the only local Indonesian speaker and naturally did all the interpreting. It was agreed to help her and she postponed any operation.

As none of the other five sponsors would set foot in Coombe Springs, a plan was worked out to divide Bapak's week commuting between Colet Gardens in London and Coombe as JB had meanwhile lined up 300 applicants for Subud, virtually overnight. Later he told me the situation was impossible and offered to put his entire premises *and staff at Bapak's disposal if Bapak would remove to live there. He did but I could not and would not - and they all started learning Indonesian...*

Fenwick and Hoare regarded me as having engineered the entire sinister plot and never saw or spoke to me again. Bennett used my absence and Bapak's virtual dependence on him to exert his influence to the maximum, progressively and methodically wiping out all possible traces of my association with the movement. The rest is known to you.

Hallinan introduced the Kibbles to Ronnie when the Bissings returned to Cyprus.

,,,Subject to the proviso that I refuse to enter into any further correspondence with the public or unknown persons on details of the above, I should have no objection to publication of the above account in the Subud magazine. When I assert that I believe all facts therein to be true and correctly remembered it may be recollected that nobody has ever known me to tell a lie about Subud and my place in it during over 50 years - and that my memory remains excellent and unusually retentive. It is made before God - for me that is much more answerable than any statutory declaration, I have no ambitions left in this world, I lack nothing that I need, I ask for nothing from anyone and I do not care who does or does not believe it. But I do care about my own responsibility to make one effort to set the record right as the wildest science fiction proliferates on all sides. I might die tomorrow, so I entrust this document to you to publish if and where you please without distortion or any curtailment that might lead to misunderstanding or ambiguity.

I believe you to be an honest man and a sincere friend.
Let me know in advance what you decide to do.
Regards

Husein
Kaneohe, Hawaii 11 April 2001

Extract 13 - **More on Husein Rofé**

Husein Rofé is a major player in the history of Subud, first of all because he was the first Westerner to have been "opened" by Pak Subuh in Djogjakarta and he was the first Westerner to carry Subud outside Indonesia to Japan, Hong Kong and then Cyprus. And finally to England!

Furthermore, as can be seen in the preceding extract, it was Husein Rofé who not only opened John Bennett, but also Aubrey Wolton, Reginald Hoare and Ronimund von Bissing, all students of the Gurdjieff methods and people who had worked under Ouspensky personally.

I count myself very fortunate to have been able to have had even a brief conversation with him at Coombe Springs and even more fortunate that I corresponded with him in 1958 and still have his letters. Luckily for me he is a voluminous letter writer, and these letters give an insight into his character.

What is certain is that though Rofé opened Bennett they never liked one another. That can be seen from the account that Bennett gave in *"Witness"* of his own opening. And of course, those who met both men in 1957 could see clearly the total physical and psychological differences between the two men. Bennett was an enormous man, some 6ft 3". He was a commanding personality. He was also clumsy and untidy in his dress. On the odd occasion that I saw him dress up in a dinner jacket it seemed almost funny, so out of character. One could never chat with him. One was always aware of the Work.

Husein Rofé on the other hand was not a bit like that. When I first saw him, he was dressed in smart tropical suits, and I noticed at once the expensive watch with a gold strap. He was then with a slight build and Levantine features. When he gave you his attention it was done with a smile to put you at your ease. He was a totally different personality to Bennett.

Now Bennett was a distinguished scientist and also a considerable linguist. Certainly he spoke French well enough to lecture in it; he spoke Italian, he spoke Turkish since at one time he had headed the British Secret Service in Constantinople, he had learned Russian, he even knew some Tibetan and I believe he could speak German. We used to say he could speak 20 languages, I say "we" meaning the young men who lived at Coombe Springs, but I have no idea what is the truth of that. Perhaps for us his most amazing performance was to learn Indonesian in some 3 months to the extent that he was able to translate for Pak Subuh, which is and has remained a sore point with Husein.

If Bennett could speak 20 languages, he could claim to be a linguist of some distinction. He once said to me that after the first five the others became easy. But Husein was in another league. He was and is a linguistic genius. I have a list of some 90 languages that he can speak. Actually that is not strictly true, as he himself pointed out to me. With some 30 of these languages he has recourse to a dictionary!! He is only fluent in a mere 60. I have been to his house in Sussex and one room is surrounded on 3 sides entirely by bookshelves and every one of those books is a dictionary. Since he runs a translating service, by which he keeps himself alive with the help of his assistants Riza and Yacin, he is constantly receiving faxes from all over the world. In any one language he may have 20 different dictionaries, in order to cope with engineering terms, chemical terms and technical terms of all kinds.

In 1993 I heard quite by chance that he was in England and phoned him to ask to meet him again. By this time he had completely forgotten me and the brief correspondence of some 3 letters that I had had in 1958. It was with some difficulty that I eventually got to meet him, since he was suspicious of people who wanted to waste his time in any way. He was a very busy man.

Once however he was assured of my continuing interest in Subud he relaxed with me, and there seemed never to be enough time for the conversations that we had. After a while we also met on holiday in the south of France. My wife, Eileen, also found him to be a totally charming person, always solicitous for our welfare, always proffering new insights, or new books, or different places of interest to visit. He was an inveterate traveller with an insatiable appetite for history in the places he visited.

Once when we were at Eze, the famous mediaeval hilltop town, we passed groups of people of different nationalities. Husein would break into Chinese or Japanese. One time we went over the border into Italy where he treated Eileen and myself to lunch and to a display of his Italian. Of Bennett's Italian he said that he, Bennett, had once joined in a conversation "quite well." One time when he was in Algeria a policeman speaking Arabic stopped him, who then complimented Husein on his command of the language. "You speak Arabic very well." "And so do you," Husein replied quickly.

On another occasion he was in Northern Spain and was eavesdropping on a conversation, by a group of men at another table. They accosted him. "Do you speak Catalan?" "No," Husein replied, "but I do speak French, Spanish, Italian and Arabic and I was therefore able to understand all that you said."

I once asked him how he came to learn his languages and in what order. Writing from memory now without recourse to notes he said something like this. Because his father lived in Egypt, he started with four languages, Arabic, Italian, French and English. He went to an English Public school and while the French lessons were on, he amused himself by learning Hebrew. He then learnt German and Dutch, then Russian, then he learned three Scandinavian languages all at the same time. After that I cannot remember, except I know that he certainly learned to speak Turkish, Chinese (of which varieties I am not sure) Japanese and of course, Indonesian. And Greek, I must not forget.

It is curious that Bennett should write of the "two Rofés." Of course there were two, just as there were two Bennetts and there are undoubtedly two Bright-Pauls. Just because a person starts on the Way, on a spiritual path, on a search for the Realities, does not mean that they have all at once become perfect. Of course not! Why else would people seek a means of self-perfecting if they were already purified? So it is a pity that after all this time that Husein feels badly done by Bennett, but then perhaps he had cause. That is not my affair. All I know is that Husein is by any standard a very remarkable person.

Like all linguists, he also had a wonderful command of his mother tongue, so it is appropriate at this point that we should see his own account of meeting with Pak Subuh and being opened in Jakarta.

The following is an extract from his book *"The Path of Subud."*

"A few nights later, in mid-January of 1951, I cycled across Djogjakarta after dinner, and arrived at Pak Subuh's home for my initiation. A number of Javanese turned up and sat silent and motionless in the sitting room, some with their eyes closed. I had never seen any women present on these occasions, and did not know if this was due to the Islamic segregation of the sexes or the nature of this particular form of mysticism. I was later to learn that this discipline was available to both men and women, but that Pak Subuh's wife took the women.

"Pak Subuh now entered the room and called me out, together with one other pupil who was popularly supposed to have been one of the most apt. This pupil, Sudarto, was about 32 years old and had been with Pak Subuh since the age of eighteen.

"We walked round to the back of the house and entered a garage that was covered with carpets, but otherwise quite bare. I was asked to remove my watch and any hard breakable objects in my possession.

"I was now asked to sit cross-legged on the ground and that I should try to relax my mind and body completely and to still thought.

"I closed my eyes and after a few seconds I was aware that Pak Subuh was intoning the Fatihah, or initial sura of the Quran, in Arabic.

"But now I was aware that something very strange was occurring. It was as if a powerful electric current was vibrating through my forearms. Suddenly a force quite independent of my own volition caused my hands to separate, my arms slowly expanding until they were stretched horizontally. They remained thus for a few minutes then dropped naturally to my sides. A little later Pak Subuh called out to me and I opened my eyes. The ceremony was over.

"In the sitting room I reflected on this odd experience. I was feeling quite strange and had no idea what had happened to me since nothing like this had ever occurred before. There was still a tingling sensation in my arms. I had not moved them at will, and was quite sure no human force had done so. What then had been this strange movement? When Pak Subuh returned to the room he explained.

"Man, he said, contacts God when his thoughts, desires and imagination are totally quiescent. I had been in such a state, since thought had completely ceased for a few minutes. This had enabled the divine Power to awaken within, and this Power would guide my every step on the spiritual path. Normally, human movements are the results of intention, they come from man, but this had been provoked by the Divine, not the human will.

"A few days later a couple of elderly Javanese entered his home to tell Husein that his arrival had interested them greatly. Apparently as far back as 1936 Pak Subuh had told them that one day a man would come from the West, of Syrian descent, speaking many languages, and this would herald the dissemination of Subud throughout the world. This struck Husein as very strange as fifteen years before he had been but a schoolboy.

"During the second session, which started under the same circumstances as the first, my experience was different. There were no arm movements, but instead of this my trunk began to twist and rotate rhythmically in an anti-clockwise direction. After a few minutes, this came to a stop and was replaced by a similar clockwise movement.

"It was not long before the content of the exercises developed into a dance—not of the western type but the traditional slow postures and gestures of the classical Eastern dance. I found that I could recapture and demonstrate these experiences sometimes, though much was only obtained under the control of an inspiration which I could not command.

"A more interesting series of exercises involved the voice, both in speech and song. Suddenly one night I sang involuntarily some ancient Eastern chant which also was suggestive of India, and this was followed by others of Jewish, Islamic, Javanese, Chinese and other types which I could not identify.

"At times when my voice was exercised I began to stammer out syllables with the ineptitude of a babe. It seemed that one had to grow up again as a little child. In the exercises I had to learn to speak all over again; I never used my own language."

It is recommended to the reader that they obtain and read the whole text of Rofé's book. The above selection has been made to show simply the experiences that Husein underwent, and which any member of Subud will immediately recognise. Everybody's exercises are individual, but there are some similarities. In my own case, it was some time before my voice was exercised and it is curious that I also speak in many languages, but rarely if ever in English. One day when I was to visit his home, Husein asked me to latihan with him. Since he was such a linguist I could not help asking after the exercise what I had said, hoping, such is our vanity, that it might be something special or profound. He was exceedingly bored with this request— oh! everyone asks me that! He went on to say that he thought they were primeval languages, but he did say that I had spoken seemingly about the Prophets in Japanese.

I think it was in '95 that I was able to arrange a luncheon at the Aurora Hotel in Windsor, where Husein Rofé was the guest speaker. Over the years, the groups had proliferated and many of the Subud members had never met Husein, some barely knowing of his existence. But then by the nineties there were also many people who had never met Pak Subuh and who were opened. And likewise there were many children of Subud parents, who did not need to be opened in a formal way, though most of them so elected.

Extract 14 - **Robert Prestie**

My great friend Bob Prestie died in the spring of 2002. Some time before, my wife Eileen and I had visited him in Las Vegas and stayed in his condominium. At this time he was, like his father before him, suffering from macular degeneration. On account of this, I had to read aloud a part of his book. In June 1957, he sent me the text of this book *"The Robert Prestie Autobiography"* which he gave and entrusted to me. It is a remarkable story, which I will endeavour to get published.

Very early in his life he had remarkable spiritual experiences, as the result he trained to be a monk. When the war came along, he joined the Royal Canadian Air Force, was shipped over to England, where he flew many bombing missions over Germany in Lancaster bombers. One incident that was never recorded in his book concerned a buddy of his who went absent without leave, and was determined to find a way back to Canada. Bob persuaded him to return to the squadron. The very next day, he was to see his friend blown sky high as the bomb load on his Lancaster exploded on the ground. This was one incident that Bob could never write about.

Hearing that J. G. Bennett was lecturing in New York, Bob accepted an invitation to come to live at Coombe Springs, where it was that I met him. I think that everyone who met him would claim him as a friend. He was that kind of guy. He was good-looking, he was a great dancer, ice-hockey player, in fact he was a good all-round sportsman, tennis, golf you name it. He was also a very talented musician of both jazz and classical music.

So he came to work at Coombe Springs to study the Gurdjieff methods and to do a great deal of work on the building of the dormitory block, and later the Djamichoonatra, the nine sided hall. He came for a few months but stayed for years, eventually getting a job in television, where he was able to use his previous experience. At length, feeling that he had learned all he could from John Bennett, he was about to depart for the mystic East to fulfil a yen that he had long nurtured. Bennett persuaded him to stay and that is where he enters the matter of this book: -

"We have a man coming from Indonesia who is bringing us some

My Stairway to Subud

spiritual work. I think this will interest you, so don't leave. He is coming in May sometime. I will let you know when."

It turned out that Pak Subuh, Ismana, Icksan, Rahayu and Rofé were arriving. Rofé was the man who had initiated all this. He had contacted the group leaders of the different major groups in London of the Gurdjieff people.

The group from Indonesia arrived on the 22nd of May 1957. Rofé apparently had acquired a small flat in Willesden. John Bennett told me that Bapak (Pak Subuh) was going to have a meeting with some men and probably ladies also. This was to take place the next

Robert Prestie

day, which was May 23rd. I had a show to do that night so I didn't think I could make it. At one time I had done a favour for Mike Sutherland, who was another producer/director friend of mine. He had to do something once and I did a show for him so he owed me one.

I picked up the phone and called him and said, "Mike, I have a show to do Wednesday night. It's all blocked out and all set. The production assistant knows all about it. So since you owe me one would you mind doing this for me?" "Sure, you're right. I do owe you one and I would love to do this for you."

So on May 23rd I hailed a taxi and went to this flat in London. I walked upstairs to this small flat and went into a tiny room. There was Hoare, Bennett, Bissing and a few other leaders of the Gurdjieff groups. Then there was this small Indonesian man whom they called, Bapak, Pak Subuh. I found out later that Sumohadiwidjojo was his real name. I know that for a fact, as I had to spell it an endless amount of times. Anyway, there was Pak Subuh and his wife Ibu, Icksan and his wife Ismana, a young couple who came with them and Rahayu, who was Ibu's younger daughter. The men were all sitting around together, no ladies. Just sitting there, so I sat down. No one said anything. It must have been about 6 o'clock in the evening and we just sat there. The other people were sort of chatting a bit.

Husein Rofè, whom everyone called Rofé, had arranged all this and he was doing the translating. He informed us that Bapak was waiting till the birds stopped singing. So we were just sitting there when Rofé said, "Ok, men, come into the next room." There were five or six of us who went into the next room. Then he said, "Take off your shoes and take off your jewellery, your watches, rings and what not, and stand over here."

So we stood in a line and there was Bapak, Icksan and Rofé in front of us.

Rofé said, "Now close your eyes, trust, submit and receive."

Trust? I trusted God all the time and I wanted to receive God all the time, of course. So I closed my eyes. A few seconds later, the same experience that I had had when I was twelve came through me. It just shattered me and threw me to the floor. I was sitting in the lion posture, on my knees, with my head down on the floor and my body began to vibrate and vibrate. I could feel this vibration like crazy. Gradually it subsided and I had this feeling of things being lifted off me. My gosh, all this garbage was being lifted from me. I felt exhilarated, euphoric and it felt fantastic. It was so good, so good!

I remembered when I was young and falling asleep, sometimes I would leave my body and float up to the ceiling and I would be watching my body go to sleep. I remember the lifting of my spirit out of my body, like this separation of spirit from body. I was floating there enveloped in this warm glow of love and peace and understanding and it was total bliss.

I began to mumble in some strange sounds. I don't know what the language was. The next thing I heard the word "Finish." Well, I did not want to finish. I loved this. I wanted this to go on and on and on. It was fantastic. Whatever this is, it is marvellous. It felt wonderful.

So we all stood up and retrieved our shoes and watches and whatnot, and we came back to the little room where we were sitting before. There was Bapak. He looked at me and we just nodded at each other.

Rofé said, "You had an experience."

I said, "Yes, I did and it was marvellous."

So Rofé told Bob to return the following Thursday when he had further experiences. Then he thought to himself that they were meeting in a tiny flat, whereas every weekend there were all those Gurdjieff students going to Coombe Springs. Now Bob knew nothing of the situation of the Ouspenskeyites vis-à-vis Bennett, and fearing nothing he rang Ronimund von Bissing, suggesting that he take Bapak and his party to Coombe Springs. He told Bennett, who said simply "Oh? Do you think so?" Little did he realise that at one stroke, he had severed the Gordian knot. And through him, at least in some small part, Pak Subuh's party came to stay at Coombe Springs in the flat in the west wing.

Later Bob went back to the States and was instrumental in setting up the Subud Groups in San Francisco and Los Angeles, ready for Pak Subuh to come.

Bob has another claim to fame, in that he married the famous authoress Taylor Caldwell. She was actually his second wife, but all that is another story that is told in his own words in his autobiography.

Extract 15 - **Soeparto in Japan**

There was a wonderful article in the Subud Chronicle of March 1961 entitled "Bapak's assistant comes to Tokyo" by Rin Jubishi. I will extract a piece of it concerning Mr Soeparto: -

One other unforgettable reference made by Bapak's assistant was to testing. The problem of testing has long been one of the most controversial topics in our Tokyo's Helpers' Meeting held every month. Some were of the opinion that we were not mature enough to trifle with testing. Others suggested that we should not venture to test from mere curiosity. Some others preached the importance of exercising testing in its simplest forms. However, Mr Soeparto simply "demonstrated" testing whenever a new question arose from somebody's mind. In fact he seemed to continue his testing every instant while listening to our multifarious queries. He even explained what testing was in a "kindergarten" manner, as follows: -

"As you know every part of your body should take part in the worship of God. But, you know, most of your parts are reluctant to do so. So, look here." Pointing to his own nose, he continued: "Oh my friend nose, will you show me how you worship God?"

His nose moved in a strange manner, which invited laughter from us. Then he gazed at his right hand, saying: "You too, my right hand!" His hand jerked, showing a joyful dancing movement. He even tried with his voice. "My voice, show me your way of worshipping God," he requested. A sweet heavenly song come out.

This is a very interesting variation on the testing that Bapak did with us in the very early days soon after being opened. The ability to receive these tests depended on the degree to which a person was purified, the degree to which a particular organ was alive. The Indonesians who had exercised with Bapak for a number of years had a remarkable ability to test at will and in all sorts of circumstances, as is illustrated by the above vignette.

Extract No 16 — **Bapak in Paris**

There is a wonderful talk by Pak Subuh, his second talk in Paris, which appeared in the Subud Chronicle of March 1961. When I first got to know Icksan Achmed he constantly referred to *"pembersihan"* or purification. In the West we have a rather sentimental idea of purification. In Subud, however, purification has a very definite connotation, referring more to the bringing alive of the separate organs. This is well illustrated by my first excerpt from this talk:

"Continuing about the work of the inner Power, it first of all pierces the coarse barrier, that is the energy at work in man when he walks, gesticulates and the like. Everything must be penetrated by the inner Power. And why? Because through touching and being touched impurities (faults) enter into our inner being. The sense of touch and all the five senses serve as doors for the entrance of impurities, which mind and heart transmit to our inner feelings. And these impurities have entered man's inner being; they have reached his innermost heart and filled his brain to capacity. Therefore it is necessary to cleanse away these impurities, to become pure.

The cleansing of all this has the following meaning: previously, your walk was activated by your desires; but since you have been doing the latihan it will happen at times that your walking is not activated by your desires, but, spontaneously from your soul. It is the same with your hands: previously, when you touched things, it was because you willed and desired it thus, but since you have been doing the latihan you may, little by little, touch something sometime, prompted not by your desires but by your growing soul. This goes on until the Power has pervaded all your organs, and in the end you will be able to see for yourselves that any action you may take, if it is right, is really guided by God: not your walking alone, and what you touch with your hands, but also your seeing, hearing and other functions.

This illustrated clearly that purification in Subud refers more exactly to the bringing alive of the various members, and the various functions.

In the same talk Pak Subuh makes clear something that has puzzled me for years. Pak Subuh has often said that the latihan works when the mind has ceased to work, but in my own observation my mind has often been quite active while my *latihan* has also been sometimes very active indeed. The *latihan* and my thinking and feeling seemed to be going along in parallel so to speak. In the next extract from the same talk Pak Subuh addresses this dilemma: *"Equally, if in your latihan your thought is still operating - in other words, if you remember events or things, or when your heart remembers events or things - let it happen; do not prevent it. If your heart and mind try to struggle against the activity of your thoughts, this does not lessen but strengthens this activity. Left to itself, however, it will gradually subside: the heart will cease to flow over for there will no longer be any receptacle into which the overflow of this activity can pour."*

In my experience it is strange how one's thoughts can continue and indeed one's awareness of others in the room, while at the same time being moved in various ways and being made to sing or utter sounds in different languages. As the latihan progresses it sometimes seems to change gear and the action of the *latihan* compels our attention and our feelings more and more, but the awareness of everything else, of the other members and so on never disappears completely from our awareness.

The next excerpt follows on directly from the above, but is concerned with formal worship in a Church or Temple and the *Latihan Kejiwaan*.

As for those of you who attend church or other places of worship - and many of you may be accustomed to regular attendance - there is nothing against it through what you have received in the spiritual latihan. If you feel allegiance to a church you should of course continue to attend worship. Only - while worshipping in church, Bapak's advice is that you should do whatever the service requires, but not the latihan, for the latihan is different. For if you were to break out in the spontaneous worship which comes to you in the latihan, you might startle and shock others who know nothing about it. For the latihan is worship as ordained by God Himself, whereas the services in the church and similar places are worship as organised by man; and although both forms of worship are intended for God, there is a difference between them.

The next excerpt, which actually follows directly on the above, contains something that is truly amazing, but is something that everyone who is established in the *latihan* can recognise straight away.

However, when the barriers which had obstructed your progress eventually open out before the consciousness of your inner being and you have reached the required stage, you will be able to enter into contact with your inner life whenever you wish. This means that you will be able to worship God in a dancing-hall or a market place, and of course you will be able to worship God wherever other people worship Him, as in a church. And if your neighbour worships in silence, you, too, will be able to remain silent, for you will already be familiar with the manifoldness, with the variety ways of worship and approaching God. Even - and Bapak really means what he is saying now - though you may have a quarrel or argument with a friend, this will not interfere with the worship of God, and you will remain in a state of worshipping. As it has been told in the chronicles of chivalry, a true knight will even in combat not forget to worship God; thus if he dies, he will be welcomed with open arms by God, and not out of pity.

I think that anyone in Subud can vouch for the truth of the above. I know very well that I have had strong differences of opinion with other members of the Group on policy matters, or sometimes (quite often!) with my own wife, but the worship of God is not forgotten. I have to put this in the passive tense, because it is not something that I do but more something that is there. This is difficult to explain.

Extract: 17 — *Water of Life*
The Opening of Hussein Rawlings in New Zealand

I turned up early for my opening, waiting parked outside the hall. As I sat there, reviewing talks with Helpers and questions asked, I considered a question not yet resolved. From my reading it was clear that in order for the experiences of members as reported during the latihan to actually occur, there had to be some kind of force or power at work. The process of being "opened" enabled one to engage with this force. The unresolved question was "Is the force of the latihan a force for good or evil?"

Usually I did not pray (being still in that confused state, uncertain as to whether God existed, but thinking that spiritual experience was possible!). However, as the day of the opening drew nearer, I had turned to Jesus for I thought he possessed a wisdom beyond normal human knowledge and intelligence. Inwardly I had asked that if the force in the latihan was the same or consistent with the one which he brought, to please provide a sign or somehow reveal this to me. That request had gone unanswered.

Sitting in my car I recalled this question, still hanging over me, unresolved. At that instant my head, seemingly of its own volition, was moved from its pensive position looking down over the dashboard, and raised and turned over my shoulder so that I looked through the side window and up into the sky. It had been a beauti-

ful spring day and the evening sky was clear except for one solitary cloud which I was now looking at. This cloud was in the shape of a cross, standing vertical in the sky. I looked in amazement that a cloud could be in this shape, and in such vertical alignment. As I watched, it was moving and changing very slowly (as clouds do). Slowly the shape changed as the cross-bar drooped down like arms on a body, and the top portion of the cross inclined forward resembling a man with head bowed, as in submission.

During the opening I did not experience anything in particular, but when it was over I noticed I felt very peaceful and deeply satisfied. Later that evening I realised that a burning sensation present in the region of my solar plexus or stomach for about 3 years had gone - and has never returned. This sensation had been like a smouldering fire, and nothing had been able to quench it. Doctors finding me clear of ulcers, but unable to identify the problem, had tried different medicines and pills—all to no effect—so I ceased looking for a medical solution. Whenever I listened to fine music or fasted or liberally blotted myself with alcohol, the sensation abated. Even during the last two years of my search when I gave up meat and alcohol the smouldering fire had remained. But that night, at the moment I saw it was gone, I realised this fire in my belly had been a thirst for "the water of life."

Extract 18 — ***Into The Light*** by Lucius Perham

INTO THE LIGHT

Dear reader and fellow Human-being,
(and any friendly aliens who happen to be taking their
annual holiday on planet Earth at the present time)
I really do wish you well.........

The following article, which also includes factual experience described in poetic form, is written for two essential reasons. Firstly that it hopefully may clarify some important aspects of the nature of Christ. Secondly, that it can give consolation and moral support to those people who, having had near-death, or out of the body experiences, had accounts of such quickly dismissed by skeptics, or those claiming to be experts in their field of work.

In my own case, the instance recorded was not a near-death experience, or self induced in any way. When it occurred, I was relaxed and participating in one of the Subud latihans (spiritual exercises) at a place called Coombe Springs, New Malden, Surrey, with a number of friends. As usual, after a short period of becoming at peace with ourselves, through a quiet relaxing of mind and body, we had surrendered ourselves in trust to God, silently asking for His Help and Power of Grace to work within us.

Individually, we began to receive interiorly, that extraordinary influx of spiritual nature which, in its Wisdom, seemed to understand the special requirements of the soul, and each person as a whole.

As I waited in quietness, my inner self and mind open and receptive to whatever God might work in me, the unexpected happened.

Suddenly, as I stood there patiently with eyes closed, I was aware that an inner body of light was rapidly ascending vertically out of me, moving towards an ocean of incredibly brilliant white light. At that moment, my consciousness realised it was entering into, also merging with, and expanding into this Infinite ocean of Light.

Like a rain-drop which, on falling meets the sea and becomes one with its immensity, so happened with me on a spiritual level of experience. The ocean, as I have mentioned, was brighter than the light of the sun. It was also the ocean of Infinite Pure Love and Peace, both knowing and seeing that it was everywhere, though not requiring eyes to see, as the ocean itself was the property of sight.

The universe, by comparison, is but a few specks contained within the vastness and magnitude of such power of Light, Consciousness and Love.

Regarding Christian understanding, although what I am about to mention here is of equal benefit to those of other true religions also.

It is written that we come from God and that ultimately, we will return to Him. We are also reminded that God is Love, and that there is a condition referred to as Eternal Peace.

.....Concerning Jesus, and the manner in which he is described as the Son of God. The experience granted to me, has helped me to personally know the reality of such a statement. A part of that Great Light and Love, conscious and aware of Its Godness and imbued with the characteristics of its Source, incarnated into the physical body of the person of Jesus, in order to accomplish the Creator's

wish and special purpose for Him.

This understanding given to me, as well as experienced by me in this incident, enhances my knowledge of Christ, and his manner of life and work while in this world. I sincerely hope that it may help others to overcome any doubts they might have regarding this matter.

In my own life, tangible spiritual experience has proved to be even more remarkable than science fiction. There really are degrees of beingness, and levels of existence ranging from darkness into Light, angels occupying their own sphere within the realms of Heaven.

(the poet Dante really did know a thing or two, didn't he ?)

Hopefully, my own contribution to modern day culture will be found useful, beneficial and interesting, and perhaps help society, where the need is present, to somehow regain its rightful place, as originally intended, in the Greater scheme of life.

INTO THE LIGHT

*One night, as I stood silently in prayer
the spirit which was in me
 soared aloft, as in a flash
into the 'inward' upper air
to merge with an ocean called INFINITY,
from where I perceived
 though not with 'instruments' of sight,
that I was endless brilliant LIGHT*

*Apart from this
I felt myself to ' BE ',
 for Consciousness Itself could sense and see
that I existed in that formless sea
as Love and Peace
in its Entirety........*

yours sincerely...... Lucius Perham

My Stairway to Subud

Part 3

Chapter 10

Forty-Six Year On.

It is now some 46 years since Pak Subuh first came to England in May 1957, and it is some 16 years since Bapak passed away. No longer are there headlines in the papers, as there were when the Eva Bartok story broke. No longer can Pak Subuh make those world journeys since he is no longer with us, in a physical form at least.

It might seem to those who visit the so-called esoteric book shops that Subud has vanished off the face of the earth. That is far from the case. In England alone there are some 62 groups in most of the major cities, some large and some quite small. There are groups all across the United States and Canada; there are groups all over South America; in Australia Subud is particularly strong and many Europeans who went to live in Indonesia for a while later settled in Australia. There are groups all over Europe, in France and Spain, in Italy, Germany, Holland, Belgium and Switzerland. There are groups in Greece and Cyprus. And further there are groups in India, Ceylon, Japan, and Hong Kong and of course in Indonesia itself.

What is interesting is to see the growth of new groups in lands that Pak Subuh was unable to visit, such as Russia and the one time Russian Republics, as well as many areas in Africa.

May one infer from that that Subud is growing apace? No. It is growing in some places and diminishing numerically in others, and a lot of the loss of numbers is simply through death. A lot of the original members who were opened by Pak Subuh and his Helpers have inevitably passed on and are due to go fairly soon!! Most of my friends and colleagues are in their seventies and eighties.

Has everyone who was opened stuck with Subud and continued to exercise with the *Latihan Kejiwaan?* No. From the very earliest days, in Indonesia also before Subud came to the West, there were those who were active in the organisation and active as Helpers, and those who left. There was and is no compulsion. I myself had a period of some years when I did not attend group *latihans*. I never for one moment left Subud, and was faintly amused by those who tried to get me back! Eventually my youngest daughter evinced an interest, quite on her own, to get opened and this precipitated in me the desire and need once more to get back to the *latihan,* which I did and also my wife, Eileen. Once my youngest was opened it was a great delight for me to see how readily she understood what Subud was all about.

Now in Part 2 of this book, I have put in a number of first experiences of the latihan, so that there are not only the record of my experiences of the "opening" but also of Husein Rofé, of John Bennett, of Victor Rainier Gebers, of Bill Ridwan Aitken and of William Robert Prestie, everyone of whom has been a personal friend.

Now the accounts of openings are no doubt unusual and strange, phenomenal, read from the outside, that is to say, read by anyone who has not experienced the action of the Great Life Force. *Hidup yang besar,* in Indonesian. One of my relatives once said, "What good has it done Tony, putting himself in a trance once a week?" So I have also quite often asked myself "What changes have occurred?" (Not a trance, by the way. The *latihan* is no trance.)

Actually it is not for me to answer that. It is also impossible to answer, because the *Latihan Kejiwaan* is the exercise of the *jiwa*, it is the exercise of the "inner content." What is clear is that in everyone this increases their sensitivity, their ability to receive indications. The examples of this are too numerous to mention because so many are coincidental. What is certain is that these coincidences, these inner guidances occur more and more frequently. That is, of course, if one is prepared to listen and be impelled or compelled by them. Because "The Empire Strikes Back," that is to say the Empire of the lower forces that inhabit us, does not easily give up its sway. The spiritual path is not a straightforward one. If it were, we would be surrounded by the Prophets.

It is often said that Subud is not a religion. That is absolutely so. Furthermore, not only do Subud members belong to every type of Christian denomination, that is to say Roman Catholics (I myself exercised with monks in the monastery of St. Wandrille), Protestants, Greek and Russian Orthodox, Quakers, Christian Scientists (which included my ancient aunt, who died at the age of 91) and so on, but also agnostics, which includes my own father, who also died at ninety-one, (but not before seeing the most amazing visions over a period of three days) and Muslims, Jews, Taoists, Shintoists, Buddhists, Hindus and Vedantins, and so on and so forth.

In Subud, there is no discrimination between the different religions because what comes to a person is really what is already there within him. So if a person is a Christian he will meet the real Christ within himself, and if a person is a Buddhist, he will meet the real Buddha within himself. The same if he is a Muslim, he will meet the Muslim within himself. And then, if you really know your inner self, you will be guided by the Divine Power in everything you do, because the Divine Power works in you through yourself, and whether you work in an office or drive a car or do anything else, you will be guided by the Power of God, which is always working within you and outside of you. (From an Introductory talk by Pak Subuh.)

What is more remarkable is that those who hold strongly to a religion need in no way desert their beliefs and their "credos." Not at all. In fact the action of Subud is such that a Buddhist for example will better understand the Eightfold Path; A Jew will also come to understand the inner meanings of the Torah. The same is true for every type of Christian. The Quakers search for the Inner Light. Subud will take nothing away from their great endeavours, but will enhance them. Undoubtedly they will better understand and even experience similar happenings to their great founders. Maybe, with the vibration of the latihan they will also "quake" or "shake" as did the original Shakers. Subud is not in any way inimical to religion. On the contrary, it can explain and reconcile many mysteries.

Here is a short excerpt from a talk by Pak Subuh in Santiago, Chile, in 1959, which is particularly relevant to our present times:

That is the difference between the Pharaoh and Moses, as recorded in history, or between the other leaders as Jesus and Mohammed. Those who are like the Pharaoh want power, want to subjugate their fellow beings, and want them to acknowledge their supreme power on earth. But Moses was different. Moses led and guided people to live in harmony, to feel compassion for the lives of others, to be able to truly worship God, and to believe that it is truly God who has the supreme power in human life.

This is the meaning symbolized by the story that the Pharaoh and all his troops sank into the ocean; that is to say that they sank into the current of subhuman forces that had influenced their inner feeling. However, Moses was able to avoid the current of seawater that was going to engulf him. He was able to separate the waters and escape. This means that God gave Moses the power within himself to be able to distinguish between bad and good, between that which was from a low force and that which was from a force from above—from God's will.

What is particularly interesting for those of us in Subud is the fact that Bapak was the supreme exemplar of "receiving." There are now some eight volumes of his talks. To the best of my knowledge Bapak never prepared a speech or made notes. What he spoke he received as he went along. I think, that for those of us who are Christians, it is truly amazing to see his knowledge and his insights into the life of Jesus Christ. In no way does Subud do anything other than increase one's respect and understanding of the teaching of Our Lord. In exactly the same way, Buddhists will feel about Gautama the Buddha, and Muslims about the Holy Prophet Muhammad.

Since I am not only (I hope) a Christian and a Vedantin, but also a student of the methods of Gurdjieff and Ouspensky, have I had to desert my understanding of any of these on account of Subud? Absolutely not.

Since I was a student under John Bennett of Gurdjieff's ideas, does it mean that I have deserted the ideas that I studied for some 7 years before the coming of Subud? Emphatically not. On the other hand my understanding of some of the fundamentals has of necessity changed.

What then of the cornerstones, what then of "self-remembering" and "self-observation?" Surely in Subud you do not try to remember yourselves? Not exactly, but then the whole problem in the Work was that no one was able to remember themselves. However in Subud it is often said that one can feel the "state of the *latihan*." Perhaps while I am typing this, I can feel the state of the *latihan*. When one does the *latihan* for a long time one can be accompanied by the state of the *latihan*. In my view that is exactly what Gurdjieff was after, exactly why he had exercises to help get a connection to the body. He was effectively trying to get a connection to the astral body, what is perhaps in Subud called the *"jiwa."* The big difference is that in Subud once one has been opened it is unbelievably easy to get that connection—so easy in fact that many people who have experienced this action do not appreciate just how remarkable that is.

What about "self-observation" and "work on oneself?" Well in Subud there is a totally different language, but consider the following words of advice by Pak Subuh about Religious Fasting, since many people in Subud do *prihatin* and some do *Ramadan*:

Those of us who have received the Latihan Kejiwaan have our jiwa trained, but our outer part also needs to do latihan to receive training, that is the fast. So there is nothing wrong with surrendering both inwardly and outwardly and doing something really in accordance with the path that connects the inner with the outer. So you will feel "When I am fasting how is my nafsu in relation to me?" "How is my nafsu in relation to me if I am not fasting?" "If I am fasting, how is my worship of God?" "How is my worship of God if I am not fasting?" You need to practice all that, brothers and sisters. Don't just be passive. Don't let us have the nature of material objects, not moving unless something moves them, no. We must move ourselves.

The *nafsu* are the lower forces, if you like, the mechanical or the satanic forces. What else is the above other than an example of self-observation? When I am fasting how is my *nafsu* in relation to me? I must add that when I first did the Fast for thirty days, and the truth is that I did not do it for many years, I was reminded at once of the Work that we used to do at Coombe Springs. So there are indeed efforts required in Subud, but they are efforts that arise entirely by an inner compulsion.

I must not pretend also that there are not some fundamental differences, the main one being that in Subud there are no Teachers, there are no Group Leaders, there are no gurus. In the *latihan* everyone follows his or her own latihan, everyone is doing something different. There is no director directing the proceedings. There is only receiving. There is a Teacher, but that is entirely an inner one.

Is there in Subud "friction," (*zirnofookalnian* friction) is there the struggle between "yes and no?" Well, the answer is yes, and most of the time we say "no." That is to say that if we surrender, that if we wish to surrender to the One God, well, the truth is that most of us just cannot do this, or I should say do it enough. Hopefully, we are surrendered bit by bit, according to our inner strength.

In the early days of Subud, particularly for those who had endured the rigours of life at Coombe Springs, many people felt that they had hit a spiritual jackpot. In spite of the fact that Pak Subuh assured us that we were not even in the classroom yet, but were like children peering through the window looking in at the school, it was still difficult to appreciate that there was a long, long way to go. Now that many years have passed have we reached the same impasse that was experienced by so many of the old Ouspenskyites? Indubitably not, for the very simple reason that no-one has ever depended upon anyone else. In the Bennett days a meeting without Bennett was considered a dull affair. None of the Group leaders could command our interest and attention in the way that he did, worthy as they were. It is true to say that in those days, many of us were totally dependent on John Bennett. He was our Teacher, just as Gurdjieff was his Teacher. In Subud it is totally different.

All and Everything is full of "Conscious Labours and Intentional Suffering" as being the prerequisite of making progress in the Work. No-one in Subud would remotely use this terminology, yet I will dare say that the labours of Pak Subuh were indeed Conscious Labours, and "conscious" in a way that perhaps only those who have been opened and are moved by, are compelled by an inner compulsion, can truly appreciate. And Pak Subuh is not alone. It would be invidious to name names, but there are many in Subud who command the respect of everyone, precisely because of the Labours that they perform when very often they could opt for an easy life

It is fundamental to Gurdjieff's ideas that the will of man is not free, that he is a machine reacting to external influences. Pak Subuh uses a different language but goes further, defining the forces below the Human level as the material, the vegetable and the animal forces. How far then is it possible for us to choose? It is clear that we cannot choose our own shape, our language, and the colour of our eyes. We cannot choose to remain eternally young and sexually highly desirable, but our teeth decay, our eyes grow dim, and our hair turns grey or white, or even falls out altogether. We cannot choose our talents. We are endowed with what Bennett called a "unique pattern of possibilities." We cannot choose to be wise if we are stupid, we cannot choose to be modest if we are vain. We cannot choose to be tactful if we are lacking in tact. What then, dear God, what then can we choose?

We have come full circle. When as a fourteen year old I whispered to Brooke-Little, "What is the purpose of Life?" he had answered, "To worship God." Well he was wrong and he was absolutely right. The purpose has to be to return to Our Creator. The same goes for the answer given me by the Reverend Scadding, "to love God."

Do those of us who are in Subud continue with the *latihan*? The answer is well, of course. But then how do you do the *latihan*? How do you actually start the *latihan*? As Prio Hartono said to Varindra Vittachi, "If I could tell you how to surrender it would no longer be Subud."

Back to Gurdjieff. Man has a certain choice of influences. The whole thing, all "work on oneself" consists in choosing the influence to which you wish to subject yourself and actually falling under this influence.

There it is. That indeed is our one act of choice. We can choose to do the *latihan*. We can choose to fall under a higher influence. We have no Will, but we can choose to surrender to the one Awake Will; in so far as we are able, we can choose to surrender to the One God.

Chapter 11

Pergi ke California!

There were two pieces of advice that Bapak had given me in 1957-58. The first one he gave me in the full presence of the Manchester Group as we were sitting *en masse* in his sitting room at Coombe Springs. Bapak said that Jesus Christ was the only man who had complete in himself both male and female natures, which was symbolised by the Sign of the Cross. "But as to Tony," he said addressing me directly in front of the others "he must get married!" At that time I was 28 and a Representative for Golden Valley Colours, selling Pigment Dyestuffs all over the North of England, from Liverpool across to Hull and then up to Newcastle and the Scottish border, while my works and Head Office were at Wick, Bristol.

This peripatetic type of existence, constantly staying away in different towns and cities in the course of my business, was a great help in the early days of Subud, enabling me to visit the various Northern Groups amongst others. I used to stay with the Widdringtons on their magnificent estate at Newton-on-the-Moors when I visited Newcastle and so could attend the Newcastle Group. On one occasion I also stayed with Kitty Trevelyan in yet another magnificent mansion, with great dragon's heads on the lawn. It greatly amused me to see that Lady Trevelyan, who was the archetypal English aristocrat, was also extremely to the left in politics, and the Trevelyans were also famed for rabble-rousing speeches down at the docks.

From Newcastle, I would go across to Carlisle and then south to Lancaster, where I had big customers in the linoleum business who bought tons and tons of South African Ochre. In Preston the huge Asphalt companies bought tons of Gulf Red Oxide from Musa, and in North Lancashire in the Paint industry I did good business with Leyland Paints and Walpamur, not to forget Godlass, Wall of Speke, near Liverpool. So I was also able quite easily to arrange my schedule in such a way that I could stay with my great friends, like the Bradfords at their home Catterall Cottage at Garstang. This was a large house with ample grounds where also Bapak had stayed and where Sjafruddin and Asikin were frequent visitors.

Maria and Eric Bradford became for me like new parents, as my own mother and father were away in Africa and I saw them rarely. I used to spend virtually every second weekend with them, the other being spent at Coombe Springs in the south of England. When the Midlands Rep resigned I was asked to look after Birmingham and the Midlands as well, and this meant that I was able to stay with the Essames, yet another Subud couple. It was with the Essames that I first began to watch television and to relish the current affairs programmes. I only mention this because in all my time at Coombe Springs I never watched TV and hardly ever read a paper, and only on one occasion watched a football match on screen. Subud was a liberating factor in many different ways.

As my company was based at Wick I was also able to visit the Bristol Group, making sure that my visit coincided with that of Bapak. And I did the same thing when he visited Edinburgh. Both of these are referred to in the foregoing Chapters.

Now when Bapak said to me *Pergi ke* California! You may imagine that that put me in a flat spin. The Indonesian language is such that that simple statement could be translated in a number of ways. Naturally, I asked whether I should make immediate preparations, but Bapak simply dismissed such an idea. In the course of time, a door would open and that would be that. In the meantime, he counselled *sabar,* which means patience, which has never been my strongest suit!

In the event things turned out just as Bapak had said, but in a way that was quite unexpected. A certain Ron Brandreth had come to Coombe Springs for the Gurdjieff work from the Isle of Man. He was in the Insurance business and I took a liking to him instantly. He had a girl friend in the Isle of Man, one Eileen Minay. No sooner had he settled at Coombe for the Gurdjieff Work than Subud arrived and he, like myself, was one of the first to be opened. Naturally he told his girl friend, Eileen, who promptly flew down to Coombe and was given an initial explanation by June Sawrey-Cookson. She returned a little later to be opened and also to stay at Coombe.

Unfortunately the rest of the story is tragic, since Eileen and Ron returned to the Isle of Man to get married, and on the very day of the ceremony, he was rushed to hospital, diagnosed with cancer throughout his body and given three months to live. Since I was in Manchester, I flew over to the Island several times to be with them both. Ron, in spite of his suffering, was very solicitous for my welfare, constantly explaining to me the things that the Island had to offer. In the event he lasted six months and in that time, I was to see Eileen in a special light, caring for a dying man.

It was only much later that I met up with her again and drove her south to Coombe Springs where she stayed. From there she took a job in the city, as she was expert at typing and shorthand, as one had to be in those days, before the advent of the personal computer and word processors. Still casting about for a job she applied to TWA who were recruiting Air Hostesses in England, since the Americans much appreciated the English accent and the manners of the English girls. There were hundreds of glamorous girls applying and at the end of her interviews she was told, "We'll let you know." Whereupon Eileen had the presence of mind to say, "I want to know now. Have I got the job or not?" There is nothing that the Americans appreciate more than a good closer. "You've got it!" was the reply.

Most of the time I only met Eileen when I went down to Coombe, but on this occasion, she flew north to Manchester to tell me the news. I think it was on the occasion of my next visit to Coombe that I took her out for a drink to the Duke of Cambridge, told her I had something important to say to her, and proposed in my car. Whereupon, she burst out laughing and I was somewhat put out by this hilarity and was inwardly saying, "Damn! Damn! Damn!" The next day I had promised to take her to the theatre, but in view of this refusal, I considered the theatre was off. I had not reckoned on Eileen, who reminded me of my offer with some glee, rejoicing it seemed in my discomfiture.

Some weeks later, I saw her off at London airport bound for Kansas City with a bevy of other beauties. Only then did she slip me a note to say "Yes"

Now by this time I had been seven years with Golden Valley Colours. I was earning a good income, relatively speaking, for the times. I had a car with all expenses paid, stayed in the best hotels when I wished to, and was earning good commissions with sales that had increased every year, and this in spite of the fact I had no chemistry and knew next to nothing of paint, oil and colour technology.

Eileen was some six weeks in Kansas City with some thirty English girls going through her training with TWA. During this time, we wrote each other copiously and I telephoned her from time to time. Nowadays it is commonplace to make transatlantic calls, but in those days not so. In fact one sometimes had to book a call with the operator and hang around for hours to get connected. Eventually, Eileen got posted to Los Angeles, the City of Angels.

Shortly after this, I was with the Bradfords at Catterall Cottage in Garstang, where I went to stay not just because I loved this couple as my own parents, but also because it was here that I was writing the original version of this book in longhand. And this dear couple had to listen to my writings every evening. Well, when Eileen got posted to Los Angeles, Eric turned to me and said, "Do you want this girl or don't you? There could be only one answer. The very next day I went to the American Embassy in Liverpool, and went through all the formalities of emigrating to the US of A. I also immediately resigned from my company, asking them to allow me three weeks notice, instead of the customary four weeks, so that I could avail myself of the cheaper fares.

Everything went well. I sold everything that I had except a small Oliver typewriter and took flight for America with one suitcase, one typewriter and £1,500 in cash, which in those days equalled $4,500. So it was goodbye to the Manchester Group and to the group of Helpers who had become close friends and goodbye to Coombe Springs, which had been the centre of my existence since I had first arrived there shortly before my 21st birthday.

However, the excitement of going to the New World and the prospect of meeting up with Eileen again, removed any sense of sadness at going. I was supposed to land at New York but for some reason the plane was diverted to Philadelphia, from where I caught the train back to New York. There I was to stay with my old friend Dan Cahill, who was the founder and owner of the Dharma Book Company, who eventually published my book in 1964, some years later. Now Dan was the lugubrious American who had stayed at Coombe Springs and amongst other things had worked on the Djami laying the copper roof, a skill that he had had to learn. We were not naturally drawn to each other as friends since he was taciturn and withdrawn, while I was somewhat more outgoing, but a chance meeting while in Paris on vacation changed things dramatically. Here I began to appreciate his droll humour and his dry wit. At this time, in Paris that is, he was still not experiencing anything from Subud. It was only much later when he had returned to the U.S. and rejoined the Merchant Navy, that he flew to California to have a word with Pak Subuh. By this time he had virtually given up on Subud. Quite suddenly he began to experience in such a way that the *latihan* became the most enjoyable thing in his life.

New York was unbearably humid, so I was driven out of town to meet Erling Week, whom Dan wanted me to meet. I stayed just one night before catching another plane to Los Angeles.

At LA airport I was met by Eileen, looking extremely smart in her beige and brown TWA uniform. By this time she had an apartment in 7th Street, Santa Monica, that she shared with three other Air Hostesses of TWA, two of whom were English. Eileen had in the meantime got me a tiny little apartment on 6th Street, not too far away, with a bed settee, its own bath and shower, and there was also a swimming pool for the residents. One could not help but be impressed at once at the ease with which everything was done in America. I had to pay up front a first and last month's rent and that was that. As for Eileen, she and her fellow Air Hostesses had first been shown an empty apartment devoid of furniture. When they explained that they needed a furnished place the agent took details of the furniture they needed and it was delivered that very afternoon. Shortly after this I needed to have a telephone installed, as the girls had also required. A brief visit to the Pacific Telephone Company showroom, which was completely devoid of personnel, and where I simply raised a phone in order to place my order, resulted that an engineer called the next morning, with his tools all hanging round his belt, who installed a phone and swept up any mess all in the space of five minutes! I had arrived in America!

I might also say that the weather was beautiful. It was hot but not humid, and day after day not a cloud was to be seen in the sky. I remarked on the weather casually to an American lady outside my apartment. "Yes," she said, "We've had real nice weather these last three years!!" Whereas in England, three days of sun are considered a heat wave, and anything longer than that calls forth warnings of drought.

Eileen's scheduling, pronounced skeduling, meant that she was away for two or three days at a time, as she flew to New York, Philadelphia, Miami, Kansas City, St. Louis and so on. So for my first few days in the States, I was on holiday, sitting on the broad beach at Santa Monica staring at the ocean. In England we go to the sea; it is typical of the Americans that they go to the ocean! In spite of the sunshine and the excitement of wandering around Santa Monica, very soon I was bored stiff. Besides which I needed to earn money, so I began to scan the papers.

That was another funny thing. In England, we have national papers. The Mirror, the Express, the Times and Telegraph are sold throughout the length and breadth of Great Britain. But in the States,

My Stairway to Subud

it is entirely a different matter. In England there is one time zone so that we don't even think of it, except when we have to adjust our watches one hour when we go on the continent. In the States, on the other hand there are four time zones and air hostesses have to be specially trained in order to cope with these time differences. Much later Eileen was to see the New Year in four times over, as she flew across the States. So returning to the matter of their newspapers, it was not unnatural that I had to be content with Los Angeles Times. Newspapers in the States are just enormous, and it took me some time to find my way around to the Job Vacancies columns. There I was immediately struck by the chance to earn $20,000 a year and up selling Real Estate.

One evening when Eileen was back in Santa Monica, we had started looking at a second-hand car lot, as I knew that eventually I would need to have wheels. A salesman, Bud Newby, strolled over and the next thing we knew all three of us were sitting in the front seat of a Chevrolet. In those days the nanny state had not been invented and there was a huge bench seat along the front, which easily accommodated the three of us, and of course it was automatic with power steering. Automatically I had got into the left hand side of the car, suddenly to discover that I was in the driving seat. "Come on, Tony, let's go!" yelled Bud Newby. Brushing aside my protestations that I had not driven on the right before, except on a motorbike in France, we set off on an excursion. This was my first taste of American confidence. You can do it! And I did it!

When Eileen went to the airport, she and the other girls had to catch the limo, but not long after I arrived, one of the crew members gave the girls an ancient Dodge, and as I was the only one who could drive, this gave me the opportunity to ferry the girls to the airport and also to go downtown to the Subud *latihan* with Eileen. By the way "downtown" was the centre of Los Angeles, some 25 miles away! In England, we talk of going up to town, if we mean that we are going up to London. For me, downtown meant the suburbs and not the centre.

Before we were given the Dodge, I had already rung up a Realtor in the San Fernando Valley in answer to his ad. To my surprise, he said he would see me that afternoon and described where his office was. This put me in a flat spin. I went back to Hastings Chevrolet. Across the street was a sign saying Cars for Hire, $5 and 5 cents a mile. I consulted Bud Newby about this as he sat on a bench outside his little office. "Here, Tony," he said, throwing me a bunch of keys. "Give me five bucks and take my car." Furthermore, he explained to me how to take the Freeway over to the Valley, go along Sepulveda Boulevard and turn up right to find my address.

If Santa Monica was hot, the Valley was blazing. You melted if you walked a hundred yards in the sun. My interview was successful, because it was unlike anything of the same ilk in England. I was told that I would be selling plots of land in the desert, that I would need an air-conditioned car in order to ferry my clients, but that first of all, I needed to obtain a Realtor's license. For this I would need to study and to take an exam in order to get my license. Even then it would only be a provisional license for 1 year, after which I would have to study again to take a much stiffer exam. But they would sponsor me throughout this process. So in a way I had landed a job, but like so many jobs in the States there was no salary, no car, no expenses but huge commissions once one had made a sale.

After about five weeks of studying Real Estate law, I went downtown to take the exam. I had some difficulty in this study, first of all, because I had never before read law in any shape or form, and secondly, because the American language is farther removed from the English language than the superficial similarities would leave one to believe. (Many years later, when I was 71 and bought my first computer, I encountered the same difficulty. What the heck is the default? In English one can be in default! What the heck is the Root Directory? And so on) The Americans understand their own language well, which in fact is well standardized from coast to coast through their schooling. Well I took the exam, which was full also of multiple-choice questions. This was an animal I had never encountered before, and I found, and I still find, this form of examination confusing. I failed by a couple of marks.

This meant that I had to wait another month to take the exam again. In the meantime, I was taking Eileen out on every occasion she was back in Santa Monica, and I was also getting to know her flatmates, who have incidentally become lifelong friends.

Eventually, I obtained my Realtor License while at the same time my sponsors went bust. That was a stroke of good fortune for me, as I did not really fancy selling land in the desert, and having to drive miles and miles in an air-conditioned car. These sponsors were, however, kind enough to recommend to me the firm of Gribin-von Dyl, who sold houses and had eight offices throughout the Valley.

A phone call elicited an interview with Ira Gribin the following day. That was slow by American standards, but what a relief after the mine fields that one has to go through in England with letters and CVs and let-you-knows. I revelled in the immediacy of everything.

The interview with Ira Gribin was no cakewalk. The Americans are simply not interested in English modesty and diffidence. They want confidence. They want what Gurdjieff called the sacred impulse of "I CAN." They want to hear it loud and clear. So Ira Gribin did everything he could to sell me off the job, because he wanted to get me off my seat to say, "I can do it!" I must have impressed him enough, but he insisted that I would have to move to the Valley away from Santa Monica. This I undertook to do, though with some misgiving. It meant that I would be the best part of an hour away from Eileen and her flatmates, with a drive over the mountains.

It also meant that I had to buy a car forthwith. In view of the small amount of cash that I had brought with me I was aiming at a car of around $800. I went back to Hastings Chevrolet and my old friend (by now!), Bud Newby. I had strolled around this lot a number of times and Bud had just watched me and never made a move or tied to pressure me in any way. But this time I was a buyer! Americans can just smell a real buyer a hundred yards away. Immediately he knew I was in earnest he said to me "Jump in!" and he took me in his car round to their garage. There sitting high up on a ramp was a 1959 Chevvy with white walled tyres, in light metallic blue, with the most enormous tail fins! Anyone who knows their automobiles will know what I am talking about. It was the most vulgar, the most brash, and the most exciting looking car that was ever made! I fell in love with it at once and parted with 1500 bucks just like that!

Now I had to fulfil the part of the bargain that I had made with Ira Gribin. I had to give up my lovely apartment on 6th Street and move over the mountains to the San Fernando Valley, which, to those who live in that neighbourhood, is known simply as The Valley, as if there were none other. I managed to find a lovely little Granny House at 15003 Greenleaf. The main house was owned by a legless Pole, a certain Mr. Ronk, who was confined to a wheelchair. In the middle of the garden, close to a large swimming pool, was this Granny house, which had its own lounge-bedroom, kitchen and bathroom. It was ideal. I had complete freedom to use the pool, and indeed Mr. Ronk really appreciated my bringing my friends there, especially Eileen. Also Bob Prestie later came over and he would immediately swim ten lengths without stopping, before shaking himself like a spaniel. At the bottom of the garden there was a long garage at the end of which there was another apartment all wood panelled, that had once been the library of the film star, James Stewart.

I was soon assigned to an office at Canoga Park, though first of all, I had to undergo some practical training with a fiery little tutor, one Guy Halperin, in Panorama City. There I was initiated into the whole practical business of selling Real Estate and in particular of selling "homes." We did not sell houses! Also I had to learn all about their special loans, like FHA and GI loans, as well as the conventional ones, running at that time at 6.6%. I also had to learn mathematics American style. I was used to Interest equalling PRT over 100, whereas Guy Halperin used a simpler more direct method. By the way in 1961 it was not only before the age of the PC, but it was also before the age of the Calculator. One still had to be able to work out percentages quickly and accurately.

Very quickly after a couple of hours in class, which normally started at 8 in the morning, one was out on the road. I had first of all to "caravan" all the homes that were listed in my office at Canoga Park. These were my stock, so to speak, but one could also caravan homes that were listed by other Realtors, if one liked to look of them, and one would leave one's calling card on the mantelpiece. At the same time while caravanning one had to look out for "homes" that had outside a sign saying, For Sale by Owner. This sign was for us an invitation to call and we were trained to try to make an appointment for a call in the evening when both husband and wife would be at home. I should mention that in most of the houses, the wife would be at home. All the houses had both an outer door and a screen door to stop insects flying into the house. So the housewife could safely open the front door while the screen door was still locked. Sometimes I would get invited into the house, with the words, "C'mon in! You're letting the heat in." It was that hot and everywhere there was air-conditioning.

All the Realtors in the Valley worked on a 6% commission. That is to say, that it would be 6% to Gribin-Von Dyl, in my case. If I listed a property and someone else sold it, I would get 20% of the 6%. In other words if a property sold at $20,000 (which was an average price in those times) then the commission for the company was $1200 and my commission would be $240 whoever sold it. However, if I sold my own listing, I would get an additional

38%, making 58% in all, or, if you can't work that out, a total commission of $696.

Obviously, the trick in all of this was to get as many listings as possible, so that your colleagues and other Realtors were selling for you, while you worked on something else and made your own sales.

The training took several weeks in Panorama City, while I was introduced to the colleagues in my own office at Canoga Park. The office was very simple, comprising about 10 desks with a passage down the middle. Outside there was parking space for our cars and those of visitors. I was introduced to the others in the office, including my manager Ed Morawey, a Pole, who sat on a chair at the back of the office, while I was right in the front with one Ruthie Brackman just across the aisle from me. This was very fortunate for I was soon to find that Ruthie was the most brilliant salesperson that I was ever to meet.

It is difficult to describe just how it feels to be on commission only, when one had been used to a salary, a commission, expenses and a car, as is normal in England. Besides which the sun was blazing, the valley was gloriously beautiful, the homes were out of this world and I was madly in love! It was a sort of intoxicating cocktail. It was easy to forget, if momentarily, that I needed to make sales in order to survive. And I was English. At five o'clock I would begin to pack up and then drive over Topanga Canyon the long way to Santa Monica. In those days Topanga was a completely wild canyon, and once one left the valley there was nothing until one reached the outskirts of Santa Monica, an hour's drive away. This was before the age of the hippies and flower power. Young Americans all had crew-cuts, many had become millionaires while still in their twenties, and they all believed whole heartedly in the almighty dollar. It was at the end of the age of complete confidence.

In a way, I epitomised something typically English. We English prize leisure. We prize our free time. Work is something to be got through, before we get to our tennis club, or to golf, or the opera or the wine bar, whatever it is to which one is inclined. But Americans are suckled on success. They start thinking about how they can make it almost before they've left their mother's breast. They are almost instinctively entrepreneurial, and for us amazingly egalitarian. For them it does not matter whether one is Jewish, Hispanic, Anglo-Saxon wasp, Irish Catholic, Russian, Italian or whatever, all that matters is that one has energy and that one has the energy of success. Gurdjieff had said that the world is divided into three zones. In the East feelings and sensitivity are most developed; in Europe it is thought and the intellect; but in America it is the moving motor centres, it is above all the place for action. Small wonder that the Americans had effectively conquered the world (and this was long before Afghanistan and Iraq) not by any military might, but by the power of the almighty dollar.

Very soon I had to shed my English skins, at least the outer ones, a bit like a snake. Survival was all. But when Guy Halperin in the course of our training said that we should take one day off per week, I wondered what he was talking about. He was serious! Gone was the holy weekend, which for so many Englishman starts at noon on Friday! In fact the one day when work was compulsory was Sunday, the day of the Institutional ads. That was the day when we all had to be in the office, for that was the day when a full page spread was done for each office, and it was the traditional day for Americans or at least Californians to house hunt.

It worked like this. If one had a listing, which was in the ad, then any call that came on the ad came to the listing person first. Otherwise, we took the calls in rotation. It was not long before I had a listing of a little two-bedroom log cabin up in the Chatsworth Hills, listed at $10,500. It pulled like crazy. This meant that I often got the first calls. My job then was to pitch my customer into the office, where upon I took him in my own car up to this little jewel on the Wohelo Trail. It took me best part of an hour to get there and when my client observed that there was brush all around and a high fire risk with little hope of getting insurance, I had to drive them all the way back again to the office. (It did eventually sell!)

In the meantime the other guys and dolls had been taking my calls and making sales. Not for one moment were they going to drive all the way out to the Wohelo Trail. No Sir! They qualified their clients.

It is just difficult for us back here in England to imagine just how ruthlessly, but how skillfully these colleagues of mine qualified their clients. What was a joy to behold was Ruthie Brackman herself in action. "Come in, you two kids," she would say to a couple of grey-heads as she motioned them to a chair by her desk. "Why!" they would laugh, "we haven't been called kids in years!" Then Ruthie would set to work. How much had they got to put down? Had they come from back east? Had they already sold? What was their income? (She had to know this in order to tell what sort of loan they could qualify for.) Only then would she take them in her car, to the homes for which she had an outstanding and prodigious memory. But all her qualifying questions were done with the sweetest of voices—she was just helping them not only to find the home of their dreams, but the one that they could afford.

Now in California, at least in 1961, there was no such thing as gazumping as we know it in England. If a client came in "as listed" the salesman could fill in the form, which was in triplicate, and the sale was made. The sales person could then go round to the house concerned with a sold sign and shoo any other salespeople out of the house.

I quite often saw Ruthie bring her clients back in to the office and they would sit by her desk. Ruthie would have her pen out in her hand and the triplicate pad open on the desk. "Well, Ruthie," the clients would say, "We just love that house. We would like to make an offer on it." At this point Ruthie's pen would be laid down on the desk. She would explain to them the loan of record, the amount that the seller would be able to take away from the sale; she would say that the "home" was listed so tight that you could not slip a nickel under the door. And then she waited. Finally the couple would say, "Go ahead!" and Ruthie would take up her pen and write.

Sometimes she would make 3 sales of a Sunday, more than the rest of us put together. For the rest of us, it would be a great day if we closed one sale.

In the brilliant sunlight it was quite a pleasant occupation, driving around and caravanning all sorts of homes that were absolutely beautiful to my English eyes. It was not too long before I made my first listing. I made the appointment in the morning to return in the evening when the husband was at home. Having made the appointment it was almost expected of the salesman to make the listing. And the salesman had one great advantage, or rather more than one. The salesman had buyers. The salesman also knew what were called the Comparables. (This was pronounced compaire-ables!) The Realtors in the Valley all belonged to the Multiple—that is to say, that all the listings of all the Realtors went to one central office. The salesman could then know ahead of his client what was the asking price of properties down the road, but more importantly he could also know precisely what they had sold for. Armed with this information, he could list "tight."

On the morning after my first listing, my manager, Ed Morawey, accompanied me to the home to measure it up with me. We were not only measuring the rooms, Ed was also checking out whether I had listed too high. Well, indeed I had, and after a few days I had to go back and get the listing down to a saleable price.

The speed with which homes changed hands would surprise people in England very greatly who often have their homes on the market for months. Happily, I have unearthed the complete record of the sales that I made. Example: 3 bedrooms 1 and 3/4 baths in Canoga Park, Listed May 20th, Sold May 24th.

Another example of interest to people in Subud is 23010 Dolorosa, listed by me on June 2nd '61 for $20,950. A group from our office went out early that evening to caravan the home. As they returned, Ruthie Brackman also returned to the office and enquired: "What's with Tony's listing?" They all agreed that the house was an unusually charming rustic in Woodland Hills and that it was really sharp. On that, Ruthie returned to her car and immediately went to inspect the house. When she returned she said to me: "Tony, I am going to sell your house." With that she got on the phone and called a prospect. Unusually for her, she gave the clients the address and told them to drive there straight away, as the house was so hot, it was going to burn down! Ruthie had to pick up her son from school. She returned to the office an hour later, when she got a call from her clients. Would she take in an offer? No way! The deal was signed and sealed on the morrow—listed June 2nd, sold June 3rd. Oh Yes! The house belonged to Livingston Dodson, one of the LA Subud Group.

As I said, I had to shed my English skin. I had to begin to work like an American, or rather I should say like a Californian. To illustrate this point, one Sunday we were all in the Office as normal and it was raining. This was completely abnormal. The brown hills suddenly turned green, the gutters were awash with water. The drains were so wide that a small body could easily have got washed away down them. And the Institutional ads were not pulling. We sat around playing cards.

I could not stand this so after a while I went to a tract (estate for you limeys!) where I had door-knocked before. That had been also part of our training—one simply knocked on doors to find out whether people were looking for a new home or wanted to sell. So I simply knocked on the door of a home where I knew that the couple were looking. I had recently listed a lovely property with a very pretty yard (that means garden) with a Japanese style bridge in the back. The couple were at a loose end too and jumped in my car to have a look at this house. No. I had flipped, but they did not. And why?

It took me a little time to realise that they lived in a Modern with beam ceilings. I will have to translate that into English. By beams, the Californians did not mean what we mean, as we think of the blackened oak beams of so many country pubs. No, they meant that there was no ceiling, so that you could see the joists or rafters. (In the valley, 99% of the homes were single storey, what in England we call bungalows.) And the house, instead of having the wooden tiles that typified the Rustic, had great white shiny rocks on the roof.

So I took them to another property that I had listed. This time it was a true 4 bedrooms modern. The furniture was low and sparse and they flipped. It was the same style as their own, the selling couple were young, there was the extra bedroom, but there was no pool. I took my couple back to their home. They wanted to buy the property if only it could have a pool like their own. I returned to the 4 bedroom Ponty, measured the yard, got an immediate quotation for a pool (remember, this was on a Sunday) and returned to my would-be buyers. Ok! The house was listed at $19,500. Would they take an offer? Would they take $19,000? I knew they would, but I upped them to $19,250 to be sure. So I wrote up the purchase of the home, and returned to my sellers. They signed off at once and the deal was closed. But my work was not finished. I returned to my buyers and listed their property at $18,250. So I then returned to my office. Each office had a sort of telex machine, which would chatter away as sales were made in the other 7 offices. This time I was able to feed in both a sale and a listing on a very wet Sunday.

A few days later, I was awakened when I had already gone to bed. It was another salesman from another Realty who had a buyer for my property. His buyer was coming in low to a GI loan, about $17,500. He was asking me to come over and help him present and close the deal. Of course, I was to represent the interests of my client. I think in this case, they had already waited 2 or 3 weeks and they were getting anxious. Once I was sure that the buyer was genuine and his finances checked out, I got up, went with the other salesman to my clients and we closed the deal about 11 o'clock at night! In that way I had lost one English skin and had become a Californian!

My Stairway to Subud

There is one other great difference to selling property in California and in England. And that is the Escrow companies. When the deal was made the salesman would put the deal of both Buyer and Seller to one Escrow Company. That meant that the salesman had control of the sale all the way to completion. If the Escrow Company found a difficulty, say there had been a Judgment against one of the parties, and there was difficulty in arranging a loan, the Escrow Company would inform the salesman and discuss ways out of this dilemma. This did away with all the business of to-ing and fro-ing that we have with solicitors in England, who sit on their fat bottoms writing letters to each other, fleecing their poor clients for all their worth. The Escrow Company dealt with all the legalities, and to my mind, performed in a wonderful, helpful, open way without any of the esoteric jargon so beloved of the legal profession in England. (Of course, I am generalising. Of course, not all solicitors are sharks or deliberately obscurantist, but there are a few. Yes?)

Incidentally, the rain that year resulted in a number of mud slides. The Californians love to build their luxury homes on the hillside. At this time, a number of people were crushed to death in their homes while they slept.

The commissions that we were paid were only normally paid on the completion of a deal. I was awaiting completion of my first deals when I had to pay my monthly rent. Unfortunately, although I was only a few dollars short, the Bank of America bounced my cheque. In England, I might have had a curt note from the Bank Manager drawing attention to my overdraft, but in California it did not work like that. I had no option but to go to see Ira Gribin and his partner Lou von Dyl. They promptly advanced me $200 to save the day, but they also took the opportunity to give me some advice! Wow! I was burning my gas! I was spinning my wheels! It was all good-natured stuff and it was all on equal terms. They wanted me to succeed, and in no way was I on the carpet in the way so beloved of English Sales Managers.

Incidentally no good salesman in the States would ever consider becoming a Manager! For them, a Manager is someone who is more or less a failed salesman. You can see their point.

One final point about Real Estate and the Multiple—the Multiple used to run breakfast meetings for all the Realtors in the Valley. At this breakfast meeting one could Pitch a Listing! This meant that one could go up in turn to the head of the long table, where there

My Stairway to Subud

would be fifty to one hundred Realtors and one could spout forth about the virtues of a particular listing that one had made. This invariably resulted in many salesman caravanning your listing and they would call you up or leave a note on your desk to say, "Terrific listing, Tony!" Can you imagine such a thing happening in England? Of course, all the properties were very new, 3, 4, 5 years old. If a property was more than 10 years old, the sales sheet simply said "older."

Some ten months went by in this way, all the time I was courting Eileen and together we would go downtown to the *latihan* in LA. By this time, the Popes had also come from England and had taken a place in a little canyon near Santa Monica. Also our great friend Peter Kermode, the impecunious, had also arrived. I tried to rush him into any old job, but he was having none of it. He was a sculptor and soon landed a job with Walt Disney making enormous models. It was not till very much later that I realised what an enormous talent he had. Sjafruddin also passed through, and I have a photo of him at Van Nuys airport with the Popes and the Jameses. Lonard James was a salesman at that time, selling light aircraft, again on commission only. I did not envy him his job, which seemed a lot more difficult than my own. He took us all up for flight, my first and last time I have been in such a tiny plane.

The LA group was very large at that time. We made a few friends, notably with the Jameses, and also Erling Week passed through, but I was pre-occupied with my job and courting Eileen. It was not until April 25th 1962 that Eileen and I finally got married.

It was an unconventional wedding to say the least. There were six other Air Hostesses, my best man, whom I hardly knew, and Livingstone Dodson from the LA Group. And there was no one to give Eileen away, as she walked into the Church supported only by her colleagues. In hindsight, I don't know how I managed it. I had a hazardous commission only job; I was fairly broke and ahead of me lay the prospect of taking a further and much more difficult exam to retain my Realtor's license. Furthermore, since my parents had been abroad almost the whole of my life, I had been at a boarding school from the age of four, and then at Clayesmore from 13 to 18. Not long after this, I had found Coombe Springs. So I was used to living in Institutions of one kind and another.

Eileen, on the other hand, came from a close-knit family in the Isle of Man, with her aunt and uncle living next door and her cousin, who was more like a sister. She understood very well the mores and general behaviour patterns that were expected of people, whereas my own upbringing had been unconventional, to say the least. I imagined that Eileen would soon come round to my way of thinking in almost everything. I could not have been more wrong!

So after a brief honeymoon where we drove up to San Francisco, via San Luis Obispo, and back down the Pacific Coast Highway again, Eileen came to live with me not in the small Granny house, but in a larger place at the bottom of the garden, which had once been James Stewart's library. Luckily Eileen, by this time, had acquired an amazing second-hand Cadillac which she would drive over the mountains to LA Airport with her accustomed verve, and, no doubt, with her accompanying Guardian Angel!

Two incidents happened fairly close together at this time. While at Indianapolis airport, her Boeing was just taxiing off, when she detected the smell of fire. Opening the loo door she found it was ablaze. She seized the fire extinguisher and sent a fellow air hostess rushing up to the cockpit to warn the Captain. The first Officer came sauntering down and then realised that there was a real emergency, as the cabin was filling with smoke. Immediately the flight was aborted, and the passengers evacuated down the chutes. This prompt action on the part of Eileen, no doubt saved the Boeing. As a result of this, we were both invited to a meeting in St. Louis where we were to meet Mr. Frankum and other bigwigs of TWA. We had no idea that this meeting was called specifically in order to honour Eileen Paul. (In California, I was known as Tony Paul, the guy with two first names!) In this event, there were many speeches with some hundreds present in a huge ballroom. Eileen, herself, was called upon to speak, after which we were both invited to a small dinner party with the aforesaid bigwigs. Alas we had both eaten earlier before the meeting, and I was able to do less than justice to an enormous peppercorn steak!

Not long after this, Eileen was in another incident at Chicago, where her Boeing slewed off the runway and almost piled into the adjoining Freeway. Luckily, the deep snow prevented a further mishap, but it took hours for the plane to be dug out of the compacted snow. This did shake her up a bit. A visit to the doctor resulted in the advice that she should lay off for 1 month. At the end of which time, when she visited the doctor again, he smilingly told her that she was pregnant.

So very soon after getting married, I had to face my responsibilities, for which in all honesty I was ill equipped. The prospect of my second exam was looming. In the heat, I was finding it difficult to study. In California at that time, it would cost $1,000 to have a baby. With two incomes our life would have been quite easy, but to rely solely on my commissions was a prospect that was too daunting.

In the event we decided to pack up and return to England. I wrote to Pak Subuh to tell him what we had decided and had a nice letter back. Pak Subuh approved. I had not asked what I should do and I think that Bapak always would approve anything that a person had decided on their own. It was perhaps a type of diplomacy. So we arrived back in England in December, taking the Polar route, touching down briefly at Montreal.

My Stairway to Subud

Chapter 12

Return to England

It was not unnatural that we should head for Kingston-on-Thames, as Coombe Springs lay on the bus route between Kingston and New Malden, and as both Eileen and I had lived at Coombe at one time or another and for me it was a natural stamping ground. We knew that we would have a number of old friends in the vicinity like Robin and Denia Mitchell, who later changed their names to Abdurrahman and Rohana, when they went to live at Cilandak. Eileen had actually shared a flat with Rohana Mitchell for a while before leaving for the States.

Besides which Coombe Springs was still functioning as the Headquarters of Subud in England, as can be seen from the following extract from the SURVEY BY THE CONSULTANT of 1960-61 for THE INSTITUTE OF COMPARATIVE STUDY OF HISTORY, PHILOSOPHY AND THE SCIENCES, which was the grandiloquent title by which Coombe was known. This was a typically Gurdjieffian type of title, since Gurdjieff's own place in Fontainebleau had been called the INSTITUTE FOR THE HARMONIOUS DEVELOPMENT OF MAN. Of course all these names were just a cloak for the real work that went on there. At one time Bennett had said to me that I was an "All-the-rights-possessing-Brother" (a direct quotation from *"All and Everything"*) before sending me off on some menial task.

The position of Coombe Springs vis-á-vis Subud can clearly be seen by the above-mentioned report, which was, of course, written by Mr. Bennett himself:

"The Institute had since 1957 provided a home for Subud in England. It had organized two world journeys for Pak Subuh and finally it had undertaken to administer and house the Congress. This work was undertaken in pursuance of the task to which the Institute was dedicated, namely research into the factors that permit the spiritual development of man. The Institute could not have opened its doors freely to Subud unless it had been free from commitment to any narrow interpretation of it Aims and Objectives.

The immense promise of Subud and the hope that it offered of making available to all people a simple, practical and non-sectarian way of spiritual development, led the Council to devote the resources of the Institute which had been built up over the years to the furtherance of Subud."

He continues later in the same report:

"We are constituted as a body for research and are recognized as a charity. As such we enjoy certain privileges, such as exemption from income tax, and we have corresponding obligations. Our field of research is defined as psycho-kinetics, that is the study of those factors that lead to the development and retrogression in the spiritual life of man. Most members of the Institute have experience of Subud, and are convinced that it is an extraordinary, if not unique, factor for spiritual development. Having found Subud, the Institute accepted the obligation for helping to make it known and established, but this did not change the character of the Institute itself as a society devoted to research.

"It so happens that such societies are within the general plan of Subud as described by Pak Subuh himself. At the Subud Congress Pak Subuh said that the Subud members should form groups of specialists whose aims are to advance their knowledge and improve their skills..."

The Subud Chronicle had been set up and was produced at Coombe Springs, with various well-known journalists on board, such as Bill, later Ridwan Aitken, and Hartley Ramsey. Coombe also undertook the reproduction and distribution of the *Pewarta*, the Subud journal produced by the International Secretariat in Jakarta.

I mention all of this to show just how deeply committed Mr. Bennett was to ideals of Subud, often having preceded Pak Subuh on his world journeys in order to lecture and explain Subud to large audiences, most particularly in the States and in Australia, prior to Pak Subuh's arrival. In fact Chapter 6 of this book shows just how Bennett led his own direct pupils into Subud, and how he was instrumental in going before Bapak in many places. Mr. B. as we called him, had an exceptionally imposing presence, and he was also an extremely good lecturer. He not only lectured in the States and Australia but also he lectured in Paris in French. He also had an interview with Steve Allen, the celebrated American talk show host, in which he gave one of the very best expositions of the principles of Subud, which is still valid today. I have such a recording in my possession.

So Eileen and I quickly obtained a maisonette in Kingston, with a typical forbidding landlady who made it clear that she would not

My Stairway to Subud

allow children, but failed to notice that Eileen was already some months pregnant. I immediately bought a second-hand Zephyr with which we went to the Isle of Man for Christmas in order to visit Eileen's parents.

After California with its continuous bright sunshine, with its houses which were all so new and so wonderfully equipped, with wall-to-wall carpets and "sprinklers front and rear," England seemed very grey and drab and the homes ill-equipped and tiny. We quickly found also that very few salesmen in England, certainly in the Department Stores, knew their products, which was in great contrast to their counterparts in the States. When we tried to get a TV on a month-to-month basis we were told that there was "no demand." In fact very soon we found that there was "no demand" for just about everything. England was very much in the grip of the "it won't work here culture." Enterprise seemed dead and conversation centred around the last night's TV show, still black and white in those days.

I quickly got a job up in London letting apartments at exorbitant rents. These old-fashioned, ill decorated places filled me with no enthusiasm, and my colleagues seemed a collection of "spivs," so that lasted only a few weeks. With the approach of fatherhood, I desperately needed a job, and I soon secured a post with "The Imperial Life Assurance of Canada." This post offered me a temporary salary of £120 a month, which after three months went up to £130. However this was only a temporary measure in order to allow one to get settled and make some sales, upon which one reverted to commission only.

By this time Eileen and I had moved out of our maisonette into a first floor apartment in Kings Keep near the Surbiton Assembly Rooms. If the move to California had burnt its brand into my soul; if marrying Eileen had made a total difference to my life; then the birth of my son Richard on March 22nd 1963 capped it all. In Wimbledon, Eileen had prepared everything in pink convinced it would be a girl. When Sister Camillus came to me and made me sit down for the news, she said, "Mr. Bright-Paul, you have a son." I must have seemed really stupid, as I struggled to take this in. I was so used to Eileen being right in all her premonitions that I burbled "A boy?" as if in disbelief. I had to be assured that this was so.

When within a few days I collected Eileen from the hospital we had to stop outside Mothercare in Kingston on the way home in order to buy a pram and a playpen and various other necessities, concerning all of which I was woefully ignorant. If I was totally unprepared to be a father, Eileen, on the other hand, was instantly and totally a mother, knowing by instinct everything that had to be done. However, I very soon became the dottiest and proudest father there could ever be.

By this time, I had made some progress with Imperial Life. I changed the old Zephyr for a new Mini, in those blessed days a mere £400 with petrol 4 gallons for £1! And I had made my first sales.

The training with Imperial Life was truly excellent. I remember that before I had left for California an Insurance salesman had called on me and left a leaflet. After he had gone I read this literature and was very impressed with it. But the salesman never returned and so he never made a sale.

Dickie Richards, my Training Manager, impressed upon me the importance of Income. The arguments for the taking out of Life Insurance were based upon trying at least to replace the income of the deceased. In order to get this over one had to take some rather dramatic actions, in so far that one had to picture what the situation would be had the principal earner in the family passed away the night previously. Exactly what would the situation be? What was the minimum income on which the wife could survive?

Luckily for me these arguments made sound sense, without which I would not have been able to pursue this profession. Even so, in spite of the training and in spite of my previous experience in four previous sales jobs, I still made mistakes. The principle one was that in the beginning I rang up old friends and asked them out for a drink or whatever, and only later in the course of conversation mentioned my new business. Of course, I was lost, completely on the wrong foot.

At length, I took a deep breath and did as I was trained. I rang one of my old friends and told him straight away that I was now with the Imperial Life Assurance of Canada and that I had some ideas that I would like to discuss with him. To my utter amazement he said that he had been thinking of taking out some Life Assurance for some time, so I agreed to meet him up in Hampstead that evening. When I put the phone down I danced round the office much to the amusement of the secretary bird. I have made my first sale, I declared. How did I know? Well, I did know, and that evening I made my very first sale to one Patrick Wynne, now Luqman, one of my friends from the Coombe days with whom I had had a great holiday hitchhiking in France.

The one great advantage that I had in England compared to California was that I knew a great many people. I had a number of friends and they have remained my friends to this day, and I also had a great number of acquaintances. When one goes to a new country as we did to California there is a great hole in one's background that has to be filled. Even so I still did pretty well in California. But here in England I was able to take advantage of the fact that I knew a great many people, and the Register of my sales that I have recently unearthed reads like a Who's Who? of Gurdjieff and Subud people.

My success was such that it was not long before I was on Commission Only once again. Imperial Life ran wonderful conventions for their more successful agents, and I was able to take Eileen with me on a wonderful visit to Amsterdam and the Daffodil Fields one year, and another time we had had a trip to Killarney. There were usually about 80 people on these trips which would be two or three nights away and they were great fun, especially for the ladies who had a chance to put on their best gear for lavish dinners and receptions.

My success was such that who should call me but J. G. Bennett himself, though selling to him was like selling to a typhoon. He insisted on grabbing papers out of my hand so that he could read everything for himself, and then congratulated me on being a natural salesman! It is sometimes said that people are either auditory or visual, meaning that they can take things in more easily through their ears or through their eyes. Undoubtedly Bennett had to see things. Much later I had a boss who was the opposite. No written memo would move him and you had to explain what you wanted with him face to face. All good salesmen know this fact and try to cover it by making their presentations both auditory and visual.

It is interesting that Bennett himself was fully in favour of Life Insurance, but mostly from a savings point of view. In Imperial Life we were trained to sell on Death Benefit, and only if that failed did we sell on savings, since there was inevitably some Death benefit thrown in. Much later I remember selling to a man who owned a building company in Bath. All my arguments to him concerning the situation of his wife and children in the event of his premature death proved of no avail. As far as he was concerned if he were to pop off suddenly his wife would have to look after herself. But when I explained the guaranteed loan values, which are a feature of the Canadian policies and the fact that they could be used as collateral, he signed up with me without too much demur. In fact some years later, when I moved to the West Country, he offered me a job and I worked for him for a few months.

So while Eileen was fully occupied looking after Richard, I was fully stretched selling Life Insurance in order to bring the bacon home. While I had some success nevertheless it was always a financial struggle, just to buy things like a fridge and a washing machine. We certainly got by, but without a lot to spare. In those days one could buy enough fish in Kingston Market for a good meal for 2 shillings, that is 10p in today's money!

In the meanwhile, I am talking now about 1963-4-5, the structure of Subud and Coombe Springs was changing. In particular the feelings of John Bennett himself were gradually changing in regard to Subud, he who had written *"Concerning Subud"* and *"Witness,"* he who had thrown himself totally into Subud, who had led his legions in, (who had joined Subud largely on his say-so and out of respect for him), he was cooling off.

There were many and various reasons for this gradual change. Subud had now been in existence in the Western world for some 7 years. Those who had experienced strongly in Subud had already become entirely independent of Bennett himself. Many of them had already headed off to Indonesia to stay at Cilandak; some to visit and others went to live there. Bennett had read the early copies of my own book and had even tried to help me get it published in England by sending it to Paul Hodder-Williams of Hodder and Stoughton, his own publishers. So he knew very well its content and even teased me by saying that now that Subud had come I no longer needed Mr. B. I was covered with confusion in making my protests. But what he said was exactly true, not only in my own case but in the case of many others. That does not mean that we were not grateful to him and indeed that we are still grateful to him even to this day. That is especially true of those who studied under him the Gurdjieff ideas.

However there was now a large body of people who had entered Subud not through Coombe Springs and not through the Gurdjieff work. In fact these people were at pains to make clear that there was no *per se* connection between Subud and the Work.

At the same time there were many who had not experienced

strongly, or perhaps not at all, and who still needed a Teacher and who wanted to depend on Mr. B. This was precisely what Bapak had warned me about, not to depend on anyone. He even said that we should not try to be like Bapak, that in the *Latihan Kejiwaan* we are introduced to our own real selves, that we were all different, in a word that we should all fulfil our own potential, or in Bennett's words the *"pattern of possibilities."*

It is easy enough to understand this, it is easy enough to understand that those who had experienced little would also hanker after having an external aid, an external Teacher, for this had been at the root of not only of Gurdjieff's teaching, and is also the basis of Yoga and the basis of Sufism. I am of course speaking of the true Yogas, like Raja Yoga, which are a means of making Union with God, and not the exercises that are taught in the West, which are derived solely from the postures of Hatha Yoga. In all these disciplines it is emphasized that an experienced Teacher is necessary, someone who could show the Way. Besides which there are some who by their very nature are followers and need to lean on someone. Bennett by his very nature was a leader and wanted to help.

It is easy enough, it is indeed facile, to say that Bennett needed to teach, that he needed to have disciples. That might have been true psychologically, (who are we to judge?) but what was also true was that Coombe Springs also needed finance and upkeep. So he also needed pupils, I believe, purely from a financial point of view. I have put in the words "I believe" advisedly, since of course, I know nothing of his personal finances, and I doubt whether he made a fortune from his writing. However, the finances of Coombe Springs itself are a matter of record and I have several copies of the minutes of the Council Meetings.

What is much more surprising in the case of Bennett is the degree to which he had committed himself to Subud not only in his world wide journeys, in his introductory lectures ahead of Bapak's visits, but also in the extraordinary experiences that he had personally. Here is Bennett in Cilandak with Bapak and a small group. He had been in Australia for the first big openings and Bapak had invited him to Cilandak on his return journey. Here he recounts one of his experiences: -

"Instead of replying directly, Pak Subuh began to tell the story of his own illumination. He described the night of June 22nd 1933, when he was overcome by such weakness that he thought that he must die. He lay down and his breathing stopped and he thought to

himself: "Soon my heart will stop, and I shall be dead." The next he knew was that he was out of his body and above the houses. He could see his mother go into his room and find his body laying, but not touch it. He went on to speak of his journey that he had made through and beyond the solar system and the mysteries that had been revealed to him.

"As he was speaking I noticed an unprecedented change in my own state of consciousness. I was no longer myself, but merged into the others. My body was not "my" body. I was aware of the inner state and even the thoughts of the others. I saw that most of them were in the same state as I was. Two were left outside, and I saw that it was because they had not abandoned their self-will. They were concerned with their own importance, with the place they occupied in Subud. They were afraid that I might somehow diminish their importance by what I was doing in the West. These thoughts made them opaque. The others were transparent as if made of light. I saw that they were free from self-will and were quite without concern about their own position or anyone else's."

Perhaps even more striking is the experience that Bennett relates in *"Witness"* when he had gone to Mexico to a group that had been well prepared by Mrs. Stella Kent, a former pupil of Maurice Nicholl. Bapak's party had arrived. On Good Friday, Bennett was doing *latihan*. He goes on:

"In the midst of the latihan I became aware of Jesus on the Cross and was raised up and entered His body, and looked through his eyes upon the maddened and uncomprehending crowd below. I became aware of the dreadful stench and of swarms of flies over the Body. Everything in me was outraged and disgusted. There was no mercy anywhere, nothing clean. And I knew that Jesus was aware of it all and infinitely more: all of human uncomprehendingness stretching away in time and place. I was aware also of the immensity of that love that could see all and forgive all. I noticed that my arms had been raised and that I was involved in the Crucifixion. Then I fell into a kind of unconsciousness in which everything became remote, and out of the darkness a brilliant light emerged, growing brighter and more and more glorious. In this radiance I was aware of the Other Nature of Christ; the glorious Divine Nature, untouched by anything that exists. Gradually the radiance rose higher and higher above me, and I was left behind. I became myself again, wondering what might be the meaning of what I had lived through."

With such remarkable experiences, with his closeness to Pak Subuh where he was often the interpreter, so quickly had he learned Indonesian, that one could never imagine that he would leave Subud. And in fact I always understood from the correspondence between himself and Pak Subuh that he had resigned as a Helper and that was all.

But the truth is that it went much deeper than that. The fact that Bennett continued with Groups of a sort for the people who were disaffected with Subud and wished to continue the Gurdjieff Work put him on a collision course with those who were not only totally Subud, but also had no relation to Coombe Springs whatsoever. This meant that he was deemed to be "mixing." The very nature of the Subud latihan meant that there were no Teachers and no teaching, just receiving. All the structure to which we are accustomed of leaders and lead disappeared and so the natural discipline that had kept Coombe Springs in place began to fracture.

Bennett expressed this dilemma better than I can:

"...but among those who had continued to practise the Latihan for two years and more, there was an unmistakable awakening of the religious sense: that is of a real and personal relationship with God. It was just this that made them feel that they no longer needed any human help.

This was admirable, but it was also devastating. We are accustomed to achieve our purposes through the exercise of authority, and the relationship of leader and led. The active minority, the oligarchs, and the passive majority, the demos or proletarii, had, for two and a half millennia, retained their relative status through all the changes of political and social forms. Those whom Subud had awakened could no longer tolerate this relationship. But if authority goes, society must either fall into chaos or rise into harmony. We could not tell which fate awaited the Subud Brotherhood."

Some years ago Kieron O'Byrne who had been in Liverpool in the same sort of position that I had been with the Manchester Group sent me a paper called *"Slaloming through the Boulders,"* explaining how he also came to leave Subud, though he continued to latihan on his own privately from time to time. I quote from the middle of this paper.

"At one time, so the story went, it seemed that Coombe had been

virtually taken over by Beatniks (this was the time of the Beat generation, before the hippies), who, so it was said, did nothing towards the maintenance of the house and grounds, contributed even less financially, then laid it all at the door of Subud. They were following their own indications by not working or making any contributions.

We in the brotherhood were a very liberal minded set of people, reflecting something of the attitudes of the times. In general, we thought that if someone asked to be opened then we would never have questioned their motives. And if members didn't feel inclined to help with anything, well that was just part of the process that we were all undergoing. We would never have dreamed that people would use the Subud brotherhood as a free ticket for bed and board. Even if they had, we would have reasoned, the latihan would soon show them a new path."

So it was that this alleged Beatnik invasion of Coombe was mentally tolerated by those of us not involved in the proceedings.

Later we learnt that not only was Mr. Bennett again running Gurdjieff groups, which seemed very much at variance with Subud, but that, as some report had it, Subud people were no longer welcome to use the latihan facilities at Coombe. This information, true or otherwise, only served to fuel this anti-Bennett attitude now being voiced in Subud. To my mind, if that were true, then it seemed at variance with what I remembered of a public meeting, held on the completion of the great hall, which was then named the Djamichoonatra, Mr. Bennett had then presented this building to Pak Subuh for the use of Subud.

There is some dispute over whether the Djamichoonatra or indeed the whole of Coombe Springs was given over to Subud, in view of subsequent events about to be related. However we can refer to the words of John Bennett himself in this respect, on page 349 of *"Witness,"* and the reader may interpret these words as he wills:

"A few days after the Gurdjieff anniversary, we invited Pak Subuh and his family to the Djamichoonatra, where, on behalf of the Institute, I offered it to Subud for any purpose it might serve. During the short talk that Bapak then gave, I became convinced that the building was contributing to the sense of harmony that we all felt..."

When Subud had started in England the old Gurdjieffites who had invited Pak Subuh imagined that they would bring to him people who were already prepared—that is to say, those who were already in the Work. They were therefore quite unprepared that Pak Subuh should say that Subud was open to anyone who asked to be "opened," and indeed there was one group who exercised in Ouspensky's former house in Colet Gardens where only specially chosen and vetted people were admitted. We, who were at Coombe Springs in those heady days of 1957 heard little about this group and really could not care less. I knew that Asikin sometimes went up there as a Helper and that he told me that it was not right. There were plenty of things "not right" in the eyes of the Indonesians and it is difficult to appreciate a totally Indonesian Subud attitude. They would often allow something to happen even though they did not approve. It is typical also that when Mr. B. would give explanations of Bapak's explanations, Pak Subuh, himself, did not approve this, but said nothing.

So it is not surprising that a great number of people came to be opened on the say-so of their friends and for a variety of reasons. It is likewise not surprising that a lot of silliness should occur. That is to say that a lot of people began to receive "indications" and to act on them in a perhaps irresponsible way. Or perhaps not, who am I to judge? But I take one more example from *"Slaloming through the Boulders."*

"...Ron was thought by some of us as having a quality of receiving better than most. He started to receive that he should give up his job and wait for God's guidance. This he did, in spite of the fact that he had a wife and a school age daughter to support.

In some ways, I was partly responsible for what happened next. One evening after the latihan, Ron informed us that he had received that he and his family should go down to London. Without it being said, it was apparent that he would need assistance in travelling to London. It also seemed that I should be the one to help with this.

So one day I took off work and drove them and their baggage down to London. Now we did not know where they should go, so in the end I drove them to where Varindra Vittachi lived, in Muswell Hill. He wasn't at home when we arrived but a small hotel close by was recommended. I dropped the family there, gave them a little money and started back home. On reaching Liverpool I went straight to Subud House to pick up my wife...

...And what happened to this family? (In this case I have omitted

their names.) Well, they moved around the British Isles and other places, were housed by various Subud members until the financial burden of these three extra mouths to feed proved too much and they were asked to move on. At one point in their perambulations they lived for several months on one of the Caribbean Islands and I think they also lived in America until their benefactors' money ran out."

This sort of behaviour did not only occur in England. There was a very amusing article in the Subud Chronicle by Isaac Gerson, showing that the same sort of behaviour also occurred in Ceylon, by people justifying all sorts of actions that arose from their own desires, by claiming that it arose from "indications from within."

Was it this sort of behaviour that led to Bennett cooling off from Subud? Even now when I look back on his writings, when I read the glowing accounts of the 1959 Congress, where he showed his evident respect and love for Pak Subuh and his admiration for the ways in which Bapak had answered so many questions, when I remember how he had said to me in the garden at Coombe on the occasion of his birthday, "I never thought to see such a thing in my lifetime!" When I think of all this, I find it difficult to reconcile myself to the events that followed.

What is certain is that while Patrick Wilson was acting as Warden at Coombe Springs, JGB prevailed upon the Bradfords of Garstang to come south and to reside at Coombe. In a sense, it was Eric's job to cleanse the Augean stables of the layabouts—the aforementioned Beatniks— who had taken advantage of the house and grounds. It was no doubt a "labour of Hercules."

During this time 1963-64 I was personally much concerned to establish myself in my job with my young son and wife to care for. Certainly I remember taking Richard in his carrycot to Coombe Springs and Bennett getting on his knees to examine the baby more closely, as was his wont. Also there was a lot of correspondence between Bennett and Dan Cahill in the States, the owner of the Dharma Book Company, at this time. Dan was very keen that I should represent Dharma in England, but Bennett opposed this idea, writing that "Tony is not a team player." I could take no exception to that!

Only many years later was I to read in the excellent anthology compiled by Ilaine Lennard, entitled *"In Those Days"* the transcript of the exchange of letters between John Bennett and Pak

Subuh. With the permission of Ilaine Lennard I am inserting here the entire script of the letter dated 18th December 1964.

Kepada Bapak jang Mulia,

Will Bapak kindly give me a decision about my position as a Subud helper? Elizabeth joins me in asking this question.

Husein Rofé opened me in 1956 and in June 1957, Bapak made me a helper-opener, the first that he appointed in England. Since then, I have myself opened many hundreds of people all over the world and have been present at perhaps two or three thousand openings with Bapak and others. I have continued to open people here until recently, but now feel my position needs to be made clear.

One reason for this is that I have heard—though not directly from Bapak—that Bapak does not agree with the way the work is now going at Coombe.

I would, therefore, like to explain what has happened. After nearly five years' experience of Subud during which time I was relying exclusively on the latihan for my spiritual development, in other words, I did not do any kind of spiritual exercises except the latihan, I discovered that things were not going rightly with me. I was growing weak and lazy and not fulfilling my duties in life properly. I tested about this and received a very clear indication that I should return to the spiritual disciplines that I had been practising before Subud came and that I had learned mainly from Gurdjieff. When I began once again to practise these disciplines my state improved and after a few months I was convinced that this was the right thing for me, and I have continued ever since.

Meanwhile, a number of other people were having similar experiences, and many came to ask me for advice and guidance. I did not say or do anything until I was fully convinced by my own experience that work on oneself in a disciplined way is really necessary. Before the end of 1962, I had no longer any doubts and therefore I agreed to begin once again to arrange groups and start movements classes for all those who wished to participate. The movements I refer to are those which Bapak himself saw quite often when he was here in 1957.

Now, at the present time, more than a hundred people who have been opened in Subud are coming regularly for psychological groups or movements classes at Coombe Springs and in London.

From my careful observation I am quite sure that these people are deriving benefit and hardly anyone who has started coming to these groups has stopped because they felt in difficulty from the side of the Subud latihan. More recently, that is, in the last year and a half, I have come into contact with a Source of the ancient Sufi Tradition, which has strengthened my conviction that the work requires something more than the practise of the latihan alone, and this is the chief reason that I am writing to Bapak now.

If Bapak has no objection to my continuing the work of the groups and the movements and similar exercises at Coombe Springs, I am quite willing to remain as a Subud helper; but if Bapak does not agree with this, then I would ask him to allow me to cease to be a Subud helper, so that there can be no ambiguity in my situation. I want to feel that I am quite free to tell people that my experience has proved to me that one cannot have a balanced spiritual development without properly regulated disciplines.

Elizabeth, who has read this letter, asked me to say that she would like Bapak to decide about her also, as she is in the same position as I am. We both of us wish to express our gratitude to Bapak and Ibu for what they have brought us. We were very sorry not to have the chance to speak about these questions when we met Bapak in Paris this year: but well understand that he was busy with the problems of Subud International Services and other matter connected with Administration and Finance. We hope that all goes well with Bapak and all his family, and that he will be able to visit us again before very long.

Sembah sudjud, John and Elizabeth Bennett.

I have read and re-read this letter many times. One little sentence keeps bothering me. *I was growing weak and lazy and not fulfilling my duties in life properly.* Really Mr. B.?!! It is just impossible to imagine John Bennett, that great workhorse, being weak or lazy. Then again, *I discovered that things were not going rightly with me.* It does not seem to have occurred to him that it might well have been precisely because he had started again Work that came from the "outside," from the heart and mind, that he was feeling at odds with himself. That the two kinds of work do not mix is clearly illustrated in the reply by Pak Subuh:

Cilandak, 13th January 1965

Dear Son,

Your letter of December 18th 1964 has been safely received by Bapak. You are hereby informed that the information that you have received from someone, as you mentioned in your letter, is correct. It is quite true that Bapak does not approve of a helper mixing theories of spiritual teachings with the Latihan Kejiwaan of Subud.

As you know the Latihan Kejiwaan of Subud does not come about from the efforts of the heart and mind. Rather does it come from the Grace of God through our complete surrender to His Will. Thus, as a matter of fact, the only principle of the Subud latihan is total surrender to the Power of Almighty God. This means that we surrender ourselves inwardly and outwardly with sincerity and submission, to the power of Almighty God, and we do not use our minds. And since the awakening of the inner feeling is brought about by the Grace of God, it is clear that our worship of Almighty God is itself guided by Him. Certainly if the Latihan Kejiwaan of Subud which we receive and practise arises from the very beginning due to the power of Almighty God, our worship will naturally be directed towards the One who guides us: Almighty God Himself. This is the aim and principle of the latihan kejiwaan that we have received. Therefore, if we still use our heart and mind in receiving the latihan kejiwaan of Subud, it means that we do not really believe in the Greatness of the power of Almighty God.

We have been convinced by the proofs that we have received that if the latihan kejiwaan progresses slowly it is not because God denies us His Grace, nor is it because the latihan we have received is the wrong way. Rather it is because our own state is such that we cannot receive smoothly. This is evidence of the greatness of God in that His guidance is adjusted according to the ability of each one of us to receive, because He is All-knowing and All wise.

This is Bapak's explanation to you. Bapak does not want to prevent a Subud member from mixing spiritual teachings with the latihan kejiwaan of Subud. But, Bapak does not know why, but he feels that it is a great pity that such a member still does not understand the truth of the latihan kejiwaan of Subud which exists by the Grace of Almighty God. But son, Bapak does not want to bind anyone and make him feel unfree. He may act as he likes. But if such a member is a helper—which means that he is in fact Bapak's helper—and Bapak himself is the guide (pelatih) of the Subud Spiritual Brotherhood and the first one to receive the latihan kejiwaan of Subud, it will be very strange if his helper who has the responsibility to help with the Latihan Kejiwaan of the Subud brothers, still uses something else. This is why Bapak does not approve of, nor permit, helpers acting not in accordance with the duties and responsibilities of a helper of the Subud Spiritual Brotherhood.

And now, Son, regarding yourself: if you still wish to use something else other than what exists and occurs in the Subud latihan, Bapak accepts the resignations of yourself and your wife as helpers of the Subud Spiritual Brotherhood.

Bapak thanks you both for what you have done during this time of responsibility as helper of the Subud Spiritual Brotherhood. Besides this, Bapak, still as your father, prays that you and your family will always be well and happy.

From Bapak.

So Bennett resigned as a helper, but the big drama was yet to come. Marjorie von Harten and Melissa Marston McLeod were two sisters who were in the work with Ouspensky at Lyne, where Melissa also knew von Bissing, though such was the discipline there that they rarely spoke. Marjorie died some years ago but Melissa is still alive in her 97th year, and has given me permission to quote from her book. The sisters were the children of one Charles Marston, the son of John Marston, the founder of Sunbeam cycles in Wolverhampton. Relatively speaking I think one could say that they were rich. However it might be, they travelled extensively, whether to the Holy Land, to South America to visit the Mayan pyramids, in fact they travelled all over the world with consummate courage visiting all sorts of archaeological sites. The extent of these journeys can be read in the book *"My Life a Spiritual Quest"* by Melissa Marston McLeod. I have had the good fortune to be able to visit Melissa from time to time at her home near Guildford. After her studies with Ouspensky she joined up with Bennett in the period when they were making visits to Mr. Gurdjieff in Paris. Like Bennett she was also opened in Subud and travelled again widely in the early days helping in the formation of various groups abroad, in North America and South Africa.

Now Melissa was a member of the Council and also a major contributor to Brookhurst Grange, the Subud Nursing Home that was set up, but which later failed. She has remained even to this day very catholic in her appreciation of all those interested in things of the spirit, whether it is the Shivapuri Baba, or Sy Baba, or Mother Meera.

Now Bennett in his letter to Pak Subuh referred to a Source of the ancient Sufi Tradition, and this was none other than Idries Shah. It was Mr. Reginald Hoare who first told Bennett about the existence of this man. He was convinced that Mr. Shah had been sent west by an esoteric school in Afghanistan. Idries Shah never claimed to be a Teacher, but he did say that he had been sent by his own Teacher and that he had the support of the "Guardians of the Tradition." I quote now directly from p.210

"Due to extreme pressure from Mr. Shah, Mr. Bennett understood that Mr. Shah not only wanted the use of Coombe Springs, but he wanted the property himself, not only access to Mr. B.'s pupils, but the right to take under his own wing any that could be useful to him. This could be the chance for Mr. Bennett to liberate himself from any attachment to it - he had lived there since 1941 and expected to die there, and he was deeply attached to it all and especially the Djami which was his own inspiration. Nothing could be harder than for Mr. Bennett than to walk out and leave it all.

By June 1965 Mr. Bennett had to convince his Council that it was right to let Mr. Shah have Coombe Springs, and later that summer the last seminar was held and Mr. Shah came to talk to the students, where he conveyed to them the importance of his mission and created a sense of urgency. In October of that year, an Extraordinary General Meeting of members was held to give away their most valuable asset, Coombe Springs. There were, of course, some members who wanted to compromise, but Mr. Shah insisted that it should be all or nothing. Finally the decision was taken and preparations were put in hand for its inhabitants to move out. Mr. and Mrs. Bennett found a small house at 23 Brunswick Road, Kingston."

There was at least one voice that was raised in objection and that belonged to my great friend, the truly honourable Warden, Patrick Wilson. Was he the lone voice who cried out that Coombe had already been given to Subud? Certainly, if not the totality, certainly the remarkable nine-sided building, built in the form of the enneagram, had been formally given to Pak Subuh by Bennett himself.

I have heard three accounts of that extraordinary Extraordinary Meeting. I was told by one person, who does no wish to be quoted, that when Bennett handed Idries Shah the deeds, Shah handed them back, whereupon Bennett duly scratched something out and wrote in the name of Idries Shah. Another account that I had from Richard Bigwood was that Mr. Bennett wanted to hand over Coombe but still as a centre for psychokinetic studies, as per the constitution. Idries Shah wanted none of that—if it was a gift then it had to be a gift without conditions. My friend, Kieron O'Byrne, also volunteered that there was some difficulty owing to the constitution of the Institute as a charity.

I never have met this Mr. Idries Shah. I did call one day at Coombe Springs, which was empty save for him and one John Bullock. I asked John what exactly happened with Idries Shah, whether he held groups meetings and so on. I gathered that he simply told everyone to get on with their own business, and John Bullock being in the Work naturally assumed that this was all part of the Sufi treatment.

Certainly Mr. Idries Shah got on with his own business and with the uttermost speed. Within months, two months, three months, the real estate was sold, the Djami was pulled down and destroyed and 28 luxury homes were built on that site. Only the Spring House built by Cardinal Wolsey remained and remains to this day.

It is interesting to see how these events are viewed from another perspective, that of George Bennett, the elder son, whom I have known all these years, since I remember Elizabeth sitting in on our group meetings prior to his arrival in this world. I remember him as a boy at Coombe Springs, and certainly there was one time as a lad he once had an interview with Pak Subuh to ask his advice. Both George and Ben travelled with Elizabeth and John Bennett on some of the journeys round the world. Those who know George always feel that he is very open, but naturally he takes the part of, and is protective of, his father's good name. This is how he saw the events just related, culled from "http://www.bennettbooks.org/AboutJGB."

Then later in 1957, Bennett shook the whole place up with his involvement in Subud, a spiritual movement that had newly arrived from Indonesia. For a number of reasons, Bennett felt that Gurdjieff had expected the arrival of a teaching from that country; and having tried the Subud spiritual exercise himself, he threw himself with characteristic energy into helping Pak Subuh, the movement's founder, disperse his teaching. He travelled extensively to spread the Subud message, both with Pak Subuh and on his own. He learned Indonesian and was so able to translate Pak Subuh's lectures into various languages. Bennett's own introductory book, Concerning Subud *sold thousands of copies worldwide.*

Some of Bennett's pupils were dismayed, and his enthusiasm for Subud deepened the divisions with some of the other Gurdjieff groups in London and Paris. Subud, with its emphasis on submission to the Will of God and its reliance on a single practice, the latihan— seemed to some to be the antithesis of Gurdjieff's methods for spiritual awakening and many people left the Coombe Springs groups. Others, however, came in large numbers, and for several years Coombe Springs was the headquarters of the Subud movement in Europe. It attracted serious seekers and sensation seekers as well as unsolicited newspaper headlines. But by 1962, after devoting himself selflessly to its growth and expansion, Bennett left the Subud organization, feeling that a return to the Gurdjieff method was necessary.

But by the mid-60s, although the work at Coombe had gathered new momentum, Bennett was ready to make another change. He and his groups had become involved with Idries Shah (who is now very well known as an exponent of Sufism, but who was then just establishing himself in England), and once again Bennett offered his help. Along with the Institute for Comparative Study, he proposed giving the whole property of Coombe Springs over to Shah. It seemed a ridiculous notion, for the land was becoming very valuable, but nevertheless, in the Spring of 1966 the gift was made. But, after Bennett and some of the Coombe Springs residents had moved into a house in the neighbouring town of Kingston-on-Thames, Shah, subsequently, and in short order, sold Coombe Springs for a housing development!

So ended a remarkable piece of history for many hundreds of Seekers after the Truth!

Chapter 13

Family Matters

Just how my ancient Aunt Belle came to be opened in Subud, I cannot now remember. I cannot imagine that I persuaded her in any sense, since she had her own very distinct views on life and death, and her own views on religion in particular. In my pacifist days, after leaving Claysmore and while working as a navvy I had lived with her and her lodger, a Welsh teacher. During this time I had had many conversations with her and mostly they were about Principle. She was a devout follower of Mrs. Baker Eddy; in a word she was a Christian Scientist. Through her, I did attend one lecture, which was formal in the extreme. The talk lasted exactly one hour, including a very brief introduction. It was well prepared and so neat, so clean and so well mannered.

So how exactly it came about that my ancient Aunt at the age of 89 or 90—I cannot be exact—asked to be opened, I cannot remember exactly. Nevertheless, ask she did, and Margaret Wichmann, who had done so much to look after Mrs. B. at Coombe, and Maryam Kibble, duly made their journey to 15 James Lane in Leyton, E.10 in order to perform the opening. (Incidentally, both these ladies went later to live at Cilandak, in the early pioneer days.) This was shortly before the demise of Coombe Springs, for my ancient Aunt came to stay with Eileen and myself in Kings Keep, when Richard was 1 year old, that is in 1964. I was curious to know how she reacted to the opening and all she said was "What beautiful singing!"

Our flat was centrally heated, whereas 15 Jimmy, as we called it, had gas lighting. When I lived there there was a wonderful kitchen range, all shining black, which never went out and kept the whole house warm. The tiny kitchen then was a cosy and jolly place and was used as the sitting room, the front room only being opened up on formal occasions. But as she grew older my Aunt replaced the range with a gas stove in the little rear kitchen and some of the soul went out of the place.

Eileen and I used to visit her from time to time, not very often I regret. In those days before any motorways it was a long haul to get to the East End. So that when my ancient Aunt came to stay with us for a few days in Surbiton in a centrally heated flat, she was just like a little girl, absolutely delighted just to be warm. Those who have seen the series *"Upstairs Downstairs"* will recognise

My Stairway to Subud

how it must have been for those who worked downstairs, for that was exactly the lot of my Aunt. She was a maid in some big house in London, cleaning out the grates and lighting the fires. When the master and mistress were out she would steal some time at the grand piano. Eventually she learned to play the flute when in her thirties to such a degree that she was employed to play in the pit at music halls, and eventually succeeded in obtaining a post in the first women's orchestra, which played at the Queen's Hall. On one occasion she went to the ballet a Sadler's Wells and was driven all the way home to Leyton in a Hansom Cab, that is, a horse drawn vehicle. One of the male members of the orchestra accompanied her and attempted to kiss her goodnight, but she would have none of it. He was a married man!

I think it was Maryam Kibble who collected my Aunt from our flat and took her to Coombe to exercise in the Djami, but she did not comment on the experience. She was the eldest of the children. She had three sisters of whom I met only Aunt Ruby, the youngest, and she was seven years older than my father. For a large part of her life, she devoted herself to caring for my grandmother, who was bedridden. Her life was one of absolute service, but she never complained. She was intensely interested in ideas and used to love to listen in on the discussions between my father and his friends, when he was a young man. In spite of her poverty, her place was immaculate, all the linen ironed with the old flat irons, before the age of electricity. And as for her, she was always interested in everything, always merry, always gay, before that word came to be defiled and have a totally different meaning.

At the age of ninety-one she died, an old lady with the soul of a little girl. May God bless her and may she rest in Paradise.

If the opening of my Aunt, who was such a devoted Christian Scientist was strange, the opening of my father in Cape Town was even more so—there could be no chance of my influencing him by proximity at least. We were separated by thousands miles and we were separated by more than that. Throughout my whole life, I doubt whether I spent as much as six months in his company. As a young man, he had worked mending telephones in London on a pushbike, before gaining a Silver Medal, which enabled him to get a post in the Colonial Service and to get posted to Ceylon, where he married my mother. When I was young, he was already Chief Post and Telegraph Engineer in the Gold Coast, only returning to England every eighteen months for short stay. When the war started and I was nine, he had to hasten back to Africa and I did not see him again until I was sixteen. He did not stay long in England but retired first out to Mombassa, then Dar-es-Salaam and finally Wynberg, Cape Town. In each of these places, they had the old-fashioned manual telephone exchanges, in which my father was an expert. Cape Town was the very last, so my father went on working into his eighties.

Now whereas my ancient Aunt Belle was devoutly religious, my father, on the other hand was truly agnostic, I might even call him consciously agnostic. He was weaned on George Bernard Shaw and H.G.Wells and all his friends were inclined to the Left, more or less Fabians. So how it came about that my father got opened, I cannot for the life of me remember. Saxon Aldred, who was one of the young men at Coombe, with whom I once went on a holiday to the South of France, (two up on his 350cc AJS) was and still is an organ builder. He met my parents while doing a job in South Africa.

The curious thing was that my father apparently had no reaction to speak of in the *latihan*. Nevertheless, my agnostic father, who himself declared that he had no clairvoyance, no religious or mystical leanings whatsoever, quite suddenly had a series of amazing visions and experiences, the like of which I have heard no where else.

There are quite a number of people in Subud who have left their bodies; some have travelled great distances and at great speed beyond the solar system. My father's experiences were not quite of that ilk, but were nevertheless extraordinary. One day in his late eighties he had been unwell and off his food for a few days. He had a flat in Wynberg, one floor up. My mother had died and he had a housekeeper, Milly.

Well one morning he woke up and found that there were two Indonesian gentlemen in his flat prostrating themselves. He waved his stick at them. Milly entering the lounge from the opposite side could see nothing. Then my Dad found that he could see right through Table Mountain and could watch the ships on the other side. Then when he sat down ladies in Edwardian dress came floating into the flat and sat opposite him. On one occasion a cat entered the room and my father bent down to stroke the cat, which arched his back as if he was a cat in reality. On another occasion he saw builders building a rough wall outside his flat, he saw bullock carts below such as were used by the Boer voortrekkers. The amazing thing about all these visions is that he recounted them to me on tape cassettes, which I still have. This was a way we had of corresponding with one another, and he eagerly looked forward to the tapes that I sent him. This meant that I could question him about his experiences, and ask him whether they influenced his views of the after-life.

When I listen to these tapes, when I think of how little I ever did for him, I am ashamed. Though he was going blind and although he was fairly deaf, all these tape cassettes that I am listening to again some twenty-five years after his death are filled with joy. What a wonderful life he had, he declared. How lucky he had been. Every letter declared his interest in our house, in the work that Eileen was doing, and he followed every thing that my son Richard was accomplishing. Never on any tape, never was there any moan or railing against fate. As to his own death he already talked about that with equanimity.

Not long after Aunt Belle's visit to us, she died at the age of ninety-one. We were still in a rented flat and Eileen was determined that we should buy a house. As good fortune had it Kingston Borough were at that blessed time offering 100% mortgages, we were able to buy a little house near the gates of Richmond Park for the sum of £4,675. Our friends the Mitchells amongst others were corralled in to paint the interior and to overcome the garish mix of colours, which we inherited. Shortly after our move, our daughter Lisa was born in January 1966.

My job selling Life Insurance was going pretty well, as well as it needed to support a growing family. In less than 2 years we sold up and bought a new house in Walton-on-Thames, making a small profit of a few hundred pounds on the first little house. It was not long before we decided to make another move, a much larger one, when we bought a house in the extremely charming village of Blagdon, in Somerset, some twelve miles south of Bristol. This was a much more major move, which involved my changing offices, as I now had to work out of the Bristol office of Imperial Life. I also had a new young manager who was less experienced than me. In Kingston, my manager was Adam Holberton, who was quite a character. He was a brilliant salesman and knew well his Life Insurance and the law pertaining to the same, but he often rubbed me up the wrong way. He would come to my desk and we would have a row, I would follow him up to his office where we would have another blazing row, then he would come down to my desk again and we would go out to lunch together, almost arm in arm. He was irritating, he had dirty fingernails, he read smutty magazines, drove his Mini-Cooper S like a maniac, but he was stimulating. It is curious but when he was my manager, I could work like fury, even though he roused me to fury on occasions.

In Bristol on the other hand, my new manager was more in awe of me than I of him. That was no good for me at all. And gradually I lost interest in the job, and it was a grind to go out at night into Bristol, where also I had very few contacts. Of course, there was the Bristol Group and I was able to catch up with my old friends the Penseneys and the Leasks.

We had barely been in this idyllic place one year, before I changed horses and began selling filing cabinets for The Shannon Limited. After some five years of selling Life Insurance it was a bit of a relief to have a job that could be done in normal daylight hours when offices were open, and it also supplied an extra car, which was a great blessing. It also meant that I could enjoy social occasions without "prospecting." In life insurance in those days, we were always on the lookout, always looking to exchange addresses, so that at some future date, I could ring up for an appointment. It was a relief not to have to do that any more, though the pressure to make sales appointments in the day was still the same.

We were expected to spend Fridays making appointments by phone, and the Sales Manager could later call you at any time to spend the day with you, unexpectedly. I must have done fairly well, since some 10 months after beginning with The Shannon Limited I had a call from a Mr. Smalley, the Sales Manager in London. He wanted a Manager for the Leeds Branch. He liked a man who knew his own mind, and he wanted an answer on the morrow.

Now of all the places we had lived since California, this house in Blagdon was the one that Eileen liked the most. Everybody loved to visit us because of the idyllic surroundings. Richard was going to the village school, and beginning to talk broad Somerset. We had also met up again with Enid Temple-Cotton, who invited us to stay at the Fruit and Flower Farm at Branscombe, an offer that we accepted and where in fact we spent holiday after holiday.

The idea of going back to the North again, after my seven years in Manchester did not appeal. But we were both influenced by a curious happening some days before Mr. Smalley's offer of promotion. A young girl gypsy called at our door one day, saying that she was the seventh daughter of a seventh daughter, and she had something to tell us. No sooner had she begun than her mother appeared and thrusting her aside, told me that we would not be going to

My Stairway to Subud

Australia (we had in fact been discussing this possibility and Richard had even written about it in his school book) that I had never worn a helmet, and that this house we had we were going to leave and so on an so forth. It was a truly dramatic encounter with these two gypsies. Furthermore she rounded on Eileen to say that she must never stand in my way.

So, though we were both loath to leave our lovely house, the very next day I accepted the offer and agreed to move north. There was another factor. Eileen gave birth to our third child, Alexandra. She was the only one at whose birth I was present, all dressed up in a gown. That same day, I had made a decent sale of some steel desks to Rolls Royce! So now there were three mouths to feed.

I had to go north ahead of Eileen and scout for properties. Eventually we found a house in Knaresborough, and missed out on one in Harrogate, because the vendor upped the price by £300 at the last moment. I was scandalised and would have none of it. This was just prior to the first great housing boom. We bought at about £6,000.

The departing Sales Manager in Leeds undertook my training for a couple of weeks. Immediately I came to see the vast difference between the Yorkshireman and the West Countryman. The West Country is known as the salesman's graveyard and for good reason. The Bristolians and those of the surrounding areas would be very charming but were very difficult to nail down. Have I got a prospect? Well, it was difficult to say. I would not say they were sly, but there was born within them a native cunning. The Yorkshireman on the other hand was proud of his brass. When one came to the showroom and asked the departing Manager the delivery time of a certain large filing system and then left, I was appalled. Why had my manager not closed the sale? Why had he not taken the order? But, my manager protested, he had the Order. The man had left his card and that was it! I had never before appreciated what a difference there is between the regions of England.

Eventually, Eileen joined me in the North and I would go to the Bradford Group on occasions. My son Richard soon began to talk like a tyke, my daughter Lisa went to her first school, and Eileen was much occupied with number three, who was at a most charming stage.

In sales there is always pressure and Mr. Smalley never let up. He would ring daily to get a progress report. I soon learnt that it was fatal to admit that there was nothing much on. So I always had a

My Stairway to Subud

list of prospects by the phone. Sales Managers only like good news, even if it's just a cloud on the horizon. Over him was a Sales Director and he was even more fearsome in a different way. Luckily, I was helped by a curious factor, which was Rowntrees of York. I managed to sell them a great number of desks. For some obscure reason, the Directors of Shannon wanted us to sell their files and filing cupboards above all, but once I got into Office Furniture, I had found at last something that I could sell with pleasure.

We were up in the North for a couple of years. One day I had to attend a Sales Conference, which was held in a hotel in Richmond, Surrey. When I rang Eileen that evening to say that it was balmy warm, that I had strolled by the river and heard the owls hooting, her discontent boiled over. She did not care for Yorkshire and wanted south again. So it was that somehow or other, I managed to get a transfer back to London, and we bought a little house in Farnborough for some £10,000.

Each time we moved we went to a different Subud group, though I must say that I never felt at that time that I belonged to a "group." I felt strongly that I belonged to the Subud Brotherhood firstly, and to a local group only secondly. At that time there was a group that met in the Friends Meeting House in Guildford. I liked this group very well. Since there was only one place for the *latihan*, the ladies exercised first and the men followed later. Though this was inconvenient for some, from the time point of view, it had nevertheless many advantages. While the men were waiting they could chat or prepare themselves. When the ladies came out they prepared tea, and so at the end of the *latihan* there was a certain amount of socialising. I personally thought that this was all to the good, that the men had a time to be by themselves and likewise the ladies, and we all had a chance to be together if we were so inclined. This meant that we got to know each other rather well.

In my outer life things changed. We moved house yet again, but this time within Farnborough to a house with a large garden, which we still have more than 25 years on. The Shannon Limited for whom I worked was taken over by Carson Office Furniture of Basildon. I was transferred into Carsons, without a by-your-leave, and my pay simply emanated from Basildon. I began to work out of a lovely showroom in Victoria and covered South West London. This was a period of intense activity and my sales and income rose year by year. At the same time, the demands of a young family never ceased, and one after another the kids went through sixth form, then University, each one of them getting good degrees.

In the mean time on the Subud front, with the demise of Coombe Springs, the whole centre of gravity of Subud changed. Pak Subuh made one world journey after another, and planeloads of people went to visit him in Cilandak for various Congresses or to stay there for *Ramadan*.

The absence of Coombe Springs as a meeting place left an emotional hole for many people, and I am bound to say that many, many years later my closest friends are those with whom I worked and struggled in the days before the advent of Subud. The exceptions to that are those Indonesians whom I met with in the early days, such as Haryono and Ismana and my dear friend Asikin.

I saw Pak Subuh on several of his visits to England. Eileen and I once went to Redington Road, Hampstead, when Richard was very young. Ibu took him in her arms and made a great fuss of him. I was outside when Pak Subuh passed me, accompanied by Pak Usman. Bapak invited me upstairs but I declined, fearing that Eileen would not know where I had gone. Usman then tore me off a strip, to use the colloquial, and it is true that for many years I felt that I had lost an opportunity. Many years later I was to meet Usman and to remind him of his rebuke.

In spite of attending various odd gatherings at Tunbridge Wells or Slough, it sort of got around that I had left Subud. People began to ask me when I was coming back. This amused both Eileen and myself. We had not flown to Cilandak for the simple reason that with our growing family we could not afford to. At the same time, there was something within me that rebelled against the current fashions. Many people changed their names to Subud names. Bapak himself explained vividly that there was no compulsion about this, but that some people, for example, might have been given a name of a famous film star (say, Marilyn Monroe) while by their inner nature they were more inclined to be a nun!! Much laughter. There were many people who hated their names and were very pleased to change and be given a Subud name. Bapak himself said that my name should begin with P., but though Haryono used to call me Petruk, who was a sort of clown in the *Wayang,* I could never bring myself to ask for a new name. I have often wondered whether I might have made some sort of spiritual progress had I done so.

Some people went farther than name changes, since they changed more than once and adopted Muslim names. Again I felt I could not do that. Some people also became Muslims. I did not feel that

My Stairway to Subud

I had to become a Muslim, because I felt internally that I already was one, that I revered the Holy Prophet Mohammed, just as I revered the Holy Prophets Abraham and Moses, and of course our Lord and Saviour, Jesus Christ. All these Prophets of God I knew to be so far above me that any arguments about allegiance to one or another seemed to be to be totally without meaning. I was sure that there was a Communion of the Saints, and that it was impossible for the Prophets of God to disagree one with another. I felt absolutely sure that it was only us humans, living on a very low level, who could misunderstand their great messages.

Of course those who went to Indonesia and decided to become Muslim officially and to espouse Islam, also had to be circumcised! I have heard many an amusing tale about just that. My friend Kieron O'Byrne was attracted to Islam, but protested that he was already circumcised. When he was told that that did not count, he asked what else would they cut off!!!

So I, just by nature, could not join in any fashion. Furthermore Pak Subuh in all his talks was emphasising more and more the need for "enterprises." And certainly many major enterprises were undertaken. One of the chief of these was a large conference centre cum hotel called *Anugraha* in central Surrey near Englefield Green. Many people sunk large sums in this enterprise, some mortgaging themselves up to the hilt. It is sad to say that in spite of many efforts, in spite of a truly unique system in the dome devised by the Architects, Lambert Gibbs, amongst others, this major enterprise finally failed, just as had the Nursing Home, Brookhurst Grange, and also Whatcombe House in Dorset.

It is only at a distance of time that I have come to realise that Pak Subuh not only introduced us all to a special Gift from God, namely the *latihan,* but he was also introducing us to a profound social change. At the time it had appeared to me ludicrous that so many ordinary financial decisions were taken as the result of "testing" instead of more normal commercial and common sense means. As Bennett had said we are so used to the relation of leaders and lead, we are so used to people arguing their corner, whether in politics or in company board rooms, that it is difficult for us to comprehend working from "right feeling." This was indeed the social revolution that Subud was internally attempting. That it should fail, or appear to fail so many times does not mean that the attempt to work together in this way was a failure. I believe that very few were sufficiently advanced to be able to "test" or to receive in a way that was totally without self-interest, which was obviously the *sine qua non* of success.

I suppose it was because I distanced myself from many Subud activities that some people assumed that I had left Subud, and even, much to the amusement of my wife and myself, urged us to return. In fact, we attended groups wherever we were, such as the Exeter Group when we stayed at Branscombe with the Temple-Cottons. In those days both Richard and Lisa were playing in the LTA tennis tournaments all over the place.

However, in 1987 when Bapak died, it is true that for a period of some years, maybe five years, I simply stopped attending *latihans*. There were many people of the *anciens*, the original clique of ex-Ouspensky followers, who had turned to Idries Shah, with the notable exception of Ronimund "Hubert" von Bissing, though Idries did try to influence even him. The experience of the *latihan*, the memory of my first doubts and then the truly explosive opening when Icksan stood in front of me, could never be set aside. I simply felt that I could exercise by myself as Sjafruddin had told me and I was confident that the latihan would continue within me by itself.

There is an amusing story of a certain lady who went all the way to Indonesia to ask Bapak whether she could now be closed! Bapak had made clear already that though someone might leave the organisation of Subud, once opened they could never leave the Spiritual Brotherhood. This is something that I believed then with all my heart, and believe now even more.

In 1978 when son Richard was 15 years old, it turned out that my father at the age of 91 was failing, and had been taken into a Nursing Home. During many years Eileen and I had kept up with the Coles and with the Whiffens, both old friends from the Coombe days, all of whom had been opened in Subud. Edgar and Eleanor Coles had a big house with a lot of land some miles south of Haslemere and we were fairly frequent visitors there. Edgar had been a broker at Lloyds and Eleanor had at one time worked for Robert Donat the actor, and had virtually been nanny to my friend, John Donat. Now Edgar was always inclined to be visionary, even in the days before Subud, and was convinced that certain people were reincarnations of historical or Biblical people of the past. Eleanor had by this time acquired a sort of direct line to Almighty God, to whom she referred fairly often among her well-heeled friends. We all knew this particular foible of hers, which caused some amusement. However, I personally have reason to be grateful to both of these people. We had Edgar and Eleanor over to dinner at our semi-detached house in Farnborough. How the subject got round to my father, I cannot remember. Eleanor, at once, said that I must go out to Africa to see my father. This was impossible; we had no savings, we lived hand to mouth. On this Eleanor turned to Edgar, who pulled out his cheque-book and wrote me a cheque for £500 on the spot.

I almost delayed going, since I was investigating cheaper flights, but Eleanor urged me to depart at once, and Eileen agreed to be left on her own with the kids and my manager in London gave me leave of absence.

I flew first to Johannesburg to stay a night with my sister Cynthia and my brother-in-law Derek, before proceeding to Cape Town. After one night in a hotel I managed to find lodgings with a lady who also spoke Afrikaans and had a small Volkswagen. How it all happened I cannot remember. She simply put the Volks at my disposal and I was able to walk or drive to the Nursing Home. On arrival there, I was to suffer a certain disappointment on the first day. My father had gone blind and deaf. He just did not recognise me at all. The next day I called again, and this time I cleaned out his hearing aid, which was clogged with wax. Suddenly he knew it was I and sat bolt upright in bed, declaring to all and sundry in the ward, "It's my son, it's my son, Tony." "Now," he went on, "we can have a conversation."

Every day after that, when I visited him he was able to sit out on the veranda and we could converse. We covered many topics. However, when I asked the nurses what was wrong with my father, they replied, "Nothing. He is dying from old age." I was curious to know how he felt, and so I asked him indirectly if his visions that I have recounted earlier had altered his views in general. He answered me straight away, "Tony, I am not afraid to die." I felt immensely proud of him then and still do more than 25 years later. After three weeks I had to return home and left him in the home. On March 22nd, my son's sixteenth birthday, I had a call to say my father had passed away.

Bapak once said to me, "As the soul of the son goes up, so does the soul of the father, even to seven generations back." This has always struck me as a most wonderful idea that I have never heard of anywhere else, except in Subud that the progress the soul can make on this earth can affect the dead, although perhaps it is the origin of prayers for our ancestors. Most people seem to think that the dead can perhaps help the living. But if what Bapak said to me is the truth, and I believe it is, then I hope and pray that for my father's sake, and for his forbears, that I may make at least some small progress while on this earth.

One very curious thing that I must remark on, I trust without causing offence, is something that Bapak said to us in regard to bringing up Subud children. Everyone wanted to know what they should do as parents to bring their kids up. Bapak on the other hand insisted that the Subud child would know, that being born with an awakened soul, would choose his or her own path unerringly. I think we all imagined that this meant that they would all become Subud members actively, but that has not always happened. As far as our own kids were concerned we did our best not to influence them in any way and each one of them quickly learned how to "paddle their own canoes." At the age of sixteen, my son Richard became noticeably independent of us, making his own decisions in everything, with a calmness and courage that I truly envy. Since then he has been extremely successful and wealthy compared to his parents. He learned to fly in the University Air Squadron, he is a daredevil skier, he has been on safari and has an enduring interest in bird and wild life and now has taken to underwater scuba diving with expeditions to Australia and the Red Sea. Nothing seems to worry him, and everywhere in business or in leisure he always seems to land on his feet.

My elder daughter got her degree in Music, is clearly very happy at being a Mum with two young girls, has a great and abiding interest in plants and flowers and is almost Buddhist in her attitude to all living creatures, conspicuously being unwilling to kill a spider or a fly.

Neither of my elder kids is in the Subud organisation, though they certainly must have heard about it as kids, both the Work and Subud.

My youngest daughter, Alex, who got a first-class honours degree in Psychology, in spite of prolonged periods of ill-health, however, began to evince an interest in all things paranormal, such as the crop circles, ley-lines and so on and so forth, what we privately called the "weird shit." However, she went on to read my book and then challenged both my wife and myself, "If Subud was all that I had said, what were we doing about it?"

It was about 1987 that I had stopped going to *latihan*. But apart from the fact that I had grown somewhat stale and the *latihan* had become samey-samey, a development had happened on the home front. For years my wife had struggled to support the pound with every sort of endeavour that a housewife could do from home. She had been an Avon lady and became a Manager, she had promoted catalogues, she had sold Shaklee vitamins, all of which endeavours had been attended with some success. However in early 1957, she was introduced to Jean-Pierre Sand, a company selling true French perfume, and this had been set up on a multi-level basis. The success of this company was legendary. Hundreds of people deserted their former MLM groups, bringing with them their downlines. The success of this company was staggering, particularly for the heads of the lines. Eileen did very well and as a result we enjoyed several trips abroad to the factory at Metz and to the perfume fields at Grasse, as well as visits to Paris. Some three or four busloads would go on these trips, all expenses paid. It was extremely good fun, but the thing that was required for success was a lot of work in the evenings.

So successful was his company that before long some of the most successful deserted to set up rivals, and instead of selling genuine French perfume they began to sell cheaper synthetics, with the result that within some 5 years the whole market was destroyed. This had been for a time a most exciting endeavour. It also coincided with a period when we had had to move out of our house for several months because of subsidence.

When my younger daughter began to evince an interest in ideas and more particularly in Subud and began to question us more seriously about it, and when I realised that she would certainly wish to be opened, I decided that I must quickly get "cleaned up." The Guildford group had ceased to exist as such, but I quickly found that there was a group that exercised at Chobham and another at Sunninghill, near Ascot.

I first went back to the group at Chobham, where I knew Howard Paice from of old. There were just four men in the group. As soon as the exercise started, my own *latihan* commenced just as if I had never been absent. It was a matter of great joy to me. After the exercise someone whom I had not met previously wanted to test something. He then told a long tale about the job he had that he did not like and about other possibilities that he was not sure about. What he wanted to test was likewise not too clear. This was just the sort of thing I realised that had put me off before. On the one hand, I rejoiced in the *latihan* itself, on the other hand this muddled request for a test reminded me strongly of former feelings. I turned

My Stairway to Subud

to the man concerned and asked him how long he had been in Subud. When he replied "thirteen years," I asked him how come that he should ask such questions. If he did his *latihan* sincerely as Bapak had told us then surely he would know the answers without having to ask the Helpers. It was as if I had never been away!

I was extremely fortunate in finding the Ascot Group, since in the main venue there was quite a large number of men and the exercise was very free. Since I had formerly been in the famous or infamous "O" group, depending on your point of view, I appreciated a venue where there was sufficient space to move about and where there were others who were moved to sing and speak. Very soon, I was asked to become a Helper again, though in fact I had never relinquished my Helper's card of 1958, signed by Pak Subuh himself, J. G. Bennett and Pierre Elliot as secretary. To my surprise, within a week or two, my wife Eileen announced that she was coming with me, so we together became active members again.

During this time my daughter was undergoing her three-month probationary period. When the day came for her to be opened I drove her to the group and waited outside in the car. It was a Wednesday evening, normally for the lady helpers. After some half an hour or so my daughter rushed to my car. "I don't know whether I have been opened," she said, her eyes wide as saucers. I could not help laughing inside. The next day was the normal *latihan* evening and so we all went together, Alex, Eileen and myself. After the latihan Alex said to me, "It's alright, Dad, I have been opened."

It was many years before I had an explanation of these enigmatic statements. Through reading of my book, she had expected everything at once, all singing all dancing so to speak. Whereas for many people the *latihan* starts quietly, and as explained before some people do not experience anything for quite a period of time, and have to be counselled before beginning to have patience. Happily for Alex, her early experience was indubitable for her and was in a way familiar, reflecting experiences of her childhood.

Within a very short time, a number of her young friends also elected to be opened and underwent the probationary period. This illustrated clearly that new members are the ones to bring other new members. It is often the initial change in a person that is the most striking.

The opening of my daughter Alex ignited in me a renewed enthusiasm for Subud, though I still found it difficult to enter into any-

My Stairway to Subud

thing to do with the organisation. I still relied heavily on my early and personal experiences with Bapak and Ibu, with Sjafruddin and Asikin, with Icksan and Ismana, and with Haryono. Simon Milan said that I was caught in some sort of time warp, and I guess he was right. In a short few years, I was out of touch with many of the events, many of the enterprises that had taken place in Subud. Also another curious thing was that in England the numbers had declined and were continuing to decline, very often simply by the death of the original members. On the other hand it appeared that Subud was starting up in all sorts of parts of the world, such as Russia and the Eastern bloc countries and in Central Africa. Bapak had said that we should not proselytise, though the decline in numbers has caused many of us to wonder why. On the other hand, it seems that Subud will start up just in those places when people are ready.

Once my daughter was opened I felt a great urge to contact again all my old friends, particularly those who had been opened in 1957. I began telephoning around, not just in England, but also all over the world. Suddenly I had the idea that I would invite all these old friends of mine to a pot-luck party.

There must have been some magic around at that time, because the response was truly amazing. It is one thing to invite people to a party from all round England. Kieran O'Byrne came from Liverpool, Ilbert Collingwood from Perthshire; Marie King came from the Isle of Wight together with Melissa Marston McLeod. That was fair and far enough. However, I also rang Bob Prestie in the States and it was typical of Bob that he had no hesitation that he would fly in. Peter Norman Kermode in Los Angeles agonised that he would love to come, but could not, but he did! As for Luqman Wynne whom I tracked down to Brisbane, Australia, I woke him from sleep in the early hours. No, he was skint (penniless or broke in American slang) it was entirely out of the question.

July 11th 1993 duly arrived and was a blistering sunny day, England at its very best. The guests began to arrive for lunch. I had already picked up Bob from Gatwick. Our great friend Dr. Mitchell arrived with daughter Lorna, luckily in England, from New Zealand. While welcoming my guests at the front of the house there was an odd fellow with a sort of rucksack with white hair that I did not recognise. Suddenly recognition came—it was Luqman Wynne, formerly Patrick, with whom I once had a holiday in France, hitchhiking. He had come after all from Brisbane, having flown to Japan and then all across the Russias to come to a pot-luck party! So

My Stairway to Subud

I had guests from all parts of England, from New Zealand, from Nevada, from California and from Queensland, Australia. The von Bissings could not make it from Switzerland, nor Richard Bigwood from Southern Ireland, nor Victor Gebers from Zululand. And Varindra Vittachi had died shortly before, whose funeral I also attended.

I have to say it was a great party, which went on for several days. It was a great party because all the people knew each other and had not met for many years. They had all been opened in 1957. Some of them had stayed with Subud and some of them had left. I made no distinction. As far as I was concerned they were all Seekers of the Truth, most all had been in the Work, and for me whether active or not, every one of them was a member of the spiritual brotherhood of Subud.

Peter Kermode and Luqman Wynne stayed with us for several days and Bob Prestie in the International Hotel nearby. Haryono wrote me to say that surely we had "laughter and tears" and asked why we had never been to Indonesia and invited us to his home.

Chapter 14

Retirement—A New Beginning

On the 21st of November '93 I retired or I was retired from my job with Carson Office Furniture at the age of 64. I say "was retired" because strictly speaking I had one more year to go. However the Sales Director wanted me out. He had new products, which were just being launched, and he wanted new blood. Whatever the reasons he wanted me to go. Those with long memories will remember that the years '90, '91 and '92 were the years of the recession. Up till that time my sales had gone up and up and my income also. In the years of recession my income plummeted, as everyone was holding on and sales were hard to come by.

It just so happened that I was in a pension scheme where my pension was based upon the best three years in the last five. Had I stayed on one more year it would have been a disaster for me financially. As it was, I was given a handsome watch, the company made me a gift of the company Sierra that I was driving, and I was able to take half my pension as a lump sum, pay off my overdraft, which had accrued owing to the recession and take a reduced pension. Furthermore, my sales director, one Alan Trotter, who was renowned for his personal driving ambition, also agreed to my carrying on selling Carson Office Furniture privately for a derisory commission. On top of that, I was allowed to keep my old customers! He was so much taken up with his new ranges that I had a free hand to sell the ranges with which I was familiar. It took me a little time for all of this to sink in. I had been 25 years with this company and during this time I had made a great many sales, some of them very large. Westinghouse Systems in Chippenham, I had kitted out entirely with desks, chairs and filing cupboards for over 300 people. I had done Lambeth Borough, the Electricity Council, and sale after sale to Southern Water. Of course, some of these clients were moribund, but one or two were very much alive. What had seemed to be a disaster turned out very well. (Perhaps it was the working of the *Roh-el-Kudus*.)

I quickly made some fairly substantial sales and had to form myself into a company, choosing the name Bright Interiors. I had become a sort of roving rep, working on commission only. I had barely been on my own for 2 months when I had a call from the sales manager of Vector Seating, a company that I liked well and whose products I had already sold. He came to visit me in my home and at once offered me a 50% commission to sell his chairs. Now Alan

My Stairway to Subud

Trotter of Carsons had insisted that Carson would do the invoicing for me, which pleased me no end, as I was thus not involved at all in VAT. So I turned to the sales director of Vector and agreed his terms, providing only that Vector would invoice on my behalf. He agreed this with alacrity, although in fact it was a very unusual arrangement. Most dealers bought the products and sold them on. They had to have a staff and showrooms and they of course invoiced their clients whom they guarded jealously. I had no showroom of my own, no secretary and did no invoicing. On the other hand I still made free use of the Carson showroom near Portland Place as well as their designers. It was a brilliant arrangement.

Sometimes a dealer would crash owing their suppliers considerable sums of money, and this had happened fairly often during the recession. It was said that some 25% of all Office Furniture Dealers in London had gone under during the recession, and this in turn had put many manufacturers in grave danger, as they were often owed thousands of £s which they could never recover.

I was never in this position. In fact my suppliers soon owed me substantial sums, but I only got my commissions once the end-client had paid up. It took me a little while to make clear my position to such customers as Southern Water, to whom I had sold a great number of desks already. They were quite happy to carry on buying through me, once they realised that Carson would invoice them and Carson fitters would fit the desks. However I had never formerly been able to get hold of their chairs business. One day I took a chair down to my contact there, and he was so intrigued by my demonstration that he asked whether he might keep the chair on trial. This had been my intention all along. Furthermore I offered him there and then a 40% discount. Since I was getting 50%, I could afford to give 40% and make my self a 10% profit. It was well worthwhile, as in the following years I sold them over 300 chairs. Much the same thing happened at Westinghouse in Chippenham.

In this way I was able to supplement my pension, particularly in the first year before the State Pension kicked in. And in the course of time I managed to increase my derisory commission of only 3% to 5% with Carson.

It was not very long after this that *Ramadan* came round. A lot of people in Subud kept *Ramadan*, but I had never done so. Pak Subuh had emphasised so much in the beginning that we should simply persevere with the latihan and I fully believed and hoped that all would come right if this was done sincerely, that is to say by following it and not making anything up. Besides which I never relished the idea of fasting where memories of fasting at Coombe loomed in my mind. Many Subud members, however, would make the trip to Indonesia, especially in order to join in the fast of *Ramadan* at Cilandak.

However this year, although I had reached the age of the climacteric, both Alex and I decided that we would undertake this fast. It was quite an experience. In the first place I made a great mistake. As we were not to eat anything between sunrise and sunset, in fact not before an hour and a quarter before dawn, we both arose early and then eat an enormous breakfast in order to see us through the day. That was a fatal mistake! By eleven o'clock in the morning, I was already dying of thirst.

Now most people who are not Muslims simply believe that the fasting is simply a matter of not eating, not letting anything pass one's lips, between sunrise and sunset. However we soon found that there was a great deal more to it than that. During the time of the fast one had to refrain from gossip, from criticism of other people, to refrain from sexual activity, and that included not using one's eyes in an unbecoming manner. In modern day language, that meant not looking at members of the opposite sex in an appraising way.

The idea was that the fast would also weaken the *nafsu*, that is, the lower forces. It was also explained that those who kept the fast for the full thirty days would experience great benefit. Furthermore, there was a tradition that during the fast the gates of Hell are locked and for anyone who followed the fast in every way prescribed, then all their sins would be forgiven. I must say that this last was a great incentive!

The Messenger of Allah said: the one who fasts during Ramadan with faith and seeking reward from Allah alone will have all past sins forgiven; and one who passes Lailat ul-qadr in prayer with faith and seeking reward from Allah alone shall have all past sins forgiven...(hadith recorded by Bakhari and Muslim)

I am bound to say that I derived much benefit from the fast. It reminded me so much of the Work. Here was an outward effort. One needed to make a decision to fast and that was that. And the effort to comply with the inner and not just the outer requirement of the fast produced in me that old friend "self-observation." But the biggest and most immediate benefit for those who were following the *latihan kejiwaan* was an immediate sharpening and deepening of the latihan experience itself.

With the exception of one year when I knew circumstances would make it very difficult or impossible, I have kept the fast every year since then. I have to admit that I look on the approach to *Ramadan* with some foreboding, since I am normally fairly self-indulgent with cups of coffee and the odd snack.

The other immediate effect of fasting in this way is the expansion of time. Without eating or snacking there is a lot more time. I find that I can work particularly hard during this period and complete a lot of tasks that I have neglected or deferred. Some people do not do this, sitting about and being quiet all day. Personally I find any inactive periods rather hard to bear, as one then begins to look forward to sunset and almost count the minutes down.

One unlooked for bonus is the relation towards others who are keeping the fast. Once my doctor, Dr. Ahmad, knew that I kept *Ramadan* his attitude towards me and my family became noticeably more caring! Ditto the local Tandoori who always gave me a special welcome when they realised that an English Christian was also keeping the fast. I know that Christians have Lent and for some it is a serious business. But in Islam the fast is obligatory. There can be no doubt that keeping the fast in the formal way that it is done would be a wonderful way to bridge the gap between Islam and Christendom. Just imagine if the Archbishop of Canterbury and the Pope were to enjoin on their congregations to keep the fast in the prescribed manner, then surely Christendom and Islam could be united in the worship of the one God.

Of course, there are still those who say that the Muslims worship Aller! (I have deliberately misspelled *Allah*, because that is how the ignorant often pronounce the word). But those with understanding know that there are many names for God, as *Jehovah, Yahweh, Brahman, Ahura Mazda, Gott, Dieu, Dios, Tuhan jang Maha Esa*, to mention just a few. It is time now for all of us to realise that we all worship the One God, unless of course we reserve our worship for Manchester United or some other modern day idol! As Christians we say, "I believe in one God, the Father Almighty, Maker of Heaven and Earth" and in Islam they say "There is no God but God, and Mohammed is His Prophet." The truth is that all who believe and who understand with all their being that there is One God are united. But there are still those who believe that their particular revelation, their particular Prophet is superior to any other, emphasising the divisions rather than the unifying factors.

There are two traditions that are followed at the end of *Ramadan*. One is to buy a new set of clothes and to wear an entirely new outfit. This is something that I especially looked forward to. It is of course symbolic; it is to symbolise that one is clean and that one has made a new beginning. The second tradition is not one I looked forward to, though it sounds simple enough. The tradition is that one has to ask forgiveness from one's wife, one's family, one's friends and acquaintances, for all the slights and hurts that you may have caused them. If you, my readers, think that that is easy, believe me you have never done it! At the end of *Ramadan*, at the feast of *Id-ul-Fitr*, Bapak would insist on everyone there and then on the spot to ask forgiveness of all around.

You try asking your wife for forgiveness. The last time I did that she laughed—just as she had when I first proposed to her!!

The author and his wife on an anniversary jaunt to London

Chapter 15

Wisma Subud, Cilandak, Indonesia

In 1995 I was able to realise a dream that I had had for many, many years and that was to go to Wisma Subud, the large complex at Cilandak Barat, in Jakarta. By taking half my pension as cash, I was enabled not only to pay off my overdraft, but also to have a few thousands in the bank. For the first time I was in a position to realise my ambition. Besides which all our children were now grown up and had flown the nest.

What precipitated my decision was a letter from Haryono, Bapak's son, whom I had known well in the early days when he had first married Ismana. He wrote to ask why I had never visited Cilandak and invited us to stay at his home in Jalan Berlian. This invitation might have just lain dormant in my mind had it not been for Ilaine Lennard the then Editor of Subud Voice. She mentioned to me that there was a meeting of the World Subud Council in Cilandak in June of that year.

It so happened that some three months earlier, Eileen and I were in the Isle of Man to attend a family celebration. During a discussion with her cousin Ann, Eileen mentioned that we were thinking of going to Indonesia. I immediately jumped in and gave a specific date for our departure, something that I had not previously discussed with Eileen. Oh! So you have a date? Yes, indeed, we had a date.

Now all my life I have been a tennis nut. I had played a lot at Clayesmore, then forgot all about it while I lived at Coombe, then my interest flared up again when Richard was 11. In the following years, I was to take him and Lisa to umpteen LTA Tennis Tournaments, and our summer holidays were scheduled to fit in with the tournaments we wanted to play. However, I had heard that Haryono was a very keen golfer. Once Eileen had agreed to our departure date, the very next morning I made a date with a professional for my first lesson at 8 o'clock in the morning. Returned to the mainland I bought a course of six lessons, which included a 7 iron, with which I practised diligently for the next three months.

The time finally came for our departure. Apart from trying to learn to play golf at the age of 65, I was also learning to speak *Bahasa Indonesia* by forced marches. Happily for me Maria Gibbs loaned me her excellent Linguaphone course, and I was able to play the recordings in my car *ad nauseam*. At the end of the time I was certainly not able to speak Indonesian, but I could get by with some of the simple things like *Berapa harganya*? How much is it? and *Tidak mengerti*, I don't understand. We had, of course, had to take all the necessary jabs and been warned not to drink the water.

Nothing, however, can prepare anyone for the East who has never been there. We had no idea even how far Wisma Subud was from the airport, so we were much relieved to find Haryono waiting for us at the airport with his Mercedes. How we found him, how he found us, amongst the milling throng, I do not know. The crowds were immense, the heat was intense, though it had been raining and it was already dark. Besides which I had not seen Haryono for some 35 years.

Now I have already quoted from the letters of Rainier Victor Gebers concerning the hospitality and the kindness that he experienced from Subud members. Over the next two weeks that was my own overwhelming impression. An hour's drive through the centre of Jakarta took us due south to Cilandak Barat and to Harjono's home, where we were also to meet Ismana once again. From there, once showered, we drove across to the complex of Wisma Subud where a cafe had been set up, prior to the start of the World Subud Council. I believe that the actual number of official delegates was something like 25, but in typical Subud fashion, another 100 had booked in as observers. While having a meal, Haryono disappeared on business and suddenly the heavens opened. The deluge fell with such intensity that within a few minutes the roads were under 1 or 2 feet of water. Haryono's son came to fetch us in the Mercedes.

The next day was the one and only available day before the Council proper started, and Haryono had arranged for us to play golf at his club. It is difficult to describe the conditions to anyone who has never been there. In the West, in England and in the States, we are all used to living in certain well-defined areas. There are areas of Council Housing; there are areas of small owner-occupied houses often semi-detached. Then as one goes up the scale there are clear areas of the more affluent middle classes, then there are the private roads and the estates of the wealthy. Not only in private housing, but also in shopping areas, the distinctions are clearly maintained.

In Indonesia, however, such clear areas did not seem to exist. Wealthy homes sat cheek by jowl with hovels. Even in the main shopping areas with giant malls and huge glitzy department stores, one could find immediately outside a little shack, where someone was selling rice dishes.

The golf club, when we arrived, was magnificent. Haryono strode off ahead of me, while Eileen tagged along behind. The golf clubs were still in the boot, so I wondered what was happening, as we did not go into the clubhouse to book in, as I was expecting. We simply walked to the first tee. Suddenly two fellows in red shirts carrying our clubs joined us. These I understood were our caddies!

Since I was really only a beginner in the world of golf, never before had I had a caddy. I was about to tee off with a 3 wood, when my caddy handed me a driver. So driver it was. Luckily the first couple of holes went quite well for me, before Harjono's superior experience and skill began to show, and I began to melt with the heat. In the meantime my caddy prompted me on every shot. Nine iron here!

In the river there were boys diving for errant golf balls, and we were assailed periodically by boys trying to sell us the balls they had retrieved. After nine holes we retired, as by this time what little skill I had had entirely deserted me. Besides which it was difficult to understand how anyone could play in such heat and such humidity.

After a second night in Harjono's home, we moved into the complex proper, where we stayed with Maryam Kibble, next door to Asikin. That was not before a memorable breakfast when I was with Ismana while she was frying eggs, and telling me about her visions of the Prophets. I won't go into the details, but how often does it happen that over cooking eggs, someone tells you of their having seen Moses and Jesus and Mohammed! Some things are secrets of God!

Now Maryam Kibble was one of the ladies who had opened my ancient Aunt Belle. Furthermore she was one of the very first western ladies to be opened, since she had lived formerly in Cyprus, where it was that her husband was opened by Husein Rofé, prior to his coming to England. This was about the same time that Husein was also getting to know Baron Ronimund von Bissing, and also the time when Husein had opened Meredith Starr. So it was extremely interesting to meet Maryam again, whom I had known formerly as Olive Kibble, and to hear of her early experiences of Subud, and her account of the first arrival of Pak Subuh at Rofé's flat in Dartmouth Road.

My Stairway to Subud

Wisma Subud is a sort of private estate, bordered on one side by the Jalan Fatmawati, an extremely busy thoroughfare now. At one time this land had been way out in the country. The centrepiece of the estate is the huge latihan hall with attendant offices. Near the entrance is Pak Subuh's own house, and throughout the estate are a number of houses owned by Subud members. It covers an area of several acres with winding roads. There is a lovely *pendopo* at one end, that is a meeting area open on all sides—very typically Indonesian.

The distance from Maryam Kibble's house to the cafe near the entrance was barely more than 150 yards, yet the heat was so intense and the humidity so great that I found I needed to change my clothes after breakfast! And indeed, I began to change my clothes four times a day, till Maryam remonstrated with me! She had provided us with a delightful room, with air-conditioning and a large fan in the ceiling. In the heat of the afternoon, we both would attempt to sleep with both the fan and air-conditioning at full blast, while geckos skittered over the ceiling.

As Eileen and I were both simply observers we did not take much part in the formal Council meetings and workshops. On the first day we were all crowded into Bapak's House and I was standing with a group near the stairs, when I heard a voice say "Tony." I turned round quickly and it was Ibu Rahayu, whom I had not seen also for some 35 years. For an instant, I saw her surrounded by a sort of wraiths of blue mist, which is the best way I can describe it.

A little later we were to meet Asikin again. "Oh Tony, where have you been all this time?" Of course, I had known Asikin as a young man of great sensitivity, whom Sjafruddin was wont to tease gently. Now he was married to a German girl, and had a son and a daughter. Our old friendship renewed instantly, as it did with all the old friends we were to meet in the next few days.

We had hardly been a few days into this Congress when an opportunity occurred. At Harjono's house we were introduced to Pak Muninjaja who was over from Bali, and who was returning there right away. We had hardly known him for five minutes before we were invited to visit him in Denpasar, Bali. How it all happened so quickly is amazing. Asikin helped us through a Subud friend in a local Travel Agency and suddenly we found ourselves bound for Bali on Garuda Airlines. Actually the plane was delayed a couple of times in Jakarta, taxiing to the end of the runway and then depositing us back into the airport lounge. This meant that we ar-

My Stairway to Subud

rived some hours late in Denpasar and Muninjaja was nowhere to be seen, and we did not even know his address. Finally he arrived and took us back to his house.

The immediate impression of Bali is one of colour. Everywhere people are wearing bright colourful costumes. Also while Java is predominantly Muslim, Bali still has a predominantly Hindu culture. Also while there is an Indonesian language, *Bahasa Indonesia,* one must remember that many people in Java speak Javanese, and of course in Bali they speak Balinese.

We could not help but be struck by the huge gates that were here and everywhere in front of the houses, and indeed at Muninjaya's house, workmen were working on the front of the house doing intricate carvings in the soft soapstone.

We had barely arrived and been introduced to Indra, Muninjaja's wife, than we were out on the main road watching a huge procession going by. We had arrived on the same day as a visit by President Suharto! The heat was intense and the road was crowded on both sides by thousands of onlookers. Suddenly, I was taken to a booth by the side of the road, where I was interviewed by radio Bali, and had to stammer out a few words in Indonesian. *Pertama kali di Indonesia; pertama kali di Bali.* First time in Indonesia; first time in Bali. I managed to get away with a few simple phrases.

After the procession had passed, we walked on to a huge bazaar. The crowds were so thick that I was all the time concerned not to lose sight of our hosts. Eventually we returned home for a meal, before setting off again to go to the theatre! We went in Muninjaja's car, surrounded it seemed by a hundred thousand motorbikes, all locked together in a huge logjam. Eventually we arrived. The theatre was in the open air, and we had to push our way in to wooden benches at the top of the amphitheatre, where smiling faces readily moved up and made room for us. The stage had a magnificent backdrop like a massive temple soaring high into the sky.

Happily Eileen had her video camera with us, so we were able to record the voices, the *gamelan* music, and the dramatic Balinese voices on the stage. The whole production was totally amazing and like all things Indonesian went on for hours. We did not stay till the end, but returned to Muninjaja's home for the night. Jokingly, I asked what time was breakfast and I thought he was kidding when he said five o'clock! The night was so hot that we slept on top of the bed without any covers.

My Stairway to Subud

In the morning, I rose early and sure enough, breakfast was at five. Eileen was still abed. A little later I noticed that Indra was cooking a chicken, and at eight o'clock in the morning we all ate lunch, Eileen included. This explained their schedule, which is somewhat different to the European norm. After this we were prepared to go out for the day and Muninjaja and his wife put themselves entirely at our disposal the whole day.

Bali is divided into eight kingdoms and Muninjaja was the son of one of the Rajas. Our journey took us first to the north of the island, stopping here and there to visit a temple, and then on to a large lake in the shadow of Mt. Batur, in a very volcanic area. On the return journey we called in at his father's palace and met his mother and brother. Once again there were these huge ornate gateways. The palace itself consisted of a series of low buildings, with open sided verandas. It was totally different to anything that can be seen in the western world.

Everywhere we went, Muninjaja was at pains to explain everything to us, as we visited ancient villages and temples. Finally we were taken to the new *latihan* premises, which were still in the process of construction, and we were able to join in the *latihan* there with the Balinese members.

After a couple of days we returned to Java, flying first into Jogjakarta, where we had been booked in to a truly luxurious hotel. One of the Subud Bali members was an official with Garuda Airlines, and so we were given rather special treatment in the lounges and first class seats on the planes. We were met at the airport by a guide who explained that he was to be with us for the next two days. He insisted that it had all been arranged and so we went along with it. The next morning he called to take us first to a Batik factory, then on to the famous Buddhist temples of Borobodhur. This is something quite out of this world. This enormous edifice contains the statues of hundreds of Buddhas often enclosed in a sort of semi-open bell.

The following day we visited a silver-working factory, before going on to the Hindu temples at Prambanan. Then back to Jakarta and we took a taxi to Cilandak Barat and Wisma Subud.

The Subud Council was still in progress and all the entertainment that had also been arranged. Unfortunately, Eileen was suffering from an upset stomach and missed the *wayang*, the famous Indonesian puppets show. But we were able to see an evening of Indonesian dancing, and Haryono was at pains to point out to me the character of Petruk, which was the name he sometimes called me.

Everywhere we were to meet old friends, like the Popes and the Mitchells who had both lived at Cilandak, and also to meet new friends. I was particularly interested to meet Brodjolukito and his French wife. I heard that Brodjo completely washed his house out every day! When he turned up to a function he was immaculately dressed. Happily for me an arrangement was made that I should read his book, which had been written in English, but had some quaint phraseology. I attempted later to put it into English English. Brodjo was a person who "saw" things. More or less whenever he attended a funeral he would see the dead person. One of the more extraordinary things in his book was his account of doing the *latihan* in a graveyard in the south of France, when on holiday there. He recounted that in many cases the graves opened and the people came out. They had not realised that they were dead! His book is quite unique, even in the somewhat abbreviated version that was eventually published.

His Chapter on *The Relationship between Man and Woman* is also striking, so I will quote a few lines from it: -

"As far back as we can see in time, no woman has been more celebrated than Mother Mary, who, after bringing forth Jesus Christ on Earth, regained her virginity. A woman of high and noble birth can regain her virginity after she has given birth to a child.

Apart from Mother Mary no other woman has been known for her high state of completeness. From Adam upwards, no other woman prophet has been known.

It is a man's duty after he has taken a woman, after he has had intercourse with her, to make her whole again. That is to say, to make her back into her virgin state. A man who takes a woman for intercourse, at that very moment she becomes his wife.

When a man and a woman have reached a certain state in the spirit, any relationship they may have is always witnessed by their ancestors. That is because this relationship has spiritual consequences in that it might bring both branches of the ancestors to a higher state or a lower level."

It is evident that the foregoing cannot possibly be understood by a western literal mind. How is it possible, one might ask, to regain virginity? It is difficult enough for people to accept the Immaculate Conception. Then again, could it be really true that our ancestors may be watching us as we make love? Who knows for sure?

Here is another excerpt from the same Chapter:

"In the present time the rules and customs of the past seem to have withered away into nothing. There seems to be no conception of the correct relationship between male and female. The idea that a man should take to wife a woman when she is still a virgin seems to be fast disappearing. It is an "orthodox" view that men seem no longer to regard as important. They accept the present situation, regardless of the fact that any female who has had sexual intercourse with a man or men, will bring with them the dirt that she has received from previous encounters.

At the time of death the woman's soul enters the man's soul to go to the man's destination. If everything is fortunate, then certainly everything will go well. If not, they will have to purify their souls in the hereafter.

Lucky are those who are acquainted with the latihan."

I am not competent to comment on the truth or otherwise of what Brodjo has written, which is indeed strange to western ears. However what is certainly true in principle is that the universe is dramatic, and that causes will certainly have effects. Nowadays it is common for people to have "partners", that is to say that they are living together. As Husein Rofé had also pointed out, from the cosmic point of view they are in fact, if not in law, married. As to the idea that the male and female soul will join in the hereafter, this reflects what Bapak had also said to me, that Jesus Christ was the only person to have complete within Him, both male and female natures.

Brodjo was a very gentle person, who has now departed this world.

One day, towards the end of our visit I was sitting on a bench outside the *latihan* hall, with a small group of people, amongst whom was Pak Usman, drinking cold tea. Here he was dressed casually, but I reminded him of the time years back in Redington Road that he had rebuked me when I turned down the opportunity to talk with Bapak. This time he laughed, as if to reassure me that we all made mistakes. I was instantly attracted to him as we fell easily into conversation. Usman had accompanied Bapak on many of his world journeys. He also told me in detail of the time in Singapore when Icksan Ahmed had died, and how Bapak had asked him to accompany the body back to Java, as it had to go by sea.

Usman could not stand false sanctity and referred to himself as a "broad Sumatran." He had that outgoing nature that made people wish to be in his company. It is curious that while I was getting to know Usman, my wife Eileen, quite independently and at exactly the same time was getting to know his wife, Aminah, whom she had met in a helper's group.

During the Congress, Haryono himself moved easily from group to group, a bit like an invisible man. That is to say, that here was Bapak's son, who was so completely modest and so self-effacing that I think that many of the foreign delegates hardly noticed him. That was OK by me and my old friend Dr. Mitchell, since we were often able to sit with him at lunch table and so on. Some years later, when he and Ismana stayed for a few days in our house, I once tackled him over this characteristic, saying that I would have to speak up for him, to which he quietly replied: "I have Ismana." I think he is a man so innately modest that he camouflages himself behind a quirky sense of humour.

While at Cilandak I found that I could sense people in an extraordinary way. And I mean extra-ordinary, because the words that I have to use can barely convey what I felt. One day Asikin recounted to us the story of his first journey to the West, of his stopover in Cape Town where he had his first encounter with apartheid of which before he was completely unaware, then his coming to England and Coombe Springs. He also told us of the death of Sjafruddin. Now the curious sensation that I had when speaking to him was that he was very wide. That he was wide, wide open.

Now when I was speaking on the rare occasion with Ibu Hardiyati, another of Bapak's daughters, I had the impression that she was very tall, and it was a surprise to me much later in England to realise that in fact she is far from tall. I also felt that she was very deep, as if I was standing in front of a deep, deep lake. With Ismana on the other hand I just felt dynamism, absolute dynamic action.

I had come to Indonesia and for me the most important thing was to meet my old Indonesian friends and to make new friends of those who had been close to Bapak. But it was also great to renew my old friendship with Dr. Abdurrahman Mitchell, who had been at Coombe many years before, who had lived in Indonesia for some time and who had been Bapak's doctor. He was a veritable fount of knowledge. Then again we met Salamah and Abdullah Pope, who had been in California when we were there, and who had also lived in Indonesia at Wisma Subud. Abdullah also told us of his experience of leaving his body when on the operating table. He could see the nurses trying to catch his arms as they were flailing about as he was given electric shocks, while it seemed he was a hundred yards above.

We left Jakarta after barely two weeks in Indonesia. Amongst other things we had also been to Cipanas to visit Bapak's tomb, outside of which both Icksan and Sjafruddin were buried. We had been to Bali, we had visited Borobodhur and Prambanan near Jogjakarta, we had seen a Balinese theatre, Javanese dancers and the *wayang*. But the most important thing was that Subud was vibrantly alive. Bapak may have died some years previously, but the action of Subud, the action of the latihan was undiminished. Furthermore there were many (who were opened) who had never met or seen Pak Subuh.

Chapter 16

Beyond the White Magician

It is ironical that I should have to turn to the words of John Bennett to bring this book to a conclusion. When Bennett had given over Coombe Springs to Idries Shah, it was not long before he set himself up again in a large house at Sherbourne in Gloucestershire.

I did go there once, as did my friend Ronald Leask. It was like being taken back in time, as no one even looked up from the tasks in hand, everyone intent on remembering themselves. After Subud, there was just too much "seriosity," to use the word that Bapak had coined.

My friend, Simon Penseney, also an old Coombe hand, visited him a month before his death. Passing him on the stairs, Bennett turned suddenly to Simon and said with great emphasis, "Have they forgiven me?"

Was this a *cri de coeur*?

Simon was very keen that I should read *"The Masters of Wisdom"* before I finished this book. And I did, and once again fell under Bennett's spell. How can one resist when he covers the whole spiritual history of life on this planet? Much that he wrote cannot possibly be challenged unless one has a profound knowledge of the history of Central Asia. Everyone has heard of Abraham, and Moses, and Jesus and Mohammed. How many, however, have heard of Ubaidallah Ahrar of Tashkent, who died in 1490? In any case, the theme of the book is largely about the necessity of preparation, and it is typical that even in writing of Jesus Christ there is the idea that he was a member of the Essene Brotherhood and was prepared by them. This is totally at variance with what Bapak constantly reiterates about the Prophets, namely, that they had no schooling, no special preparation, but what they received they received directly as a Gift from God.

Fascinating as is this book, and also various excerpts that Patrick Wilson was kind enough to supply me from various of Bennett's writings, I still prefer what Bennett wrote in the book, *Concerning Subud*, which I believe is still one of the very best introductory books on the subject.

The question is still: Does one need a Teacher? Does one need a

Guru? It was the constant theme in the Gurdjieff work, that a Teacher was necessary. It is the same with Raja Yoga. It is impossible to undertake these disciplines without a *Guru,* who really understands the techniques and who has himself made some spiritual progress. All work in the Way can be described as "working from without."

John Bennett understood the distinction between working from within and working from without and expressed it better than can I. I will quote from page 107 of *Concerning Subud:*

Worship and Magic.

The latihan cannot rightly be understood unless we clearly distinguish between magic and worship. Magic is a real power, and so far from belonging to a dead past, it has never been as widely practised as at the present time, although it is called by other names.

Magic is the use of forces that act upon man through the lower parts of his nature. There are four such forces:

1. The Material Forces. These come from the attraction exerted upon man by the energies in the material world. They are properly called "Satanic Forces" and those who employ them are "Black Magicians."

2. The Vegetable Forces. These act upon man through his instincts. They are natural forces, and those who use them are "Red Magicians."

3. The Animal Forces. These act through the emotions and passions of man, and those who are able to manipulate these forces are known as "Yellow Magicians."

4. The Human Forces that act through the nature of man himself. Those who are able to use these forces are called "White Magicians."

In all magic without exception the action is by one man upon other men.

Bennett goes on to show how advertising is a form of black magic, as it makes use of the suggestibility inherent in all people from their attachment to material possessions. Likewise political propaganda is also a form of black magic.

Red Magic, he explains, comprises all forms of hypnotism and suggestion that act primarily on the nervous system and the blood, where the initiative is always transferred to the practitioner.

Yellow magic comprises nearly all forms of spiritualism, as well as spiritual healing, clairvoyance and telepathy.

It is not my purpose here to discuss these forms of magic, which the reader can undertake himself or herself. However what Bennett says about White Magic is germane to the theme of this book and explains better than I can the position of people like Gurdjieff and Bennett himself. So I will quote again, from page 110.

"White magic, properly speaking, comprises all forms of 'working from without' that are directed towards the improvement of man's nature. The spiritual guide or teacher is a white magician. He helps his pupils to acquire control over their own human and sub-human forces, but since they more or less depend upon him and his initiative, the relationship is still that of magic. The really good white magician takes every opportunity of throwing his pupils back upon their own initiative, and refuses to take away their freedom even if they wish to lay it in their hands. Thus the teacher becomes a true spiritual guide only when he ceases to be a magician. He may find it necessary to use magic up to a point, in order to help people who cannot help themselves, but as soon as he gives even the smallest help beyond what is indispensable his white magic becomes a destructive influence that arrests the progress of the soul.

It will be clear now that all forms of magic are essentially opposed to the true worship of God. Worship is a state of complete freedom and full consciousness, in which the soul is aware only of the Power of the Holy Spirit. No lower power can come between the soul and the Holy Spirit, and yet all the lower powers are themselves brought into harmony with the soul that turns towards its Maker. This comes through the vivifying power of the Great Life Force that flows back towards its Source in and through the act of worship. It soon becomes evident to all trainees that in the latihan there is no diminution of freedom or loss of consciousness. In so far as we are aware of the existence of others, they enter our consciousness as beings passing through the some process as ourselves. If they appear to us to be influencing us or influenced by us, the latihan itself either stops or loses its power. We can thus verify in the most direct man-

ner that there is no magic in the latihan. The ideal state for man is to live wholly without magic. This is non-identification or non-attachment—that is, complete freedom and full consciousness. It is theoretically possible to go by way of magic to attain freedom from magic, provided that we understand at all times that magic is the use of the lower powers of the essence. It is better if we can find the way to dispense with magic altogether."

Thus Bennett. We who studied under him have nothing to forgive. We have only gratitude that we were led beyond white magic to the *latihan kejiwaan,* where we depend upon no man, but God alone.

Some Paragraphs on Surrender

From the talks given by Pak Subuh to the Congress at Coombe spring in 1959.

So the essence of surrender is that at the required time—when you are opened and later, when you do the latihan—your heart is empty and void of everything: your hopes, wishes and desires, including your wish to surrender to God. For when you wish to surrender, what is wishing is simply your heart.

The truth is that in the latihan, according to God's will, you should simply be aware of your whole being and not think about anything. Movements will then arise from within your being. And the arising of these movements within you means that you are surrendering to God; in other words, that you are allowing whatever God wills and the working of the Great Life Force within you. (Think of it) like this: it's as if you are with someone else, and whatever they do to you—they raise you up, they hold you, guide you, or whatever—you don't resist; you simply submit to whatever they want to do with you. That is what true surrender to God is like.

This is the meaning of surrendering to the greatness of God. But do not forget that the most important thing in the latihan and in receiving the contact is not the surrender but the fact that, by God's will, the current of God's power flows through the opener to one who is being opened. Their feeling is spontaneously awakened within them and the activity of their heart, thinking and desires stops.

Bapak says this because many people besides us also practice surrender. Their surrender may be a finer quality and more real than ours. But because it is not yet God's will to channel His power into their being, even though they surrender every day and every night—you could say they surrender to God a thousand times— there is no result. So it is clear that the most important thing, which results in the reality of receiving the latihan—meaning surrender that is accompanied by a contact with God—is not your surrender but the opening. That is to say, it is the current of the force that flows through the body of the opener to the body of the person being opened.

Extract: Argument and Anger

From Bapak's Talks, Volume 4, San Francisco 13th July 1959

Clearly, this spiritual training penetrates all activities of human life on earth, enabling you to worship and turn to the greatness of God in every situation. For example, when you have an argument with someone, your arguing will be filled with the worship of God. So, in the course of the dispute you will be aware of the truth; you will know the right way to argue and how to finish the argument. Then, when the arguing is over, you will embrace one another.

Brothers and sisters, don't misunderstand and think that the prophets had no passions and never became angry. Oh, when the prophets were angry, they were very angry. Yes, really! But the prophets' anger was filled with faith, it was filled with the worship of God, so they were able to feel and remind people of what was right and wrong.

Clearly, then, you don't have to get rid of your passions or put them aside. But you do need to stop them at times when you are receiving what God gives you, so you can receive that clearly and properly. Later, when the process is complete, you will be able to use your passions when they are needed. So you won't be angry all the time—every day. No. There are times when anger is necessary. Yes, necessary. But what Bapak means by necessary is that you are angry when you have to be—when someone has done wrong. If they haven't then you don't get angry. It's like that.

Extract: Your Human Soul

From Bapak's Talks, Volume 4, San Francisco 13th July 1959

That is why in Subud you need to be purified and prepared, so that eventually you will be able to understand and know how to use everything you need. The mistakes you have made through misus-

My Stairway to Subud

ing all the necessities of life are simply because your feelings, heart, brain and thinking have been under the influence of the low forces, which still rule within your being. That is why the whole of you needs to be awakened, so that you will get to know and recognise what has become the inner content of yourself. Once you recognise and know that content it will become aware, and by itself will return to the place it should be. Then you will meet your human soul within you, which should be in its rightful place.

From that position, you will be able to know how the material, plant, animal and human forces variously influence the action of your will. As Bapak is always saying, if you reach that state it will not be through using your heart and mind. The only way you can receive it is to have patience and trust, do the latihan diligently, and obey God's commands.

As Bapak has said earlier, it is the nature of the heart and mind to be always at work, and they don't want to stop working. So if you let your heart and mind go on and on, as long as you live you will never find truth or peace. Moreover you will become confused in your life and in your feelings; especially if your heart and mind want to go fast, to be better or more famous than others. Such wishes only block your path, and obstruct the progress of your soul and the cleanness of your inner feeling.

Later, when you have comprehended what Bapak has been saying and have reached the required stage, you will feel really free in your way of worshipping God. For, when you are asleep and when you are awake; in the course of your work and when you are traveling; when you die; in everything there will be no space left or empty. You will always be filled with the worship of God. Then when the time comes for you to die—whether you die in the street, at home, or in the forest—you will be in the same state: that is, you will always be in the lap of God, always before God, because everything in you worships God.

Ballerina and Culture

From Bapak's Talks, Volume 4, San Francisco 13th July 1959

That is why all of you in Subud really need the purification of your inner feeling. It is to prepare you, in order that in your life you may worship God and be aware of the life of your inner self; and not be closed up by everything you have become accustomed to.

So, for instance, suppose you are a ballerina: when you perform in a ballet, it will not be the desire of your heart but the power of God that makes you do it as you do, so all your actions become worship. That is to say, your legs and your hands an your whole body become aware of the greatness of God. When that happens, when the dancing is from the soul and by the will of God, you will be able to feel it. Both those who see it and the one dancing will feel peaceful and alive. This is indeed what is needed by humanity, and this is true culture. However, generally these days, people are not looking for this kind of culture, but for culture produced and refined by the thinking mind and by the passions. That is very different from the living culture that you will encounter in our Subud latihan, our worship of God.

Here is another example. Suppose someone is ill—seriously ill: perhaps if you dance the ballet before that person, he or she may become well. Why? Because your dance is not ordinary dance, but a dance of worship, as when you do the latihan Subud. Bapak once tried something similar when he visited a sick person. Bapak did not touch the person at all—he was some distance away—but he sang. After Bapak had finished singing he left, and the person said, "Hearing that singing just now made me well again." But don't get the idea that Bapak cures people just by singing. Don't do that, because then people will be asking Bapak to sing everywhere.

Extract From the Life of George Fox

Being set at liberty, I went to the inn where Captain Drury at first lodged me. This captain, though he sometimes carried it fairly, was an enemy to me and to Truth, and opposed it. When professors came to me, while I was under his custody, and he was by, he would scoff at trembling, and call us Quakers, as the Independents and Presbyterians had nicknamed us before. "http://www.strecorsoc.org/gfox/" \l "fn105" [105] But afterwards he came and told me that, as he was lying on his bed to rest himself in the daytime, a sudden trembling seized on him; that his joints knocked together, and his body shook so that he could not rise from his bed. He was so shaken that he had not strength enough left to rise. But he felt the power of the Lord was upon him; and he tumbled off his bed, and cried to the Lord, and said he would never speak more against the Quakers, such as trembled at the word of God.

Another Extract From the Life of George Fox

At another place, I heard some of the magistrates say among them-

selves that if they had money enough, they would hire me to be their minister. This was where they did not well understand us, and our principles; but when I heard of it, I said, "It is time for me to be gone; for if their eye were so much on me, or on any of us, they would not come to their own Teacher. For this thing (hiring ministers) had spoiled many, by hindering them from improving their own talents; whereas our labour is to bring every one to his own Teacher in himself."

This remarkable extract when George Fox was in America near Rhode Island.

Though George Fox always talked in strictly Christian terms, his understanding of Christianity was on a very mystical level, and particularly the idea that man could have his own internal Teacher. *"...whereas our labour is to bring everyone to his own Teacher in himself."*

Yet another wonderful extract from The Life of George Fox:

http://www.strecorsoc.org/gfox/" \l "fn176" [176]

"Next morning, some of the chiefs of the town desired to speak with me, amongst whom was Colonel Rouse. I went, and had a great deal of discourse with them concerning the things of God. In their reasoning they said, 'The gospel was the four books of Matthew, Mark, Luke and John'; and they called it natural. I told them, the gospel was the power of God, which was preached before Matthew, Mark, Luke or John were written; and it was preached to every creature, of which a great part might never see nor hear of those four books, so that every creature was to obey the power of God; for Christ, the Spiritual Man, would judge the world according to the gospel, that is, according to his invisible power. When they heard this, they could not gainsay; for the Truth came over them. I directed them to their Teacher, the grace of God, and showed them the sufficiency of it, which would teach them how to live, and what to deny; and being obeyed would bring them salvation. So to that grace I recommended them, and left them."

Extract From a Talk given by Pak Subuh on the 11th August 1959:

You, who are amongst the first to be rescued in this way, and who have received help from God within yourselves, have been able to sense how God in His greatness is working within each of you. So you can witness that there is within you an energy, a higher power that always guides you, which enables you to feel and experience—to a greater or lesser degree—the change taking place in your own being.

If Almighty God has given this to us—all of you—it must also be God's will that this should be given and transmitted to others, especially to those who have really gone wrong and are deeply under the influence of the material forces. Therefore if you do not share this gift with others in our society, you are committing a sin; because you have received something and are not using it. So it is clear that the transmission to other people of this infinite life force you have received is an unconditional obligation, willed by God for the accomplishment of an order in human society in which happiness and harmony may be established.

About Hummingbird Books—

Hummingbird Books

Hearing the news that Muhammad Subuh Sumohadiwidjojo had passed from this world on the morning of 23rd June 1987, we were overcome by a deep sense of loss. In a moment the old familiar world had disappeared. Saddened we drove up to Lake Anza in the Berkeley hills. On our return to the house, Stephanie and myself saw a beautiful hummingbird in our porchway trying to fly through the glass window. I cupped the tiny bird in my hands and released him outside where he flew high up into the sky. For some reason this small incident gave us a feeling of hope and consolation which we connected with Bapak's passing.

The Amerindians have long known and celebrated the fact that the Great Spirit speaks to us through the wonders of Nature. The small and the beautiful have their quiet voice and sometimes when we too are quiet we may hear the joy and sweetness in their song despite the confusion and clamour of our world.

We gratefully dedicate the Hummingbird Book Series to the memory of Bapak.

Rachman Hopwood
Berkeley, California 1987

A message from the Undiscovered Worlds Press

UWP is an online publisher specializing in books and articles dealing with: Spirituality, Speculative Archaeology, Ancient Mysteries, Ancient Civilizations, Personal Accounts of dealing with the Miraculous, Aspects of Subud Culture. In fact, any subject that reveals or expresses an Undiscovered World.

Our aim is to publish material that uplifts and nourishes the human spirit. We aim also to do our best to rescue those stories and books— the *Hidden Gems*— that have slipped beneath the sands of time and are in danger of being forgotten and lost.

We at UWP are interested in your book and story proposals. Please send us an email with a synopsis of your story or book.

Free downloads of selected articles and books are available on our website.

Website: www.undiscoveredworldspress.com
Email: admin@undiscoveredworldspress.com